# God's Gamble

*The Gravitational Power of Crucified Love*

GIL BAILIE

# God's Gamble

The
*The Gravitational Power*
of
*Crucified Love*

 Angelico Press

First published by Angelico Press, 2016
© Gil Bailie, 2016

For information, address:
Angelico Press
4709 Briar Knoll Dr.
Kettering, OH 45429
angelicopress.com

978-1-62138-222-5 Paperback
978-1-62138-223-2 Cloth
978-1-62138-224-9 eBook

Cover Design: Michael Schrauzer
Cover Image: Antonio Ciseri, *Ecce homo*, 1871

# CONTENTS

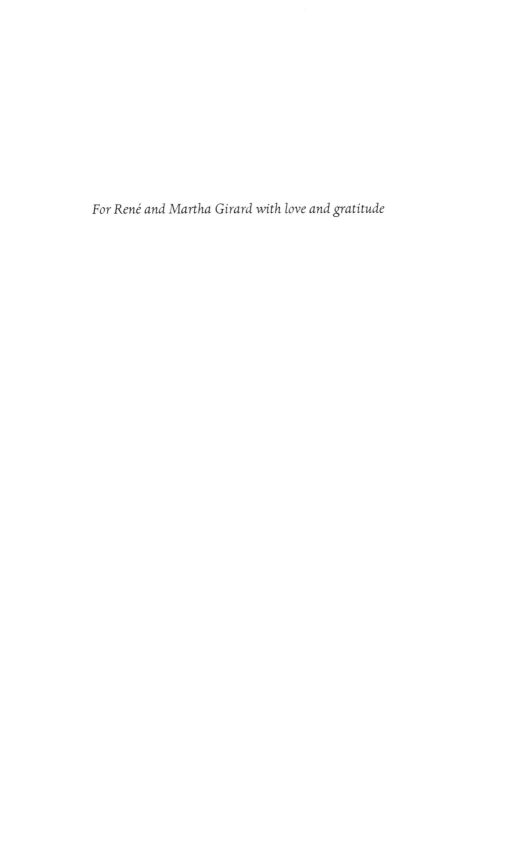

*For René and Martha Girard with love and gratitude*

He was at the very end and here at the same time,
He was at the very end and then at the same time.
He was in the middle and simultaneously at one
   and the other end.
He alone
Of all men.[1] —Charles Péguy


It seems both presumptuous and foolish to assert that one single figure who is bound to disappear farther and farther into the mists of the past is the authoritative center of all history. . . . Can we cling at all to the straw of one single historical event? Dare we to base our whole existence, indeed the whole of history, on the straw of one happening in the great sea of history?[2] —Joseph Ratzinger (Benedict XVI)


The Christian answer to this contemporary challenge is a confession of faith: there is no superseding Christ, he is the fulfillment of all things, he is Alpha and Omega, the last end of the world as he is the spring of its eternal youth. . . . For Christians, the structure of history is complete, and its decisive event, instead of coming last, occupies the central position. Nothing can ultimately go wrong.[3]—Jean Daniélou, S.J.

1 Charles Péguy, *The Mystery of the Charity of Joan of Arc*, trans. Julian Green (New York: Pantheon, 1950), 110.

2 Joseph Ratzinger, *Introduction to Christianity*, trans. J.R. Foster (San Francisco: Ignatius Press, 1990), 193.

3 Jean Daniélou, S.J., *The Lord of History*, trans. Nigel Abercrombie (Cleveland: Meridian Books, 1958), 82–3.

# Acknowledgments

SO MANY people have contributed spiritually, intellectually, and materially to the writing of this book—some by their presence in my mind as much as by more obvious contributions of which they might be aware—that any attempt to list them would be inadequate. Though there are some whose contributions I cannot fail to mention, I trust that the many others who deserve mention will know how sincerely grateful I am for their friendship and encouragement.

I owe a debt of gratitude to René and Martha Girard that I cannot hope to repay. Their friendship buoyed me at every stage of this project. René's passing from this life prior to the publication of this book adds to the sadness I feel at the loss of his warmth and kindness.

Without the constant support of my friend and colleague in the work of *The Cornerstone Forum*, Randy Coleman-Riese, this book could not have been written. I am deeply grateful to Randy for his extraordinary example of Christian faith in action and for all that he has done to foster the *Forum's* work. I want to thank Jennifer Bledsoe as well for all that she is doing to help Randy in the work of the *Forum*. The contribution that my friend Caroline Gissler has made to this book cannot be overstated. Caroline spent long hours critically reviewing the manuscript during its preparation, and her wise counsel and steady hand—her editorial gifts and her familiarity with the sources on which this book draws-have been invaluable.

A loving family is so precious a gift that it sustains everything that one does in life, and I have been blessed beyond measure with a loving family. Should the reader of this book derive from it any wisdom or insight, part of the credit goes to my gracious wife Kathleen, my children Allyson, Hunt, and Aña and their wonderful spouses and children, from whom I have learned what love means.

iii

# Prologue

THOSE READING these words have been in my mind and heart throughout the writing process. Alas, a writer will have the privilege of actually meeting only a few of his readers. It is a fundamental principle of a Catholic sensibility, however, that even relationships as seemingly one-sided and tenuous as that between the reader and writer of a book enjoy a reciprocity of which neither may be sensible, but which nonetheless may bear fruit in the lives of each. I want to speak directly to the readers of this book, with whom over the years of its gestation I have increasingly felt a bond. I hope the possibility of a rapport of sorts between myself and my readers will not be jeopardized by the fact that everywhere other than in this prologue, I have avoided the first-person singular.

The use of the editorial "we" in the chapters below is not a supercilious affectation. Nor is it a subtle attempt to conceal the personal character of these reflections or avoid the personal responsibility I bear for what is written here. This book is written in the first-person plural because I am fully aware that my very personality is not mine alone. This book, no less than the life of its author, arose from countless encounters and relationships—whether personal, literary, ecclesial, or sacramental. The voice with which I speak is traceable to countless others under whose influence I have been fortunate to fall. Even when one has been vouchsafed an insight for which he knows of no precedent, it is prudent to attribute what appears otherwise to be originality to the author's inadequate recollection of influences that have long since been integrated into his own worldview and the literary habits by which he expresses it

The use of the first-person plural is especially apposite in my case, for I have spent much of my life collecting and commenting on the literary, theological, anthropological, and cultural genius of my betters. Over the course of many years, I have doubtless internalized these sources, and it would be discourteous not to acknowledge their presence in some small way, as the use of the authorial "we" does. In a more important sense, however, the plural pronoun represents an ecclesial rather than a merely authorial "we." I am neither a clerical homilist nor a lay preacher, but I identify with what Emery de Gaál has said of them:

> [B]oth the clerical homilist and the lay preacher allow the individual "I" to be spelled with a lowercase "i," so that the universal "we" of the creed may shine forth. This subjective "i" is aware that in the Greek original the creed began with "we believe." The lowercase "i" of the homilist or lay preacher finds its proper context, authority, and thus authenticity, in the lowercase "w" of the ecclesial "we."[1]

It is my hope that the use of the plural pronoun will be a repeated reminder that, even though this is an intensely personal book, it is not a book of personal opinion. Rather, it is a sprawling florilegium consisting of fragments retrieved from the great tradition and its latter-day custodians and arranged so that the reader will have some sense of a larger and more elusive mystery. Whatever its shortcomings, and whatever its readers make of it, my persistence in bringing this book to completion was aided by my sense that it is a book that no one else could write. Others have written and will write better books dealing with the themes herein explored, but it was given to me to write precisely this one, and I am grateful for the gift of perseverance and inspiration that made it possible for me to do so.

Later in this book I quote a beautiful passage in which Hans Urs von Balthasar employs the metaphor of a symphony. In keeping with this marvelous image, I might say that I have tried to gather what I consider to be reliable voices from the Christian tradition, broadly understood, ancient and contemporary, and to arrange them into a kind of polyphonic ensemble. The reason for this approach is not just my deference to penetrating insights of those more worthy of my readers' attention than are my own,

---

1 Emery de Gaál, *The Theology of Pope Benedict XVI: The Christocentric Shift* (New York: Palgrave Macmillan, 2010), 235.

but because I want this book to give its reader some sense of the great cloud of witnesses on which Christian faith can and should draw for its continued vitality. If I am neither a clerical homilist nor a lay preacher, neither am I formally trained in theology. And yet I find my own vocation limned in the vocation of the theologian as defined by Cyril O'Regan, namely that of "remembering the live voices of the tradition as they witness to the mystery of the triune God revealed in Christ, as they attest to the logic of love."[2] In warrant of both my efforts and my limitations, I offer these words from the pen of Blessed John Henry Newman:

> Without deciding whether or not it is advisable to introduce points of theology into popular works, and especially whether it is advisable for laymen to do so, still, if this actually is done, we are not to expect in them that perfect accuracy of expression which is demanded in a Latin treatise or a lecture ex cathedra; and if there be a want of this exactness, we must not at once think it proceeds from self-will and undutifulness in the writers.[3]

My ultimate aspiration in this book is perhaps best framed by Søren Kierkegaard's famous distinction between an "admirer" of Christ and of Christianity and a "follower" of Christ. I hope it will not betray the chiseled clarity of Kierkegaard's distinction to say that his categories are arrayed on a continuum. Just as it is possible for a follower to devolve into an admirer and thereafter to take the next easy step into faithlessness and the secular wasteland that it fosters, it is sometimes the case that one comes to Christian faith by first recognizing it from afar, so to speak—by seeing its effect on Christians, by appreciating its capacity to give a rational account of itself, by its demonstrable moral and cultural benefits—thereafter to arrive at faith itself and become a follower of Christ. In any case, this book is written for those like its author who are unsatisfied with being what Kierkegaard calls an *admirer*, in the hope that they might find between the covers of

---

2 Cyril O'Regan, *The Anatomy of Misremembering: Von Balthasar's Response to Philosophical Modernity* (New York: Herder & Herder, 2014) 110–111.

3 John Henry Newman, "On Consulting the Faithful in Matters of Doctrine," *Conscience, Consensus, and the Development of Doctrine*, ed. James Gaffney (New York: Doubleday, 1992), 398.

this book reasons to try, at least, to become a *follower* of Christ. Writing it has helped move its author along that spectrum; I pray that it might do so for some readers as well.

It is one thing to propose, as I do, that the truth revealed by Christ is the anthropological key for understanding the human drama and deciphering the postmodern malaise. It is another thing to bear witness to that claim with conceptual and linguistic tools that are unavoidably ill-suited to the task. But that is precisely the challenge which Christianity has faced for two millennia. An essential feature of Christian faith, however, is the confidence that the Spirit, whom Jesus declared would lead us gradually to the whole truth, will accompany the Church through history and inspire an ever deeper understanding of the truth revealed by Christ. There is no reason to doubt that in our own time the Spirit will awaken the necessary wherewithal for facing the exigencies of our particular moment in history. Indeed, in what follows, we will be drawing generously on the work of two men—René Girard and Hans Urs von Balthasar—who have opened new paths into what is arguably the most audacious of Christianity's claims, namely, that Christ, the incarnate Logos, is the Alpha and Omega, the source and the destiny of the created order itself. Using the insights of Girard we will look for evidence—elusive though it necessarily must be—of Christ at the dawn of the human race and the emergence of the human person. We will consult the work of Balthasar to suggest a variation on an Omega Christology, namely, that every person who ever lived or ever will live will be met by Christ at the moment of death. A corollary to this claim is one no less audacious: that the key to understanding the structure, meaning, and trajectory of human history can best be delineated by reading the Old and New Testaments from the perspective of a theological anthropology informed by the work of both Girard and Balthasar. The middle chapters of this book will take up the task of defending that proposition.

In his own famous gamble, Blaise Pascal reasoned that every life amounts to a wager as to whether or not God exists, and that the rational choice is to believe in the existence of God, for if that belief is false far less is lost than if one's gamble on the nonexistence of God turns out to be wrong. Not everyone will be persuaded that Christ is who he said he was and that Christianity is the driving force in human history, but I would hope that very nearly everyone might come to wish that it were true. Like Pascal's wager, I think it highly likely that anyone who chooses to live *as though* what is here being proposed is true would thereby enjoy a happier, deeper, and more fulfilled life. I believe what I have written, but should I be wrong, as surely in places I am, I do not think that those who think me right will be damaged by having thought so.

# Why Bother? Why Get Married? What are Families For?

Our times are becoming increasingly timeless in the sense that so few now have a knowledge of history that most lack a clear sense of where they or their civilization stand in history: they belong to no story or history. The civilization is becoming more and more objective in the sense that fewer and fewer have a rich interior life or a sense of their own distinctiveness, and increasingly one's norms are absorbed from cyberspace.[1]—Glenn W. Olsen

A NUMBER of years ago a fascinating essay by journalist David Samuels appeared in *The New York Times Magazine*. It was a clever, tongue-in-cheek, anecdotal, and autobiographical essay about the hazy social and moral landscape in which Samuels and his contemporaries were foraging for spiritual nourishment.

By the time my girlfriend and I broke up, I had concluded that the problem wasn't just sex, or high-pressure careers, or guilt, or the takeout food cartons in the fridge, or the boredom inherent in serial monogamy. Our inability to imagine a future together was not ours alone. It was a symptom of a larger fracture or collapse, involving however many hundreds and thousands of people in their 20's and early 30's who seem to lack any sense of necessary connection to anything larger than their own narrowly personal aims and preoccupations. In the aftermath of the civil rights movement, women's liberation, the movement from the cities to the suburbs, the birth of rock-and-roll and other changes, basic laws of social gravity had lost their pull. We were free to be white or black, gay or straight, to grow our hair long,

---

1  Glenn W. Olsen, *Beginning at Jerusalem: Five Reflections on the History of the Church* (San Francisco: Ignatius Press, 2004), 99.

shave our heads, meditate for days on end, have children or not, drink bottled water, work out at the gym, watch television until 3 in the morning and otherwise exist outside the traditional roles and close, gossipy communities that had burdened and constrained our parents growing up in Brooklyn or the Bronx.[2]

One of the things that makes Mr. Samuels' article historically emblematic is that at its center is an attempt to understand the meaning of a broken relationship. This break-up, we are told, was not due to the things that at first seemed to have contributed to it: "the boredom inherent in serial monogamy, . . . the takeout food cartons in the fridge," or any other issues over which the couple might have regularly disagreed. Of course, we are never told what the real reason for the breakup is except that it coincided with an inability to imagine a future together and that something seems to have gone wrong at the cultural level. It would take us too far afield to further explore this matter, but it should at least be said in passing that as a culture slips into crisis, relational difficulties, most especially sexual relationships, are the first to show strain. Observing an earlier stage of our present cultural crisis, G.K. Chesterton noted: "Everything has been sundered from everything else, and everything has grown cold. . . . This world is all one wild divorce court."[3]

While enjoying an extraordinary degree of what he and his contemporaries believed to be freedom, Mr. Samuels quite obviously felt that that freedom had been purchased at a high cost. The freedom Mr. Samuels and his friends enjoyed had a worm at its core the nature of which they were not quite able to comprehend:

> This freedom from the gravity of age-old constraints was accompanied by a weightless feeling that attached itself to even the most fundamental human decisions. Why bother? Why get married? What are families for? What was new about these questions was that they didn't have answers, or that the answers they

2 David Samuels, "In the Age of Radical Selfishness," *The New York Times Magazine*, October 17 (1999).

3 G.K. Chesterton, *What's Wrong with the World* (San Francisco: Ignatius Press), 88.

did have were so multiple and contingent and arbitrary that they never really felt like answers at all.

Here we have a glimpse into the spiritual emaciation that is taking place beneath the hustle and bustle of our joylessly materialistic, hyper-sexualized, and functionally irreligious world. It is a world in despair even when it remains unconsciously so. It is a world of weightlessness, of "the unbearable lightness of being," a fragmented world characterized by what the French theologian Henri de Lubac brilliantly termed "the waning of ontological density."[4] A forlorn sense pervaded Mr. Samuels' article. Whatever the putative benefits of having been freed from tradition, that freedom has been accompanied by the loss of a sense of being part of a larger story in the context of which one's life might make sense, a story about why we're here and what we should be about while we are, a story that demands something of us and that situates our lives in a living historical drama in which what we do has both meaning and consequence. The loss of a sense of a common historical narrative is exactly what has occurred in our time. In his 1929 book, *Progress and Religion*, the historian Christopher Dawson recognized this underlying problem and anticipated the existential ramifications which were to puzzle Mr. Samuels seven decades later:

> The achievement of the last two centuries would hardly have been possible had there not existed a view of the universe and of the nature of reality which was easily comprehensible to the average man and equally accepted by the men of science. At present no such common world view is possible, and modern science is poised insecurely on the verge of a metaphysical abyss which is continually threatening to engulf it.[5]

---

4 The word ontology and its cognates will recur throughout our explorations, almost always in the context of our inquiry into the dawn of humanity, where we distinguish *cultural* origination and *ontological* origination, the former referring to the emergence of the rudiments of human social collaboration and the latter referring to the origin of human nature or the human person. When de Lubac speaks of the waning of ontological density he means the experience of existential insubstantiality, which is the starting point of our own inquiry in this chapter and the next.

5 Christopher Dawson, *Progress and Religion* (Garden City, NY: Doubleday & Co., 1960), 180.

In light of technological powers and genetic experiments in which the moral implications and historical consequences are as disturbing as they are incalculable, Dawson's concern about the metaphysical abyss over which he saw science poised is prescient indeed. But the edge of that same metaphysical abyss is crowded with people unaware of how they got there, and whose options seem disconcertingly multiple, conditional, and arbitrary. Why get married? Why bother? What are families for?

Samuels' anomie is experienced by countless numbers of his contemporaries. Nonetheless, as a diagnostic key the "radical selfishness" of the article's title is far too banal. It is almost as useless as the litany of cultural changes ostensibly associated with the onset of the malaise Mr. Samuels laments: the civil rights movement, women's liberation, the movement from the cities to the suburbs, the birth of rock-and-roll. What the article fails to analyze, however, it ingeniously depicts. It begins with a lament over the breakup of a relationship, a vague and undefined relationship that seems to have dissolved for reasons that are not entirely clear. Reference to the demise of the relationship flows seamlessly into a brief discussion of the kind of freedom enjoyed by many young adults in our society today. Those less advantaged are doubtless constrained in ways that bright and well-educated young professionals are not, but the disconcerting nature of freedom as it is understood in contemporary popular culture no doubt remains problematic even for those with less latitude for indulging themselves.

We return, then, to the question, not so much of problematic relationships, of these the world has always consisted, but of a fundamental misconception of the idea of freedom, one in which freedom and the responsibilities entailed in committed relationships are seen as antithetical. At one level, of course, there is truth in this assessment, but it is a truth based on a very weak understanding of freedom and its spiritual depth. Our civilization rests on the strength of the natural family and on the willingness to sacrifice freedom, understood in adolescent terms, in favor of freedom freely subordinated to the responsibilities of loving service. The latter form of freedom has been hallowed in those cultures that have had the great good fortune to have fallen under biblical influence. The situation Mr. Samuels describes results from the attenuation of that influence, and it arguably has a more deleterious impact on non-believers than on religiously serious Christians and Jews. Christians, by definition, carry the Christian ethos within themselves and their worshiping communities. On the other hand, when Christians fall under the influence of the superficial spirit-of-the-age anthropology that regards freedom as a synonym for the unencumbered life, they pay an especially great price. Even though what Hans Urs von Balthasar said of Christians has at least broad social applicability to non-Christians as well, he was right to underscore the particular danger contemporary culture poses for Christians. "There may be many sorts of sociological reasons why men today are so reluctant to commit their whole existence," wrote Balthasar. "But if they see that in this the axe is laid at the roots of their existence as Christians, then they have cause for reflection."[6]

The "wild divorce court" of which Chesterton spoke is as corrosive of human community and human happiness as it is lethal to the Christian vocation. But there is more at stake in this "wild divorce court" than the domestic tranquility or the degree of personal satisfaction that accompanies it. Wrenching as they are, the symptoms of this widespread lassitude must not be mistaken for its essence. Mr. Samuels was documenting the attenuation of the bonds of relationship and the growing reluctance to unreservedly take on the responsibilities they entail. To his credit, however, he seemed to realize both that it was a far broader and deeper crisis and that beyond its interpersonal ramifications, it represented a perilous anthropological experiment which Western culture had rather cavalierly undertaken:

> It is hard to put my finger on exactly when this change was set in motion, or what the larger forces behind it might be. Only that the old rules no longer apply, and that coherent narratives, the

6 Hans Urs von Balthasar, *Elucidations*, trans. John Riches (San Francisco: Ignatius Press, 1998), 304.

stories that tell us who we are and where we are going, are getting harder and harder to find. There is the decline of organized religion and the nation-state, the failure of politics, the reduction of human behavior to chemicals in the brain, the absence of the sense of common purpose.

Coherent narratives, "the stories that tell us who we are and where we are going, are getting harder and harder to find." Here we have a hint of the yawning abyss on the edge of which many of Mr. Samuels' less attentive contemporaries continue to celebrate the unfettered autonomy about which he was perceptive enough to express misgivings. How many people today, especially young people, live without a palpable sense of common purpose, bereft of a story about why they are here and how they should behave while they are? What if, Mr. Samuels asks, "the freedom to rearrange reality more or less to our liking is the only freedom we have?" A distressing number of people have come more or less to that conclusion.

In 1964, during the Second Vatican Council and decades before he was to become Pope Benedict XVI, Joseph Ratzinger preached a sermon before a congregation of Catholic students in which he said:

> [M]en are unable, of themselves, to give any meaning to their individual and collective stories. If they were left to their own devices, human history would run out into nothing, into nihilism, into meaninglessness. No one has grasped this more profoundly than the poets of our time, who feel and live in that solitude of man left to himself, who describe the boredom and pointlessness that are the basic sense of such a man who becomes a hell for himself and others.[7]

David Samuels may not be a poet, but he can be counted among those who came to recognize the boredom and pointless-

---

7 Joseph Ratzinger, *What It Means to Be a Christian*, trans. Henry Taylor (San Francisco: Ignatius Press, 2006), 61–2.

ness of people left to their own devices and who "lack any sense of necessary connection to anything larger than their own narrowly personal aims and preoccupations."

As the civilization that formed around and was formed by Catholic Christianity has slowly de-Christianized itself, those charged with assessing the crisis in the midst of which we now find ourselves have tended to do so by defaulting to a set of morally feckless and anthropologically dubious assumptions about history and the human predicament. We remain baffled by the most distressing developments of our time because many of those surveying them—whether historians, journalists, or commentators—rely on intellectual presuppositions and epistemological reflexes left over from the European Enlightenment of the eighteenth century and the modernist dogmas and nihilist gestures into which they morphed in the nineteenth and twentieth. In the absence of a more penetrating analysis, we casually assume that the contemporary predicament can be both assessed and rectified by recourse to political, economic, sociological, or psychological ingenuity. Of course, each of these interpretive tools sheds some light on our world, but it is increasingly the case that the more serious and more historically emblematic the event is, the more likely that it will be recalcitrant to both analysis and remediation when analyzed exclusively with these now rather shop-worn and ideologically encumbered social sciences.

"The communities to which men belong in the democratic world," writes the French political philosopher Pierre Manent, "no longer command them."[8] As Manent takes pains to point out, these communities include not only the family, the nation, and the Church, but that vast community that supplies the ballast for any social arrangement that hopes to have stability. "[T]he past itself, as the community of those who are dead, has lost all commanding authority, whether in the social, moral, political or religious order," Manent writes. "[I]t is now only the ensemble of 'places of memory' open to a kind of historical tourism." Manent laments, not only that contemporary literature has taken as its appointed task the unmasking of the "deception of

8 Pierre Manent, "Modern Individualism," *Crisis Magazine* (Oct. 1995).

human bonds, the lie of love, the inanity or deceptiveness of language," but also that the teaching of history in the West is today largely characterized by what he calls a "negative anthropology, supported not by faith, but by distrust."

> This movement opposes and substitutes itself for the two great authorities which previously nourished literature: the Greek and Roman models, on one hand, and the Christian Scriptures on the other. There is no longer heroic conduct, no path towards wisdom, no journey of the soul towards God, but quite exactly a "voyage at the end of the night" in which it is a matter of discovering finally what it is to be a pure individual, beyond any social bond or even any language.[9]

In his study of the work of Hans Urs von Balthasar, Cyril O'Regan offers this echo of Manent's assessment:

> It is not an accident then that the Enlightenment spawns a culture of deracination, for prescribing the move beyond roots is essential to the Enlightenment ethos. On behalf of modernity the Enlightenment presents the license to forget as essentially a matter of being human. The roots to be forgotten are endless and include the nation, ethnic group, community, physical place, social and gender roles. The Christian tradition is, of course, an object of such forgetting, indeed historically the prime one, since it represents an obstacle to the Enlightenment ethos in general and the imperative to forget in particular in the memory enacted in liturgy, in its customs and cults which bring the past to bear on the present, and its commitment to particular beliefs and values that appear to have timeless sanction.[10]

The liberationist cast of modern thought has driven moderns and postmoderns into the cul-de-sac of autonomous individualism, where, as Manent asserts: "Men do not have any natural connections." But there is more, and here the French philosopher is especially percipient: "Just as for Kierkegaard, to be a Christian is to become a Christian, for the modern man conscious of himself, to be an individual means to *become* an individual, and to become

---

9  Ibid.

10  O'Regan, *The Anatomy of Misremembering*, 12.

more and more an individual." This incessant demand that one become an individual requires not only that he eschew all affiliations or any associations that might limit his spontaneity, but also that he ceaselessly distinguish himself from other individuals whose examples he might otherwise be accused of mimicking. The unremitting pressure to demonstrate one's independence from the social influence of others causes the self-styled individual to resort to more and more idiosyncratic social gestures in appearance and behavior, all of which will be traceable to a model who is being emulated but whose influence is unacknowledged or camouflaged to prevent both the imitator himself and his observers from recognizing the mimicry underlying his labored pantomime. The secret mimeticism beneath the surface of the assertion of autonomy drives the process toward ever more desperate gesticulations of authenticity which in fact amount to an open declaration of its opposite. On the social level, the end result is a spiritual alienation from oneself and from a healthy social matrix, an alienation from which relief is often enough sought in crude and ultimately violent forms of social solidarity. Thus it is that the effort to demonstrate one's individuality is proof of its attenuation, from the later stages of which the erstwhile individualist may well seek relief in mass movements of the most dubious kind. Eric Hoffer once observed that when the attainment of individual self-respect is thwarted, "the nationalist spirit of the people becomes more ardent and extreme."[11] Whenever in what follows we speak of the late modern aspiration to autonomous individuality we mean our critique to include the danger of the social aggregation of alienated individuals into virulent and violent collectivities, the analysis of which awaits us in the following chapter.

---

11 Quoted: *The Viking Book of Aphorisms*, ed. W.H. Auden and Louis Kronenberger (Viking Press, 1981), 233.

# The Emergence of Homo Sapiens

What is it that makes Girard's theory presenting *Homo sapiens* as
the emergent religious animal so illuminating and so cogent?
We might answer briefly: because it meets, better than any other
known theory, the two primary requirements resting upon any
theory of emergence: it accounts for both the most significant
continuities and the quantum leap involved in the passage from
animal to human. More than that: it holds these two vast and
complex imperatives of understanding together according to the
simplest form of reciprocity. It is a beautiful theory in the sense
that $E = mc^2$ is a beautiful theory.[1]—Paul Gifford

UNTIL his retirement in 1997, René Girard held the Andrew B.
Hammond Chair of French Language, Literature, and Civilization at Stanford University. In 2005 he was elected to the French
Academy. On his death in 2015, a fellow Frenchman compared
him to the great historian and moralist Alexis de Tocqueville.
Whereas Tocqueville saw aspects of the American social arrangements of which the Americans themselves were unaware, Girard
performed the same role with respect to human culture as such.
His work in the fields of literature, the humanities, and social science led him to recognize some quite obvious but rarely thematized anthropological facts: namely that above and beyond
instinctual appetite or what the philosophical tradition calls natural desire is a form of desire that profoundly shapes and fairly
defines human motivation, namely mimetic desire, desire
aroused by another's desire and that easily leads to rivalry with
the model whose desire one imitates. This bears on the question

---

1 Paul Gifford, "Homo religiosus in Mimetic Perspective," *How We Became
Human: Mimetic Theory and the Science of Evolutionary Origins*, ed. Pierpaolo
Antonello and Paul Gifford (East Lansing, MI: Michigan State University
Press, 2015), 309–10.

of hominization inasmuch as culture became necessary for survival precisely when the instinctive dominance-submission mechanisms that served to curtail violence in the animal kingdom proved inadequate to that task in the case of a creature endowed with seemingly insatiable, metaphysical, and fickle desires, all too prone to replicate the desires of others. We will turn to the question of hominization—the birth of humanity—below. Here we will give a brief overview of Girard's essential insight.

Human desire, Girard argues, is always aroused, redirected, and intensified by the desire of another. We desire what we see another desiring, striving to obtain, or enjoying. Two children in a room full of toys inevitably want the same toy, and the more emphatically each expresses a desire for it, the more the other desires it and the more heated the rivalry between the two becomes. Far from outgrowing our childhood predilection for imitating the desires of others, experience teaches us to engage in the mimetic contest in ever more subtle, complex, and self-deluding ways. Every reaching for a desired object or gloating over its possession amounts to a public declaration of the object's desirability. Those who witness such a gesture will be encouraged by it to desire the same object, depending more on the prestige the model enjoys in the eyes of the imitator than on the inherent desirability of the object. The second aspirant for possession of the object will find himself in conflict with the one from whom he learned to desire it. The resulting conflict will have two social ramifications. First, the desire for the object will be intensified by the proximity of a rival claimant—proximity understood in both the physical and social sense. Secondly, the escalating desire of the rivals will further glamorize the object of desire, not only in the eyes of the existing rivals, but also in the eyes of onlookers, who will tend to imitate the intensifying desires of the existing antagonists and join in the struggle to possess the object. As more rivals enter the fray and the conflict grows more intense and polyvalent: the rivals will become increasingly more obsessed (negatively) with each other than they originally were (positively) with the object over which the rivalry began. It is at this point that the phenomenon loses its center and takes on a life of its own. As long as all rivals are preoccupied with the object of desire, the social drama has a focus and therefore a degree of rationality. With the intensification of the rivalry, however, the rivals shift their attention from the object over which they are in conflict to the most proximate rival for its possession. Thus, by a process that Girard has masterfully thematized, there comes into being a completely undifferentiated and increasingly violent brawl over precisely nothing, now operating in predictable ways toward a predictable outcome.

Once the passions born of mimetic rivalry overwhelmed the instincts that kept them in check in the animal world, the survival of primitive humanity depended on the acquisition of cultural procedures for constraining these passions. The question is: How can such violence be transformed into the nascent social consensus upon which conventional culture depends? The fiercer the conflict, the more susceptible those caught up in it will be to mimetic suggestion. The penultimate stage of the crisis consists of innumerable concurrent rivalries, each merging indistinguishably into others in its vicinity. Though purely the product of mimetic reciprocity, these conflicts are characterized by what, for simplicity's sake, we can call *accusatory* gestures. For each rival will behave as though his immediate *bête noire* is the ultimate adversary, the one responsible for the overall crisis. As the binary rivalries escalate in intensity and contaminate each other, those caught up in them grow more susceptible to mimetic suggestion at the same time that accusations most likely to be imitated grow both more fantastic and impassioned. If nothing arrests the process, it is inevitable that one of the "accusations" will eventually be expressed so ostentatiously that those in its vicinity will succumb to its mimetic effects and redirect their own animosity accordingly. Whereas an *acquisitive* gesture, when imitated, leads to envy, rivalry, and conflict, an *accusatory* gesture unites those who surrender to its mimetic appeal, lending the accusation a moral certitude directly proportional to the degree of social unanimity it generates. The logic of the mimetic phenomenon, in the absence of any countervailing force, will lead inevitably and precipitously to complete social polarization, or in Girard's phrase: "unanimity minus one."

In the eyes of the terrified mob, the hapless creature who has suddenly become, to borrow a phrase from Shakespeare's *Hamlet*, "the observed of all observers" is catapulted into the status of a metaphysical being—a superhuman monster. The social apotheosis of this unfortunate creature survives his death at the hands of the mob, for his death coincides with the startling transformation of the terror of violence into the peace of a community unified by its single-minded goal of destroying the monster. So abruptly is the victim's monstrosity turned to beneficence that the valence of his metaphysical status is simply reversed. In the bewildered eyes of the newly formed community he is seen to be a god, thanks to whom the community has mysteriously been saved from the terrors that prevailed while the god was threatening destruction.[2] Quite logically, the beneficiaries of this blessed peace replicate as best they can the process that produced it. They reenact the drama in rituals of blood sacrifice; they recount the event that turned madness into peace in their myths, and they establish taboos to prevent a spontaneous eruption of this crisis. Archaic religion is born.

Writing before René Girard made bolder and more creative use of the data, Mircea Eliade was nevertheless forced by this data to reckon with cultural-founding violence. He writes, for instance, that "according to the myths of earliest cultivators, man became what he is today—mortal, sexualized, and condemned to work—in consequence of a primordial murder; *in illo tempore* a divine being, quite often a woman or a maiden, sometimes a child or a man, allowed himself to be immolated in order that tubers or fruit trees should grow from his body. This first murder basically changed the mode of being of human life."[3] Stories about sacrificial victims allowing themselves to be immolated can be regarded with deep suspicion. The myth of the willing vic-

---

2 There are, of course, countless variations on this scenario, as would be expected in light of the fact that the unwitting purpose of each interpretations of the event is to veil the truth from the eyes of those now enjoying the social benefits of his death.

3 Mircea Eliade, *The Two and the One*, trans. by J.M. Cohen (New York: Harper & Row, 1965), 98. Quoted: *Myths, Rites, and Symbols: A Mircea Eliade Reader*, vol. 1., ed. Wendell C. Beane and William G. Doty (New York: Harper & Row, 1975), 254.

tim is embedded in sacrificial thought. An aside is in order.

A typical example of the kind of collective misrecognition that congeals into a myth of the willing victim surfaced with the publication of Mala Sen's *Body: Death by Fire: Sati, Dowry Death and Female Infanticide in Modern India*, a book about an immolation that occurred in northern India. Sen's book was reviewed by the *London Financial Times* journalist, Joan Smith, who wrote:

> The event that prompted Mala Sen to write this book took place in the north-western state of Rajasthan, which borders Pakistan, in 1987. An 18-year-old woman, Roop Kanwar, whose husband had died suddenly, was burned alive on his funeral pyre in the village of Deorala in front of a large crowd. After her death, she was hailed as a Sati Mata, which translates as "pure mother," even though she was childless, and a shrine was set up on the site of her immolation. A social worker who visited the village a few days later found most of the inhabitants insisting that Roop Kanwar's death was "a voluntary act of heroic courage" which had turned her into a goddess and given her the power to answer their prayers. The man was unconvinced, especially when a very different version of the story began to emerge, in which Roop Kanwar had been buried under a heavy load of firewood to prevent her escape.[4]

Those who think that societies that worshiped goddesses rather than male gods were *ipso facto* more solicitous of the welfare of women would do well to consult the anthropological data on just how these goddesses came to be worshiped. In these cases there were, alas, no investigative journalists, and it would be most prudent for those who were drawn together by virtue of the victim's immolation to avert their eyes from details incompatible with the religiously transfigured account of it.

Thanks to the Christianization of the West and the quasi-Westernization of the world, at this point in history the unanimity— or near-unanimity—of the community in cases such as this will often depend in part on subtle coercion, fear of reprisals, and other ways of enforcing adherence to a mythological remem-

---

4 Joan Smith, "Burning Issue of Women's Rights," *Financial Times of London*, March 31 (2001).

brance. Even when these things are factored in, however, the myth that emerged in the aftermath of the murder of Roop Kanwar and the speed with which it apparently emerged cannot have been something that was merely imposed on people who knew otherwise. Clearly here, as even more surely in the ancient world, the violence aroused a social predilection for its own mythic misrecognition. Vestiges of similar myths and rituals suggest that antiquity is littered with events much like the one that occurred in Rajasthan in 1987.

According to the pioneering study of the ancient city by the French historian Numa Denis Fustel de Coulanges, the ancients "stood in fear" of all things religious and—more to the point— "dared not reason upon it, or discuss it, or examine it."[5] Consistent with this is the anthropologist Walter Burkert's observation that: "Sacrificial killing is the basic experience of the 'sacred,'" and that "the strange and extraordinary events that the participant in the sacrifice is forced to witness are all the more intense because they are left *undiscussed*."[6] Myth excels in narrating the past without actually discussing its core moral reality, the discussion of which would destroy the efficacy of the ritual repetition of the event in question.

To clarify: like Burkert and Fustel and many others, Girard uses the term *sacred* to designate the primitive forms of sacrality rooted in violence. In anthropological discourse this designation is unproblematic. As we will note in later chapters, the terms *sacred* and *sacrifice* touch on matters of perennial importance to mankind, and they cannot and must not be expunged from our vocabulary simply because, speaking strictly anthropologically, the forms these deeply imbedded human predilections took in antiquity were sacred and sacrificial only in the crudest and most morally troubling ways. The fact that we have the moral clarity

5 Numa Denis Fustel de Coulanges, *The Ancient City: A Study on the Religion, Laws, and Institutions of Greece and Rome* (Baltimore: Johns Hopkins University Press, 1980), 159.

6 Walter Burkert, *Homo Necans: The Anthropology of Ancient Greek Sacrificial Ritual and Myth*, trans. Peter Bing (Berkeley: The University of California Press, 1983), 3; my italic emphasis.

to recognize the darker features of the primitive sacred is due to the biblical revelation, but again, as we shall see, the Christian revelation not only exposes what is most troubling about the sacred and the sacrificial, but it brings into the world new and deeply meaningful experiences to which these terms can legitimately be applied without invoking the primitive and unsavory connotations associated with them in pagan antiquity. In what follows, however, we will often use *sacred* and *sacrifice* to refer to the primitive forms of these things.

Archaic religion, the emergence of which marks the birth of culture itself, was born of the transfiguration of violence into religious awe and holy dread, the moral effect of which was to erase the truth about the victim on whom the violence of the community fell. Our most ancient ancestors, in other words, prevented violence precisely by *pre-venting* it onto expendable victims and thereafter ritually reproducing the catharsis with which the original violence was concluded, thereby rejuvenating the social solidarity it produced. We will have more to say about catharsis in a later chapter.

Morally and epistemologically, the frenzied mob has eyes that cannot see and ears that cannot hear; they "know not what they do" (Lk. 23:34). So abruptly is the terrifying chaos replaced by an intense and never before experienced social solidarity, that the survivors ascribe religious meaning to its dénouement. The newfound community attributes its otherwise inexplicable peace to the death of the victim, who is deified according to an interpretation that our primitive ancestors would have found quite plausible. The victim, who in life was a metaphysical monster, is transcendentalized in death while retaining his terrifying potential. This interpretation of the event gives rise to religious anxieties that are propitiatory rather than pious, for our ancient ancestors saw the gods as a threat to be kept at bay by apotropaic offerings of blood—ritual replicas of the murder, which brought a social crisis to a cathartic dénouement and conjured a community into being by providing it with a god to worship, fear, and appease. Fustel expresses the matter succinctly: "Neither did the gods love man, nor did man love his gods. He believed in their existence, but would have wished that they did not exist. . . . His great inquietude was lest he might incur their displeasure. He was occupied all his life in appeasing them."[7]

Moreover, the ritual reenactment of the originally spontaneous violence, itself an act of social mimesis, demanded the highest degree of scrupulosity. Every ritual particular was to be performed with utmost attention. Again Fustel provides the overview:

> The slightest gesture of the one who performed the sacrifice, and the smallest parts of his costume, were governed by strict rules. . . . The nature of the victim, the color of the hair, the manner of slaying it, even the shape of the knife, and the kind of wood employed to roast the flesh—all was fixed for every god by the religion of each family, or of each city. In vain the most fervent heart offered to the gods the fattest victims: if one of the innumerable rites of the sacrifice was neglected, the sacrifice was without effect; the least failure made the sacred act an act of impiety.[8]

Inasmuch as the myths that recount such events are massive misrecognitions of what actually happened, they vary considerably from one cultural setting to another. One of Girard's great contributions was to detect the underlying unity of these mythological accounts, recognizing in each the role of all-against-one violence in the generation of humanity's original cultural structures. The relationship between archaic rituals and the myths that provided their narrative template is obvious. The challenge early researchers faced was that of discerning the nature of that relationship. The Enlightenment bias had ill-prepared the late nineteenth century anthropologists for reckoning with raw religious phenomena, and seeds of today's preoccupation with "texts" were already germinating, the intellectual residue of the Reformation subordination of altar to pulpit. The prevailing bias gave rise to an assumption about the relationship between myth and ritual, namely that the myths came first, born of nothing more troubling than the creative imagination of our ancestors, the rituals being merely later dramatic performances of the mythic narra-

---

7  Fustel de Coulanges, *The Ancient City*, 159–60.
8  Ibid., 160.

tives. Confronted with the ubiquity of blood sacrifices and myths, for example, Mircea Eliade's surmise was typical.

> The exemplary model for all these forms of sacrifice is very probably a cosmogonic myth, that is, the myth that explains the Creation by the killing of a primordial Giant: his organs produce the various cosmic regions. . . . In general, the cosmogonic myth has been shown to be the model for all myths and rites related to a "making," a "work," a "creation." The mythical motif of a "birth" brought about by an immolation is found in countless contexts.[9]

Alluding almost as gingerly as the myths themselves to the violence they reenacted, Eliade assumed that the myths preceded the rituals. According to this assumption, myth, the story of origin, has no origin itself. It is the pure product of human ingenuity, a naïve idea for which both rationalism and romanticism had a peculiar weakness. This assumption precluded the recognition that both rituals and myths are the vestigial residue of an actual violent event, the event that either brought the community into being or rejuvenated it by terminating a crisis that would have otherwise destroyed it.

"The worshiper experiences the god most powerfully," writes Walter Burkert, "in the deadly blow of the axe, the gush of blood."[10] The gods, from all appearances, demanded blood. Ritual sacrifice was clearly how the world worked. Human and animal sacrifice, observed the German ethnologist Adolf E. Jensen, and all the ritual customs related to it, "are not individual cultural elements, which have come together more or less accidentally in a cultural group." They are all, Jensen argues, "to be derived from a central idea, namely that of a divinity who was killed and who by his death established the present order of existence of the world."[11] Or as René Girard succinctly put it: "Mak-

---

9 *Myths, Rites, Symbols: A Mircea Eliade Reader,* vol 1, ed. Beane & Doty (New York: Harper & Row, 1976), 215.

10 Burkert, *Homo Necans,* 2.

11 A.E. Jensen, *Die getötete Gottheit: Weltbild einer frühen Kultur,* Stuttgart, 1966; quoted: Raymund Schwager, *Jesus in the Drama of Salvation* (New York: Crossroad, 1999), 127.

ing gods by killing victims is the human gesture par excellence and, each time that they do it, human beings widen the gap between themselves and the true God a little more, they take part in his murder."[12] We pause to underscore the significance of this remark: The killing of victims produced the false gods of pagan antiquity, but in killing these victims our ancestors took part in the murder of the true God. But the birth of the new gods depended on the complete misrecognition of the fact that the true God was murdered in the process. We will draw out the staggering implications of this observation in a later chapter.

Humans are, indeed, *homo religiosus*, religious by nature. Nonetheless, it counts as more evidence of our fallen condition that the first social manifestation of this most precious human capacity was a tangled skein of fear, ferocity, violence, and superstition. That humans are intrinsically religious beings is hardly an unambiguous source of reassurance. Rather it simply means that if we are not rescued from our self-absorption and pseudo-religious exhilarations we will fuse them into an intoxicating idolatry that—to adopt a T. S. Eliot trope—will famish the craving it promises to feed and ravage the world in its desperation.

There are two very distinct ways in which religion in the ancient world was radically different from the religious practices with which those living in our culture might be familiar. First, far from being objects of piety and affection, the gods of the ancients were dangerous and deadly. Appeasing them was the primary business of religious ritual. Occasionally, to be sure, these dangerous gods could be coaxed into bestowing a favor on their supplicants, but it was their more dreaded and predictable wrath that inspired the supplication, evoked the deference, and compelled the ritual scrupulosity. Secondly, religion in the archaic world meant something nearly incomprehensible to those who associate the term with the sober decorum of Christian liturgies or synagogue Judaism. The gods of antiquity were for the most part dreaded figures that had to be kept from visiting their worshipers

---

12 René Girard, *When These Things Begin: Conversations with Michael Treguer*, trans. Trevor Cribben Merrill (East Lansing, MI: Michigan State University Press, 2014), 77.

with scourges by ritual offerings of blood, which reenacted the darkly veiled event that gave rise to both the gods and the worshipping community in the first instance. Intimately linked with the sacrificial rituals are the taboos required to prevent a spontaneous eruption of violence and the myths that recount the founding violence so as to flatter the victimizing community and erase the truth about the victim—the truth being that he or she was some hapless wretch on whom the mob fell in its capricious frenzy.

The New Testament offers the outlines of a demonology of sorts, which becomes immensely important in bringing to light the process that leads to the unanimous immolation of a community's victim. The word devil, *diabolos*, means to throw across (*dia* "across" and *ballein* "to throw"). The devil sows discord by fostering and festering division. When this division produces a level of animosity and mutual antipathy requisite to the demonic dénouement, the devil assumes a new guise and becomes, so to speak, Satan, the accuser. The agitated and socially fractious community fashioned by the sower of discord is now unified by the work of Satan. The accusation finds mimetic replicators whose accusations find even more replicators. The end result is unanimity minus one. The social harmony that the *diabolos* undermined by sowing discord, Satan restores by means of an accusation directed toward a single victim or helpless minority. Thus do the "kingdoms of this world" come into being, human cultures whose prince and operating principle is "Satan." However reluctant one might be to invoke a malevolent metaphysical entity in this regard, little less can do justice to the impersonal, autonomous, and seemingly inexorable way that man's misdirected mimetic passion moves toward its predictable conclusion unless deflected or defused by the mob's unlikely recognition of its own sinfulness or an equally unlikely empathy for the accused—sentiments aroused by biblical thought generally and Christianity especially.

That the first rudimentary forms of human culture came into being in the midst of an event that is structurally identical to the Passion Story might be expected to eventually attract Christian attention. Hans Urs von Balthasar has spoken of "the watermark of the Cross on creation," which serves as a Catholic corrective to the dreary Darwinian exultation of the savage fecundity of tooth and claw. What Balthasar saw in the endless devouring of the weak by the strong, and the surrendering of life by the decrepit to the vigorous, was the paschal drama blindly performed by creatures incapable of the non-instinctual acts of self-sacrifice with which humans would one day be able to ennoble it. In a comparable way, Girard has explicated the cruciformity of culture, providing us with the anthropological analogue to Balthasar's watermark of the Cross on creation.

To suggest that what Girard calls the surrogate victim mechanism is what made human culture possible may seem baffling to those unfamiliar with his work and the anthropological data for which it accounts. But it is no more baffling than the related Christian claim that humans have been freed from the power of sin and death by a victim whose innocence neither the religious and political powers that sanctioned it, nor the excited mob that demanded it, were capable of obscuring. The central event of the Christian drama reveals the truth about how (fallen) human culture and religion came into being, "things hidden since the foundation of the world" (Mt. 13:35). In light of the foregoing, at least anthropologically speaking, *the* "sin (singular) of the world" (Jn. 1:29) can be seen as the endlessly reenacted drama whereby the community purges itself of its *sins* (plural) by offloading the animosities born of these sins onto one figure—the "scapegoat." In revealing the innocence of the Victim on Golgotha, and thereby progressively crippling the efficacy of this preternatural ruse for taking away *sins*, Christ, the Lamb of God, takes away *the sin* of the world, which is precisely fallen humanity's way of turning sins into an unearned and delusional experience of moral righteousness at the expense of its victims.

Beginning with discoveries and insights gained from the careful reading of first literature and then anthropology, Girard turned to the Scriptures, only to find there an anthropological perspicacity that completely distinguished this tradition, and in light of which the continuity between the Old and New Testaments came more clearly into focus. Girard saw the mounting chorus of anti-sacrificial admonitions issued by the prophets and the sympathy for the victim found in the psalms and wisdom literature as evidence of the Bible's religious and moral movement toward the culminating, history-altering revelation of the Cross. Those who might regard Girard's work as the reduction of the mystery of Christian redemption to a moral repudiation of an odious example of human sinfulness are mistaken. Not only has Girard shown how profoundly and unavoidably humans are implicated in the sacrificial paradigm, but his discovery of these things was accompanied by the deepening of his Catholic faith, sacramental participation, and personal piety—indicative of both his humility and of the gravity of the anthropological conclusions to which his research led him. Notwithstanding his own religious faith, in the interest of having his anthropological discoveries taken seriously by those who instinctively recoil from any hint of Christian special pleading, Girard tried to defend his work exclusively in terms intelligible to the social sciences. This doubtless involved some sacrifices, as those privileged to know him personally are aware. The theological reticence and the associated argumentative constrictions that Girard adopted professionally, far from being a sign of timidity, were part of an effort to make even non-believers aware of the uniqueness and universality of Christian revelation.

More than once, Girard told this author that he felt that his chief intellectual challenge seemed always to elude him, namely, accounting for his insight into the fundamental role of mimesis in human life and human affairs in such a way that its profound meaning would not be camouflaged by its seeming obviousness. In an interview conducted some years ago, Girard mused about how daunting that challenge was:

> The mimetic hypothesis makes me think not so much of a very tangled ball of twine but rather of a road map that has been folded over on itself so many times that it's just a little rectangle. To use it, you have to unfold it, and then fold it up again. Clumsy people like me can never find the original folds, and the map soon tears. . . . If I could do just one thing in the time I have left, I would like to learn to unfold and refold my road map in such a

way as not to tear it. If I managed to do this, I could then write an apology for Christianity that was accessible to so-called uncultivated people, to those who probably aren't wrong not to have followed any of what's been happening over the last thirty years in the social sciences and philosophy.[13]

What this casual and off-handed remark conveys is that Girard's insistence on demonstrating the scientific basis of his anthropological insights can in no way be taken to suggest that his intellectual aspiration was purely scientific, far from it. To "write an apology for Christianity" accessible to the average person, Girard revealed to his interviewer, was an underlying aspiration of his later career.

The future Pope Benedict XVI, writing in the last decade of the twentieth century about the role the Creeds play in opening the true meaning of the Scriptures, resorted to a compelling metaphor that is equally applicable to Girard's work.

> [T]he Creeds, as the fundamental form and the lasting crystallization point of what would later be called dogma, are not an addition to Scripture but, rather, the common thread leading through them; namely the canon made within the canon; Ariadne's thread, so to speak, which allows Theseus to walk through the labyrinth and makes its plan recognizable. Consequently, neither are they an external clarification added to what is unclear; rather, they are precisely a reference to the self-illuminating *Gestalt*, the highlighting of the significant form that allows the reader to see the clarity of what is authentically scriptural.[14]

With his mimetic theory and his theory of cultural founding violence, Girard found an anthropological Ariadne's thread running through biblical literature, which he would come to see as both scientifically distinct from the creedal thread to which Cardinal Ratzinger had alluded and entirely compatible with it. In much the same way that Ratzinger found in the creeds the key to the unity of the biblical canon, Girard's anthropological insights

---

13 Ibid., 127–128.

14 Joseph Ratzinger, *Dogma and Preaching: Applying Christian Doctrine to Daily Life*, trans. Michael J. Miller and Matthew J. O'Connell, ed. Michael J. Miller (San Francisco: Ignatius Press, 2011), 29.

allowed him to read the scriptural canon as a single story—in fact the original story, the story to which all the other (mythological) stories (unwittingly) point.

Though anthropological thought is itself an intellectual extension of the process of cultural decoding that the biblical tradition inaugurates, the new science, suffused as it was with Enlightenment prejudices, has been tardy in reckoning with the anthropological mother lode Girard had discovered the Bible to be. The animus against Christianity with which modern social science was infected predisposed early researchers to see the structural similarity between myth and gospel—namely, a social crisis leading to the immolation and religious apotheosis of a single victim—as further confirmation of the mythic nature of Christianity and as further grounds for dismissing Christian claims of uniqueness and universality.

Under the circumstances, the Christian reluctance to acknowledge the similarity between myth and gospel was perfectly understandable. Even though Christians had from the beginning seen Christianity as the culmination and purification of both pagan and Hebraic religion, they had also insisted on the utterly unique revelation of the Cross. The anthropological discovery of the paschal structure in extant remnants of archaic religion appeared to present a serious challenge to the claim of uniqueness. This difficulty was compounded by the fact that the defense of Christian uniqueness would increasingly have to be made in a world that was becoming one large electronically linked Areopagus in which Christian truth-claims had to be made within the hearing of countless people, cultures, and religious traditions to whom these claims seemed both ludicrous and offensive. Embarrassed by this new situation, many Christians have chosen the line of least resistance, adopting an ahistorical status-quo pluralism ideologically averse to any criteria that might compromise their multicultural *bona fides* by putting either Christianity, or the cultures under its influence, in a favorable light vis-à-vis other traditions and cultures. This ideological sentimentality makes a mockery of the Christian catholicity it nevertheless parodies, and to genuflect before its fashionable slogans is to shirk the perennial Christian obligation to proclaim the Good News of Christ to the ends of the earth. If the prevalent trend is to be countered, its feigned neutrality exposed for what it is, and the true uniqueness and history-altering centrality of Christ crucified proposed afresh, then, as Girard argued, the issue must be joined on precisely the question of the structural similarity between gospel and myth. This was no small challenge given the scope and seeming incoherence of the anthropological data.

It is clear that Girard did not set out to discover the pagan foreshadowing of the Christian revelation. Until his work led to that discovery, the sheer variety of evidence and its apparently complete incompatibility with Christianity would have dissuaded such an attempt. The distinguished French theologian, Cardinal Henri de Lubac says this about man's ancient religious rituals and myths:

> [W]e can certainly see the mystical aspirations of which history gives us so many examples—some curious, some magnificent— that bear witness to that destiny for which God has made us, but we can only do so by projecting upon them the light of our faith. Taken literally in themselves, especially when it comes to the theories commenting on them and systematizing them, we should be equally justified in condemning them as the absolute antithesis of Christian salvation.[15]

In fact, archaic religion was both the absolute antithesis of Christian salvation and a crude groping toward it. "What might quite rightly seem after the event and allowing for some fundamental changes," de Lubac writes, "as having been a 'preparation for the Gospel,' is also, and in fact primarily, an obstacle to it."[16] The fact that man's first forms of religious life might be seen either as crude parodies of the Christian revelation or as preparations for it is surely fascinating. Balthasar had recognized this, and he, like Girard, saw it as evidence for the very Christian uniqueness that many anthropologists and social scientists thought it disproved.

15 Henri de Lubac, *The Mystery of the Supernatural*, trans. Rosemary Sheed (New York: Crossroad Herder, 1998), 222.

16 Ibid., 223.

> It does not matter whether or not [the Cross of Christ] resembles the myths of dying gods, for why should not the myths be a feeling after, as it were, an empty form of that which must occur in true history and yet which cannot be imagined in historical terms?[17]

We should not allow Balthasar's phrase "in true history" to go unremarked. For it is precisely the true history of the world that we seek, the one true story in the context of which all the other stories can find their rightful place. Paradoxically, therefore, it was by completing the work of researchers who thought they were disproving Christian claims of uniqueness that Girard has been able to substantiate these claims decisively. Nonetheless, the very fact that in reasserting the uniqueness of Christian truth-claims, Girard cited the evidence adduced by others to prove that Christianity was just another myth was bound to arouse suspicion among more traditionally minded Christians. Girard nevertheless insists that one has to begin with the similarities between myth and gospel in order to bring out the true and radical differences. If myth and gospel are dealing with two totally different realities, as many Christians had tended to argue, then the differences between them are as theologically nugatory as the similarities are intellectually inconsequential. The difference between them can be significant only if they deal with the same fundamental event, and especially if myth and gospel respectively offer radically different interpretations of that event, one true and one false. In myth, the victim is "guilty"—that is, the victim's death is justified—and the victimizing community is exonerated. In the Gospel, as we know, the victim is innocent and the community culpably oblivious—"they know not what they do."

The innocence of someone unanimously condemned by an enraged mob strikes anyone living in a culture under Christian influence as hardly more than common sense, so aware has Christianity made us of the perversity of precisely that scapegoating scenario. And yet the moral visibility of the scapegoat represents the single-most historically significant anthropological breakthrough in human history. So prevalent today is the solici-

---

17 Balthasar, *Elucidations*, 51.

tude for "scapegoats" which Christianity bequeathed to the world that this moral attentiveness is routinely hijacked and redeployed as a highly selective and politically correct critique of Christianity itself. Given the Christian origin of René Girard's intellectual instincts and the explicit Christian implications of his scholarly discoveries, it is somewhat but not altogether surprising that some have found no better use of his work than to deploy it in the re-adjudication of Christianity's historical failures. Beyond that, an over-the-counter version of Girardian thought has proven attractive to those smitten by the victimary thinking that is so fashionable in the redoubts of contemporary liberalism, and according to which Girard's work is more or less reducible to a moral judgment on scapegoating and its seemingly obvious political implications for all institutions other than those enjoying a "progressive" dispensation. To the enforcers of the new post-Christian order, Christian truth-claims are insufficiently respectful of contrary truth-claims, and Christian moral principles are the perpetuation of Christianity's longstanding insensitivity to those with differing moral assessments. Thus it is that Christianity's creedal truth-claims and traditional moral principles have been castigated by appeal to the work of a man who was himself brought by that same body of work to a deeper Catholic faith and to regular participation in the most traditional of Gregorian liturgies.

Christianity's adversaries have recently sought to appropriate the moral seriousness, the theological depth, and the cultural beneficence of Christianity, even as they have disparaged the source of these blessings. This effort is roughly analogous to a scene in the Fourth Gospel in which Jesus—the Way, the Truth, and the Life—offered to set his Jewish audience free from a bondage of which they were completely oblivious. In the spirit of their age and ours, they took umbrage, insisting that they were already free, and asserting their Abrahamic patrimony in warrant thereof. Recognizing the violence latent in their sudden antipathy, Jesus, conceding that they were *descendants* of Abraham, insisted that they were nevertheless not *children* of Abraham. For their sudden bristling indignation was evidence that they were succumbing to precisely the sacrificial reflexes from which Abraham was turned away by the angel on Mount Moriah.

> You belong to your father the devil and you willingly carry out your father's desires. He was a murderer from the beginning and does not stand in truth, because there is no truth in him. When he tells a lie, he speaks in character, because he is a liar and the father of lies. (Jn. 8:44)

The devil, says Jesus, has been a murderer, a liar, and the father of lies, "from the beginning." According to the latest science, the birth of the cosmic order occurred billions of years ago, at which the entire material content of the universe appeared in "a trillionth of a trillionth of a trillionth of a second." For billions of years thereafter no creature existed who was capable of prayer, sin, or sanctity. Quite obviously, the beginning of which Jesus spoke was the beginning of (fallen) human culture. René Girard's work is indispensable to the anthropological elucidation of this Johannine text. If this murderer has been lying and murdering "from the beginning," the beginning of human culture must have been a murder concealed by a lie. And, however this demonic force might be understood in moral and doctrinal terms, it is clear from this passage, numerous other biblical texts, and Girard's cultural anthropology that reference is being made to socially fractious mimetic entanglements that culminate in violence. There isn't the slightest doubt that the moral responsibility for sin lies with each individual, but it is also the case that an element of mimesis is almost always present in our individual sinfulness, and that the social aggregation of sin is the key to the spontaneous mimetic phenomenon by which the sins of the many are transformed into a violent consensus, the unanimity of which is experienced as restoration of the community's moral rectitude and social harmony.

The beginning of which Jesus speaks in John's Gospel is the beginning of human culture, about which we today know a good deal more than did our ancestors. The faithful ascribe the perspicacity of the Bible to divine inspiration, and the more one delves into the Scriptures the sounder this attribution appears to be.

There is today, however, perhaps one prominent feature of the biblical narrative that does not enjoy the esteem that Girard and most of the faithful have for the Bible as a whole, namely the Genesis accounts of human origins. These obviously imaginative accounts of the dawn of humanity seem utterly useless in trying to access the beginnings of our unique and sin-shackled species. In what follows we will take a closer look.

# Toward a
# Theological Anthropology

Christian principles, ultimately grounded in Christ as Word, are
replete, and show their plenitude in their ability to assimilate
and transform non-Christian culture to which they do not bear
an antithetical relation given the internal link between creation
and redemption.[1]—Cyril O'Regan

CATHOLIC Christianity has distinguished itself by respecting,
from its very beginnings, the quests for truth latent in pagan religions and ascendant in the pagan philosophical tradition that
tried to extricate itself from the superstition that characterized
pagan religiosity. Joseph Ratzinger, before and after he assumed
the Chair of Peter, has often called attention to the fact that the
early Christians were eager to take advantage of the truth-seeking protocols developed by the Greek philosophical tradition.
David Bentley Hart has expressed this well: "Christians rejected
nothing good in the metaphysics, ethics, or method of antique
philosophy, but—with a kind of omnivorous glee—assimilated
such elements as served its ends, and always improved them in
the process."[2] The eager assimilation of Plato and later Aristotle,
the theologically and philosophically fruitful study of Greek
metaphysics, and later still the hard sciences and the social sciences—these were products of the "omnivorous glee" which animated those who had discovered—or were in the process of
discovering—the intellectual Rosetta Stone: the Logos made
flesh. Nor did the early Christians fail to notice in the mystery
cults and pagan religions traces of what Augustine called reli-

---

1 O'Regan, *The Anatomy of Misremembering*, 97.
2 David Bentley Hart, *In the Aftermath: Provocations and Laments* (Grand
Rapids, MI: Eerdmans, 2009), 12.

31

gious yearning (*desiderium*) and inchoate but genuine insight, bound up though these things were with dubious superstitions.

Saint Matthew's story of the magi can be seen as an implicit recognition of the value of all serious truth-seeking enterprises— the ardor of the quest tending to compensate in the long run for the deficiencies of the religious, philosophical, or scientific presuppositions by which it might have been hampered at its outset. In suggesting a collaboration between Christian theology and the social science of anthropology we are simply being faithful to a long tradition. In fact, of course, Christian theology has had a long engagement with anthropology, albeit for the most part with a philosophical anthropology rather than with the social science that goes by that name today. It is to René Girard's credit that he recognized and systematically demonstrated the theological pertinence of the discoveries of field anthropology that others had regarded as antithetical to Christian truth-claims.

Examples abound of the "omnivorous glee" with which Christians continue to collaborate with serious truth-seekers from other traditions and with those relying on epistemological strategies unique to their disciplines. Addressing the scientists and theologians gathered by papal invitation at the Vatican Observatory near Rome, Saint John Paul II said:

> If the cosmologies of the ancient Near Eastern world could be purified and assimilated into the first chapters of Genesis, might contemporary cosmology have something to offer to our reflections upon creation? Does an evolutionary perspective bring any light to bear upon theological anthropology, the meaning of the human person as the *imago Dei*, the problem of Christianity— and even upon the development of doctrine itself? What, if any, are the eschatological implications of contemporary cosmology, especially in light of the vast future of our universe? Can theological method fruitfully appropriate insights from scientific methodology and the philosophy of science?[3]

As his reference here to theological anthropology suggests, John Paul II's eagerness for collaboration extended as well to the findings of the anthropological sciences. Approaching the dia-

---

3 Quoted: Edward T. Oakes, S.J., *Infinity Dwindles to Infancy* (Grand Rapids, MI: William B. Eerdmans, 2011), 435–36.

logue between theology and anthropology from the other end: René Girard once gave an interviewer his assessment of the theological and philosophical context in which his anthropological work should properly be seen:

> In my view, we have here a new illustration of a very great traditional idea, reason and faith upholding each other. *Fides quarens intellectum* and vice versa. That's a Thomist way of reasoning, I think, but it's applied to a domain—anthropology—that in Saint Thomas's era didn't exist in the modern sense. And, once more, it's a question of the Light that is at once what must be seen and what makes it possible to see, *Deum de Deo, Lumen de Lumine.*[4]

Many of those most familiar with Girard's work and anyone who knew Girard personally would probably second the American philosopher Fred Lawrence's exclamation: "What more could an orthodox Roman Catholic theologian ask for?"[5] Girard has made anthropological contributions that are destined to play an important role in the recovery of Christian self-confidence on which so much now depends. John Paul's successor to the Chair of Peter has suggested that the collaboration between theology and anthropology can lead to "the truly most exciting part of Christian faith,"[6] and it is in dialogue with the anthropological work of René Girard that some of the truly most exciting parts of Christian faith are likely to be rediscovered in the years ahead. As we will suggest in more detail below, the same can be said of the theological anthropology of Hans Urs von Balthasar. Notwithstanding the sweeping claims made by each of these original thinkers, and despite their distinctive approaches, they each provide "a painstaking, difficult, and ever-incomplete hermeneutics of the human condition."[7] Girard's intellectual legacy constitutes a social science with intriguingly Christological ramifications.

4 Girard, *When These Things Begin*, 98.

5 Fred Lawrence, "Philosophy, History, and Apocalypse in Voegelin, Strauss, and Girard," *Politics and Apocalypse*, ed. Robert Hamerton-Kelly (East Lansing: Michigan State University Press, 2007), 125.

6 Ratzinger, *Introduction to Christianity*, 212.

7 *How We Became Human: Mimetic Theory and the Science of Evolutionary Origins*, ed. Antonello and Gifford (East Lansing, MI: Michigan State University Press, 2015), xli.

For instance, a good case can be made for seeing Girard's work in light of the passage in the Vatican II document *Gaudium et spes*, which recent popes have declared to be the lens through which to see the true meaning of the Council as a whole: "The truth is that only in the mystery of the incarnate Word does the mystery of man take on light."[8]

Girard's long-time friend and fellow member of the French Academy, Michel Serres, called him the Darwin of the social sciences. It is also the case that Girard's work can serve to extricate us from the dismal anthropology to which Darwin's irreligious reductionists have insisted that we accommodate ourselves. Be that as it may, there is, of course, no inherent necessity for harmonizing biblical, theological, and doctrinal truth-claims with the findings of anthropological science, any more than the biblical account need necessarily be harmonized with evolutionary biology. And yet, beyond the fact that the truth of revelation and the truth of reason and science cannot be at odds, however dissimilar their methodologies might be, Christians have special reason for encouraging a collaboration between theology and anthropology. For Christianity stands or falls on the mystery of the Incarnation, where the human and the divine are opened to one another, and as a result of which, as some of the most distinguished Catholic theologians of recent memory have insisted, every theological statement is also an anthropological one. To the extent that these two structures of thought intersect, they can arouse in one another a welcome spirit of inquiry. Moreover, it may well be the case that these disciplines remain estranged from one another, not fundamentally because of their disparate methodologies, but, ironically, because of a reluctance on the part of the biblical and theological representatives to give full voice to those themes that, though theologically essential, are so likely to confound and alienate their dialogue partners. that setting them aside in the interest of collaboration has seemed only prudent under the circumstances. It is almost certainly the case, however, that the dialogue between anthropological thought on one hand and theological and biblical thought on the other will

8 *Gaudium et spes*, §22.

again bear fruit only when the Trinitarian, Christological, and paschal character of the latter is brought fully to the fore.

Theology has been known to accommodate itself too readily to the native tropes of its dialogue partners—in both the social and hard sciences—whose worldly respectability theologians often seem to envy. A number of the Church Fathers gave too much ground to Platonic and Neoplatonic presuppositions, and scholasticism's rationalistic excesses are well known. More recently, the adoption of Enlightenment protocols in the exploration of Christian doctrine and scriptural exegesis—their technical benefits notwithstanding—has demonstrated that care must be taken in appropriating the fruits of the social sciences, lest in doing so people of faith inadvertently succumb to the hermeneutical suspicion with which modern and postmodern thought is often infected and which has a corrosive effect on Christian acumen.

Aidan Nichols, O.P. is surely right when he writes: "The knowledge that faith brings is not, evidently, of an academic kind. It is knowledge of love for us of the One who is Alpha and Omega, our absolute Source and unconditioned End."[9] Faith—specifically Christian faith—is a form of intelligence, much in the same way that music and mathematics and rationality are forms of intelligence, but it is one born, not of new ideas, but of a new mind, *metanoia*. The knowledge to which Christian faith gives access is far from that to which speculation and curiosity aspire. Reason at prayer is far more genuinely fruitful than the kind of deracinated rationalism or untethered romanticism that has come to replace it in our post-Christian context. As is true of other structures of thought, the intelligence of Christian faith can be deployed in both rudimentary and highly sophisticated ways. Like the other forms of intelligence, Christian intelligence can be manipulated, made to serve unworthy ends, and otherwise betrayed. It has its charlatans.

While the epistemological powers of Christian faith are quite extraordinary, staggering in many ways, they are distinctly Chris-

---

9 Aidan Nichols, O.P., *Figuring Out the Church: Her Marks, and Her Masters* (San Francisco: Ignatius Press, 2013), Kindle edition, §167.

tian. Not only do they aspire more to truth than to speculative knowledge of the truth, these powers often operate most fruitfully in what we might call an incarnational modality. The natural form of Christian intelligence is that of a truth-seeking seed quietly deposited in the heart of those forms of intelligence with which it enters into collaboration, often quite unnoticed. One thinks of Johann Sebastian Bach, Joseph Haydn, Michelangelo, Caravaggio, Maximus the Confessor, and countless others. Subtract the role that Christian faith and the truth-and-beauty-seeking aspiration it plays in the lives of so many gifted people and the world will watch helplessly as the great cultural treasures, works of art, and moral achievements that have ennobled us recede, only to be replaced by gestures of unlovely cleverness, the hermeneutics of suspicion, and their misbegotten offspring.

More theological candor regarding Christianity's unique and uniquely participatory epistemic resources is therefore to be welcomed, however confounding this might be to those quick to level the unfounded charge of fideism. At its deepest level, Christian intelligence is liturgical and dramatic. Precisely because of its inaccessibility to those outside its orbit of assent, bridges must be made where common ground can be found with seemingly more straightforward epistemologies. This is especially true when it comes to the field of anthropology, for Christian theology is, as Balthasar argued, a meta-anthropology. Without betraying the proper degree of rational rigor, however, the modality of inquiry proper to the mutual interrogation of theology and anthropology will necessarily have an evocative quality, one that is appropriate to mysteries such as the birth of the human race and the death of the human person, issues to which we will turn below.

Mystery, of course, is not a synonym for a problem for which a solution has yet to be found. Mystery is not something that is simply unknown or even unknowable. Rather it is something that is knowable but not reducible to the known. It is the shimmering essence that endlessly excites the longing to know. The more that is known about a mystery, the more mysteriously it glows with the promise of what is yet to be known. Knowledge of such mysteries—however much intellectual energy is exerted in acquiring it—is always experienced as a gift of grace. These are hardly the assumptions of contemporary social scientists, nor are they proper to their enterprise, but Christian thought misrepresents itself if they are set aside for diplomatic or inappropriately deferential reasons.

If the creative engagement of theology and Girard's mimetic theory is to bear fruit, it will be by being a truly collaborative dialogue. Any attempt to homogenize the discourse, whether in favor of theological or anthropological categories, will be counterproductive. Just as Christian self-understanding would be deprived of an enormously significant resource were we to ignore or underestimate the contribution René Girard has made, maladroit efforts to retrofit theological truths in the interest of aligning them with what Girard calls "mimetic theory" will hamper rather than further the rich and potentially enriching dialogue between them. This collaboration will require both mutual respect and—most of all—patience.

Inasmuch as Girard's work has focused attention on the inordinate power of mimetic or imitative desire in human affairs, there are theological and, indeed, Christological reasons for asking, for instance, what, if any, might be the theological implications of the apparent intensification of desire that coincided with hominization. The species whose mimetic propensities suddenly (in evolutionary terms) overwhelmed the instinctual mechanisms for keeping the violent potential of these propensities in check is the species whose members behave as though their deepest desire can only be fulfilled by imitating another. The ostensible object of human desire, once acquired, straightaway loses the aura that surrounded it prior to possession when it was refracted through the lens of another's desire. Humans, in short, desire something both unknown to them and inaccessible to the strategies of acquisition that desire sets in motion. We are creatures in whom has been implanted and to whom has been entrusted a world-consuming desire, and if misdirected, it will sooner or later lay waste the world. Christ came among us precisely to intensify that desire, to free it from the idols of its own making, and to orient it toward its true and proper object. The point is that the anthropology of desire leads to fresh theological and Christological insights.

That the higher primates exhibit greater and greater mimetic predilections should not cause us to discount the evidence of a qualitative shift in mimeticism coincident with hominization. In clear contrast to what exists in the animal world, human desire is unlimited, insatiable, and intensified by the desire of others. The foregoing suggests that humanity is intrinsically endowed with an inextinguishable longing. Christianity, in affirming this anthropo-logical fact—and affirming as well that nothing in this world can fully and finally satisfy human desire—concludes quite obviously that it is either a curse that destines us to futility and disappoint-ment or it is, at bottom, a desire for God—however fickle and inevitably squandered on inappropriate idols it might be. More-over, Christianity recognizes that the Incarnate Christ, in intensi-fying desire, restoring its metaphysical meaning, and redirecting it toward its proper object is indispensable to the true restoration of the human vocation.

The ultimate meaning of the sharp rise in mimeticism in homo sapiens is not its biological origin or evolutionary utility, but its ontological ordination; not what occasioned its evolutionary emergence, but what might be its ultimate end. To what consum-mation might our mimetic proclivities be ordered, and to what, in the fullness of time, might they eventually lead? The answer to which we are led when relying on a collaboration between theol-ogy and anthropology is that we are made to respond to the invi-tation "follow me." Every interesting person we meet or to whom our attention is attracted seems implicitly to be issuing that invitation.

Were theology and anthropology to collaborate in rendering a Christological account of creation and hominization, the result might well be a fresh rediscovery of "the truly most exciting part of Christian faith." All the more is this collaboration pertinent today, for the world-historical shifts that are now underway can-not be adequately reckoned in geopolitical, economic, or socio-logical terms. Whether in response to the worldwide cultural crisis or in the interest of rediscovering Christianity's uniqueness, what is most needed today is a theological anthropology, not one, of course, that can or should resolve all the issues man faces as he attempts to appraise his predicament, but one in which sci-ence, philosophy, and theology work together.

# Toward a Theological Anthropology

For Christians, today's many challenges are accompanied by theological opportunities arising from three serendipitous developments: recently acquired anthropological insights, the Second Vatican Council's implicit call for a more full-bodied theological anthropology, and the powerful case made by Hans Urs von Balthasar for a theo-dramatic anthropology. Providentially, as the last Council was concluding, Girard was beginning to account for the anthropological treasure trove amassed in the nineteenth and twentieth centuries in ways that were enormously congenial to their theological appropriation, and Balthasar's massive theological enterprise and his call for a theological anthropology was beginning to command the attention it is destined to receive for centuries to come.

There are all manner of discoveries that indicate the existence of human culture—language, graves, tools, and so on—but the question is: What would constitute the most indisputable and at the same time the most ancient evidence of rudimentary human culture? The answer is evidence of ritual sacrifice. Girard's research helps us recognize the cogency of this criterion. The *esprit de corps* that coincides with the spontaneous polarization of violence onto one victim may well have occurred—and no doubt did occur—thousands of times in countless places and over a very long period of time before those it momentarily gathered into an *ad hoc* community were able to cobble together the ritual wherewithal for sustaining that social consensus over time; thereafter the elementary cultural roles and institutions of primitive humanity slowly developed. Quite obviously, the question of hominization is not entirely answered by this.

When and how the threshold from animal to human existence was crossed is a mystery known only to God. We are here posing more modest questions. We are trying to locate, theoretically to be sure, events that, were we able to pinpoint them, would count as indisputable evidence that humans walked the earth. However inaccessible such evidence might be in actual fact, it is worth asking what might theoretically constitute credible grounds for believing that the threshold from animal to human existence had actually been crossed, events anterior to the origin of tools and graves. Girard has both accounted for the available data and provided a convincing account of *cultural* origination. While it is common sense to recognize primitive ritual as a clear indication of human culture, Girard's analysis shows the proximity of culture formation and ritual sacrifice, suggesting that, were we able to locate the first such sacrifices, we would be very close to the moment of cultural hominization itself, ritual sacrifices being reenactments of the collective violence that produced the first rudimentary experience of social solidarity.

While the creation stories of ancient peoples constitute a rich treasure trove of anthropological evidence concerning the birth of human culture, they do so precisely by being of no value whatsoever in our quest to understand the origin of the human as such—the origin of the human person. The science of anthropology, struggling under the Enlightenment biases that prevailed at its birth, is no more helpful in that regard. Yes, we understand that language acquisition is key, as was tool-making and forms of social collaboration that depended on language, but these markers and others that anthropologists use to locate the origin of our species seem to locate something posterior to hominization itself. When we find tools, language, graves, evidence of rudimentary social arrangements, we have good reason to conclude that hominization has occurred. As for the event of hominization itself, the anthropological sciences have not been particularly helpful. To catch a credible glimpse of what the actual event of hominization might have been we turn, not to the most ancient myths, but to the sober reflections of ancient Hebrew authors who were drawing on a rich religious tradition that had grown increasingly wary of the religious practices of their pagan contemporaries. The creation stories that have been collected and redacted in the first chapters of the Book of Genesis draw on anthropological insights of far greater value than many have been willing to acknowledge.

The effort to account for hominization—the birth of human personhood—is necessarily conjectural, unable as we are to rely to any significant extent on empirical data. Girard has given us the most plausible theory for the origin of *culture*. What hypothetical discovery would constitute reliable evidence for the first appearance, not of human culture, but of human *nature*—or the human *person*? There are two possibilities. Either the first human who ever lived crossed the threshold from the animal to the human realm *before* the violent event at which human culture originated, or the birth of human culture and the birth of human personhood as such were essentially *simultaneous*. In Girard's own work, his unapologetic claims for the centrality of the Christian revelation notwithstanding, he limited himself to the issues of culture formation, satisfied to have recognized the immensely important link between cultural origination and the Paschal drama at which its mystifications were finally shattered. In our attempt to mutually engage the theological and anthropological disciplines, however, we will separate the question of what we might call *ontological* hominization from that of cultural origination. Nor will we ignore the essential biblical principle of original innocence, itself indispensable to the biblical insistence on the goodness of creation and a precondition for making sense of the Christian doctrine of original sin.

There are two possible ways to reconcile the biblical principle—as narrated in the Genesis account of the paradisal garden—with the anthropological data suggesting the violent origins of human culture. The easier of the two would be to be convinced—whether by anthropological evidence or the mythopoetic perspicacity of the biblical narratives—that human nature, the human person, appeared prior to the "Fall" into sin and violence. The evidence for this is likely to be convincing only for those whose sacramental sensibilities have survived the acids of modern thought and the toxins of postmodernity. We will begin by presenting this evidence. In due course, we will take another look at the violent origins of culture precisely to determine whether or not it is possible—without abandoning the principle of prelapsarian innocence and the goodness of creation—to affirm that both human culture and human persons emerged at the moment when the first victim was immolated by a mob. These two parallel lines of inquiry are undertaken in an effort to enrich and integrate our understanding of both the anthropological data for which Girard has so impressively accounted and the biblical traditions and theological doctrines which Girard's own intellectual journey led him to embrace.

We began with David Samuels' lament that "coherent narratives, the stories that tell us who we are and where we are going, are getting harder and harder to find." We turn now to the biblical tradition, the anthropological irrelevance and intellectual dubiousness of which is regarded by many as indisputable. Surprisingly, however, we want to show that the outlines of the universal human story can be found there, a story which traditional Christianity sees as a story with distinctive Trinitarian and Christological features.

"Once we know that God has redeemed and divinized the world in Christ," writes Balthasar, "the immediate issue of that knowledge for human understanding is the recognition that everything in history and nature, as far back as the act of creation itself, must be intelligible in this perspective, which excludes all others, and that it could not be otherwise."[10] And so we might appeal to a sensibility that Balthasar found in Maximus the Confessor, one in which the earthly paradise only interests the seventh-century Byzantine monk "as the starting point of the world's history, as the place of the fall." For Maximus, "it is only by glimpsing the ultimate goal that he hopes to make contact with lost origins, never by looking backward."[11] If we look backward to the origin, we do so with all the advantages that accrue from having caught a glimpse of the decisive turning point. Moreover,

---

10 Hans Urs von Balthasar, *The Glory of the Lord: A Theological Aesthetics, Vol. III: Studies in Theological Style: Lay Styles,* trans. Andrew Louth, John Saward, Martin Simon, and Rowan Williams, ed. John Riches (San Francisco: Ignatius Press, 1986), 293.

11 Hans Urs von Balthasar, *Cosmic Liturgy: The Universe According to Maximus the Confessor,* trans. Brian E. Daley, S.J. (San Francisco: Ignatius Press, 2003), 180.

the light this turning point sheds on both originality and finality leads us logically to consider the Last Things. The intimate link between eschatology and originality cannot be forgotten.

Even though the discovery of intelligent life elsewhere in the universe would pose no more threat to Christian faith than has the discovery of the evolutionary process by which biological adaptation occurred, astrophysics is narrowing—to the point of inconceivability—the chances of discovering intelligent life in the vast space-time expanse of the cosmos. This being so, we can either treat the existence of the only creature who longs for meaning as an utterly meaningless cosmic fluke, or we can humbly acknowledge that we have been inserted into the cosmic maelstrom for a reason and turn our attention to discerning what that reason might be. Even though 13.8 billion years that have transpired since the birth of the cosmos constitute an admittedly protracted overture, the details of which need not concern us, nonetheless, we have every reason to suspect that this process was ordered toward what appears to be the one creature in the universe capable of prayer. Our story, therefore, begins long after the mysterious origin of the material world. It begins, as so many good stories do, *in medias res*—in the middle of things. It begins with hominization.

Girard's theory of human origins has tended to corroborate a rather Hobbesian picture of the lives of our most ancient ancestors, repudiating the sentimental Rousseauesque myth of peaceful origins, and properly so. Attempts to find evidence for peaceful primitive societies or even to imagine them—once the perennial hobby of Western romantics—are, of course, doomed. However lacking the anthropological evidence in its favor might be, an indispensable element in the biblical account of creation is the principle of an original prelapsarian goodness. It has long served as a bulwark against Gnosticism's perennial assault on Christianity's respect for both nature and history. In light of the contemporary renewal of that assault, this is no time to make unnecessary concessions.

## Original Innocence

The first human did not have human parents.

This statement, so simple, so logically incontrovertible, might stir us from the lazy crypto-Darwinian presuppositions with which our age and our thinking are so suffused. Implicit in these presuppositions, though almost never made explicit, is the assumption that our species developed slowly from that of our primate ancestors. There is hardly a more unquestioned dogma than that. It is based, however, on the assumption of the quasi-human status of the creature who served, according to this theory, as the intermediate stage in this process. In other species such an assumption is unproblematic, but to transfer this idea to the consideration of human origin is both naïve and dangerous. Virtually all ancient cultures regarded the inhabitants of alien cultures as being, at best, quasi-human, and for millennia the institutions of slavery and concubinage have been premised on a similar assignment of ontological insufficiency to certain designated persons. There has probably never been a time in human history, however, when the idea of quasi-human existence—of a creature who is potentially human, but not yet fully human, or once human, but no longer so—was more fraught with danger. Today precisely this notion is creeping into issues of great moment. The moral and legal status of the human embryo, the fetus, the child in the womb, the severely handicapped, the demented and decrepit—are today being questioned, and any suggestion of an indeterminate stage during which someone with a human mother and father is not yet fully human or no longer so may well be the source of the twenty-first century's greatest horrors.

Of course, the findings of science are not, and should not, be determined by the political problems that might flow from them. Nor, however, should we assume that the question of hominization is one for which the unaided scientific paradigm, as currently construed, has sufficient competence. The humanity of those with human parents is indisputable and irrevocable, but there had to have been a moment or moments when someone born of a highly evolved higher primate became human postpartum. However happy one might be to acknowledge the role of genetic adaptation in biological development, it is an indisputable fact that the first human on earth did not have human parents. The age and origin of our species continues to be debated, and we can leave that debate to paleoanthropologists. The important point is precisely the *point* at which hominization happened, for the transition from the non-human to the human was a punctual event. Balthasar has put the matter succinctly: "We may say, then, that subhuman nature is related to man, and the history of nature to the history of man, in a manner analogous to the relation of the Old Testament to Christ. In each case there is a slow approach and then, at the end, a leap."[12]

It is precisely such a leap that science has ignored or dismissed as fanciful. As Pierpaolo Antonello and Paul Gifford write in the introduction to *How We Became Human*:

> Culture, morality, religion, the symbolic order: all are explained as a function of encephalization and the growing neocortex. Or else they are referred, by way of explanation, to the transformation of the larynx and the vocal apparatus (which seems at best one enabling condition). . . . Characteristically, the emergence and evolution of culture are seen as linear and progressive, a form of "phyletic gradualism," involving no "punctuated equilibria," or "quantum leaps."[13]

In the concluding essay in the volume he co-edited, Paul Gifford returns to the ineluctable but elusive *event* of hominization:

> As brain size increases, therefore, and mimetic capacity with it, there must come a point of critical phase change, rather like the one envisaged in René Thom's catastrophe theory, where a relatively minor incident, or series of them, can trigger incalculable consequences in the system of reference, disrupting group understanding, destabilizing the social community, and opening up an entirely new set of potentials and probabilities—which

---

12 Hans Urs von Balthasar, *A Theology of History* (San Francisco: Ignatius Press, 1994), 144.

13 Pierpaolo Antonello and Paul Gifford, "Introduction," *How We Became Human*, ed. Antonello and Gifford, xxii.

here means all the things making up what we commonly refer to as cultural development and civilizational advance.[14]

This is a remarkably insightful comment, but it concerns chiefly—if not exclusively—the process of *social* hominization, behind which we are trying to peer in order to better account for the event that coincides with the birth of the human *person*. Doubtless this event took longer than the trillionth of a trillionth of a trillionth of a second during which the created order came into existence following the Big Bang, but it didn't take all day. It occurred, as Claude Levi-Strauss put it, at a single stroke. The question is: Was it a stroke of luck? Was it a stroke of genius? A stroke of lightning? Was it a loving stroking of a cheek? Or was it the stroke of a crude, makeshift weapon conveniently at hand at the propitious moment?

"Catholic theology affirms that the emergence of the first members of the human species (whether as individuals or in populations) represents an event that is not susceptible of a purely natural explanation and which can appropriately be attributed to divine intervention," said the Catholic Church's International Theological Commission in 2004. If it is true that the moment of hominization eludes a purely natural explanation, René Girard has offered what appears to be a purely natural explanation of the origin of *culture*, something so indispensable to human existence that it must have been virtually, if not precisely, coincident with hominization itself. There are only scant biblical allusions to the prelapsarian paradise, which innocent humans might have at least momentarily enjoyed, and absolutely no anthropological, archeological, or ethnographic evidence thereof. We will come back to that question in due course.

Meanwhile, however, evidence does exist, and René Girard made it his lifework to amass and synthesize it, indicating that the first human cultures emerged when the first humans almost literally stumbled upon the process whereby recurring eruptions of collective violence could be brought to harmonious conclusion by transferring the hostilities onto a single victim. This pro-

14 Paul Gifford, "Homo religiosus in Mimetic Perspective," *How We Became Human*, 311–12.

cess was not the product of thought or planning. It emerged, as Girard has shown, quite spontaneously due to the enormously surcharged mimetic or imitative propensities with which this strange new creature was endowed. The spontaneous nature of this seminal, culture-founding event is made clear from the abundant evidence for it over the entire spectrum of archaic cultures. Moreover, and more to the point, the pivotal, culture-founding event—repeated no doubt countless times wherever creatures were brought to this threshold by the sudden intensification of their mimetic propensities—occurred quite literally at a single stroke. To suggest that the process of cultural hominization Girard has brilliantly theorized may, in fact, include an element that "is not susceptible of a purely natural explanation," is not to dispute Girard's findings, but rather to ponder some of their theological ramifications.

Girard's theory of culture formation provides us with an exceedingly reliable marker for the origin of human *culture*, namely the existence of ritual sacrifices. The challenge, however, is to reconcile Girard's anthropology of violent origins with the biblical principle of the prelapsarian goodness of creation and the original innocence of humanity. There are, we will argue, two ways to reconcile them. The first assumes an event anterior to the cultural hominization that Girard has theorized. The second way of reconciling a strictly anthropological account of human origin with the theological and biblical account assumes that they occurred simultaneously. This will require an extended defense to which we will turn in a later chapter. Each of these addenda to Girard's theory leaves the mimetic analysis perfectly intact while reconciling it, in the first case with the Bible's creation narratives broadly understood and with their Trinitarian implications brought to the fore, and in the second case with a Paschal theology and the doctrine of the pre-existing Logos. For each of these unavoidably theoretical accounts of the origin—not of human culture, but of human nature there is a specific marker, corresponding to the ritual sacrifice that serves as a definitive marker of *cultural* hominization. Were we to discover, on one hand, evidence of *non-instinctual acts of self-sacrifice*, or, on the other hand, indications suggesting the existence of the *moral conscience*, we could confidently pronounce the creature who performed such acts or who exhibited such moral scruples to be a fellow member of our species. We want to explore these two markers of hominization independently. The premises on which they are based are sufficiently distinct to foreclose any attempt to integrate them seamlessly, and we will make no such effort. What each of these approaches has is both a degree of plausibility and the punctuality which we have argued above is demanded by any attempt to locate the emergence of homo sapiens. For the purpose of exploring the first possibility we will turn to the Genesis accounts of creation, and, for the second, we will rely on anthropological insights from Girard, his intellectual predecessors, and certain New Testament texts.

## Genesis as Evidence

We will now turn to the Book of Genesis and specifically to the literary *locus classicus* for the initial encounter between theology and anthropology, no doubt less central to that encounter than the Passion story in the New Testament, but nonetheless an essential starting point. If a collaboration between theology and anthropology is to bear fruit, arguably the greatest initial challenge is that of reconciling the Bible's mythopoetic but nonetheless scripturally venerable account of hominization with what anthropological intelligence can reasonably surmise about human origins. Initially, there are, it seems, three major difficulties to be met. In light of what we know and may presuppose about human existence, our inquiry confronts the seeming contradictory witness of the biblical account of the following essential matters: the Genesis account of prelapsarian goodness and innocence, the Bible's characterization of death as the punishment for the first sin, and, finally, the testimony of both the Old and New Testament to the effect that all of humanity has inherited, in some mysterious way underscored in the Pauline and Augustinian tradition, the curse associated with the first sin. Can these bedrock principles be defended in a way that is broadly intelligible? Here is where the alliance between theology and anthropology can be most fruitful. The preliminary task is to find a shared focus that these two quite dissimilar disciplines might jointly ponder and scrutinize, and, for that purpose, the obvious place to begin is the creation narratives in the Book of Genesis.

As impressive as are René Girard's theoretical insights into the origin of human culture, and as convincingly as his mimetic premise accounts for the origin of human social and psychological life, Girard offers little in the way of insight into the origin of human *nature*, or, perhaps better put, the emergence of the human *person*. However powerfully Girard's mimetic theory corroborates Christianity's truth-claims, it does so by beginning with anthropological data and turning subsequently to biblical texts for corroboration and explication. By beginning with the Genesis story of creation, we may well be laying ourselves open to derision. One of the many reasons why deracinated Enlightenment rationalism is in such a crisis today is that its scorn for the very idea of revelation has driven secular reason first to vulgar materialism and then to nihilism. As such, it has annealed itself against rescue by the tradition in alliance with which philosophical reason has historically been most fruitful. The very idea that the world—including man—would be better known by knowing something, however incomplete, about the God who brought it into existence seems to most a quaint remnant from the past, as is any suggestion that knowledge of God would depend on an initiative on God's part, which is what the word revelation means. It is nonetheless essential to biblical thought that man's conspicuously unique situation is the effect of a divine intervention at the very moment of hominization.

By proposing a joint theological and anthropological reflection on the Genesis account of hominization, we are, of course, in no way trying to argue that the creation stories in Genesis are factual in the explicit historical sense. Our purpose is to explore portions of the Book of Genesis in dialogue, not only with Girard's anthropological findings, but also with the theological doctrines born of Christianity's fidelity to scriptural revelation and the historical exigencies that gave rise to it. On the issue of the relationship between the Genesis account of creation and hominization, and the anthropological data, the question could be stated this way: Can the anthropological data for which René Girard accounts so cogently be transposed into the mythopoetics of Genesis in a way that is faithful to the truth to which each of these thought forms bear witness? Or, conversely, can the theological and anthropological premises of the Genesis narrative be expressed in terms intelligible to secular social science and plausible from the perspective of its epistemological disciplines?

The idea that language evolved from the grunts and groans of our most primitive ancestors has just enough plausibility to be taken for granted. Undoubtedly the first forms of language were inelegant and crude, but language is integral to the event of hominization. Like hominization itself, it must have been a punctual event. In other words, whatever noises the immediate predecessors of our species might have made, language that formed the first rudimentary culture must have erupted in response to an event with a very significant emotional valence. In what follows we will explore two possible scenarios in which the most rudimentary form of language—and therefore the most rudimentary form of culture—might have occurred. We will then consider how each of these scenarios might have provided the context for the transition from pre-human to human existence.

# "It is Not Good
# That Man Should Be Alone..."

> It is clear that a conscious subject can only awaken to himself
> and his distinct selfhood if he is addressed by one or more others
> who regard him as of value or perhaps as indispensable.[1]—Hans
> Urs von Balthasar

"IT IS not good that man should be alone" (Gn. 2:18), the Lord
says to Adam in the Genesis story, a textual cornerstone of biblical anthropology. The significance of this verse from chapter two
of Genesis comes to the fore only when read in the light of the
verse in the first chapter of Genesis, which is the literary source
of an even more uniquely biblical principle, namely that humans
are made in the image and likeness of God. For Christians the
larger meaning of this verse emerges from what is revealed in the
Christian New Testament, that the God in whose image humans
are made is a Trinitarian God, a God who, prior to creation, is a
community of such unimaginably generous love that the sources
of this love are consubstantial. In the words of an early creed:
"God is one but not solitary."[2] As the first Christians began to
work out the theological implications of the events on which
their faith was based, the incipient outline of the Trinitarian doctrine began to emerge. It is unsurprising that Christians turning
to the Hebrew Scriptures in an effort to ascertain the prehistory
of the Incarnation were quick to notice a grammatical hint of the
Trinity in this critical verse in the creation story where God
speaks in the first person plural. "Let *us* make humankind in *our*
image, according to *our* likeness" (1:26). The next verse in Genе-

---

1 Hans Urs von Balthasar, *Theo-Drama: Theological Dramatic Theory, Vol. III:
The Dramatis Personae: The Person of Christ*, trans. Graham Harrison (San Francisco: Ignatius Press, 1992), 205.

2 *Fides Damasi.*

sis returns to the more conventional singular subject, a philologi-
cal anomaly that might be taken to suggest the presence of a
mystery that no extant linguistic resources were capable of faithfully rendering. Modern exegetes offer various interpretations,
and most would be embarrassed to give weight to the suggestion
of a Trinitarian innuendo.

The Church Fathers, however, were considerably less reluctant
to take advantage of serendipitous textual anomalies than are
theologians living in the aftermath of the historical critical exegesis of the last century and a half, many of whose practitioners have
a rather cramped view of the scope of divine inspiration. The
Fathers were generally both more docile and more daring; more
docile with respect to the text and more daring with respect to its
Christological and Trinitarian implications. While accepting with
appreciation many of the technical achievements of the modern
exegetes, we follow the Fathers of the Church in our gratitude for
textual windfalls of the sort that the Genesis author has here provided. One need not enter into the strictly exegetical arguments
to observe that there is no place in Scripture where an intimation
of intra-divine relationality would have more anthropological
implications than this one in Genesis. For if humans are made in
the image and likeness of God, then human nature and the
human vocation will be radically different depending on whether
that God is a divine monad, a pantheon of gods forever vying with
one another, or a divine *communio* in no need of creation, but
nonetheless overflowing with a self-communicating love. "Let *us*
make man in *our* image, after *our* likeness" (Gn. 1:26).

At the center of Christian theology—whose anthropological
probity we are here exploring—is the Cross and the Trinity, the
former: the history-altering event whose manifold ramifications
we will continue to explore in subsequent chapters, and the latter: the ultimate explanation for why the public execution of one
man could have had such ramifications. Without the Trinity and
the Cross we simply cannot fully appreciate the greatness of the
human vocation and the tragedy of the human predicament. So
indispensable are the Trinity and the Cross to a better understanding of our unique place in the created order that we will
more likely locate the event of hominization itself by being alert

for any traces of our Trinitarian provenance and any adumbrations of the Paschal Drama, which unsealed the mystery of history and opened a path back into the Trinitarian existence for which we were made. We are aided here by the Genesis author. That we humans are made in the image and likeness of the God who summoned us into life and who, in the same verse that expresses our divine provenance, speaks in the first person plural, is a theological gift containing within it an anthropological one which it would be foolish and discourteous to refuse.

One of the problems we have pondering the mystery of the Trinity is the name we have given it, which tends to focus our attention on its least essential and most easily distracting feature, namely the numerical one. The Trinitarian doctrine is fundamentally about the nature of God and only secondarily about the economy by which that nature operates, which we are ill-suited to imagine. "*The* Trinity," writes Rémi Brague, "is the manner in which God is one." It is a "way of saying that 'God is love.'"[3] The God revealed by Christ overflows—even within the Godhead—with generosity and love. Quick to connect theology with anthropology, as is most essential, Brague adds a comment that is especially apropos to the topic at hand: "The way in which God is one is not without implications for the way in which we have to conduct ourselves. And 'implications' is too weak; 'imperatives' is better."[4]

Then-Cardinal Joseph Ratzinger insisted that the communion of Persons in the Trinity constitutes man's "basic anthropological shape."[5] In assessing this basic anthropological shape, the Genesis story contains treasures galore, if we but take the time to extract them. Of course, a truly Trinitarian understanding of the God in whose image and likeness man is made comes into focus only with the Incarnation of the second Person of the Trinity. A Trinitarian theology necessitates a Christological anthropology, for

---

3 Brague, *On the God of the Christians (and on one or two others)*, trans. Paul Seaton (South Bend, IN: St. Augustine's Press, 2013), 67, emphasis in the original.
4 Ibid., 68.
5 Joseph Cardinal Ratzinger, *Truth and Tolerance: Christian Belief and World Religions*, trans. Henry Taylor (San Francisco: Ignatius Press, 2004), 248, my emphasis.

the self-donation within the Trinity illuminates the overflowing of the Trinity in the Incarnation of the one who, "though he was in the form of God, did not count equality with God a thing to be grasped, but emptied himself" (Phil. 2:6–7). Creatures made in the image and likeness of such a God will have an ordination to self-gift written into their spiritual DNA. "The trinitarian love is the only ultimate form of all love," writes Balthasar, "both the love between God and men, and that between human persons."[6]

If, in the first chapter of Genesis the source, whom most exegetes call the priestly author, had God declare—in the first person plural—that man was made in the image and likeness of his Creator, the author of the second account of creation in Genesis chapter two has God announce that, "It is not good that the man should be alone; I will make him a helper fit for him" (Gn. 2:18). In drawing out the anthropological ramifications of this text it is difficult to avoid a degree of humor. Why is it not good that man should be alone? If he needs a helper, with what exactly does he need help? This is prior to the Fall. In the prelapsarian paradise there would presumably be very few chores, and certainly no onerous ones. Why does man need a partner? Why is it not good that man should be alone? Precisely because he cannot fulfill his true human vocation in solitude, for he is made in the image and likeness of a God who—even within the Godhead—is a communion of loving self-gift. It is in the image and likeness of such a God that each of us is made. We carry an ineradicable divine imprint, the image of God, even though, in our obstreperousness and pride, we have corrupted the likeness. Since it is not good that man should be alone, God chose to make a helper and a partner for him.

> *So* out of the ground the Lord God formed every beast of the field and every bird of the air, and brought them to the man to see what he would call them; and whatever the man called every living creature, that was its name. The man gave names to all cattle, and to the birds of the air, and to every beast of the field;

6 Hans Urs von Balthasar, *The Glory of the Lord: A Theological Aesthetics, Vol. VII: Theology: The New Covenant*, trans. Brian McNeil C.R.V., ed. John Riches (San Francisco: Ignatius Press, 1989), 484.

*but* for the man there was not found a helper fit for him. (Gn. 2:19–20; emphasis added)

Again the temptation to humor is irresistible. Immediately after declaring that he would make a helper and a partner for Adam, the topic turns to animals of the field and the birds of the air. Did the Lord God lose his train of thought? What is going on in this text? Why this seeming *non sequitur* about animals, birds, and naming? It is not, apparently, a question that is exegetically resolvable. It is a dramaturgical matter. The link between these two seemingly disparate topics comes to the fore when we emphasize, as we have, the words *so* and *but*. In sharing his name with Moses on Mount Sinai, the Lord had opened up the possibility of communication between humanity and God himself. Thus does the Bible understand the meaning of names. They are not mere labels used to prevent confusion between and among objects; they are the precondition for genuine communion between subjects. As soon as mention is made of what John Paul II—in his magisterial *Theology of the Body*—called "a suitable partner," Adam is presented with creatures, which he is expected to name. In naming each creature, Adam is essentially trying to establish a relationship with a suitable partner, but it is to no avail. So the interlude in which Adam named the animals of the field and the birds of the air is an essential element in the story. For the suitability of the partner for Adam consists of both a subjective and objective dimension. Only another creature made in the image and likeness of God will be suitable for the self-gift to which humans are called. As Balthasar has written:

> Even Adam, according to the legend of Paradise, although created in the fullness of God's grace, had an unsatisfied longing until God had given him Eve. Adam transcended and sought through the whole of nature—naming and hence knowing it— looking for that which would bring him fulfillment and completion. He did not find it. It is strange that human nature, obviously quite different from the animals which were already created two by two, has to long for the other.[7]

7 Hans Urs von Balthasar, *Man in History: A Theological Study* (London: Sheed and Ward, 1968), 84–5, emphasis added.

The delay during which the man named creatures and, in the act of naming them, found them unsuitable represents the preliminary awakening of his longing for such a partner. In order not to present the man with a suitable partner before his ardor for such a partner has arisen and grown acute, we have the interlude of naming. Each creature is given a name, but none is found capable of reciprocity. The end result of the naming is that the man is now conscious of his longing for a partner. The Genesis author has chosen this parade of creatures unsuitable as partners and helpers for Adam as a way of alluding to what John Paul II called Adam's "original solitude," a solitude that is pregnant with a longing for communion, a longing that is ultimately a longing for God but also for a human *communio*, a partner in relationship with whom some intimation of the Trinitarian mystery might be experienced. It is just such a longing, and not the expansion of the creature's cranial cavity, that constitutes the precondition for the discovery of other-directed self-sacrifice which uniquely distinguishes our species.

The man not only needed a partner, he needed a *suitable partner*. Suitable for what? If he needed a partner, why couldn't his partner have been another man? And why was he limited to one partner, not, say, five? Everyone knows the answer to this, but not everyone is willing to acknowledge it. In any case, the Genesis author knows, and the God of the Bible under whose inspiration he was writing knows that what the man needed was one partner, and only a partner who was ontologically the same and intrinsically other, for nothing less than this would awaken the man to a life lived in keeping with his Trinitarian provenance.

It is important to note that this singularly unique and intimate communion for which the man now longs, however corporeal and underwritten by sexual ardor it is, has a theological pedigree and is oriented to a theological end. It has, we would say, an intrinsically sacramental character. Made in the image and likeness of the Trinitarian God, the man longs for a communion analogous to the inner-Trinitarian *communio*, and like the Persons of the Trinity, the union for which Adam has his longing awakened is one in which the *otherness* of the partners is essential to and proportional to the ardor that attracts them one to another. This takes us back to the first chapter of Genesis and to the verse with which we began. At this point we can better appreciate the biblical verse that is at the very heart of the anthropological crisis of our time. The verse reads: "So God created man in his own image, in the image of God he created him; male and female he created them (Gn. 1:26)."

The same verse that declares that God created humanity in His image immediately speaks of humanity's sexual complementarity. Did these two things just happen to appear in the same verse by chance? Are they related to one another? What does the fact that we are made in the image and likeness of the God whom Christians would one day realize is a Trinitarian God—a God of self-donating communion—have to do with the fact that we exist in sexual complementarity? Of course if you ask a deracinated secular evolutionary biologist to account for sexual complementarity, you will be told, quite rightly, that sexually differentiated species enjoy an enormous genetic advantage over forms of life that reproduce by parthenogenesis or asexually. With the genetic experimentation vastly sped up, evolution leaps forward in those species that reproduced sexually. That is where the evolutionary biologist would likely leave it. Who can argue with that? Well, perhaps one could hazard a quibble, not with respect to the biological sciences as such, but with a presupposition buried deep within them; namely, one could quibble with the assumption that natural adaptation is driven by forces that have no intrinsic meaning for the species in which they occur, no *telos*, no goal toward which they are ultimately oriented, and that the purpose of sexual differentiation and sexual complementarity is the survival of the species. Anyone who has ever been seriously in love knows better than that. The first thing we notice and the only thing that we will never forget about a person is that he is a boy or man or she is a girl or woman. Nothing is more primary, and we unsuspectingly betray the ontological and spiritual essence of this distinction, as Erich Przywara has pointed out, by confusing it or conflating it "with 'the vegetal-animal form' of 'male and female.'"[8] This is the category mistake that the evolutionary sciences so often commit

8 Erich Przywara, *Analogia Entis*, trans. John R. Betz and David Bentley Hart (Grand Rapids, MI: Eerdmans Publishing, 2014), 561.

and on the validity of which today's sexual revolutionaries are
gambling their happiness, their peace of mind, and the health of
the culture they will leave in the aftermath of their recklessness.
The categories of man and woman are not reducible to the categories male and female in sub-human species. The conflation of
these categories has led to anthropological blunders and the social
and spiritual suffering to which such blunders inevitably lead.

Nature is ordered to its own transcendence, and the emergence
of sexual differentiation and sexual complementarity cannot be
properly comprehended without reference to an ordination
beyond biological survival. Not only does the survival of the species require their cooperation, but unless the man and the woman
find one another—there being in the Genesis author's account no
other suitable partner in the garden—their human vocation would
remain inchoate and their ontological potential unactualized. It
seems to us that the implications of this are clear: our incomplete-
ness as isolated individuals in need of our complementary *other*—
in the most concrete physical sense—has as its ultimate purpose,
not simply the evolutionary advantages that all sexually differentiated species enjoy, but a communion between the man and the
woman that has, in addition to an inseparable procreative purpose, a "sacramental" one toward which our natural instincts
incline us, but which these instincts alone cannot achieve.

Creation takes time, and God gives it time. The intrinsic sacramental significance of the conjugal relationship, intimations of
which are present from the moment members of our species first
appear, fully emerge only over many millennia. In fact, even after
it has been recognized, celebrated, and endowed with the religious significance proper to it, this ennobling and all important
element in human sexuality can be obscured and even lost when
its religious and cultural supports are compromised, attenuated,
or disparaged. But when the biblical God declares that "it is not
good that man should be alone" (Gn. 2:18), the goodness that
depends on human relationships is not limited to either the personal happiness of the individuals involved or the survival of the
species of which they are a part.

> But for the man there was not found a helper fit for him So the
> Lord God caused a deep sleep to fall upon the man, and while he

slept took one of his ribs and closed up its place with flesh; and the rib which the Lord God had taken from the man he made into a woman and brought her to the man. (Gn. 2:20–22)

The biblical author's anthropological insight that "it is not good that man should be alone" is presented in a dramatic rather than a discursive form. We might better appreciate the implications of the story of the woman being made from the rib of the man by seeing the rib as metaphorically analogous to what is typically symbolized in our time by the heart, especially if we see the heart, not as the seat of the emotions and even less the source of sentimentality, but—as many ancients did—as the source of a wisdom and understanding greater than that arising from cogitation alone. Were we to transpose the symbolism into one more expressive of its inner meaning, therefore, we would read that God took the heart out of the man and put it into the woman. This gives the man's exclamation, with which this passage dramatically concludes, added resonance. It is significant that we are told that the man named the creatures, but we do not hear him speak. This suggests that the mere labeling of speechless creatures has failed to awaken the man's inner essence. The first human words in the Bible are spoken by the man only when he enters into a spiritual communion with another, the woman. Upon seeing the woman, the man says: "This at last is bone of my bone and flesh of my flesh" (Gn. 2: 23).

Defined as the ordination toward transcendence and the capacity for love, the event of hominization will forever elude detection, but there could not be a more existentially convincing depiction of the *awakening* of humanity's Godlikeness than that given in the Genesis account of the recognition by the man of the woman. One former member of the Catholic Church's International Theological Commission, Anthony Kelly, put the matter succinctly: "Human loves sacramentally prefigure a final form of loving as a sharing in the ultimate being-in-love that is at the heart of Trinitarian life."[9] If the nuptial union of the man and woman has a hidden Trinitarian character, all the more obviously

9 Anthony Kelly, C.Ss.R., *Eschatology and Hope* (Maryknoll, NY: Orbis Books, 2006), 168.

it has a Paschal dimension. The love between the man and the woman, writes Rémi Brague, "is crowned with the sacrifice that prefers the other to oneself."[10]

We can read the Genesis author's description of the man's "This at last is bone of my bone and flesh of my flesh" experience as an anthropologically acute and mythopoetically felicitous account of the birth of self-sacrificial love. For in the Genesis account we have a glimpse of the moment when love appeared in the world for the first time, suffused as it was with religious longing. The assertion that man is made in the image and likeness of God is surely the greatest revelation of the Old Testament, but it comes fully to light only with the New Testament revelation of the divine Trinity, which is the true and only basis for the paramount revelation that God is love. Inasmuch as the very doctrine of the Trinity arose from the Christian attempt to understand Christ, the Trinitarian inference in Adam's exclamation carries with it a latent Christological one as well. Being a Christian, Joseph Ratzinger observed in a 1964 homily, "means, constantly and in the first instance, letting ourselves be torn away from the selfishness of someone who is living only for himself and entering into the great basic orientation of existing for the sake of another."[11] Whatever degree of animal tenderness we may find in the non-human world, it falls short of the "great basic orientation of existing for the sake of another" with which the man's exclamation in the Genesis story is redolent. Though sexual attraction can and often does precede such a moment, it is not to be thought the natural extension of sexual arousal. No less reliable a source than Henri de Lubac has warned against regarding eros as "preparation for and commencement of agape." Eros is, as de Lubac has written, "the indispensable subsoil from which agape will be able to blossom,"[12] but that blossoming awaits precisely the prevenient grace that we are positing as the moment of hominization. Benedict XVI expressed this with characteristic

10 Brague, *On the God of the Christians (and on one or two others)*, 61.

11 Ratzinger, *What It Means to Be a Christian*, 56.

12 Henri de Lubac, *Theological Fragments,* trans. Rebecca Howell Balinski (San Francisco: Ignatius Press, 1989), 88–89.

elegance when he wrote in *Deus Caritas Est* that *"eros* and *agape*—ascending love and descending love—can never be completely separated. The more the two, in their different aspects, find a proper unity in the one reality of love, the more the true nature of love in general is realized" (*Deus Caritas Est*, §7).

Inasmuch as we are trying to conceive of a threshold event that "blossoms" into an aptitude for and aspiration to non-instinctual acts of self-sacrifice—our marker for the existence of mankind—we think that sexual attraction qualifies as the experience most likely to have prompted our ancestors to step across that threshold. Quoting in passing the Russian philosopher and theologian Vladimir Solovyov, Balthasar writes:

> The true lover "actually sees something, perceives with his eyes, something other than that which other men see": he sees the ideality that is the true reality; in an inchoate way he sees the beloved person as God sees him, which is indeed the only way God wills to see him. And to let this ideality be true, to make it true, is "the beginning of the visible restoration of God's image in the material world."[13]

Nothing is more elusive than the beginning of something unprecedented. No one seeing a chrysalis or an acorn for the first time could imagine the culmination toward which these life forms are intrinsically ordered. Upon reading the Old Testament, no one who had never heard of Christ or Christianity could predict the content of the New Testament. Upon reading the New Testament, however, Christians and many who are not Christians can look back on the Old Testament in astonishment at how all its central themes converge and are brought to unsurpassable completion in Christ. Analogously, inasmuch as the Cross is the world altering instance of the self-gift of which Adam became at least momentarily capable, and inasmuch as Jesus revealed the eternal self-gift within the Divine Trinity, a Christian would be perfectly right to regard the man's "This at last is bone of my bone and flesh of my flesh" as the first faint adumbration of the distinctively human vocation.

---

13 Balthasar, *The Glory of the Lord*, Vol. III, 348–9.

We began with the statement that the first human did not have human parents. It is imperative to add that to be regarded as a member of the human species, worthy of respect commensurate with that status, the only criterion is that one has human parents. A human is someone who has human parents, and he or she has that status from the moment of conception. The age, level of development, or degree of incapacity or decrepitude can in no way alter that status. That said, and emphatically so, it is also the case that the fulfillment of our human vocation—though our membership in the human family is unalienable from the moment of conception—awaits the discovery, usually and most properly awakened by the mother's loving gaze, of a communion with another.

Whatever he lacked in scientific or historical erudition, the author of the second chapter of Genesis intuitively understood both that, though the man was in possession of all the neurological wherewithal requisite to human existence, the full actualization of his humanity awaited the moment when he came out of himself and discovered the mystery that was his true calling: self-sacrificial love. Even though the Genesis author could depict the essential punctuality of the moment of hominization only by eliding any reference to parenting, there is no reason to doubt that the more typical situation in which the bonding event occurs is the moment of the exchange of loving gazes between a mother and a child. Freed from the demands of scientific rigor, the author of the second chapter of Genesis was able to depict the essence of the creature made in the image and likeness of his (Trinitarian) Creator with great loveliness and poignancy: "This at last is bone of my bone and flesh of my flesh." This "one flesh" *communio* is the most reliable indicator that the transition from pre-human to human existence has occurred. Since it is impossible to find empirical evidence of this event, our debt to the biblical author is all the greater, for he has given us a glimpse of what no social science can corroborate. Yet it constitutes the most plausible evidence at another level of reflection for what the subjective experience accompanying the moment of hominization must have been.

While the appearance of the first human—the first creature capable of participating in the Trinitarian mystery of loving self-donation—is beyond the capacity of empirical science, the biblical story of creation recounts the original experience of loving self-donation located beautifully and meaningfully in the context of the nuptial mystery. It is essential to note, of course, that the true and deeper meaning of nuptiality—as the manifestation in human affairs of the Trinitarian mystery of self-donation—can be expressed in both a conjugal and a celibate form, the essence of each being self-giving commitment to another. The relationship between the man and the woman is distinguished by the fact that it is the *communio* prepared for, and enhanced by, an especially powerful instinctual drive. This graced elevation of *eros*, however important from an anthropological point of view—especially for the recognition of the profound meaning of conjugal *communio*—might not be fully volitional and meritorious, due precisely to the instinctual impulse by which it is aided. Relationships involving similar levels of self-sacrifice but unreinforced by instinct—the consecrated life of virginity or celibacy, for instance—might well represent nobler instances of the self-sacrificial life. In either case, however, eros understood in its fuller and broader sense than is typical of our lustful and listless age is operative at the inauguration of the journey toward its final fulfillment in what Balthasar has called "the Inner-Trinitarian-Ecstasy."

The Genesis story provides, therefore, the narrative wherewithal for formulating an entirely plausible theory of hominization, one that is far more profound in its subtlety and emotional verisimilitude than any of the theories claiming more empirical justifications. Just as we posited the existence of non-spontaneous rituals of blood sacrifice as the hypothetical proof of the existence of the first human cultures, so we can propose as confidently the emergence of non-instinctual acts of self-sacrifice as the hypothetical proof of the existence of human beings as such. Whatever rare acts of self-sacrifice might be found among the birds of the air and the animals of the field, it is only with man that *non-instinctual* forms of self-sacrifice can be found. Moreover and more to the point, the most likely context in which the ardor for self-donation might emerge with sufficient force to have ontological consequences is the sexual attraction between the man and the woman. It is here, and uniquely here, that nature—in the form of an instinctive drive for sexual gratification—is most likely to have been touched by grace and transformed into the ardor for self-donation so marvelously captured by the exclamation: "This at last is bone of my bone and flesh of my flesh." Balthasar writes:

> Not only is the eros between human beings the basis that permits God to impress his own agape on the human person; the encounter face to face between man and woman is also the basis that permits the possibility of such a face to face encounter between God and humanity.[14]

The nature of sexual attraction makes it most propitious for receiving the grace that would elevate and ennoble it, and the sexual decorum on which every society in history has insisted, about which the biblical tradition is especially adamant, serves to foster the longing for spiritual communion and the life of self-gift that it requires. The nuptial mystery—into which Adam is drawn by the grace of God and the loveliness of the woman—gives us a glimpse, therefore, of that "inner-Trinitarian ecstasy" toward which creatures made in the image and likeness of the Trinitarian God are intrinsically ordered.[15] That the essence of this ecstasy is the willingness—nay, the eagerness—to perform acts of self-sacrifice is made explicit when Balthasar writes: "Seen with the eyes of faith, bliss and sacrificial self-abandonment are identical."[16]

The biblical text provides what no social science can provide, a scene of prelapsarian goodness which is at once phenomenologically plausible, edifying, and weighty with contemporary implications. The paradisal tableau the biblical author gives us is not societal peace of the sort that Western romantics once sought with such naïve credulity, but a single intimate society—the *com-*

---

14  Balthasar, *The Glory of the Lord, Vol. VII*, 484.

15  Inner-Trinitarian Ecstasy"—a phrase used by a French Jesuit [Jean Galot], whom Jacques Maritain quoted and Balthasar found useful and which was quoted by Aidan Nichols, *No Bloodless Myth: A Guide Through Balthasar's Dramatics* (Washington, DC: The Catholic University of America Press, 2000), 210.

16  Hans Urs von Balthasar, *The Glory of the Lord: A Theological Aesthetics, Vol. I: Seeing the Form*, trans. Erasmo Leiva-Merikakis (San Francisco: Ignatius Press, 1989), 236.

*munio* between a man and a woman, and more precisely the fleeting but ontologically decisive moment when, by the grace of God, the relationship between them—readied by sexual ardor and, for at least one nanosecond, uncontaminated by sin—transcended the instincts that occasioned it.

Humans have an intrinsic longing for communion with God analogous to the longing of the man and the woman for the "one flesh" *communio*. But lacking the physicality that served to channel the attraction of the man and woman and that preconditions its sacramental elevation, the inherent longing for God is squandered on idols from which it can only be rescued by a mimetic model who is both fully human and indistinguishable from the God for whom the human heart longs. The Christ, who is for mankind what the woman was for the man in Genesis, is precisely the crucified Christ, whose pierced heart corresponds to Adam's opened side. The former no less than the latter suggest the ontological coexistence discernible both in Adam's "This at last is bone of my bone and flesh of my flesh" (Gn. 2:23) and in Saint Paul's "I live, no longer I, but Christ lives in me" (Gal. 2:20).

Strange as it may seem—and despite the fact many trace its origin to Arab sources and that there are variants of it wherever one looks in history and in today's world—"romantic love" became a major and defining phenomenon only in those cultures that fell under Christian influence. Whatever its origin, the poetry of the troubadours—a number of whom became Cistercian monks—celebrated the chivalry of the man and the spiritual and mystical essence of the love between the man and woman. Then as now, such sentiments easily devolve into a parody and then into the romanticizing of illicit assignations, bawdy sexuality, or gnostic delusions of one sort or another. But the maxim that the corruption of the best is the worst applies here as elsewhere. C. S. Lewis was surely right when he wrote:

> It seems—or it seemed to us till lately—a natural thing that love (under certain conditions) should be regarded as a noble and ennobling passion: it is only if we imagine ourselves trying to explain this doctrine to Aristotle, Virgil, St. Paul, or the author of Beowulf, that we become aware how far from natural it is. Even our code of etiquette, with its rule that women always have pre-

cedence, is a legacy from courtly love, and is felt to be far from natural in modern Japan or India. Many of the features of this sentiment, as it was known to the Troubadours, have indeed disappeared; but this must not blind us to the fact that the most momentous and the most revolutionary elements in it have made the background of European literature for eight hundred years. French poets, in the eleventh century, discovered or invented, or were the first to express, that romantic species of passion which English poets were still writing about in the nineteenth. They effected a change which has left no corner of our ethics, our imagination, or our daily life untouched, and they erected impassable barriers between us and the classical past or the Oriental present. Compared with this revolution the Renaissance is a mere ripple on the surface of literature.[17]

As the cultures that have been to some extent Christianized renounce their Christian patrimony, romance is dying and sex itself is becoming boring. That is because there is a deep and abiding relationship between, on one hand, the spiritual ardor of romantic love, the nuptial mystery that suffuses it, and the self-sacrificial joys of familial life; and, on the other hand, what Balthasar calls the "inner-Trinitarian ecstasy" for which only Christians can give an adequate theological accounting. Balthasar writes that the "highest realization [of the relationship between the man and the woman] is . . . an extreme achievement that is made wholly possible only within Christianity."[18] This is so precisely because the nuptial mystery is the outcropping in this life of the Trinitarian Mystery, which it is the unique historical privilege and responsibility of Christianity to make palpable to Christians and credible to the world.

Just as the Spirit remains in the background of the love between Father and Son, the Divine Trinity remains in the background of the seemingly binary structure of the conjugal relationship. As Balthasar puts it: "In the highest, fulfilled rela-

17 C.S. Lewis, *The Allegory of Love: A Study in Medieval Tradition* (New York: HarperCollins, 2013), 4.
18 Hans Urs von Balthasar, *Explorations in Theology, Vol. III: Creator Spirit*, trans. Brian McNeil, C.R.V. (San Francisco: Ignatius Press, 1993), 17.

tionship between man and woman, the divine . . . can blaze forth and make itself present . . . [making it] possible to experience the origin of all good as something that has drawn close."[19] One thinks here of the lines from William Butler Yeats' poem *All Souls' Night*:

> Two thoughts were so mixed up I could not tell
> Whether of her or God he thought the most,
> But think that his mind's eye,
> When upward turned, on one sole image fell;
> And that a slight companionable ghost,
> Wild with divinity,
> Had so lit up the whole
> Immense miraculous house
> The Bible promised us,
> It seemed a gold-fish swimming in a bowl.[20]

These lines bring out a fascinating feature of the mystery brought to light by Christ and his Church. The deepest truths of orthodox Christianity are found, not at the farthest remove from idolatry and heresy, but in dangerous proximity to them. In many cases, the greatest Christian truths have to be wrenched from the clutches of idolatry and heresy with which erstwhile Christians have allowed them to become commingled. One can feel in these lines from Yeats the tension between the recognition of the truly transcendent experience of agapic love and the tendency to give an entirely erotic interpretation to the experience.

We have been dwelling on the intrinsically Trinitarian structure of the nuptial experience, for which Yeats' "slight companionable ghost" might be considered a subtle allusion. In addition to this, however, there is the *slight corporeal guest* who may arrive on the scene with no subtly at all nine months later. And these two "triangles" so to speak—the sacramental and the domestic—are intimately related: the openness to grace in one and the openness to children in the other being two aspects of the same thing. Balthasar quotes a passage from Richard of Saint Victor's treatise

19 Balthasar, *Explorations in Theology, Vol. III*, 33.

20 *The Collected Poems of William Butler Yeats*, ed. Richard J. Finneran (New York: Scribner, 2008), 227.

on the Trinity that is most apposite:

> When two love each other, exchanging the gift of their heart in intense longing, and love flows from the one to the other and from the other to the one and thus in each case tends in an opposite direction toward a diverse object, there is indeed love on both sides, but the partners do not yet love with each other [*condilectio*]. We cannot say that they love with each other until the two love a third in harmonious unity, lovingly embracing him in common [*socialiter*], and the affection of the two surges forth as one in the flame of love for the third.[21]

In other words, the nuptial mystery is the outcropping in this life of the Trinitarian drama of mutual self-donation in whose image and likeness we are made. It is essential, however, that we remember that we could never have suspected the Trinitarian architecture that underlies and underwrites human existence and the human *communio* without the revelation of Christ, the eternal *Logos* made flesh. Adrienne von Speyr has captured this mystery magnificently:

> To be two means, in the long run, death. One and one, face to face forever, lead ultimately to the exhaustion of love. A third is always necessary to keep the love between two alive, a third that reaches out beyond the two who love one another. A task that fills and occupies them, a spring that feeds their love, a common interest, something or other to stimulate them, that leads them on, that makes a breach in the circle, an occasion for the eternal renewal of their love. Something that touches both of them and in that way keeps the relationship alive. . . . That is why everything living is three, participates in the three, and must be taken up and plunged into the Trinitarian life if it is to live.[22]

---

21 Richard of Saint Victor, *De Trinitate III,* 19; quoted: Hans Urs von Balthasar, *Theo-Logic, Vol. II: Truth of God*, trans. Adrian J. Walker (San Francisco: Ignatius Press, 2004), Kindle edition, §513.

22 Adrienne von Speyr, *The Word Becomes Flesh; Meditations on John* 1–5, trans. Sr. Lucia Wiedenhöver, O.C.D. and Alexander Dru (San Francisco: Ignatius Press, 1994), 26.

# The Fall

HOWEVER irreversible the hominization event might have been, it is perfectly clear that the intense predilection for self-giving borne aloft by sexual ardor and surcharged to some degree by physical attractiveness, is evanescent. The debt it owes to comeliness and instinct must eventually be paid. As Balthasar puts it: "Earthly eros as an 'atmosphere' blooms but briefly, and every man has the duty to compensate its withering by the force of his love, to endure it, transformed, with renewed vitality through the moral power of the heart."[1]

For love to appear in creation, the creature in whom it appears had to be free, free in a way that no creature ordered entirely by instinct could possibly be. One could say that God's great gamble was in giving humans freedom, but it was a necessary gamble. Not only is freedom indispensable to the creature whose unique vocation is love, but only a creature thus endowed with freedom has the capacity to seek out and to recognize truth, goodness, and beauty (mysteries to which non-human creatures are oblivious) and to say "Yes" to the God who has left these traces of divinity in our midst and inscribed a hunger for them on our hearts. We have been given freedom so that we might one day—or everyday—pronounce a heartfelt "Amen," becoming thereby conscious participants in the hidden liturgy that is the true engine of world history. But the great danger is that the freedom necessary to the fulfillment of the creature's vocation in love will be used haphazardly and self-referentially. Of course, given the inevitably mimetic matrix in which self-will is exercised, it is never entirely self-will, but rather an aspiration aroused, redirected, and distorted by the

---

1 Hans Urs von Balthasar, "Revelation 23 and the Beautiful," *Explorations in Theology, Vol. I, The Word Made Flesh* (San Francisco, CA; Ignatius Press, 1989), 124.

counter-will of another. Armed with the mimetic insights that Girard has placed at our disposal, therefore, we return to Genesis and the story of the Fall.

> And out of the ground the Lord God made to grow every tree that is pleasant to the sight and good for food, the tree of life also in the midst of the garden, and the tree of the knowledge of good and evil. . . . And the Lord God commanded the man, saying, "You may freely eat of every tree of the garden; but of the tree of the knowledge of good and evil you shall not eat, for in the day that you eat of it you shall die." (Gn. 2:9, 16–17)

What light, if any, does this story shed on the question anthropology exists to address? What does it tell us about humanity's origin, destiny, and interim predicament? At one level, it suggests that the act of reaching for the good as though it were on sale at a carnival, the effort to take possession of what is true and beautiful, violates the very conditions under which these things are offered to us. And unless we restrain our desire for exclusive possession of what can be received only as a gift, we necessarily infect the good for which we long with a taint of selfish willfulness, which is the seed out of which evil grows. We might transpose the Genesis narrative into discursive prose this way: unlike any other known creature, man, having been freed to a very large extent from the instinctual constraint that ensures the integrity and survival of non-human species, faces the necessity of ordering the freedom that is indispensable to the supreme human vocation: namely participation in the economy of Trinitarian love.

We hear of peace and justice, and we realize how imperfectly we have achieved either, or even how egregiously we have thwarted them out of avarice or intemperance. But these essential human goods depend on order, and it is the nature of the order to which our lives are sub-ordinated that is decisive. To live an orderly life is to live in an ordered world, and there is no order without a spirit of deference. Whether this deference is free or forced may bear on how just the order is, but an aversion for deference as such is the recipe for the kind of chaos that is prelude to moral anarchy and political tyranny. The paradisal order enjoyed by our first ancestors, according to the Genesis author, has the

Lord God as its architect and precondition. Then something awakens in those who have lived in this perfectly and blissfully ordered garden, an unwillingness to accept the prerequisites for that order. The paradisal inhabitants snatch at an ersatz form of freedom thereby surrendering the freedom that requires docility and patience.

Both wisdom and holiness—and all the spiritual riches that flow from them—depend on an original act of deference and sub-ordination. The tree in the garden can be seen as the archetypal representation of the norm to which the only free creature in all of creation is asked to defer, a gesture indicative of the creature's recognition of its metaphysical dependency. The perennial reason for humanity's rejection of this ontological subordination to the Creator is the presumption—practically the defining assumption of the modern age—that the freedom with which humans have been endowed is incompatible with any norms other than those freely chosen by each individual. To live according to that assumption is to expect a kite to soar to great heights by cutting the string that seems to restrain it.

The story of the serpent's seductive suggestion as to the desirability of the forbidden fruit and the promptness with which the beguiling desire is imitated is proof that the author of the Fall story had both an intuitive understanding of mimetic desire and the literary ingenuity required to provide the *dramatis persona* requisite to its elucidation. One indication of this is that the desire to eat the fruit of the forbidden tree does not occur to Eve independently. Her desire for the fruit will have to be aroused mimetically, but the paradisal world would hardly have provided for that had not the Genesis author inserted a nefarious creature into the story for this purpose. We are so familiar with this story that this odd narrative contrivance doesn't appear to us as ingenious, but it certainly is. It is the Bible's first recognition of the mimetic reality of the human condition, the first of a great many biblical allusions to this fact.

It was not until the biblical journey comes within two centuries of the Christian era that the serpent in the Fall story is explicitly identified with the devil. We read in the Book of Wisdom: "God created man for incorruption, and made him in the image of his own eternity, but through the devil's envy death entered the world, and those who belong to his party experience it (2:23–24)." Envy is a mimetic vice par excellence, akin to resentment and jealousy, and conducive to hatred and eventually madness. While the conversation in the garden between the serpent and the woman turns on whether or not her violation of the Lord God's commandment will lead to death, the author of the Book of Wisdom has linked death—not with disobedience as such—but with envy, which is congruent with the fact that the first death in the Bible is a murder rooted in envy and rivalry. The death that came into the world because of the corruption and misdirection of humanity's richly endowed mimetic capacity and imitative predilection was death inflicted by fallen humans on themselves. The authors of the New Testament would develop more fully the picture of Satan as the mimetic tempter in the wilderness. But as René Girard, drawing on the more fully developed New Testament insights, has pointed out: "Both Jesus and Satan are teachers of imitation and imitators themselves, imitators of God the Father. This means that human beings always imitate God, either through Jesus or through Satan."[2] Jesus lives to do the will of his heavenly Father; Satan envies the Father and strives to trick Jesus into joining his rebellion.

The serpent's corruption of the mimetic propensity by which man has been endowed can ultimately be restored—and truth and freedom once again aligned—when man yields to the mimetic attraction of Christ, the incarnation of the God in whose image and likeness we are made. Satan is the counterfeit Christ, the anti-Christ, the personification of imitation as envy, jealousy, resentment, and rivalry, and whose essential characteristic is not open opposition but the dissimulating imitation of Christ. For Satan, divinity is something to be snatched at, and he inspires his imitators to acts of self-assertion. Jesus, on the contrary, empties himself and bids his imitators to follow him in living lives of loving self-donation (Phil. 2: 6–7).

---

2 René Girard, 'The Question of Anti-semitism in the Gospels," *The Girard Reader*, ed. James Williams (New York: Crossroad Publishing, 1996), 215.

# The Fall

Adam and Eve disobeyed the Lord's command. In stark contrast to Jesus, as described in the Letter to the Philippians, they snatched at divinity, their desire for the fruit and for godlikeness having been mimetically aroused by the serpent. To focus on the norm and its violation is perhaps to overlook the essential issue: the abrogation of the creature's trusting relationship with the Creator. That which can be received only as a gift was despoiled by the surreptitious attempt to purloin it by an act of will. The Lord, theretofore the cornerstone on whom the relationship between the man and the woman depended for its essential triadic structure, becomes the stumbling block. Humanity's essential imitative gift has been squandered on an envious and spiteful mimetic model. The catastrophe of the Fall cannot be reckoned as a simple act of disobedience, lest we reduce the existential predicament that Blessed John Henry Newman called a "terrible aboriginal calamity" to morality. For our purposes we here need to note only that the self-will that lies at the heart of sin is never simply self-will, nor can it be remedied by yet another act of self-will. Both the errant act of self-will and the remedial one are mediated.

Alas, when we humans look around we do not immediately see the Logos in whose image we are made. Rather, our eagerly imitative glance falls (pun intended)—if not on the Serpent himself—in any case on our neighbor, a neighbor who is himself dazzled and confused by the plethora of models to which he himself is enthralled. The gift of free will—intrinsically ordered to the true, the good, and the beautiful—thus dissolves into a cacophony of mimeticism, from which—if one inhabits a modern or postmodern world—one struggles to extricate himself by mimicking the very gestures of autonomy and individuality by which so many of his neighbors are attempting to convince themselves of their social independence and existential authenticity. But to attempt to find one's way out of the mimetic labyrinth by mimicking gestures of individuality or striving to be different is to enter into the more interior chambers where the dismembering Minotaur awaits.

## Death as Punishment

The punishment for eating the forbidden fruit was death. Adam died at the age of nine hundred and thirty; his sons and male descendants enjoyed comparably generous lifespans—not exactly the proximity of punishment to crime that might focus the attention of the sinner on the gravity of his sin. This, however, is a superficial way of understanding what the curse of death really is. If hominization happened, as we have argued, at a single stroke, and if it happened only when the organic and neurological preconditions for it had been fulfilled, then there was surely creaturely death prior to hominization and therefore prior to the Fall. But was there really? Did the pre-human world really know death? We will come to that. For the moment, we need not wait nine hundred and thirty years to see the deadly effects of the Fall. We needn't even wait for Abel's death at the hands of his brother. The man and the woman didn't die, but they lost touch with that within them that cannot die, and—existentially—that is a living death. The real curse of death—the curse that is the consequence of severing the relationship of loving dependence on the God in whose image man is made—is the sudden diminution of ontological substantiality as a result of which the specter of death haunts the living in a myriad of ways, directly or indirectly, throughout life. The man and woman in the Genesis story are now living under the power of death. When the Lord asked:

> "Have you eaten from the tree which I commanded you not to eat?" The man said, "The woman whom thou gavest to be with me, she gave me fruit of the tree, and I ate." Then the Lord God said to the woman, "What is this that you have done?" The woman said, "The serpent beguiled me, and I ate." (Gn. 3:12–13)

In following the serpent's mimetic suggestion and choosing to vie with God for godlike powers, Adam and Eve dissolve the original *communio* that was the essence of the paradisal state, a communion with God and with each other. The dissolution of that communion is exemplified clearly by the moral evasions and mutual recriminations of Adam and Eve in which Cain's murder of Abel is already inscribed and prefigured. Girard's description of culture-founding violence and its self-transformation into sacrificial religion and conventional culture can be read as an anthropological extension of the post-lapsarian breakdown of the first human *communio*, the breakdown between the man and the woman. "Sin . . . wounds man's nature and injures human solidarity,"[3] so says the Catholic *Catechism*. In shifting the blame for their offense and the stated punishment for it, Adam and Eve are, in effect, trying to transfer death to another. What is that if not the pagan sacrificial reflex par excellence? That is exactly what ritual sacrifice does in primitive religion, in which the only possible cure for death is death.

The *punishment* for the sin in the garden is simply the *consequence* of abandoning the Trinitarian economy of self-sacrificial love—which is implicit in Adam's "this at last is bone of my bone and flesh of my flesh"—and the renunciation of man's subjacent position in the created order, a corruption of the properly ordered relationship with his creator and the corresponding corruption of his human relationships, so glaringly indicated by the attempt to transfer both the blame for and, by obvious implication, the mortal consequences of the failed grasping at godlikeness. The *Catechism of the Catholic Church* puts it succinctly: "The harmony in which they had found themselves, thanks to original justice, is now destroyed: the control of the soul's spiritual faculties over the body is shattered; the union of man and woman becomes subject to tensions, their relations henceforth marked by lust and domination."[4]

The doctrine of "original sin" gives expression to the experience that the sinful condition is *always already*. The individual sinner, if he is at all self-reflective, realizes that he inhabits an always already morally compromised existence. (Personal sin, as distinct from "original sin," is the attempt to recover from the congenitally sinful state in which man finds himself other than by way of contrition.) Again as the Catholic *Catechism* formulates it, that prior sin, original sin, is "'contracted' not 'committed'—a state and not an act."[5] Seen in this way, personal sin is rebellion against

---

3  *CCC* §1872.
4  Ibid., §400.
5  Ibid., §404.

the conditions born of an aboriginal rebellion, and the rebel's curse is to be in secret rebellion against himself, at war with his very existence.

There is no doubt that pre-human creatures died. In reconciling this fact with the mythopoetics of the Genesis story, the Catholic *Catechism* nonetheless tells us that due to sin, "death made its entry into human history."[6] By which we are invited to suppose that though death existed prior to human sin, it had not insinuated itself into human history and infected man's existential attitude toward his temporal finitude. Animals instinctively flee from lethal threats and are quite tenacious in doing so. But animals do not brood over their impending mortality, nor are they haunted by the dark possibility of non-existence. Unlike animals, for postlapsarian humans, ontologically compromised as we are, death awakens an existential dread. In fact, it is essentially this dread that is the key to what humans mean by the word death. It is also one way to understand death as punishment for or as consequence of the sin-ridden, ontologically impaired existence that we now live. Life is lived with the certainty of death, ignore it and postpone it though we do. Whether due to grace or faith or stoicism, it is possible for humans to come to accept their deaths and die in serenity, but when they do, others look on with admiration and even astonishment, for such serenity is not the default response to death in our species. We live under the power of death, in dread of death. We cannot substantially evade the weight of mortal dread, though, as mentioned, we might occasionally experience a fleeting taste of what life without it would be. The existential dread of death is a product of the ontological tenuousness whose source is the covenantal break with the Ground of one's being that sin brings about.

The Book of Genesis provides just those hints of the fallen condition from which the basic outlines of the human predicament in any age can be limned: mimetic entanglement, dissimulation, evasion, and the tendency—essential to cultural sacrificiality—to transfer the onus born of such things to others. Having allowed the gift of freedom to succumb to the mimetic allurements of the

6 Ibid., §400.

sower of discord and envy, the man and woman renounced the Paradisal Order—the Original Logos. Henceforth, the perennial task would be that of fashioning some makeshift alternative to the ordered love on which the creature, brought into existence by that love, had turned its back.

## Divine Forbearance

The paradisal order—the aboriginal *Logos*—was just that: paradisal. The man and woman were given one insignificant constraint. Why? Let us speculate: because God endowed his one conscious and ensouled creature with freedom so that this creature could enter the school of love on an entirely voluntary basis, for love must be a freely proffered gift. But just as love depends on freedom, so freedom necessitates order. But freedom can be used to rebel against the very order that is indispensable to the exercise of freedom. The alternative to order is violence and madness. Those who think otherwise delude themselves into believing that the exhilaration that accompanies the initial phase of the dissolution of order will last, and there is in history not one shred of evidence for that belief. The garden story in Genesis is about the mimetically driven willfulness that blithely overturns a beneficent order more conducive to human happiness than anything we can now imagine. The story hardly has to be literally true for us to recognize the truth about our predicament that it reveals.

The attempted usurpation of divinity is incompatible with its intended goal. The impatience and pride that the tempter awakened in the usurpers does ontological damage to the godlikeness that is the secret to paradisal existence. The expulsion from the garden is the Lord's way of making them as aware as they are capable of being under the circumstances of the damage they have caused, as well as the biblical authors' way of alluding to the Lord's abiding solicitude. The ontological impairment, which the man and woman will henceforth suffer, will be the source of an alienation from which they will be unable to extricate themselves by their own unaided efforts. Nonetheless their expulsion from the garden is itself the first phase of the Lord's covenantal pedagogy with which they will be invited, but not compelled, to cooperate. The disenchantment of the world begins, but it begins with the very gesture of divine solicitude in which the later more explicit forms of the covenant are inscribed. Before expelling them from the garden, "The Lord God made for Adam and for his wife garments of skins, and clothed them" (Gen. 3:21).

As many exegetes have pointed out, such skins could be had only at the expense of the creature slain in order to provide them, and much has been made of that sacrificial innuendo in the course of both Jewish and Christian reflection on this verse. It is reinforced by yet another sacrificial implication. The Hebrew words for clothed (*labash*) and garments (*kĕthoneth*) are occasionally used in the Jewish Bible with ritual implications as, for instance, when Moses clothes Aaron in his priestly vestments (Lev. 8:7ff), and when he later transfers this ritual attire from Aaron to his son Eleazar (Num. 20:28). Whether one derives a sacrificial meaning from the fact that an animal had to be sacrificed to provide the skins or from the sacerdotal innuendo linking this detail to the vestments of the Aaronic priesthood that presided at ritual sacrifices, one is reminded of Origen's interpretation of sacrifice as a concession:

> Since the Jews loved sacrifices, being accustomed to them in Egypt, as the golden calf in the desert gives witness, God permits them to offer them to himself so as to curb their disordered tendency to polytheism and to turn them away from sacrificing to idols.[7]

What the first fallen humans needed far more than they might have needed garments to protect them from the elements was something to protect them from each other, which is precisely what archaic religion did for our most ancient ancestors. That is to say, it allowed them to exert a degree of ritual control over both violence and the mimetic passions in which violence incubates. Having effectively self-excommunicated themselves from

---

7 Quoted: Henri de Lubac, *History and Spirit: The Understanding of Scripture according to Origen*, trans. Anne Englund Nash (San Francisco: Ignatius Press, 2007), 291.

the paradisal garden ordered according to Trinitarian and covenantal principles that would take their ancestors millennia to
apprehend, aboriginal humans would have to cobble together
some way of ordering their world. As the Lord ushered them out
of the garden, he provided them with the thing most necessary:
religion in the form of primitive priestly vestments, the mantle of
sacrality necessary to end violence by bringing it to a cathartic
climax and by ritually forestalling its return by the exercise of
primitive shamanic and sacred authority.

Analogous forms of divine solicitude were to follow. When
Cain, the fratricide and builder of cities, murdered Abel, his slain
brother's blood cried out to God who heard the cry. Cain was condemned but protected from annihilation. Culture, notwithstanding the violence with which it came into existence, and the ritual
repetition on which it thereafter depended, was to be humanity's
spiritual life-support system. The condemnation of Cain, com-
bined with the forbearance with regard to his crime, prefigures
Yahweh's reluctant accession to the Israelite desire for "a kingdom
like the other nations have." If human freedom—the key to the
eschatological triumph of love—was to be preserved, then postlapsarian humanity would have to make the best of the clumsy
and morally odious cultural apparatus it had substituted for
paradisal docility. As Paul told the people of Lystra, in the past God
"allowed all the nations to walk in their own ways" (Acts 14:16) as
he had done with Cain, the founder of culture par excellence.

Though man is free to avoid sin, he hasn't the power to surprise his Creator by failing to do so. The Father chose us *in Christ*
before the foundation of the world, Paul tells the Ephesians (Eph.
1:4). Balthasar quotes with approval the nineteenth century German biblical translators, Valentin Loch and Wilhelm Reischl:
"God did not plan the foundation of the world and bring it to
pass without, in foreseeing sin, forming his decree for the
redemption of the world, and this through the future incarnation
of his only-begotten Son. Redemption therefore is not something
in the mind of God posterior to the creation of the world.[8]

---

8 Loch and Reischl, Die hl. Schrift (1885); quoted: Hans Urs von Balthasar,
*Explorations in Theology, Vol. I*, 22.

In light of this suggestion and with the help of the alliance of theology and anthropology, there are a number of Christian themes that might prove to be richer and deeper than many have imagined. Summarizing the way the eighteenth century Italian philosopher Giambattista Vico understood archaic religions, Karl Löwith writes, "True providence, operating in history for the preservation of mankind, deceived the first generations of men into the truth through a false religion, for they were by nature incapable of conceiving the true religion in spirit and in truth."[9] It is easier to imagine that "providence" was deceptive than it is to attribute deception to the God whose essence is self-revelation, but there is nonetheless more than a hint of truth in what Vico says. Archaic religion, indeed all religion, is an anticipation of the truth revealed by Christ on the Cross. As Balthasar puts it:

> In the structure of the world and of existence, there must be a kind of adumbration, a sketch, an inchoate intimation of the Cross, a preliminary plan on God's part that is aware of the imminent culpability of the free human being and takes account of it, without man being able to guess it, abstract it as a universal law and gain control of it.[10]

Vico suggests that—"operating in history for the preservation of mankind"—God coaxed man into false forms of transcendence in anticipation of the eventual revelation in Christ of the full and true meaning of religion, one in which "the true worshipers will worship the Father in spirit and truth" (Jn. 4:23). There is only one circumstance in which this plan of salvation would not simply be an outrage against the goodness of God. Only if every person who ever lived or who ever will live is made the beneficiary of the revelation of God in Christ, could God be good, just, and merciful. In subsequent chapters we will return to this matter of the universality of the Christian revelation.

Staying within the narrative arc of the Fall story in Genesis, we can say that the perilous world in which postlapsarian humanity

---

9 Karl Löwith, *Meaning in History* (Chicago: University of Chicago Press, 1949), 128.

10 Hans Urs von Balthasar, *Truth is Symphonic: Aspects of Christian Pluralism*, trans. Graham Harrison (San Francisco: Ignatius Press, 1987), 46.

would have to grope its way was a world unhinged, a world without order, a world forever threatened with what René Girard calls "the crisis of undifferentiation." Such was the aboriginal world, now inhabited by a creature which had slipped its instinctual leash, so to speak, a creature whose survival could no longer depend on the neurophysiological reflexes that served to limit the interspecies violence in creatures with less robust mimetic endowments. This species—as the Genesis author made clear—responded to the mimetic suggestion of the lowliest of creatures with such foolish alacrity that it threw away its own happiness in the process, as we humans have routinely done ever since. Ah, but the God who for unspecified reasons loved this creature more than all others and who would forever woo it like a jealous lover provided it with—of all things—religious vestments. The fig leaves that the fallen couple had quickly grabbed to cover their shame were all but useless for the exigencies of life no longer governed and ordered by instinct.

We conclude the exploration of the providential role of sacrificial religion with the words of Cardinal Charles Journet (1891–1975). His words are of special interest because they are the words of a theologian, not an anthropologist; words penned before René Girard began his publishing career. The important point, however, is that the cardinal's reading of salvation history is characterized by the same assimilating intelligence, the same attentiveness to the underlying scriptural leitmotif, and the same deeply Christocentric anthropology that distinguishes Girard's work. *Mutatis mutandis*, the theologian and the cultural theorist have recognized the same Ariadne's thread running not only through the Scriptures but through human history itself.

> According to the Fathers of the Church, both under the law of nature and under the Jewish law, sacrifices offered to God uncontaminated either by human perversity or by diabolic activity were acceptable to him only because he saw in them an adumbration of the future sacrifice of his Son. If the blood of Abel cried out to God, according to the Epistle to the Hebrews (12:24)

this was because, one day and still more eloquently, the blood of Christ would cry out to God. All that was genuine before Christ came, all the things that were acceptable to God, were so because he saw them already overshadowed by the cross; they were the first rough outline of what he would receive later from the supreme sacrifice of his Son. The Christian graces formed a single people, not yet visibly assembled, but already centered on Jesus. The Church was in the course of formation, advancing through the centuries toward the Redeemer. Human dignity was solicited both by divine grace and the forces of perversity; assent and refusal were, then as now, the outcome of a free interior decision; grace constantly returned to move men's hearts; and those who did not refuse it at the end already belonged to Christ, though perhaps still knowing nothing of him.[11]

Inasmuch as there were human lives sacrificed on the altars of very many ancient cultures—not to mention the countless human lives taken in the quasi-ritual pogroms, purges, and wars of our own age—very grave moral problems and theodicy issues arise concerning God's tolerance of fallen man's reliance on makeshift sacrificial regimes. We will return to these questions in a later chapter. We mention these issues here, not to impugn Journet's assessment, with which we concur, but to note that we will need to delve more deeply into the question in due course. Meanwhile we can simply cite in conclusion at this point a sentence written by Cardinal Journet, which could have been written with no amendment by René Girard: "Already under the natural law and under the Law of Moses, the cross threw its shadow over the world and brought it salvation."[12] Both Cardinal Journet and René Girard, therefore, read human history through the lens of the Cross. In what immediately follows, we will look more closely into how the sacrificial foreshadowing of the Cross actually worked. By peering into the inner workings of ritual sacrifice, we will find evidence to corroborate the mysterious designation—

11 Charles Journet, *The Meaning of Grace*, trans. A. V. Littledale (New York: Scepter Publishers, 1996), 102–3.

12 Ibid.

most clearly in the King James translation—of Christ as the Lamb Slain from the foundation of the world (Rev. 13:8).

We are keenly aware that many of those for whom we have the greatest respect, and with whom we feel the most theological accord, may fault such reasoning as attempting to elucidate theological and anthropological conundrums without adequate empirical corroboration and scriptural support. We are well aware of these difficulties, but our predecessors in the faith faced similar disconnects between the truths of faith and the worldly forms of reasoning to which they seemed, as Saint Paul famously said, scandalous and foolish (1 Cor. 1:23). A Christian proposal that deftly avoids scandalizing anyone and that awakens no accusation of foolishness, is in that degree congenial to the spirit of the age, and may be suspected of being, for that very reason, kerygmatically questionable. This can be acknowledged without the implication—which we renounce—that proposals that are thought foolish or scandalous are ipso facto valid. A proposal, Christian or otherwise, deserves to be thought through with an eye to what we know from Scripture and tradition, as well as whatever light might be thrown on these matters by relevant secular sciences.

# The Moral Conscience

We do not assent to our moral beliefs by admitting "this is true" but by feeling guilty if we fail to comply with them.[1] —Leszek Kolakowski

IN BRINGING together the Genesis author's poetic realism with the anthropological insights that René Girard has made available, we have suggested that Adam's exclamation "This at last is bone of my bone and flesh of my flesh" not only constitutes the most plausible biblical marker for the emergence of the proclivity for non-instinctual self-sacrifice, but it is also the most phenomenologically credible account of prelapsarian innocence, however evanescent it surely must have been. We suggested that nature in the form of sexual ardor—nature, that is to say, at its most mystical, self-forgetful, and other-directed attentiveness—might have availed itself of the intercommunicating grace whose origin is the Trinitarian communion, discovering in that moment self-sacrificial love, the high calling of the human person. This way of accounting for prelapsarian goodness, we suggested earlier, has a degree of emotional verisimilitude, as does the certainty that the other-directed aspiration to self-sacrifice must have quickly succumbed to mimetic intrigues, rivalries, and the assertion of self. There is, however, another account of prelapsarian innocence, and it is one that links to the question of the moral conscience. It should be noted that while Saint John Paul II sought to locate hominization in the fleeting but ontologically decisive encounter between the man and the woman in Genesis—the salient feature of which we have suggested was the awakening of the capacity for non-instinctual self-sacrifice—John Paul's successor approached

---

1 Quoted: Roger Kimball, *The Fortunes of Permanence: Culture and Anarchy in an Age of Amnesia* (St. Augustine Press, 2012), Kindle Edition §2679

the question of hominization by assuming that it coincided with the birth of the moral conscience.

A closer look at the nature and meaning of the conscience is in order, for the term is today widely misinterpreted. Though the conscience is common to all reasonably mature humans, those cultures under Christian influence are the recipients of a Pauline understanding of conscience that, in turn, was born of Paul's experience of conversion. In an address published in 1991, Joseph Ratzinger tried to clarify the widespread misunderstanding of the conscience by offering the Platonic concept of *anamnesis* (recollection) as a philosophically more nuanced substitute for the New Testament term, *synderesis*, which was later translated into the less precise Latin, *conscientia*. In his exposition, the future pope argued that the Greek term *anamnesis* was completely in keeping with the bedrock Pauline principle of a law written on the human heart. Above all, Ratzinger argued, *anamnesis* "harmonizes with key motifs of biblical thought and the anthropology derived from it."[2] This is germane to our current exploration inasmuch as we have suggested that evidence of the moral conscience constitutes proof that hominization has occurred. Ratzinger's use of anamnesis provides access, as we shall see, to an anthropologically plausible understanding of prelapsarian innocence, a recollected, not biographically experienced, state of sinlessness.

> [T]he first so-called ontological level of the phenomenon conscience consists in the fact that something like an *original memory* of the good and true (they are identical) has been *implanted* in us, that there is *an inner ontological tendency* within man, who is created in the image and likeness of God, toward the divine. From its origin, man's being resonates with some things and clashes with others. This *anamnesis* of the origin, which results from the god-like constitution of our being, is *not a conceptually articulated knowing*, a store of retrievable contents. It is, so to speak, an inner sense, a capacity to recall, so that the one whom it addresses, if he is not turned in on himself, hears its echo from within. He sees: That's it! That is what my nature points to and seeks.[3]

2 Joseph Ratzinger, *On Conscience* (San Francisco: Ignatius Press, 2007), 31.
3 Ibid., 32, my italic emphasis.

# The Moral Conscience

Cardinal Ratzinger's disquisition on the conscience posits an innocence that arises retrospectively from the realization that one is no longer innocent. Arguably innocence is never a present experience; it is the memory of a situation no longer pertaining. The Scottish poet Edwin Muir deftly captures this:

> Innocent, knowing nothing of innocence,
> We learned it from the sad memorial name
> First uttered by the offense,
> And now the two words seem
> A single, fabulous, reciprocal glory,
> A dream re-enacted in another dream,
> And all accomplished as we plucked the bough.
> Stories we know. There is another story.
> If one of you is innocent let him tell it now.[4]

Innocence is an unperturbed state of moral self-satisfaction, accessible to the mind only in retrospect, when that state has been disturbed and survives only as an intimation of something for which one has no specific memory but for which one is nevertheless vaguely nostalgic, and for the loss of which one feels responsible. No innocent child walks around aware of his innocence. Anyone older than a child has ceased to be innocent and has access to lost innocence only as a mental reconstruction based on two things: a non-innocent present condition and a sense of complicity in the loss of a prior innocence. However "innocent" an accused person might be in a limited and strictly juridical sense, original innocence and goodness as these things are imagined in the biblical context are not to be found in our world. One may experience forgiveness, or grace, or even the bitter-sweet peace of having faced the sobering truth about one's responsibility for a forfeited innocence, but innocence itself is always in the past. It is always remembered as a prior state of blessedness.

As a marker for the event of hominization, Ratzinger's *anamnestic* reading of the moral conscience has a psychological and moral

---

4 Edwin Muir, "The Other Story," *Edwin Muir Collected Poems* (London: Faber and Farber, 1984), 241.

plausibility comparable to the emotional realism of the conjugal moment of hominization which we have earlier described and which was favored by his immediate predecessor on the Chair of Peter. We can assume, however, that the awakening to a lost state of innocence is less likely to have occurred in a moment of reverie than in response to a provocation. So we are left with a question as to what that provocation might have been.

The following remarks on the moral conscience by Joseph Ratzinger give us a hint of what might have constituted the admittedly unconscious choice facing our most primitive ancestors. Ratzinger writes:

> What actually is conscience? Is there such a thing? Or, is it not just an inward-directed superego that turns the taboos of one's upbringing into divine commandments, thus making them insuperable? . . . Of course it is possible for the canonization of the superego to insinuate itself into the concept of conscience, so that it hinders individual human development. Then the absolute call to personal responsibility is covered over with a system of conventions that is falsely made out to be the voice of God, whereas in truth it is only the voice of the past, which fears the present and bars its way.[5]

It is certainly true that one's life can be hedged in by the ethical customs absorbed, often unknowingly, from one's cultural milieu and operating in ways that Sigmund Freud described in his theory of the superego. The social and ethical conventions thus interiorized may be perfectly healthy or they may be morally perverse or psychologically injurious. In any case, however, these customs might well help shape the development of the moral conscience, but they are not synonymous with it. Even where these inherited traditions are healthy, their value is limited until they are consciously appropriated and instantiated in the life of the free moral subject.

5 Joseph Ratzinger (Pope Benedict XVI), *Church, Ecumenism, and Politics*, trans. Michael J. Miller, et al (San Francisco: Ignatius Press, 2008), 163.

# The Moral Conscience

The word conscience means "knowing with." The participants and onlookers at the culture-founding event of all-against-one violence would have had to know the event with either the surviving community or with the community's victim. To the extent that they were able to know the event with the community, they would have enjoyed the social benefits of the violence. Whatever the moral benefits of knowing the event with its victim, the social consequences would have been unpleasant and, very possibly, fatal—both for the one who threatened the unanimity by drawing back from the violence that generated it and fatal for the rudimentary culture that consisted of that unanimity. Moreover, the social benefits—and arguably the accompanying psychological advantages—of knowing the event with the community of victimizers would have been so welcome and so unexpected, and the power of social contagion so overwhelming, that the very possibility of knowing the event from the victim's perspective would likely have been only a faint hint of discomfort at the victim's suffering and death, a momentary wincing perhaps and nothing more. As we shall see below, without that tinge of moral remorse, however, there would have been no catharsis, and therefore no surviving culture. So we have at least implicit evidence for a theory long favored by Girard's interpreters, namely that cultural hominization coincided with the immolation of the "first" victim—first, that is, inasmuch as it provided the existential shock that brought the a fragile human community into existence in the first instance and induced in its participants a profound sense of religious awe.

In this scenario, the conscience is detectable only as a moral aversion that remained below the level of full awareness, but without which the violence of the victimizers would not have achieved the cathartic climax that is the key to the birth of archaic religion. To the extent that those present at the event of cultural origination surrender their tenuous hold on the moral conscience in favor of the decided advantages of social peace made possible by the immolation of the victim, their conscience, in the words of Joseph Ratzinger, is "covered over with a system of conventions that is falsely made out to be the voice of God." What they hear, then, is not the cry of the victim, but the *vox pop-*

*uli* (the voice of the people), transfigured, as it would henceforth tend to be, into the *vox dei* (the voice of god). Absent an intervening event of very considerable moral unlikelihood, the asymmetrical contest between the voice of the crowd and the cry of its victim would have endured, and the occasional twinges of moral discomfort it aroused would have had precious little cultural or historical consequence. In point of fact, however, and against all odds, the reverberations of the voice of the victim underwent a remarkable amplification over time. René Girard would trace its gradual magnification back to its biblical sources in the Hebrew Bible and, most unmistakably, to the passion and death of Christ. But that part of our story awaits us in the chapters below.

## Catharsis

It is not within our powers to locate the precise moment of *cultural* hominization. It surely occurred in countless places over hundreds or thousands of years. Thanks to the work of René Girard, however, we can reconstruct the anthropologically plausible event that could only have appeared either coincident with or proximate to hominization, namely an episode of collective violence in which the mimetic dynamic driving the event has produced an all-against-one finale accompanied by a rudimentary form of religious awe. Such an event would give rise to social benefits if, and only if, a cathartic dénouement is achieved. It is when we ask about the nature of this catharsis that we discover that culture itself represents something like the fruit of the tree of the knowledge of good and evil.

The Greek word *katharsis* means purification by means of offloading or expelling. By implication, if not explicitly, Aristotle seemed anxious that the tragedians of his day take the necessary precautions to ensure the cathartic resolution of their tragic dramas, without which the drama would leave the audience socially and morally divided. He insisted that the key to a cathartic resolution was a commingling in the audience of the emotions of "pity" and "terror." Especially given the almost offhanded nature of this Aristotelian remark, we need not regard the terms he used as overly precise, and we have far less reason to suppose that these competing emotions are present in an equal degree. To ensure that the drama end in a cathartic resolution, the terror—the horror at the devastation that the victim's transgression might set in motion—would necessarily eclipse the pity felt for the victim. Aristotle's concern about the precariousness of the cathartic resolution that was so essential to the sacrificial rituals (dramatizations of which the Greek tragedians were presenting to popular audiences in a setting no longer explicitly religious) was, we feel, essentially the same as Plato's fear that the tragedians were undermining the religious piety of their audiences. In each case, these Greek thinkers were expressing concerns quite similar to those that so preoccupied the priests presiding at ritual sacrifices in antiquity. The anxieties of the priests with regard to the apotropaic rites at which they presided took the form of ritual scrupulosity, while the concern foremost in the minds of the later philosophers were predominantly social and political. Underlying the distinctive terms by which the priests and the philosophers expressed their anxieties, however, there lies the problem of catharsis. Both the priests and philosophers were intuitively aware that the ratio of what Aristotle termed "pity" and "terror" was delicate and that ritual or dramaturgical miscalculations or inattention to the appropriate balance between them might have dire consequences. The "terror"—that is to say, the horror at the potential violence unleashed by the protagonist's transgression of taboos—would necessarily overshadow, but not entirely extinguish, a trace of moral empathy for the one whose death was indispensable to the avoidance or cessation of the "plague" or violence visited upon the community by the gods or worldly instruments under their control. Only by achieving the right balance between these emotions could the ritual (in the case of ancient religious rites) or the performance of a dramatized reenactment (in the case of the Athenian theater) produce its social benefits.

In this sense, Aristotle, Plato, and the high priest Caiaphas all point to the dependence of culture on ritual catharsis and an awareness of the delicate balance between the dominant experience of righteous relief that the crisis has been averted and the subliminal sense of moral remorse for the figure whose suffering and death made that deliverance possible. No such cathartic resolution would occur if the audience felt no "pity" or moral discomfort whatsoever. The result in that case would be the cheap titillation associated with superficial Hollywood films in our day, which was an outcome Aristotle urged the dramatists of his day to avoid. It might well unite the audience in the experience of triumph or vindication, but there would be no deep or "religious" sense of the meaning of that social unanimity. It would be evanescent. It would work less like a cure and more like a social stimulant that would quickly wear off, potentially sending those it momentarily fascinated into the streets of Athens to settle scores between the dramatis personae that the drama itself failed to resolve. On the other hand, if the "pity" or moral scruples that audience felt rose fully to consciousness in the audience in general, the violent dénouement of the ritual or the drama would stand revealed as morally odious and would produce no social unanimity. Either everyone would leave—as did the crowd gathered for the "spectacle" on Golgotha—in confusion, or the onlookers would break into factions consisting of those who empathized with the victim and those who found the need to ward off some social catastrophe reason enough to withdraw and disparage any such empathy. Instead of "pity" and "terror" residing uneasily side-by-side in the breast of each member of the audience or ritual onlooker, these conflicting emotions would manifest themselves in two or more social factions, further threatening the society which it was the anthropological role of both ritual and drama to solemnly unite. Aristotle's concern was simply with the social efficacy of ritual sacrifice, the elaborate dramatized versions of which were appearing on the tragic stage. Were we to transpose that concern into the more morally animated vocabulary and operating paradigms of biblical Israel, then in place of Aristotelian terror and pity we would have something like *righteousness* and *remorse*, a sense of moral vindication, on one hand, and a sense of moral regret, on the other, the latter necessarily subordinated to the former.

Now if the event that gives rise to ritual sacrifice, one of the markers for *cultural* hominization, is also the event where traces of the moral conscience first appear—suppressed but detectable in the experience of catharsis—then we have the interesting situation of two markers of hominization, the cultural and the ontological, appearing simultaneously, precisely at an event that is a morally inverted but nonetheless structurally identical variation on the Crucifixion. One would be tempted to think of these two effects in an unambiguous way, condemning the violence and valorizing the latent traces of moral aversion that accompanied it. It would be morally right to do so, but to think this way is to rush in with a quick moral fix, averting one's eyes from precisely the tragedy from which the human race is being rescued by Christ. To segment off the putatively good interior moral misgivings from the morally tainted social solidarity is too simple. It would be to insist on a discontinuity between archaic religion and Christianity, which, however morally reassuring and intellectually tidy, would, in the end, obscure both the enormity of the human predicament and the breathtaking felicity of the Christian answer to that predicament. It would be to try to salvage Christian uniqueness by sacrificing the equally astonishing scope of Christian universality.

Not only do we have here an account of the paradisal, prelapsarian goodness of creation that retains all that is essential, but we have as well an understanding of the human conscience free from the moralism that has done almost as much to undermine the religious and sacramental prerequisites to moral health as has the antinomian relativism now so prevalent in Western culture. Conscience not only "remembers" a time when truth, goodness, and beauty were so radiant that moral scruples were entirely unnecessary, it also envisions the graced completion of our nature that beckons to us—from beyond and from within—when this will be the case once more. Conscience tells us, in then-Cardinal Ratzinger's words: "That's it! That is what my nature points to and seeks." The conscience is the uniquely human capacity to hear the divine invitation to fully actualize the dignity and nobility of the human vocation, a summons inherently and necessarily subtle because anything more compelling might overwhelm the freedom that is essential to the response it invites. At the birth of human culture, that subtle summons to a nobler and more self-giving existence was drowned out by the aggregated terrors and passions of those who, for the moment, had eyes but could not see and ears but could not hear.

Embedded within Girard's account of cultural hominization we have discovered an essential criterion indispensable to the cathartic resolution, namely a tinge of moral discomfort all but extinguished by the gravitational power of social mimeticism. We argued that this tinge of moral remorse—unconsciously sublimated in favor of the social passions that demanded, justified, and celebrated the immolation of a victim—represented the first, faint manifestation of the moral conscience. And we further argued that this moral conscience was indisputable proof that hominization had occurred.

At this point, we need only underscore what we have said earlier: that the marker for *ontological* hominization we detected in the Genesis account—the man's "This at last is bone of my bone and flesh of my flesh"—must have been an exceedingly fleeting experience, soon enveloped by mimetic desires and rivalries. The marker for the birth of humanity we found in Girard's account of *cultural* hominization was tucked away inside the fact that only a cathartically concluded event of collective violence could have produced the first intense experience of social bonding from which culture could be religiously elaborated. What these two accounts of hominization have in common is their evanescence. The spiritual communion between the man and the woman needn't have lasted more than a moment to have both served as a moment of prelapsarian goodness and had ontological consequences. The moment of prelapsarian goodness we discovered in the Genesis account was doubtless a transient one, but the social unanimity in the case of the collective murder posited by Girard could hardly have been less so. In the latter case, the tinge of moral discomfort without which no catharsis could have occurred necessarily remained inchoate, the historical journey of our species consisting of man's gradual awakening to the promptings of the moral conscience. To this need only be added what Blessed John Henry Newman famously says of the conscience: "It is a messenger from Him, who, both in nature and in grace, speaks to us behind a veil, and teaches and rules us by His representatives. Conscience is the aboriginal Vicar of Christ."[6]

---

6 John Henry Newman, "A Letter Addressed to His Grace the Duke of Norfolk on the Occasion of Mr. Gladstone's Recent Expostulation" (London: Pickering, 1875), 57, cited in the *Catechism of the Catholic Church*, §1178.

# The First Victim

Immediately after the Fall the mediation of Christ began. It worked in a very hidden manner, by anticipation. This was the age of the expectation of Christ. It was possible for men to be saved by him without knowing of his future coming, except in a very obscure and very imperfect manner.[1]—Cardinal Charles Journet

IF HUMAN CULTURE begins with the birth of religion, religion begins with the separation of the sacred and the profane, and the separation of the sacred and the profane coincides with the apotheosis or divinization of the victim. The deification of the victim could only have occurred in response to a death that was *cathartic*—that is to say, stunning in a rudimentary *moral* sense, and emotionally enthralling in a way that the killing of an animal (by another animal) could not have been; cathartic in a way that the killing of an animal by humans could be only if dramatically intensified by rituals of the sort that could only have arisen *subsequent* to the culture-founding event. Alas, an aporia arises, a chicken and egg dilemma. Were we to discover—even theoretically—the moment when the moral conscience is even faintly detectable, as it is in the experience of catharsis, then we could declare those in whom evidence of the conscience appears to be members of our species. If in Girard's analysis of the birth of human culture at the first successful transference of collective violence onto a single victim, we find traces of the first stirrings of the moral conscience, then it is quite possible that this event constitutes the moment of both cultural and ontological hominization. The conundrum that arises here, of course, is that the

---

1 Charles Journet, *The Meaning of Grace*, trans. A. V. Littledale (New York: Scepter Publishers, 1996), 93.

95

tinge of moral discomfort that betokens the presence of the moral conscience and therefore of human existence as such could have been aroused only by the death of a fellow human. If pack animals join in the killing of another animal, the result is not primitive religion; it is the consumption of the slain animal, delayed only for as long as it takes for the pecking order among the most powerful animals to be established. So have we arrived at a dead end? Cardinal Charles Journet offers a hint: "The destruction of the first state of innocence was permitted so that God might show forth his love for us, his boundless love, by giving his Son for the salvation of the world. From then on everything was to be centered on the cross: 'I, if I be lifted up from the earth, will draw all things to myself'" (Jn. 12:32).[2]

We have reason to believe that our most ancient ancestors were brought across the threshold from primate to human existence at precisely the moment when, let us say, the cry of dereliction—emanating from the suffering and dying victim in their midst—left its first moral trace on their hearts. "Immediately after the Fall," Cardinal Journet opines, "the mediation of Christ began." Might the Fall itself and the mediation of Christ have been concurrent? Might the event of social hominization—its twisted ribbons of darkness and light notwithstanding—have been made possible by the presence of *the Lamb slain since the foundation of the world*?

The victims of primordial culture-founding violence were randomly selected due to any number of purely fortuitous markers that would have given rise to their social exceptionality, but their ontological status remains an enigma. Whatever role their deaths might have played in bestirring the trace of moral discomfort in their victimizers and thereby uniting them and bringing them across the threshold of hominization, it was a hominization event made possible by the victim's exclusion from it. However emotionally intense the victim's suffering and death might have been, he would have known nothing of the moral remorse—the muffled voice of the Aboriginal Vicar of Christ—that his death made faintly audible to his persecutors. On the other hand, the trace of

2 Journet, *The Meaning of Grace*, 93–4.

moral discomfort that made the cathartic climax of the collective violence both ontologically and culturally fruitful could only have been aroused by a human victim. The question is, from whence—or from Whom—did the victim's own ontological weight come?

Before reasoning and reflecting on its validity, we will state with almost vulgar and impious inelegance the mystery we are asking our readers to contemplate: What was to keep Christ, the Eternal *Logos*—the *Meaning* of and the *Reason* for creation itself—from launching humanity on its careening course toward Golgotha and beyond by putting his thumb on the ontological scales to the advantage of the first neurologically qualified creature at precisely the moment when a mob of his fellow creatures, likewise teetering on the threshold of hominization and human in every respect, save for their as yet unawakened moral conscience, were menacingly circling, murmuring the grunting, aboriginal equivalent of "crucify him!"?

Whatever the shortcomings of this supposition, it provides a new perspective on scriptural passages such as that in the prologue to John's Gospel where we are told that "all things came to be through him" (Jn. 1:3). All the more so does it call for the reassessment of the allusion to the same Christological mystery found in the magnificent hymn in Colossians: "He is the image of the invisible God, the first-born of all creation; for in him all things were created, in heaven and on earth, visible and invisible, whether thrones or dominions or principalities or authorities— all things were created through him and for him. He is before all things, and in him all things hold together" (Col. 1:15–17).

To say that in and through Christ all things were created, including "thrones or dominions or principalities or authorities" is to say that Christ is the source of the very cultural scaffolding about which Paul elsewhere expresses such ambivalence. In conflating these primary allusions to Christian universality, one would have to say that the crucified Christ, as Paul insists, would eventually despoil the very cultural and religious structures he originally brought into being, making a public spectacle of them by nailing them to the cross (Col. 2:14–15). The implication is that the conventional cultural structures—the architecture of the kingdoms of this world—came into being in and through Christ who, in the fullness of time and in fulfillment of the Scriptures, would empty them of their sacred aura and metaphysical pretensions. This issue is a variation on the one of which we spoke in reflecting on the Lord's provision of garments of skins in the Genesis account of the Fall. In each case, we are permitted to discern an act of divine condescension to the fallen state, though the moral issue raised by the Pauline claim—whose anthropological implications Girard allows us to draw out—is far weightier than the one in the Book of Genesis.

Two questions are unavoidable, one anthropological and one theological. Especially given the cogency of Girard's account of "thrones or dominions or principalities or authorities" as the structures necessary to the maintenance of the sacrificial systems of antiquity, the first question is how exactly could all these things have their origin in Christ? The second question is the theodicy question: How could God have countenanced such a makeshift concession to human sinfulness and tolerated its violence and cruelty? Divine mercy shown to those about whom Christ would say "they know not what they do" is one thing, but tolerance for the cruelties visited upon their victims is another.

One thinks in this regard of that most remarkable and exegetically enigmatic verse in the Book of Revelation (13:8), referring to "the Lamb slain since the foundation of the world." Its textual ambiguity notwithstanding, there is no way of translating this verse that completely eliminates the suggestion that what is revealed on Golgotha has been ongoing since the beginning—that all the persecuted victims in history share in Christ's passion, their names recorded as co-sufferers with Christ on the Cross. This bewildering suggestion is made the more intriguing by the anthropological evidence that fallen human culture came into existence at precisely the moment when a suddenly hushed mob mistook its unfortunate victim for a god, a massive recoiling from a dark truth no doubt, but nevertheless one that invites reflection from the point of view of an "all things came to be through him" Christology. Blessed John Henry Newman's lapidary suggestion that the conscience is the aboriginal vicar of Christ has the ring of anthropological authenticity when specified as referring to the crucified Christ—the first foreshadowing of which was arguably the first episode of all-against-one violence that achieved a cathartic resolution precisely, as we have argued, by occasioning the first incipient arousal of the moral conscience.

Compared with the death of Christ on the cross, the first hint of the *aboriginal* vicar of Christ—the moral conscience—left no forensic evidence whatsoever, and perhaps only one circumstantial intimation, albeit an anthropologically plausible one, namely the cathartic resolution of a violent event that can justly be regarded as humanity's first attempt to rid itself of the figure who was belatedly and retrospectively recognized as divine. In other words, cultural origination coincided with the first proto-crucifixion. However incipient the moral faculties might have been in our most primitive ancestors, and however easily they might have been overridden by passions and fears, if our hypothesis is correct, neither aboriginal religion nor primitive human culture would have emerged without them. And this cultural beachhead could not have been aroused except by a Victim with greater ontological weight than any of his victimizers. The clearest evidence of this greater ontological weight is the ancient world's universal tendency to divinize its victim.

The aboriginal vicar of Christ—the moral conscience—may have first appeared at the moment when creatures, seemingly over-endowed with mimetic propensities and beset by mimetic conflict no longer superintended by animal instincts, first brought an episode of all-against-one violence bred of mimetic passions to a cathartic conclusion. In this case, the resulting culture—however incipient—would not only be one of the kingdoms of this world beholden to Satan, the accuser, but it would also be—even more inchoately—the first adumbration of the *ecclesia ab Abel*, Augustine's term for an aboriginal Christianity "hidden since the foundation of the world" (the revelation of which occurred on Golgotha), giving birth, even in its most ancient and benighted instance, to a community of those whose swords had been made into plowshares by the death of a god.

According to his English translator, one of the great achievements of Eugeno Corsini's study of the Book of Revelation was his insistence that the Greek text of Rev. 13:8 is best rendered as referring to "the Lamb slain since the foundation of the world." On the strength of that translation, Corsini writes of the just ones throughout history who suffer from the brutality of what he terms political authority:

> [T]hey participate in the divine life even before the coming of Christ because of the eternal efficacy of the death of Christ. In the *divine plan*, the sacrifice of Christ precedes the death of his "witnesses," on the *level of history* their physical death precedes his and in some way "prefigures" it. . . . In this way we can say that the death of Christ is already at work and being performed in the deaths of these innocent just. John can thus speak of the "Lamb slain from the foundation of the world."[3]

While the community of victimizers are being dragged across the threshold to hominization by the awakening of the first faint stirrings of the moral conscience—traceable to the hint of moral discomfort that made the cathartic resolution of the violence possible—the victim himself is being brought across that threshold more magnificently by the fact that "the death of Christ is already at work and [in fact] being performed" in his suffering. His death is conjoined with Christ's just as the trace of moral discomfort his persecutors experience is the incipient form of the crowing cock that brought Peter's faith to full maturity. At the *level of history*, such victims suffered prior to the Passion of Christ, but, as Corsini audaciously recognized, at the level of the *divine plan* these victims share in Christ's Passion even more intimately than did the two thieves in Luke's Gospel. They are in a very real sense co-crucified with the One of whom Job confidently spoke:

> For I know that my Redeemer lives,
> and at last he will stand upon the earth;
> and after my skin has been thus destroyed,
> then from my flesh I shall see God,
> whom I shall see on my side,
> and my eyes shall behold, and not another. (Job 19:25–7)

---

3 Corsini, *The Apocalypse*, 145–6.

These victims are Christian martyrs—witnesses whose immolation rescued their persecutors, momentarily and at no small moral cost, from even more destructive murderous madness, leaving them hushed as though in the presence of mystery. And John of Patmos insists that the names of these victims are written in "the book of life, of the Lamb that was slain before the foundation of the world" (Rev. 13:8).

If Blessed John Newman's "aboriginal vicar of Christ" attribution is valid, and if René Girard is correct in locating the origin of culture in violence cathartically resolved, and if we are right in assuming that a hint of moral transgression was indispensable to the cathartic resolution of the violence, then we have warrant for the hypothesis that the first culturally successful foreshadowing of the crucifixion of Christ had the effect of arousing in the encircling crucifiers the first hint of moral equivocation, smothered in its infancy as it surely was by the unexpected experience of communal solidarity shimmering with numinosity. Its primordial suppression notwithstanding, this trace of the moral conscience—the aboriginal vicar of Christ—remains available for activation if and when an anamnesis is triggered. This mostly dormant residue of moral apprehension would grow in strength and insistency, most markedly in the Jewish people whose historical exigencies awakened an ever-deeper apprehension of the sacrificial predicament in which they and the rest of mankind were entangled. Seen in retrospect from Golgotha and through the lens of faith—polished by Christianity's magisterial wonderment—this gradual awakening to the truth vis-à-vis the sacrificial arrangements on which conventional culture depended appears as preparation for the moment when the "aboriginal vicar of Christ," born at the first proto-crucifixion and trained in the school of Jewish history and its hard-won religious understandings, would finally break the bonds of sin. This awakening would confront Peter with the full-fledged crowing cock (Mt. 27:74), the people of Jerusalem with what had theretofore been safely buried corpses (Mt. 27:53–4), and the pagan sycophants and indifferent functionaries assisting at Christ's execution with an intimation of the Trinitarian mystery, which took Christians themselves centuries to adequately formulate (Lk. 23:47).

The difference between the victim of the first culture and the victim Saint Paul described as "the Lord of Glory" (1 Cor. 2:8) could hardly be greater. And yet, despite the difference, the fact that each, in the end, came to be worshipped as divine is far from being an uninteresting coincidence. The messengers of Jesus Christ, writes Joseph Ratzinger, found that their preaching "responded to an expectation," and that it encountered what seemed a "prior knowledge . . . found in all cultures."[4] To recognize that a victim whose innocence is utterly invisible to his persecutors is the occluded source of fallen human culture is to give anthropological substantiation to Augustine's remark: "What is now called the Christian religion had always existed in ancient times, and was never unknown, right from the beginning of human history until Christ appeared in the flesh."[5] Girard's work makes it possible to recognize in Augustine's maxim the watermark of the cross inscribed on archaic culture and religion. "There has never been a moment in history without the gospel," writes then-Cardinal Ratzinger,[6] albeit in pagan antiquity a gospel so successfully inverted that the only trace to be found is a divinization of the victim which exonerates the community, a parody, that is, of the slain Lamb who takes away the sin (and sins) of the world.

There is a scriptural hint of the theme of Christ co-crucified with human victims in the famous narrative in the Book of Daniel. For their refusal to commit apostasy, the three faithful Israelites are thrown into Nebuchadnezzar's fiery furnace. But they are found to be accompanied by a mysterious fourth figure: "King Nebuchadnezzar rose up in haste and asked his nobles, 'Did we not cast three men bound into the fire?' 'Assuredly, O King,' they

4 Joseph Cardinal Ratzinger (Pope Benedict XVI), *Values in a Time of Upheaval* (New York: Crossroad, 2006), 93.

5 Quoted: Hans Urs von Balthasar, *Theo-Drama: Theological Dramatic Theory, Vol. III,* 417, n.37.

6 Joseph Cardinal Ratzinger and Hans Urs von Balthasar, *Mary: The Church at the Source* (San Francisco: Ignatius Press, 2005), 51.

answered. 'But,' he replied, 'I see four men unfettered and unhurt, walking in the fire, and the fourth looks like a son of God'" (Dn. 3:24–25).

The story of the persecuted witnesses—Shadrach, Meshach, and Abednego—mysteriously joined by one who looks like a son of God might be read as the type for which the antitype and inverted structural analogue—with the co-suffering divine figure moving dramatically into view—is the tableau of Christ crucified between two thieves. The co-crucified Christ, who was entirely invisible in pagan antiquity—save for the impulse to divinize the victim—begins to move anonymously into view in the late-Old Testament period with the prophets—especially Deutero-Isaiah, Jeremiah, the Book of Wisdom, and here in Daniel—and is finally and fully foregrounded on Golgotha, his co-crucified companions simply framing his centrality and serving as a hint of the theme of co-crucifixion. Writes Henri de Lubac:

> [I]t is really no easier to understand how the fact that the first emergence of the idea of God may possibly have been provoked by a particular spectacle, or have been linked to a particular experience of a sensible nature, could affect the validity of the idea itself. In each case the problem of its birth from experience and the problem of its existence or validity are distinct. They are problems of a different order.[7]

In other words, behind and beneath the mental fog and moral obfuscations that give rise to pagan religion, there are hints of truth that it would be a grave mistake to overlook. De Lubac continues:

> The gods thus secretly nourished by the idea of God are parasites and prevent the true God from emerging. . . . It is only natural that the idea of God should be, at one and the same time, ready to emerge and yet menaced with suffocation; for mankind—made in the image of God, though sinful—while destined to grope its way slowly up, is nevertheless obsessed from the first moment of its awakening by a call from above.[8]

7 Henri De Lubac, *The Discovery of God*, trans. Alexander Dru (Grand Rapids, MI: Eerdmans Publishing, 1996), 16.
8 Ibid., 20–21.

De Lubac cites Maurice Pradines in a footnote: "No matter how strange it may seem, one can ask if magic did not for some time carry before the species the torch of reason."[9] In light of this, it is hardly surprising to learn that Henri de Lubac once remarked that if he had to begin his theological work again he would begin with the work of René Girard. There are many reasons for this affinity, but they are surely encapsulated in de Lubac's insistence that "it is the Cross which disperses the cloud which until then was hiding the truth."[10] Observations such as these lead to a hypothesis that both addresses the theodicy question and finds anthropological corroboration, namely that the deification of the victim—which is found throughout the anthropological record and which was hardly the only possible interpretation available to our earliest ancestors, but without which primordial religion and the human cultures that it made possible would not have come into existence—may itself have been made possible by the presence of the divine after all, the light that shines precisely in the uncomprehending darkness, emanating from the *Logos* by whom the pitiable and hapless victim was mysteriously accompanied in his suffering. Is it possible, then, that the violent catharsis and the religious awe into which it congealed were due not just to the victim's death, but to the God by whom he was accompanied, the God who, as both Balthasar and Pascal have opined, is perpetually crucified by the sins of fallen humanity? Perpetuity, of course, is hardly an appropriate way of speaking of what the Church Fathers called supra-temporality. Care should be taken when thinking of the eternal now of the Triune God in terms of before and after. As the Lord's Prayer constantly, if subtly, reminds us, God's self-giving will within the Trinity does not involve the resistances that ever plague our remotely analogous attempts to replicate it in this life. So the Pascalian idea of a perpetually crucified Christ is valid only when we do not transfer to the Cross as the image of the Trinity the suffering of Christ on the Cross on Good

9 Ibid., 22, n.17.

10 Henri de Lubac, *Catholicism: Christ and the Common Destiny of Man*, trans. Lancelot C. Sheppard and Sr. Elizabeth Englund, OCD (San Francisco: Ignatius Press, 1988), 179.

Friday. Nonetheless, in an Easter homily the second century bishop Melito of Sardis spoke of Christ in just such terms: "It is he who endured every kind of suffering in all those who foreshadowed him. In Abel he was slain, in Isaac bound, in Jacob exiled, in Joseph sold, in Moses exposed to die. He was sacrificed in the Passover lamb, persecuted in David, dishonored in the prophets."[11]

What Melito saw in the lives of the patriarchs of the past, Balthasar saw running into the future:

> Because Christ, as the crucified and risen one, is a "brother" like no other, who experiences in himself all that is done to the brothers, there is complete appropriateness in the patristic concept that the heavenly Christ continues to suffer in his earthly Church which is his body (Augustine), and indeed that it is only together with all of his perfected and risen members that he will enter the definitive state of blessedness (Origen, Lev. 7:1–2; Baehrens 6:370–380).[12]

In light of suggestions such as this, might we not entertain the possibility that the divinization of the victim by our most ancient ancestors was a beclouded but inchoate form of pre-Christian lucidity, thoroughly enveloped though it was in a sea of delusion, which nevertheless made human religion and therefore humanity itself possible. "All things came to be through him" (Col. 1:16). The primordial deification of the aboriginal victims represents the flicker of light that the darkness of human violence could not quench, a light that would fully triumph only on Golgotha.

The truth—the Logos—about the created order is that it is ordered toward the self-donation that is the reality of the Triune God as revealed by the crucified Christ. Even though we are prevented by sin from living in full accord with this ordination of our existence, the elusive reality of grace is such that not even our venality and mediocrity can entirely ward off this fact of our ontological makeup. If the Easter homily of Melito is a glimpse into one of the realities that is "not susceptible of a purely natural

11 *Christian Prayer: The Liturgy of the Hours* (New York: Catholic Book Publishing, 1976), 1983.

12 Balthasar, *The Glory of the Lord, Vol. VII*, 523, n. 8.

explanation," might it nevertheless compel us eventually to recognize its universal implications? For as Girard has shown, Christ's passion was "foreshadowed" by many more than just those eminent figures of the Old Testament enumerated by Melito. The question is just how universal is that foreshadowing, and is it limited to prefigurations of the Passion? That is to say: Is its essence persecution as such or suffering itself?

In the famous eschatological discourse in the twenty-fifth chapter of Matthew, the Son of Man comes in glory to judge the world and, to the surprise of all, announces that he was the co-recipient of both the kindness and the mistreatment shown to others: "Truly, I say to you, as you did it to one of the least of these my brethren, you did it to me" (Mt. 25:40). The question is: When does this all begin? When exactly does Christ become the secret co-recipient of the mistreatment meted out to the least of his brothers and sisters? Has this always been the case?

> "Saul, Saul, why do you persecute me?"
> And he said, "Who are you, Lord?"
> And he said, "I am Jesus, whom you are persecuting."
> (Acts 9:4–5)

"Jesus Christ," writes Nicholas J. Healy, is "God's theodicy." In him, "God himself fully enters human history and, in a certain way, unites himself with every human being and thus with all human suffering."[13] Christ's identity with sufferers cannot be limited, therefore, to those suffering persecution, for the violence that eventually falls on the community's scapegoat is simply the suffering born of sin and death turned outward on to others. Our fallen condition predisposes us to elude as best we can the suffering that is the ineluctable consequence of sin. Like the man and woman in the paradisal garden we avoid such suffering by transferring it to others. Meanwhile, as Simone Weil reminds us: "The false god changes suffering into violence. The true God changes violence into suffering."[14] Christ, who suffers with the one on

---

13 Nicholas J. Healy, "Inclusion in Christ: Background to a Christian Doctrine of Providence," *Communio: International Catholic Review*, Vol. XXIX, No. 3 (Fall 2002): 470.

14 *The Simone Weil Reader* (David McKay, 1977), 347.

whom all the unsuffered suffering of others finally falls, suffers as well with those who accept or endure the suffering that falls to them, those, that is, who take up their crosses daily. In his 1984 Apostolic Letter, *Salvifici Doloris*, John Paul II wrote:

> Christ does not explain in the abstract the reasons for suffering, but before all else he says: "Follow me!" Come! Take part through your suffering in this work of saving the world, a salvation achieved through my suffering! Through my Cross. Gradually, *as the individual takes up his cross,* spiritually uniting himself to the Cross of Christ, the salvific meaning of suffering is revealed before him. He does not discover this meaning at his own human level, but at the level of the suffering of Christ.[15]

It isn't, therefore, as Melito of Sardis implies, that Christ co-suffers only with those whose role in biblical revelation prefigure his own. Rather, he is "co-crucified" with everyone who suffers and dies. The difference is that the pre-Christian biblical figures were to one degree or another sensible of the religious meaning of their suffering, whereas their pagan predecessors were not. Christians enjoy the privilege and commensurate responsibility of being made explicitly aware of the co-suffering, precisely in order that they might assent to it freely: "Take up your cross daily."

To take up one's cross in this sense is to diminish in a small but real way the social accumulation of unsuffered suffering and unforgiven sin that, if left to accumulate, will eventually be ignited by mimetic passions and immolate victims. It is to make up for what is lacking in the sufferings of Christ (Col. 1:24). But the taking up of one's cross daily has much more than merely a moral or social efficacy. Above and beyond any such justifications, there is, as John Paul emphasized, simply Christ's "follow me," an invitation left unexplained in all likelihood because it invites us into a mystery requiring faith precisely because the life we are being invited to live—and the death at which we surrender that life back to its Source—are recalcitrant to speculative assessment. "In exactly the same way that he sacrifices himself on

15 *Salvifici Doloris*, Feb. 11, 1984, §26.

every altar where Mass is celebrated," writes Adrienne von Speyr, "he dies again when every man undergoes his death-throes."[16]

Foreign though it is to contemporary thought, it is in the school of suffering that we learn to be truly human, for it is there that we are drawn into the drama of human self-transcendence toward which our lives are ordered. Jesus learned obedience from what he suffered (Heb. 5:8), and our own suffering continues to serve as a moral purgative and an indispensable source of compassion, maturity, and sanctity. Alleviating the suffering of others is a paramount Christian duty, but today great moral catastrophes are in the making for which the apparent justification is, and we use the term advisedly and ominously, the *extermination* of suffering itself. Not only is Christianity the world's preeminent source of solicitude for those who suffer, but it is for all intents and purposes the sole source of a theology of suffering without which the unfettered determination to alleviate suffering at all costs will lead to unspeakable moral catastrophes enveloped by ideological smokescreens and the thick incense of sentimentality.

Above we have taken the risk of proposing and the pains to defend the proposition that ontological hominization—the birth of human personhood—may have been made possible by an incipient moral response to the event at which human cultural origination took place, an event which was in its essence structurally identical to the crucifixion. The jolting event that awakened the moral conscience occurred below the level of full consciousness, but it nonetheless introduced the moral ambiguity requisite to the cathartic resolution that the event achieved at the dawn of human existence. We have run an additional risk in taking seriously those biblical and theological texts which suggest that "all things came to be" through the agency of the preexisting divine Logos, incarnate in the fullness of time in Jesus of Nazareth. From these traces, we have proposed the possibility that the Lamb who has been slain since the foundation of the world has quite literally taken on the sins of the world, albeit in ways that we cannot com-

16 Quoted: Hans Urs von Balthasar, *Theo-Drama: Theological Dramatic Theory, Vol. V: The Last Act*, trans. Graham Harrison (San Francisco: Ignatius Press, 1998), 147, n. 26.

pletely comprehend, both as the co-sufferer in all suffering and as the co-crucified in every act of blind cruelty.

We have suggested two distinct but compatible accounts of ontological hominization, both of which are rendered less implausible by the existence of heretofore neglected scriptural suggestions. It is important to point out that though these ways of accounting for the emergence of mankind are meta-scientific, each is both an anthropologically threshold event and an onto-logically punctual one. Each would have occurred countless thousands of times over hundreds or thousands of years wher-ever higher primates neurologically readied for the transition to fully human existence might have fallen into a mimetic vortex from which they extricated themselves at the expense of their victim. And yet, the immensely varied settings in which they might have occurred would in no way prevent each from being the precise and punctual moment of hominization. Neither is ever likely to be scientifically confirmed, but each should be assessed in light of its plausibility in comparison with other accounts of the birth of our species.

A book that seeks to foster a renewed respect for Christianity's traditional Alpha and Omega Christology, as this one rather unconventionally does, will necessarily have to argue for the presence of Christ at the beginning—the Alpha—and at the end—the Omega—but it will also have to give an account of the central role of Christ in the *meantime*, the period between the beginning and the end. Having suggested all too hastily some ways in which a dialogue between theology and anthropology might throw light on an Alpha Christology, we will turn in later chapters to some reflections on how that same collaboration might lend credence to an Omega Christology, not by providing proof or even evidence in the strict sense but by way of a pro-posal whose persuasiveness will largely depend on whether the reader shares in the religious convictions of this writer. In the meantime, however, we will pause to reflect on the *meantime*, precisely in order to show that historical consciousness—as a pre-supposition about the world and its temporality—has itself a his-tory, that it also has an inner ordering principle. Furthermore, at the heart of this principle is a cluster of events and, more specifically, the man at the center of those events, whom our ancestors in the faith were not reluctant to acknowledge as the Lord of History. Though in what immediately follows we can do little more than gesture toward this mystery of history, we hope these gestures will lead at least some to contemplate the possibility that history is Christ-centered, Christologically underwritten, and, despite the world's perennial effort to rid itself of Christ, Christ-haunted.

# The Refusal of History

Karl Löwith correctly argued that there is no universal history without Judaism and Christianity. That is, the notion that all mankind shares in the same history, a linear history moving toward a goal, only appeared historically with the Judeo-Christian tradition.[1]—Glenn W. Olsen

[A]ll history is . . . a riddle that cannot be solved unless we plough with some heifer other than our reason.[2]
—Johann Georg Hamann

LONG AFTER our ancestors learned to keep a record of events— thus technically leaving behind the prehistoric period—they lived without what Octavio Paz, Mircea Eliade, John Lukacs, and many others have called "historical consciousness." If history is "the remembered past," as John Lukacs argues, there are nevertheless two strikingly different ways of remembering it: the mythological and the historical, and they are separated by an anthropological divide of great significance.

How and when did historical consciousness emerge, and what does its provenance tell us about the world in which we live today? In challenging a discredited Enlightenment era cliché, Henri de Lubac asked whether, in pondering the human predicament, the natural cosmos or human history provides the more dependable paradigm of intelligibility. His insight is all the more germane inasmuch as he alluded to the incommensurability of the sacrificial practices of antiquity and historical consciousness,

---

1 Glenn W. Olsen, "Christian philosophy, Christian history: parallel ideas?" *Eternity in Time: Christopher Dawson and the Catholic Idea of History*, ed. Stratford Caldecott and John Morrill (Edinburgh: T & T Clark, 1997), 138.

2 Johann Georg Hamann; Quoted: Hans Urs von Balthasar, *Glory of the Lord*, Vol. III, 250.

an incommensurability that first came fully into view in the Hebrew Scriptures:

> Is it really necessary to conclude that up to these recent centuries "humanity had dwelled in nature and was still not detached from it?" In reality, rather than animal innocence, was this not on his part the deliberate (though admittedly still instinctive) refusal of history? And was this refusal not explained by a veritable ontological thirst, by the desire not to let himself lose contact with the archetypal beings whose gestures he reproduced?[3]

De Lubac is here dispensing with the quaint idea—once widely presupposed with regard to indigenous peoples—that the religion of primitive societies and their presumed attention to nature was due to their "animal innocence." This once prevalent notion cannot survive an encounter with anthropological findings. Archaic peoples clung, not to nature, but to religious procedures that were sometimes remarkably complex. What distinguished archaic peoples from those who would one day be fascinated by them, which is to say, those with the intellectual and scientific curiosity to study archaic people, was that archaic religious life depended on rituals, the mythological interpretation of which was essential if the archetypal beings these rituals evoked, invoked, and potentially provoked were to be kept favorably disposed to their propitiators. These archetypal beings were born of violence; their sacrality was rooted in the religious transfiguration of violence whose crescendo had cathartic effects on its perpetrators and spectators alike. Archaic societies scrupulously reenacted this violence using surrogate victims, and their religious lives consisted of ritually returning again and again to the original scene. The very word, *religio*—to bind (*ligio*) back (*re*)—suggests exactly this. Thus these ancient cultures remained profoundly backward oriented. This ritualized return to a primordial past, the very essence of mythological forms of recollection, is what de Lubac perceptively characterized as a "deliberate

---

3 Henri De Lubac, S.J., *The Drama of Atheist Humanism*, trans. Edith M. Riley, Anne Englund, Mark Sebanc (San Francisco: Ignatius Press, 1995), 423.

(though admittedly still instinctive) refusal of history."[4] It is difficult for us to imagine the depth of trepidation our pagan ancestors felt when the possibility of offending their gods by neglect
loomed before them. "One of the signs of a mature spirit," writes
de Lubac, "is without doubt to renounce false forms of transcendence,"[5] precisely the forms of transcendence on which the religious lives of our ancient ancestors instinctively depended.

"Indian thought has refused to concede any value to History,"
writes Mircea Éliade, and "traditional India has had no historical
consciousness." What Éliade observed in an Indian context,
Octavio Paz saw in the archeological and anthropological data
concerning the indigenous cultures of the Americas. "Meso-
American civilization negated history," he writes. "From the
Mexican high plateau to the tropical lands of Central America,
for more than two thousand years, various cultures and empires
succeeded one another and none of them had historical consciousness. Meso-America did not have history but myths, and,
above all, rites."[6]

The consciousness of those whose rituals exist to repristinate
an aboriginal beginning is strikingly different from the consciousness of those whose acts of recollection produce moral
misgivings about events in the past—events in which they or
their ancestors actually participated and for which they feel a
genuine degree of contrition. Any realistic prospect for a better
future depends on these moral misgivings and the contrition

---

4 The term "instinctive" here is perhaps not the most helpful, inasmuch as
it suggests precisely what de Lubac is arguing against, namely that archaic
humanity remained "in animal innocence." A more apposite word might be
*reflexive*.

5 De Lubac, *The Discovery of God*, 178.

6 Quoted: John Patrick Diggins, "History Standards Get It Wrong Again,"
*New York Times*, Op-Ed page, May 15, 1996, a criticism of the cultural "convergence" theory (European, African, pre-Columbian native American) as a way
of explaining American culture.

they inspire. It is this historical form of the remembered past, and not the morally impotent mythological form, that is most compatible with human hope. Those who recall the past with contrition are precisely the ones who are able to look to the future with hope.

As long as they remained beholden to their gods and the cycle of sacrificial rituals that appeased them, our ancient ancestors lived in a cyclical and not a historical world. At each sacrifice a decision was made, usually by way of practiced inattention, and it was, metaphorically speaking, the decision as to where to put the emphasis in the drama the ritual reenacted—with the victim of the sacrifice or with the community that benefited from the victim's death. Inasmuch as our ancestors were seen as the conduit through which these visible benefits returned to the community, it was easy enough to convince the beneficiaries that the gods of the pagan pantheon required that the ritual's social benefits preempt any fully conscious misgivings about how they were obtained. For our ancestors to step even tentatively onto the path of history, they would have to break with these "archetypal beings" and, to some degree at least, renounce the false forms of transcendence that they represented. As we shall see in later chapters, the fullest and most anthropologically comprehensive story of this break with these "archetypal beings" is the one recounted in the Bible. By revealing a God who is both totally transcendent to the cosmos and active within human history without detriment to that transcendence, the biblical worldview relativized the cosmos as the locus of human self-questioning. With this disruption of the cosmic centered worldview, writes Balthasar, "a fundamentally new period dawned for man's understanding of himself and for anthropology," the primary effect of which was that one whose horizons were opened by biblical thought stood before the prospect of having "to step forth as an actor on the theodramatic stage."[7]

7  Balthasar, *Theo-Drama, Vol. II*, 394.

## The Key to Historical Intelligibility

Christianity is not one of the great things of history; it is history that is one of the great things of Christianity.[8]—Henri de Lubac

Does not world history show a theological structure, a Christological structure, and can it not be demonstrated even to the nonbeliever?[9]—Hans Urs von Balthasar

To bring into sharper focus the nature of what Henri de Lubac called the pagan world's refusal of history, we turn from the cosmic and ahistorical myths of the ancient world to the pagan world's serious attempts to enter into historical consciousness. Benedict XVI reminded us that the other religions of the world— ancient and contemporary—are "religions in waiting"[10]—awaiting the truth revealed by Christ with its capacity to draw out of these religions deposits of truth otherwise obscured by mystification and superstition. Showing the same respect for religions, ancient and modern, Henri de Lubac nonetheless insists on the futility and injustice involved in attempting to preserve these ancient and fragile cultures by insulating them from contact with cultural forces—Christian ones—that would drain their myths and rituals of the binding power necessary to sustain cultural life.

> The human inheritance these men of old have left us is a fine one—but it is short. Their religious spirit was often profound, and we should be wrong to scorn their message for us, and not recognize with the Fathers how much "preparation for the gospel" is in it. But ultimately their efforts achieved nothing. St. Thomas notes this with deep sympathy on several occasions. They never found the remedy for what Jacques Maritain so aptly calls "the great pagan melancholy."[11]

---

8 Henri de Lubac, *Paradoxes of Faith* (San Francisco: Ignatius Press, 1987), 145.

9 Hans Urs von Balthasar, *Theo-Drama: Theological Dramatic Theory, IV: The Action*, trans. Graham Harrison (San Francisco: Ignatius Press, 1994), 431.

10 In a message to the Pontifical Urbaniana University on the dedication of its great hall to Benedict XVI, October 21, 2014.

11 De Lubac, *The Mystery of the Supernatural*, 132.

The cyclical character of mythological thought dogged the efforts of even the finest of early historians. Karl Löwith points out that though classical historians recorded events with remarkable perspicuity, they had no historical consciousness of the sort that was found in the roughly contemporary Jewish prophets and chroniclers:

> To classical antiquity the course of history appeared not at all as a "course" but as a cyclic succession of identical phases, never experiencing a new transformation directed toward a definite goal in the future. Thus every idea of progress was inaccessible to the philosophers of antiquity. Even the most sagacious of them rather shared the popular belief that the contemporary state of things was far inferior to that of former times.[12]

At the risk of getting ahead of ourselves, we must not let Löwith's remark about the absence of the idea of progress in non-biblical religion leave the impression that progressivism as we understand it is the legitimate heir of biblical thought. We can here reissue Balthasar's caveat:

> It is significant, however, that this walking forward into the future is understood by Israel as a "waiting"; from time to time it is also interpreted as an active "pressing on" toward the coming salvation, but it is never regarded as a progress that can be measured. The category of "progress" is of an entirely different provenance. Originally it has no religious aspect at all; in fact, it rapidly becomes anti-religious and hence subverts religious energies in order to offer a substitute for religion. The elementally religious potentiality of the Israelite hope was bound, sooner or later, to make a pact with this spurious sister. Together they have become a driving force in world history.[13]

The inherently paradoxical nature of Christianity requires that even so lucid a corrective submit itself to a slight correction, which Antonio López provides:

> For Christianity there is a progress in the truth of what it means to be. Following Christ one is permanently growing, from one

---

12  Löwith, *Meaning in History,* 73.
13  Balthasar, *Theo-Drama, Vol. IV,* 87.

beginning to another beginning. Yet Christianity is not only a part of a larger progress, it is the goal of progress itself. Christ's presence is the eschaton (the future end) that has already taken place—the Holy Spirit will bring mankind to the fullness of truth contained in Christ.[14]

History as a literary genre begins most notably with the Greek historians, Herodotus and Thucydides. Herodotus, writing in the fifth century before Christ, begins his history by declaring the purpose of his inquiry. He wants to understand the reasons for the wars between the Persians and the Greeks in the fifth century BC. Mingled with this aim, however, is one that conceivably might be antithetical to it, namely the desire to preserve the memory of the glorious achievements of both Greek and Persian warriors and generals. In setting out "to discover the reason why they fought one another," Herodotus strove to preserve the memory of the "glorious deeds" of the warriors, an aspiration more congenial to a mythological cast of mind, exhibiting the predilection for myth over history that hounded his efforts and that kept even so great a historian from developing what Lukacs was to call historical consciousness.

Herodotus was finally unable to "discover the reason why they fought one another"; at least this is so in the judgment of the historian Charles Norris Cochrane. In the end, argues Cochrane, Herodotus could not account for the historical events he chronicled. In one way or another, he was forced to disguise his failure by turning to that staple of pagan thought: *fate* (*moira*). Cochrane insists that to understand the dilemma Herodotus and the classical historians who followed him faced and the intellectual task on which they labored in vain, one needs to appreciate how important this concept of fate or fortune eventually became in their reckonings. For classical historical thought, says Cochrane,

14 Antonio López, "Vatican II's Catholicity: A Christological Perspective on Truth, History, and the Human Person," *Communio: International Catholic Review*, Vol. 39, Spring–Summer 2012, 116.

would eventually surrender to "a quite illusory belief in luck"[15]—
an almost open declaration of intellectual and moral bankruptcy.
Here Greek historiography shows how inadequately liberated it
was from the mythological world. Behind Zeus and the pantheon of Greek divinities, writes Balthasar, there stands "as a final
authority the impersonal, unsearchable, inscrutable abyss of
being: fate. It is the question mark of fate which concludes the
beautiful, sunny poetry of the Greeks,"[16] a world, be it noted, in
which its sunny poetry was ever and again clouded over by what
Maritain called "the great pagan melancholy."

Herodotus' successor, Thucydides, who chronicled the war
between Athens and Sparta (431–404 BC) in his *History of the
Peloponnesian War*, was unable to rescue Greek historiography
from its agnosticism as to the meaning and purpose of human
history and therefore of human existence. "Thucydides assumes
a character hardly less disconcerting than that of Herodotus,"
writes Cochrane. "For the story he has to tell is that of human
reason defeated and crushed by the forces of irrationality."[17]
Cochrane sums up the situation succinctly. In the classical world,
he writes, the "quest for a principle of historical intelligibility
came to an ignominious end."[18]

According to at least one careful observer, Thucydides' quest
for a principle of historical intelligibility not only ended ignomin-
iously, but it also had an unpropitious beginning. In his introduction to Thucydides' *History of the Peloponnesian War*, M.I. Finley
writes: "There is not a sentence in the book—this cannot be
stressed enough—that states explicitly what Thucydides thought
history was about, why it was worth a lifetime of very hard effort
to write a detailed and accurate history of the war, or why that
history could lay claim to being a possession for all time."[19]

15 Charles Norris Cochrane, *Christianity and Classical Culture* (New York:
Oxford University Press, 1957), 479.

16 Balthasar, *Elucidations*, 48.

17 Cochrane, *Christianity and Classical Culture*, 473.

18 Ibid., 474.

19 Thucydides, *History of the Peloponnesian War*, trans. Rex Warner, intro.
M.I. Finley (London: Penguin Books, 1972), 13.

Although the classical historians had a gift for cataloguing historical events, if Cochrane and Finley are correct, these towering figures of Greek historiography lacked an adequate anthropology for which they can hardly be faulted, inasmuch as the key to *anthropological intelligibility* is the discovery of the Trinitarian God that was finally revealed on the Cross and that broke in on the world a half-millennia after Herodotus and Thucydides. The shortcomings of these Greek historians are nonetheless of interest to us because, to the extent that Christianity and its epistemological and moral benefits are set aside, those deprived of these things will, in the words of Joseph Ratzinger, lose their way in history and squander their cultural patrimony on utopian social experiments.

Cochrane is quick to insist that the classical world's failure to discover "a principle of historical intelligibility" was simply "calamitous, for the ideal of intelligibility thus betrayed took speedy vengeance upon its betrayers."[20] Inasmuch as the culture founded on a Judeo-Christian understanding of history is in the process of betraying the principle of historical intelligibility—precisely, as Girard reminds us, by our "panic-stricken refusal to glance, even furtively, in the only direction where meaning could still be found"[21]—we would do well to heed Cochrane's ominous warning. We will do so by asking two questions: What prevented the emergence of historical consciousness over the course of several millennia? And what eventually overcame this resistance and awakened historical consciousness?

It is highly germane to our inquiry that Cochrane finds that failure epitomized by a casual remark Thucydides makes at the end of his chronicle of an Athenian social crisis in 415 BC, a crisis related to political conspiracies lately foiled and others rumored to be in the making. As rumors spread, Athenian social consensus, such as it was, fractured and grew more and more volatile. As Thucydides put it, "every day showed an increase in savagery

---

20 Cochrane, *Christianity and Classical Culture*, 478.

21 René Girard, *Things Hidden Since the Foundation of the World*, trans. Stephen Bann and Michael Metteer (Stanford, CA: Stanford University Press, 1987), 261.

and led to more arrests being made."[22] One of the prisoners was persuaded that a confession in which he would implicate other conspirators would win his release, and, in any case, not materially worsen his already unpromising prospects. Confessing his own guilt and that of others produced a considerable lessening of social tensions. "The Athenian people were delighted at having now, as they imagined, discovered the truth, after having been previously in a terrible state at the idea that the conspirators against the democracy might never be found out." The confession having been made, the prisoner was released, and all those against whom he had given evidence of a highly dubious nature were brutally killed. Cochrane labels this event a "bloodbath," and he places remarkable emphasis on the concluding sentence of Thucydides' chronicle of it. The sentence reads as follows: "In all this it was impossible to say whether those who suffered deserved their punishment or not, but it was quite clear that the rest of the city, as things were, benefited greatly."[23]

If Cochrane's intuition is correct, the classical failure to understand what is happening in history is symbolized by a morally blasé interpretation of a blood-bath whose victims were very probably innocent, but whose innocence was regarded as less worthy of attention than the fact that "it was quite clear that the rest of the city, as things were, benefited greatly" from the violence that cost them their lives. Thucydides' moral nonchalance with regard to violence that both fell on innocent victims and was of visible benefit to the community of victimizers was a species of the tendency found throughout the ancient world to defer to the social benefits of sacrificial rituals while discouraging a moral evaluation of them. As Cochrane helps us understand, the quest for a principle of historical intelligibility comes to an ignominious end precisely when this tendency to subordinate the truth about the victims to the social benefits that flowed from

---

22 Thucydides, *History of the Peloponnesian War*, 447.

23 Ibid.; Cochrane provides his own translation of this sentence: "It is doubtful, whether the victims were justly punished, but the rest of the city at any rate was for the time being visibly helped."

their victimization is indulged. The question is, therefore, when and where and under what religious and moral imperative was this tendency resisted? When did humanity begin to free itself from the grip of the mythic and sacrificial powers which prevented historical consciousness from emerging?

In his early work on the theology of history in the thought of Saint Bonaventure, Joseph Ratzinger writes, "With his Cross [Christ] has uncovered the lost centre of the world's circle, thus giving their true dimensions and meaning to the movement both of individual lives and of human history as a whole."[24] As we shall see in what follows, the lost center of the world's circle is the event of which the Passion of Christ is one unique example, unique precisely in that it exposes what all the other variations on this event conspire to conceal.

## Getting a Grip on History

"We cannot escape the issue of a relationship with the real course of history," writes René Girard. "Indeed, we shall see that only by confronting the real course of history—which the gospel text claims to determine—can the astonishing coherence of the gospel logic be fully revealed in our time."[25] To be "equipped for working in our time," insisted Balthasar, we must "get a grip on history."[26]

We could say that human history—as the term is commonly used—began when our most remote ancestors stumbled upon what René Girard has termed the surrogate victim mechanism, the late Paleolithic discovery that, over the course of time, our

24 Joseph Ratzinger, *The Theology of History in St. Bonaventure* (Chicago: Franciscan Herald Press, 1971), 146.

25 René Girard, *Things Hidden Since the Foundation of the World*, 252.

26 Hans Urs von Balthasar, *Raising the Bastions*, trans. Brian McNeil, C.R.V. (San Francisco: Ignatius Press, 1993), 44.

most ancient ancestors slowly learned to ritualize, thereby secur-
ing the cultural beachhead that would sustain the fragile order
that the scapegoating violence first achieved. Another way of
putting this is to say that history began with the discovery of the
sacrificial procedures for warding off the apocalypse (anthropologically understood); the latter defined as violence for which
there is no adequate arresting or quarantining mechanism.[27]
Subsequent ritual re-enactments of this procedure functioned to
keep "apocalyptic" violence at bay. Historical consciousness, on
the other hand, begins with the attenuation of these same cultural mechanisms for postponing the apocalypse, at which point
the acquisition of the moral, spiritual, and cultural wherewithal
for living without these sacrificial operations becomes imperative. The beginning of history in the biblical sense, in other
words, is the beginning of the apocalypse (anthropologically
understood). That is to say, as the efficacy of the system of sacred
violence that made human culture possible begins to attenuate
under biblical influence, the apocalypse hangs in the balance:
Will the waning of the ancient system for keeping this apocalypse at bay be offset by the religious conversion of the human
heart? Or will the gradual loss of the efficacy of sacred violence
outpace man's moral and spiritual conversion, plunging the
world into cataclysms of destruction? "Christianity," writes René
Girard, "is the only religion that has predicted its own failure.
This prescience is known as the apocalypse."[28]

We now turn to a cultural world that at first sight resembles the
one we have just been considering. What is extraordinary about
the world of ancient Israel, however, is not what it shares with the
pagan cultures of its time, but the ways in which, over time, it
gradually distinguished itself from them. Whereas Greco-Roman
history was driven by an intellectual curiosity about the events
of the past, the historical chronicles of Israel were prompted by

27 For a more thorough analysis: Gil Bailie, *Violence Unveiled: Humanity at the Crossroads* (New York: Crossroad Publishing, 1995).

28 René Girard, *Battling to the End*, trans. Mary Baker (East Lansing, MI: Michigan State University Press, 2010), x.

entirely different concerns, very nearly opposite ones. In sharp contrast to their pagan contemporaries, Israel's remembrance of the past was marked by two tendencies: a faith in Yahweh's fidelity to the Abrahamic covenant, on which Jewish confidence in the future was based, and the contrition that accompanied the remembrance of Israel's own violations of that covenant. Based on the hope revived by accounts of the Lord's abiding faithfulness in the past and the realization that the Israelite infidelities were capable of being rectified, Israel took cultural risks, which would have otherwise been unthinkable, and which remained so for its pagan contemporaries. The hope that awakened slowly in ancient Israel is perhaps chief among the many incomparable contributions of Judaism to humanity. Christianity has the privilege of being the conduit through which this world-transforming hope has been infinitely enlarged, eschatologically reformulated, ennobled, and made available to the whole world. The business of theology, writes Balthasar, "is not to keep one eye on philosophy, but, with its gaze obediently turned toward Jesus Christ, simply and directly to describe how he stands in time and in history as the heart and norm of all that is historical."[29] Christ initiates what David Bentley Hart calls "counterhistory," which turns out to be, as Hart writes, "the true history of the world."[30] Rémi Brague echoes this when he writes that, "the miraculous birth of Jesus" represents "the entry into the world of a new mode of historicity."[31]

By trying, in what follows, to locate the key to historical intelligibility, we will be taking up the challenge so aptly expressed by the Cistercian Scholar, Denis Farkasfalvy, when he argues that if Christians today are to meet their responsibilities, they "must give account in a credible way of a realistic concept of salvation history which tradition posits to be in some true sense a reality

29 Balthasar, A Theology of History, 26.

30 David Bentley Hart, The Beauty of the Infinite: The Aesthetics of Christian Truth (Grand Rapids, MI., Eerdmans Publishing, 2003), 326.

31 Rémi Brague, Eccentric Culture: A Theory of Western Civilization (South Bend, Indiana: St. Augustine's Press, 2002), 59.

encompassing all forms and stages of human existence." The task facing us, he writes, is that of "tying together our understanding of the Bible and humankind's universal religious history, both in the pre-historic age and in the history of human cultures."[32]

---

32 Denis Farkasfalvy, O. Cist., "A Heritage in Search of Heirs," *Communio*, Fall 1998, 517.

# Our Father Abraham

God does not so much lead Abraham back to the *Alpha*, the origin (*re-ligio*), as forward to the *Omega*, the future fulfillment. Israel is, today as always, the alternative to *religio*: hope in the God who is coming. This is the other side of mankind's religious experience, and there is no third.[1]—Hans Urs von Balthasar

To become a Christian means entering into the history of faith that began with Abraham and, thus, accepting him as father.[2] —Joseph Ratzinger

WE HAVE tried to establish the relationship between the gravitational power of archaic society's sacrificial center and the cyclical and backward looking fixation of pre-historic thought. Cathartic sacrificial rituals were an expression of the ancient world's fear-ridden determination to re-create an imagined past and remain safely within the orbit of its protection. It is not too much of an overstatement to say that the purpose of archaic religion was to protect its participants from the exigencies of history—or, to speak in a biblical idiom, to spare them the call of Abraham or the vicissitudes of the Exodus. No historical consciousness of the sort that biblical faith has long been spreading throughout the world could have emerged as long as rituals of blood sacrifice— and the mythic forms of reminiscence that accompanied them— retained the power they had in ancient times. The pertinent question is: When and where and under the impact of what religious or moral forces would the universal sway of ritual sacrifice begin to weaken, making it at least possible for historical consciousness to emerge?

---

1 Ratzinger and Balthasar, *Mary*, 160–1.
2 Ratzinger, *Truth and Tolerance*, 97.

For history—as those under biblical influence now understand it—to begin, man would have to be coaxed out of the immediate sacrificial arena and taken out of earshot of the incessant droning of its mythico-ritual reinforcements—into a deserted place where the still small voice of God might be heard. Monotheism, writes then-Cardinal Ratzinger, "was not able to develop in the great cities and fertile countryside of Mesopotamia. No, it was in the wilderness where heaven and earth face each other in stark solitude, that monotheism was able to grow—in the homelessness of the wanderer, who . . . put his trust in the God who wanders with him."[3] Gradually thereafter, the gravitational power of the sacrificial cult itself would need to be attenuated, and those tentatively liberated from the myths and rituals of the pagan world would need to learn to live without the "sacrificial protections" by developing the capacity for self-renunciation commensurate with the loss of the cathartic power of blood sacrifice.

The story with which the biblical historical panorama begins to move from legend and saga to a narrative more likely to have evolved from actual historical events—however overlaid it doubtless was with imaginative embroidering—is the story of Abraham. For our purposes, in turning to the Abraham saga there is no need to delve into its exegetical background and peel away its several textual layers. It has been said that the *Iliad* and the *Odyssey* were written either by Homer or by someone else with the same name. The point is well taken. This story has had a major impact on the world. We hardly need to find Abraham's sandals and walking stick to discover why this is the case. It is because the saga of this ancient Bedouin has been widely recognized as the first call to a religious journey, the depth and meaning of which would preoccupy Jews and Christians for millennia and transform the world in the process. It is not unworthy of our attention, however, to note in passing that, even though the writers and redactors of the story have taken the opportunity to sing Abraham's praises here and there, for the most part the story is

3 Joseph Ratzinger, *The Spirit of the Liturgy*, trans. John Saward (San Francisco: Ignatius Press, 2000), 98–99.

conspicuously not about someone who could be regarded as an exemplary model in every sense. Obviously there is here a rudimentary fidelity to whatever scraps of historical memory were at the disposal of the authors and redactors of this story, and they are by no means all flattering to Abraham. On the glaring difference between the great religious figures of Asian religions and the prophetic figures of biblical religion, Joseph Ratzinger wrote:

> If we set the principal actors in the covenant-event of Israel against the religious personalities of Asia, then first of all we feel remarkably uncomfortable. Abraham, Isaac, Jacob, and Moses, with all their wiles and tricks, with their ill-temper and their inclination to violence, seem at least quite mediocre and pathetic next to someone like Buddha, Confucius, or Lao-tzu, but even such great prophetic characters as Hosea, Jeremiah, and Ezekiel are not entirely persuasive in such a comparison. That was a perception that concerned the Church Fathers in the meeting between the Bible and Hellenism ... before the sublimity of mythical thought, the actors in the history of faith appear practically uncouth.[4]

The biblical God appears to be far less morally fastidious than many of his worshipers, having a well-documented predilection for choosing the weak and making them strong and turning sinners into saints. Biblical faith, Cardinal Ratzinger observed, "is not primarily the discovery of some truth; rather, it is the activity of God himself making history. Its meaning is, not that divine reality becomes visible to man, but that it makes the person who receives the revelation into an actor in divine history,"[5] that is, in what Hans Urs von Balthasar called "the theo-drama" of salvation history, the true history of the world.

We will limit ourselves to only four of the events in Abraham's life and will touch on each only in passing. These events are the call of Abraham (Gen. 12:1–20), the rivalry between the herdsmen of Abraham and those of his nephew Lot (Gen. 13:5–13), Abraham's persistent defense of the innocent living in Sodom

---

4 Ratzinger, *Truth and Tolerance*, 40–41.
5 Ibid., 42.

(Gen. 18:20–33), and the binding of Isaac on Mount Moriah (Gen. 22:1–18). Abraham's entry on the biblical stage, at which point he has yet to receive his new name, is abrupt, prefaced only by the kind of genealogy that often serves as a segue in biblical literature:

> The Lord said to Abram: "Go forth from the land of your kins-
> folk and from your father's house to a land that I will show you.
> I will make of you a great nation,
> and I will bless you;
> I will make your name great,
> so that you will be a blessing.
> I will bless those who bless you
> and curse those who curse you.
> All the communities of the earth
> shall find blessing in you."
> Abram went as the Lord directed him, and Lot went with him.
> Abram was seventy-five years old when he left Haran.
> (Gen. 12:1–4)

The Bible is about being called and sent. Abram is called and sent. Moses is called and sent. Jeremiah and Isaiah and Amos are called and sent. Paul is called and sent. This is the great theme of biblical literature and of biblical faith. The question biblical people face is never, "Who am I?" It is: "By Whom am I called, and to whom am I sent?" Abram went as the Lord directed him. There is something quite moving about the simplicity of that verse of Scripture. Abram went. It is an instance, the paradigmatic Old Testament instance, of what Balthasar called "the poverty of pure readiness." The response to the call is not verbal. There is no dialogue, no fanfare, and no looking back.

The second story from the Abraham saga pertinent to our theme is Abraham's appeal to the Lord to spare Sodom from destruction for the sake of those inhabitants who were innocent of the offenses for which the Lord appeared willing to destroy the city. Abraham summons the courage to confront the Lord with the injustice of destroying the innocent.

Then Abraham drew near, and said, "Wilt thou indeed destroy the righteous with the wicked? Suppose there are fifty righteous within the city; wilt thou then destroy the place and not spare it for the fifty righteous who are in it? Far be it from thee to do such a thing, to slay the righteous with the wicked, so that the righteous fare as the wicked! Far be that from thee! Shall not the Judge of all the earth do right?" And the Lord said, "If I find at Sodom fifty righteous in the city, I will spare the whole place for their sake." (Gen. 18:23–26)

The rest of this story is well known. Abraham haggles with the Lord until he gets him to agree to spare the city if as few as ten righteous inhabitants can be found. Later in the story both Sodom and Gomorrah are destroyed in response to subsequent crimes committed when two angels visit Lot and his household. Our focus, however, is on Abraham's earlier petition to the Lord on behalf of the righteous of Sodom. We include this story among the few we are considering because it foreshadows the attention to innocent victims that would develop in subsequent Hebrew history into an ethic so incontrovertible that, in our world today, it can only be circumvented by being rhetorically appropriated by pre-designated subsets of victims, in whose interests it is necessary to leave undiscussed the victimary plight of others. In this early episode in Genesis we find the incipient signs of that solicitude for victims in the greater moral emphasis Abraham gives to the innocence of the few than to the wickedness of the many.

The final story from the Abraham saga of pertinence to our theme is best understood as preparation for the (non)sacrifice of Isaac. Its significance comes to the fore in light of Girard's analysis of the role of ritual blood sacrifice and communal violence generally in transferring the animosities born of mimetic rivalry onto expendable victims. Any effort to move away from what Girard calls the "sacrificial protections" on which ancient peoples depended would necessarily require the acquisition of morally tolerable and socially reliable ways of defusing mimetic rivalries that might otherwise overwhelm these ancient and fragile cultures. All the more fascinating in this light is the fact that the redactors of Genesis have preceded the Mount Moriah story with the story of a rivalry that erupted between the herdsmen of Abram's livestock and those of Lot's:

> Lot, who went with Abram, also had flocks and herds and tents, so that the land could not support them if they stayed together; their possessions were so great that they could not dwell together. There were quarrels between the herdsmen of Abram's livestock and those of Lot's. (At this time the Canaanites and the Perizzites were occupying the land.) So Abram said to Lot: "Let there be no strife between you and me, or between your herdsmen and mine, for we are kinsmen. Is not the whole land at your disposal? Please separate from me. If you prefer the left, I will go to the right; if you prefer the right, I will go to the left." (Gen. 13:5–9)

Moving beyond blood sacrifice in all its forms may well be *the* historical task. It is certainly a formidable one, which humanity is far from having accomplished. The difficulty in leaving sacrifice behind has to do with how sacrifice works to solve social tensions. As we have seen, the cathartic power of sacrifice has the effect of draining away social tensions that would otherwise fester, leading eventually to conflict and violence. To compromise the awesome power of sacrifice without compensating for the loss in some way is to risk plunging culture into the kind of social chaos that ritual sacrifice existed in order to ward off. If ritual sacrifice is to be left behind or, more realistically, to the extent that it is possible to leave it behind, the social tensions it eliminated or resolved have to be dealt with by other means.

Here in this story we have, therefore, what amounts to the companion piece to the story of Abraham and Isaac on Mount Moriah. In the (non)sacrifice of Isaac, the cathartic ritual upon which archaic cultures depended for purging themselves of social tensions is dramatically weakened. The move from human sacrifice to animal sacrifice entails a dramatic diminution of the cathartic potential of the ritual, and it marks the beginning of the great anthropological transition, in the midst of which we are still living, from archaic sacrifice to... to what? To non-sacrifice?

To peace? To rationality? This is precisely the point of stopping to think about this story. It helps us to understand the one thing that is most misunderstood about what is happening in the history of our time, namely that the attenuation of the ancient forms of victimary sacrifice—whether in its archaic ritual form or in any of the residual forms it takes in our world today—requires a corresponding development of another form of sacrifice, namely self-sacrifice. The proximity of these two stories is one of the most important clues to their deeper anthropological meaning.

While Lot is pondering whether to take the lands to the left or the right, Abram has already chosen between the power that belongs to him as the patriarch of his clan and the act of self-sacrifice that will preserve the peace which would otherwise have to be restored either by intra-tribal violence or some form of blood sacrifice. For Abram has before him no non-sacrificial option, and neither do we. The fact that evidence of a self-sacrificial spirit is presented in such close proximity to the story of sacrificial renunciation on Mount Moriah is yet another indication of the incomparable anthropological perspicacity of biblical literature.

Why, we wonder, has Abram relinquished his power and prerogative? He has done so in order to resolve the potentially dangerous intra-clan rivalry. Yes, we know that. But why has he done that? Is it just that he is a very magnanimous man, or that he is terribly fond of his nephew? The Bible surely has more to do than familiarize us with the personal virtues of its protagonists, which are, for the most part, not that impressive in any case. Abram has chosen the path of self-renunciation, not because he is especially virtuous, but because he has begun to place more trust in the God who accompanies him on his journey than in human strategies for ensuring its worldly success. The psalmist of Psalm 119 puts it this way:

> Remember thy word to thy servant,
> in which thou hast made me hope.
> This is my comfort in my affliction
> that thy promise gives me life...
> Thou art my hiding place and my shield;
> I hope in thy word. (Ps. 119:49–50, 114)

"It is not the special qualities of the people of Israel, inclined by interior disposition to what is new," Walther Zimmerli writes, "that causes them to look forward." Rather, it is "the divine promise that stands over all else as the prime mover."[6] Abram relinquishes his prerogative because, as the exemplary figure at the dawn of historical consciousness, his hope is in the God who called him. As Zimmerli puts it, "one can see clearly that the divine promise is the power on the basis of which the patriarchs dare to live their lives of hope."[7]

Abram is the patriarch of his clan, the Alpha-male. The prerogative as to how to solve disputes is clearly his. And yet he exercises that prerogative by simply bestowing it on Lot. Compared to the drama on Mount Moriah, this quaint little episode seems hardly worth remarking, but anthropologically the modest gesture of deference to a less powerful potential rival is an absolutely essential correlative to Abraham's inauguration of sacrificial renunciation. From an anthropological point of view, had the move away from the most emotionally gripping form of sacrifice not been accompanied by a heightened concern for resolving conflict by stepping back from mimetic rivalry, it would have been inconsequential at best and in all likelihood catastrophic. What has prevented humans from moving more gracefully and expeditiously from sacrificial to post-sacrificial ways of life is not the lack of anti-sacrificial sentiments—be they moral, political, or religious. What has slowed the process is the relative nascence of the self-sacrificial ethic without which it would be both impossible and foolhardy to leave ritual sacrifice behind. As we look back to the patriarch who would ever be remembered as Abraham, it would therefore be well for us to raise to a higher status than it has heretofore been accorded this little scene which depicts the simple act of self-renunciation, which is the absolutely essential corollary to the dramatic scene on Mount Moriah.

---

6 Walther Zimmerli, *Man and his Hope in the Old Testament* (Naperville, Illinois: Studies in Biblical Theology, Alec R. Allenson, Inc.), 53.

7 Ibid., 52.

The most famous event in Abraham's life was one for which he is not well remembered, though the story is one of the most well-known in the Bible, often referred to as "the sacrifice of Isaac." The point of the story, of course, is that Abraham did not sacrifice Isaac. The fact that biblical writers and redactors of the Abraham saga have gone to great lengths to shore up Abraham's reputation by insisting that he was *willing* to sacrifice Isaac is perhaps a hint of an original anxiety about his apparent reluctance to sacrifice his firstborn, an act far from unheard of in pagan antiquity. What would have been striking to many of Abram's contemporaries is not that he was willing to sacrifice his son, but that at the last minute he didn't do so. Conceivably, the biblical emphasis on his willingness to do so represents a very early tradition in which the failure to follow such a time-honored practice would have given rise to serious concerns, that by neglecting a religious duty that his contemporaries and social equals felt obliged to perform, he was risking the disfavor of the gods who had long demanded such sacrifices.

There are few stories of equal antiquity narrated with such heartrending pathos as the story of Abraham climbing Mount Moriah with Isaac, the boy innocently wondering what is to come, and Abraham assuring him that "God will provide" (Gen. 22:8). But the great anthropological meaning of the story is that Abraham did not sacrifice Isaac, and those who ignore this will miss its great religious meaning. It is hardly without significance that the first truly historical figure was the man whom the biblical tradition credits with taking the first important step *away* from the most dreadful form of blood sacrifice. Like so many other stories of Jewish antiquity, this one pulls in two directions. The theological argumentation is directed at proving that Abraham was willing to sacrifice his son, while the narrative dramatically awakens an emotional aversion for what seems the certain outcome. In this way it perfectly captures the reality of the religious and moral tensions at work in the period of Israelite history when this story was being redacted. A threshold was being crossed here—one accompanied by religious resistances and new moral dilemmas, each requiring a deepening of man's interiority.

Abraham broke free of the sacrificial imperatives of his day, not by smugly and breezily denouncing the sacrificial system, naively assuming it to be something that could be easily left behind. Rather, living in a world where the sacrifice of the firstborn may well have been an accepted and time-honored religious imperative, Abraham took the first decisive step in the biblical historical journey by a bold and unconventional act of religious fidelity to the God whom his actual contemporaries may well have thought demanded child sacrifice.

In the course of Israelite history, moral misgivings about rituals of blood sacrifice developed, and this is a key feature of Israel's uniqueness. The Genesis account makes it perfectly clear that what prompted Abraham's step away from blood sacrifice, however, was not his personal moral misgivings about it. For had he moved away from sacrifice just because he had developed a moral revulsion for it, he would have remained oriented to the past in the same curious way that merely political revolutions almost always are, their moral and political coherence secretly dependent on whatever "system" from which they imagine themselves liberated. If leaving the past behind is the animating principle of any moral or political aspiration, the past from which it strives to extricate itself remains the secret organizing principle of its efforts to do so. Thus it is that both the attempt to cling to the past and the attempt to be rid of it come to the same thing. As René Girard said in a slightly different context: "There is a loud rattle in the lock but the gates remain closed."[8]

In a book that purports to find elusive evidence for an Alpha and Omega Christology in the process of hominization and aboriginal culture formation, on one hand, and at the moment of death, on the other, we have paused in between to suggest that history itself and historical consciousness have been the by-product of the biblical revelation and, more specifically, of Old Testa-

---

8 René Girard, *Deceit, Desire and the Novel*, trans. Yvonne Freccero (Baltimore: Johns Hopkins University Press, 1965), 113, 120.

ment Judaism. Unfortunately, the limitations of space have made it necessary to limn the outlines of the history of the Chosen People in the Old Testament in a few episodes from the Abraham saga. We bring our all too abbreviated reflections on the Old Testament to a conclusion by turning to yet another figure, precisely the one who brings the faith of Abraham to its ultimate fulfillment, namely, Mary of Nazareth.

# Getting to Yes

René Girard lighting a candle at the
Marian Altar Abbey of Saint Germain des Prés

At the point where all roads meet which lead from the Old Testament to the New we encounter the Marian experience of God, at once so rich and so secret that it almost escapes description. But it is also so important that time and again it shines through as the background for what is manifest. In Mary, Zion passes over into the Church; in her, the Word passes over into flesh; in her, the Head passes over into the body. She is the place of superabundant fruitfulness.[1]—Hans Urs von Balthasar

THE OLD TESTAMENT is a story of a journey into hope and the trials and heart-rending prayers of those who made that journey.

---

1  Balthasar, *The Glory of the Lord, Vol. I*, 338.

It is a story of a people set apart, a people whose historical and religious uniqueness Christians cannot and must not overlook, a people with whom Christians are in an historical dialogue of greatest importance, a people in whose faith Christian faith gestated for centuries, a people in solidarity with whom Christians await the Messiah—the children of Israel for his arrival and the disciples of Christ for his return. And yet, the Old Testament is a story that by Christian standards is prologue to another one, its New Testament fulfillment, and it is best understood as such. "The historical character of the religion of Israel," writes Henri de Lubac, "can be understood in all its originality only through its consummation in the religion of Christ. We should never forget that the explanation of Judaism is not to be found within itself."[2] If by Christian estimation the Old Testament needs the New, it is not less true that the New needs the Old. Of this de Lubac's friend and theological collaborator, Hans Urs von Balthasar reminds us: "The history of Israel is unique because it is the pre-history of Christ who is unique. He needs this pre-history to be truly historical."[3]

In chronicling the waning of ritual sacrifice and mythic thinking, the Hebrew Scriptures epitomize what Balthasar calls, "the 'twilight' nature of all pre-Christian religion."[4] As Balthasar sees it, the difference between biblical Judaism and the pagan religions—and it is a massive and qualitative difference—is that "in the pagan religions, this 'twilight' feature is not subjected to any critique." Greek tragic drama, Greek philosophy, and Greek historiography, for instance, evince an aversion for sacralized violence, but they themselves remain only marginally religious, and none of them were able to bring to bear on the problem of ritual violence the moral and religious critique that is found in the Hebrew Scriptures and nowhere else in the ancient world. The sacrificial regimes of pagan antiquity may ebb and flow with religious ardor, and, over time, they may become attenuated, but this attenuation is not driven by a religious imperative as it is in

2  De Lubac, *Catholicism*, 164.
3  Balthasar, *A Theology of History*, 132.
4  Balthasar, *Theo-Drama, Vol. IV*, 216.

Israel. The pagan religions, writes Balthasar, "lack the divine barb that is applied to Israel, compelling it, in the course of a genuine theodramatic history, to utter an ever-clearer Yes or No." In Israel, Balthasar writes, "there is a kind of ruthless provocation that is designed to elicit a decision."[5]

With this implicit suggestion that the historical exigencies of the Chosen People were but the dramatic framework within which this people was slowly being prepared for a decision, we prescind from even a cursory review of these historical events in favor of a reflection on the decision that, in Balthasar's view, these events were meant to elicit. If the history of Old Testament Judaism can be read as a process of divine prodding designed to elicit a decision, the question arises: Of what would such a decision consist? The Bible is about the people of God: the Jews of the Old Testament and the Christians of the New. But decisions—most especially decisions as weighty as one for which the entire history of a people can be regarded as preparation—are not collectively made. Such a decision could be made only in a representative way on behalf of the entire community, indeed in this case, on behalf of the entire world. Our own decision to omit a more detailed review of Old Testament history in favor of a few reflections on the inner lining of this history, necessitated though it is by practical concerns, is founded on the premise that so weighty a decision could only be made by a person. So we come to the question: If Balthasar is right that the Chosen People were being subjected to a divine barb intended to elicit a decision, was such a decision ever made? And, if so, when and most especially by whom?

Just as in the Genesis account of the birth of humanity we saw nature providing the erotic ardor conducive to its graced transfiguration into genuine other-directed conjugal love and the disposition for self-sacrifice appropriate to it, so we now want to apply that same principle to the question of salvation history. The cultural analogue to the sexual attraction of the man and the woman in the Genesis creation story is, on one hand, an intensification of the spiritual hunger intrinsic to the human heart and,

5  Ibid., 217.

on the other, the long painful process required to transform stiff-necked willfulness into supple willingness.

Faced with impossibilities, Abraham placed his trust in God. He went. Not until we come to the New Testament do we see an act of faith as utterly simple and unreserved as the one represented by the words: he went. Mary, the living repository of Jewish faith and Jewish experience, a child of Abraham in the deepest sense, in responding to the angel at the Annunciation, utters words that bring the faith of Abraham and the journey of his faithful people to fulfillment. The Old Testament begins with the faith of patriarchal Abraham. The New Testament begins with the faith of the young and all but nameless daughter of Zion, Mary of Nazareth. Whereas Abraham had been promised that his cooperation in God's plan of salvation would mean that his descendants would be as many as the stars of the sky and the sands of the sea, Mary was promised a sword that would pierce her heart. As the ultimate and final expression of the Yes first elicited from Abraham, Mary's *fiat* inaugurates her pregnancy and brings that of her people to term. Writes David L. Schindler: "[Mary's] *fiat* reveals in all of its profundity what it means to be a creature. The *fiat* expresses the dependent relation on God that discloses the inner meaning of all of reality as gift, which in turn disposes one toward service."[6]

Mary's *fiat*, her total self-gift to the Trinitarian God who is nothing but self-gift, is intrinsically linked to her Magnificat. For it is her self-gift that "proclaims the greatness of the Lord." In her exposition of the theology of Adrienne von Speyr, and specifically von Speyr's Marian reflections, Michele Schumacher makes an important comment:

> Adrienne thus teaches that the most personal and personalizing activities of the human being are not primarily of his or her own doing, but rather of one's allowing to be done to oneself (*geschehen lassen*). Requiring—contrary to appearances—an extraordinary exercise of the free will, such "actions" of allowing God to determine the direction of one's own accomplishment by grace

6 David L. Schindler, *Heart of the World, Center of the Church* (Grand Rapids, MI: Eerdmans, 1996), 93.

consist primarily in the continued and generous perseverance of readiness and expectation.[7]

The scriptural aftermath of his assent to the summons of the Lord makes it perfectly clear that Abraham's "Yes" inaugurated the gradual religious maturation of the people who would one day look back to him as the father of faith. By contrast, Mary's *fiat* is quite obviously the assent nonpareil of the human race as such, precisely the pure "Yes" uncorrupted in any way by self-regard. Whereas the response of Abraham, the father of faith, was one of action involving many dramatic events great and small, Mary's *fiat* was pure assent. She brings the Yes of Abraham to its supreme expression. She consents, not to *do*, but to *be*, to be available as a vessel of divine will. Writes Joseph Ratzinger:

> The typological identification of Mary and Zion leads us, then, into the depths. This manner of connecting the Old and New Testaments is much more than an interesting historical construction by means of which the Evangelist links promise and fulfillment and reinterprets the Old Testament in the light of what has happened in Christ. Mary is Zion in person, which means that her life wholly embodies what is meant by "Zion."[8]

Concurring with his theological colleague, Balthasar writes that Mary's Yes "recapitulated (while raising to a new level) the whole Abrahamic faith of the Old Testament, together with the hope that it entails."[9] The Church was quick to recognize Mary as both the summation and epitome of Old Testament Judaism and the unsurpassable personal embodiment of the mystery of the Church. Apropos of which, those who see Jesus's heavenly Father prefigured by Abraham the father of Isaac on top of Mount Moriah, though they are by no means mistaken, might consider the more earthly analogue suggested by Joseph Ratzinger: "The parallel between Mary and Abraham begins in the joy of the promised son but continues apace until the dark hour

7 Michele M. Schumacher, *A Trinitarian Anthropology: Adrienne von Speyr & Hans Urs von Balthasar in Dialogue with Thomas Aquinas* (Washington, DC: The Catholic University of America, 2014), 157.

8 Ratzinger and Balthasar, *Mary,* 66.

9 Ibid., 9.

when she must ascend Mount Moriah, that is, until the Crucifixion of Christ. Yet it does not end there; it also extends to the miracle of Isaac's rescue—the Resurrection of Jesus Christ."[10]

As for Mary as the New Eve, both the authors of the Vatican II document, *Lumen Gentium*, and John Paul II in his encyclical, *Redemptoris Mater*, quote Irenaeus: "The knot of Eve's disobedience was untied by Mary's obedience; what the virgin Eve bound through her unbelief, the Virgin Mary loosened by her faith."[11]

Dante famously begins canto XXXIII of the *Paradiso* with the words: *Vergine madre, figilia del tuo figlio*—Virgin Mother, daughter of thy son. More than five centuries before the Church finally declared the longstanding belief in the unique ontological and moral status of the mother of Christ, the great Florentine poet penned this unforgettable tribute to her uniqueness. A Christian is someone who has met a Christian. Analogically speaking—and acknowledging the limits of analogy—this is true of Christ himself. The mystery of the Incarnation would be diminished were we to conceive of it as occurring entirely independently of the unique and irreplaceable relationship between mother and child. Mary was decisive for the Incarnation. "Jesus," writes Balthasar, "like any authentically human child, needed that call from a mother in order to acquire his human identity."[12] Therein lies the anthropological realism without which the Incarnate Christ would be reduced to yet another of the countless pagan myths of divine visitation. Christians see in Mary an ontological exception necessitated by an anthropological reality, which the Bible quietly honors: the preeminent role of the mother in the life of a child. For Jesus to have a real human childhood, he would have had his primary, pre-synagogue formation at his mother's breast, on his mother's knee, and at his mother's side. The purity of this

10  Ibid., 69.

11  *Lumen Gentium*, §56; *Redemptoris Mater*, §19.

12  Hans Urs von Balthasar, *To the Heart of the Mystery of Redemption*, trans. Anne Englund Nash (San Francisco: Ignatius Press, 2010), 51.

formation would more than compensate for whatever shortcomings he might have later encountered in his formal religious and practical instruction at the hands of Mary's husband, the rabbis, and the scholars of the Law. Both the cultural and familial factors in Jesus's formation flow through Mary, who brought Abraham's faith to completion and who submitted to the will of God so unreservedly that it was only a matter of time before Christians began grappling with ways to account for her uniqueness.

Doubtless sin distorts man's relationship with God, but we are now able to see more clearly that this distortion—though the result of "original sin"—occasions actual sins. The key to both Mary's religious and moral singularity is her unique invulnerability to the mimetic melodrama in which the rest of humanity is unavoidably entangled. "Her mind and soul," Cardinal Ratzinger writes, "are alive to the manifold ways in which the living God quietly calls her"; she is immune by graces and blessings unique to her to the mimetic distractions in the midst of which we children of Eve must struggle. As a result of this fullness of grace, Ratzinger argues, she possesses "unerring powers of discernment" and a "readiness to suffer."[13]

The alternative to faith is not doubt; it is control. Mary is the one who finally allowed God total control, and no one inwardly crippled by original sin could do so. Despite the fact that it took many centuries for the Church to formally enshrine in dogma the longstanding belief in Mary's unique exemption from original sin, her Immaculate Conception, like so many of the Church's dogmas, was fairly forced on the Church as being the only reasonable way to account for certain anthropological prerequisites for the Incarnation and their more or less obvious implications.

The Catholic must steer clear of both rationalism and romanticism. If popular Marian devotion has not always done so successfully, it nonetheless kept open what must not be foreclosed. Balthasar argues that a renewed appreciation for the role of Mary

13  Ratzinger and Balthasar, *Mary*, 68.

of Nazareth in the world-altering event of Christ came just in time to prevent "the idea of the Church from disintegrating into mediocrity and ultimately into sociology." He states: "The period of one-sidedly private devotion was a prolonged transition, mistaken in its cramped approach but not in its essence. Its persistence right up to the present time has enabled *Vatican II* once more to relate Mariology and ecclesiology."[14]

Mary's "spotlessness" is too often reduced to her moral impeccability. We would draw much closer to the mystery of her uniqueness by taking up Balthasar's simple summation of Mary as one "totally free from guile."[15] "The nearer any nature is to God," Thomas Aquinas argues, "the less inclined it is to be moved by another and the more capable it is of moving itself."[16] If we translate this into anthropological terms, we could say that the more open to the divine one is—the unsurpassable height of which is the co-existence with Christ's own co-existence within the Trinity, to which Paul alluded when he says, "it is no longer I who live, but Christ who lives in me" (Gal. 2:20)—the less mimetically promiscuous one will be, the less easily one is drawn off balance by the mimetic influence of others. Moreover, if we extract from this Thomist principle its Mariological implications, we could say that, in practical terms, what we call the Immaculate Conception means the undisturbed poise and unhindered availability of one who is not just without sin in a moral sense but without the mimetic capriciousness which led Eve to succumb to the serpent's glamorizing of the forbidden fruit in the Garden. In some remote sense, today's labored masquerade of social and psychological autonomy can be seen as an unintended salute to the only healthy person who ever enjoyed this exemption, the woman who responded to each of life's unexpected developments, not by

14 Hans Urs von Balthasar, *The Office of Peter and the Structure of the Church*, trans. Andrée Emery (San Francisco: Ignatius Press, 2007), 216.

15 Balthasar, *Mary*, §1484.

16 *De veritate*, q. 22.

reacting, but simply by keeping all these things in her heart and pondering them (Lk. 2:19).

Mary sums up in her person what it means to be a Jew and what it means to be a Christian, and it is in light of this uniquely pivotal role she plays that we have meditated for a few pages on her in place of a detailed review of the Old Testament religious journey that led to her and beyond. A toothing-stone is a stone built into one building but projecting beyond it so that it can later be incorporated into the wall of an attached building, thus adding to the stability of both structures.[17] Inasmuch as Mary is the toothing-stone in whom both Old Testament Judaism and New Testament Christianity are epitomized and forever joined, the undying relationship between these responses to the God of Abraham are best appreciated by contemplating this utterly unique woman.

We have lived with the Christian answer to the human predicament for so long that we have forgotten the question to which it is the answer. It takes no great degree of theological or scriptural learning to recognize the salient features of Christ's life without which Christianity would not exist. They are the Incarnation, the Crucifixion, and the Resurrection. So if we assume that each was essential to the rescue of the human race, we can simply ask: Why did it take these things? Why was Jesus not just an exalted messenger like Moses, Buddha, or Muhammad? If he had to die as part of his incarnation, why did he have to die at the hands of a mob, whose clamors for his death were elicited and then sanctioned by the religious and political powers of his time? And what could the reports of his Resurrection appearances have to do with the rest of us? If we would like to rediscover the spiritual shockwaves these three inextricably intertwined events sent through the ancient world, setting hearts on fire and rippling down through history, changing the world forever, we might well begin by asking: Why did it take the Incarnation, the Crucifixion,

17 I am indebted to a reference to toothing-stones made in a lecture by the Australian theologian Tracey Rowland for this apt metaphor.

and the Resurrection to save us? Accordingly, if regrettably, our review of the New Testament will not be in any way exegetically thorough or theologically encompassing. In what follows, we will limit ourselves to the three questions just mentioned, and we will try to answer them as succinctly as possible. Only after we raise these three questions and propose some answers to them will we turn to a question about something that happens in the midst of the Passion, and on which we will focus much more attention than it typically receives: Why did our redemption require Jesus's descent into the realm of the dead?

# Why Did It Take
# the Incarnation to Save Us?

IN 1997 Denise Levertov published *The Stream & the Sapphire*, in which she gave a poetic account of her 1984 conversion to Roman Catholicism. One of the poems in that volume constitutes a compelling image of the mimetic maelstrom into which we fall when we lose our grounding and our roots.

> "Adam, where are you?"
>     God's hands
> palpate darkness, the void
> that is Adam's inattention,
> his confused attention to everything,
> impassioned by multiplicity, his despair.
>
> Multiplicity, his despair;
>     God's hands
> enacting blindness. Like a child
> at a barbaric fairgrounds—
> noise, lights, the violent odors—
> Adam fragments himself. The whirling rides!
>
> Fragmented Adam stares.
>     God's hands
> unseen, the whirling rides
> dazzle, the lights blind him. Fragmented,
> he is not present to himself. God
> suffers the void that is his absence.[1]

In his 2013 apostolic letter, *Lumen Fidei*, Pope Francis provided what amounted to a prose reprise of Levertov's poem:

---

1 Denise Levertov, "On a Theme by Thomas Merton," *The Stream & the Sapphire* (New York: New Directions, 1997), 17.

Once man has lost the fundamental orientation which unifies his existence, he breaks down into the multiplicity of his desires; in refusing to await the time of promise, his life story disintegrates into a myriad of unconnected instants. Idolatry, then, is always polytheism, an aimless passing from one lord to another. Idolatry does not offer a journey but rather a plethora of paths leading nowhere and forming a vast labyrinth.[2]

Today more and more people are being coaxed into the labyrinth, the appeal of which is both uniquely characteristic of our culture and our age and symptomatic of what Newman called our terrible aboriginal calamity. These distressing developments are also the context in which the mystery of Christian redemption takes place and in light of which it makes sense.

To the images provided by Levertov and Pope Francis can be added Balthasar's colorful description of the challenge Jesus faced:

And now there he stood, at the edge of their land. How was he to go over the border? In which language would they be able to understand his message? . . . They will have to take offense at him. They will turn everything around. They will understand his sayings and discourses as a new morality and a plan to improve the world, and in his example they will see nothing but a teacher of religion.[3]

Here are perhaps the three most widely held interpretations of Christianity: Christ as the spokesman for a new morality, a plan to improve the world, or a teacher of religion. Those who interpret Christianity along these lines do not lack evidence for their views, and these views tend to soften the scandal of the true Christian claims, but in doing so, they miss the only thing that makes these claims worthy of consideration. In Balthasar's reconstruction, the challenge Jesus faced was to find a language in which he could reveal a saving Truth, to which many would prefer these mundane religious or moral tropes, but to which that Truth could never be finally reduced. Elsewhere Balthasar poses

2 Pope Francis, *Lumen Fidei*, §13.

3 Hans Urs von Balthasar, *Heart of the World*, trans. Erasmo S. Leiva (San Francisco: Ignatius Press, 1979), 61.

the same question in slightly different terms: "The first question is not, 'How can we human beings translate the one revelation of God into our many languages and thought forms?' The first question is asked by God himself: 'How shall I cause my unique and utterly determinate Word to enter into the plurality of human languages and thought forms?'"[4]

In which language would they be able to understand his message? That is the question underlying the mystery of the Incarnation. Christ was surely a teacher, and—properly understood—he was also a proclaimer of the law and the proponent of a new morality, but these things were not the language in which he communicated his everlasting message. The language he chose for the proclamation of the *Logos* that he came to reveal was neither Hebrew, Greek, Aramaic, nor Latin; nor was it the language of doctrine, prescription, or proscription. The language in which his message was delivered was the language of life itself—the Word made Flesh. *Jesus was himself the message he came to deliver.* He was the Father's language translated into the finitude of human existence. He was the Word of the Father. He was the Word He came to speak, and He spoke that Word simply by letting Himself be seen, heard, befriended, betrayed, reviled, and slain. What He did and what was done to Him was the content of His message. All of Christian theology is but the outworking of what is revealed in the life, death, and Resurrection of Jesus of Nazareth, given formal expression by the Church composed of those he chose in life and those drawn by His Spirit into the ecclesial community at and after the miracle of Pentecost, when the Word entered the disciples with such undeniable force that they, even while stammering to account for what they had experienced, spoke mere words in a miraculously compelling way. The future Benedict XVI made the startling point that: "The Creed offers no teachings of Jesus; evidently no one even conceived the—to us—obvious idea of attempting anything like this." The reason for this, writes Joseph Ratzinger, is simply that "Jesus is his teaching, and his teaching is he himself."[5]

4 Balthasar, *Truth is Symphonic*, 57.
5 Ratzinger, *Introduction to Christianity*, 203, 205.

## The Torah Written on Our Hearts

Beginning notably with Aristotle, the ancients recognized that nature involves the actualization of potential, and the term Aristotle uses for the process by which something actualized its potential is *entelechy*. The word more or less means the mature *form* of an entity toward which it is intrinsically ordered. An inanimate object can hardly be said to be ordered toward something other than itself. Such an object is simply is what it is. Nonetheless, one can say that someone might sit in his car and listen to the car radio, but the car isn't for listening to music. It is for going someplace. More to the point of the transcendent *telos* toward which those endowed with a Trinitarian ontology are ordered: an acorn contains within its nature the potential tree, and it cannot remain true to its nature by remaining an acorn. Were the acorn to have desires and were one of them to become a rolling stone that gathers no moss, its attempt to fulfill that desire would be both contrary to its nature and ill-suited to its "happiness," if we may speak of acorn happiness. The reader will have gotten the point. Luckily for the acorn, in place of desires it has DNA, and its DNA doesn't include the possibility of envying a rolling stone. Humans, on the other hand, not only have desires, but they often enough desire things and experiences and forms of gratification that are neither gratifying nor conducive to fulfillment and happiness. A further complication is that desire itself is mimetic. Our desires are aroused by the desires of others. As problematic as this particular feature of our common humanity is, it is part—a very important part—of what it means to be human. The question we now want to ask is a question of theological anthropology to which we have alluded earlier: Does our extraordinary mimetic propensity have a religious meaning?

At or very near the dawn of humanity and apparently quite suddenly, mimetic desire, rudimentary forms of which are found throughout the complex hierarchy of organic life, surged to new levels of intensity in homo sapiens, quickly overwhelming the ability of the instinctive mechanisms that had long served to limit the violence born of mimetic rivalries in the animal world. The perils of recurring crises of mimetic rivalry notwithstanding, this surge in mimeticism was nonetheless decisive for our species. Robust and nimble mimetic aptitudes are the anthropological *sine qua non* for creatures called to the affective and conceptual complexities of language communication and mutual, interpersonal self-revelation. Many will regard such developments as nothing more than evolutionarily advantageous and as containing within themselves, so to speak, no hint of either a teleological purpose or theological meaning. To come to such questions from a biblical understanding of creation, however, is to see both evolution and human history as ordered toward a consummation, experiential intimations of which are fostered by personal holiness and by the sacramental sensibilities Catholic Christianity exists to awaken.

Having used the phrase "sacramental sensibilities" and the word "experiential" in the same sentence, it is important to note what we are not saying. By "sacramental sensibilities" we do not mean emotional experience. The formal sacraments, the entry into the heart of which requires a sacramental sensibility—never correlate with the participant's emotional state. In fact, the unique contribution of a Catholic sacramental sensibility is to bring about—not an emotional experience of the sacraments— but rather a higher and richer form of assent to mysteries enshrined in the doctrines of the faith. In the matter at hand, someone with his sacramental sensibilities intact is more likely to sense that the surge of mimetic desire coincident with hominization is both anthropologically and theologically significant. For we are creatures made in the image and likeness of the Trinitarian God, the God of mutual, self-donating love, and we have been endowed with the mimetic wherewithal to respond to the living Icon of that God, should we confront a sufficiently unblemished manifestation thereof. Both the anthropological advantages and social dangers of mimetic desire are considerable indeed, but the best way to avail ourselves of the advantages and avoid the dangers is to comprehend and reconcile ourselves to the teleological and theological meaning of our inordinately mimetic nature; namely as the instrumental wherewithal for succumbing to the attractive power of Christ, the living manifestation of the Trinitarian God in whose image and likeness we are made. Above and beyond the manifest benefits and formidable dangers associated with our mimetic endowment, its religious implication cannot be overlooked. Our mimetic propensities having overwhelmed the instincts by which they are controlled in the animal world, we are a danger to ourselves and others until we fall under the mimetic influence of the *Logos* in the Flesh, the living instruction manual for human existence. So apposite to our condition is Christ, and the truth and mercy He offers, that even a brief and seemingly inconclusive encounter with Him or His Church can leave one Christ-haunted for life.

Our misuse of the freedom with which we, alone among living creatures, have been endowed could not have been unforeseen by the God who brought us into existence and fashioned us according to the divine image and likeness. The plan of redemption is embedded in the plan of creation. The theological doctrine of the preexistent *Logos*, incarnate in Jesus in the fullness of time, is from eternity the "logic" of both creation and redemption. It is the Logos who will "judge the living and the dead." That is to say, the objective measure of how well each of us has fulfilled the human vocation will be how well we have replicated in our lives the pattern, the *Logos*, the intrinsic meaning of human existence, whose bare outline is written—in the idiom of morality—on our hearts, but whose full and final revelation is constituted by the life, death, and Resurrection of Christ. To turn down the invitation to enter into the Trinitarian mystery is to turn one's back on the *Logos*, which is to say on the *meaning* of and *reason* for existence itself. The incomparable revelation of that meaning, that *Logos*, occurs in history in one unforgettable place: Golgotha. It is there that Christ makes his final case for love and forgiveness and mercy, and it is there where humans face the Loving God's incomparable appeal for reconciliation in all its unsurpassed starkness and heartrending moral beauty.

The question always is how can one respond to the vocation to godlikeness? And that is a question that must now be asked by a creature so habitually and constitutionally implicated in the Eden rebellion as to be incapable of spontaneous acts uncontaminated by the mimetic misdirection that produced that rebellion. This congenital handicap has left us morally, spiritually, and epistemologically impaired, something humans didn't have to wait for the blood, tears, and carnage of recent memory to discover. The shock of the Babylonian exile in the sixth century before Christ was sufficient to cause the prophets Jeremiah and Ezekiel to realize that nothing short of a divine reordering of the human heart was necessary if humanity was to be restored to spiritual and moral health.

> See, days are coming—says the Lord—when I will make a new covenant with the house of Israel and the house of Judah. It will not be like the covenant I made with their ancestors the day I took them by the hand to lead them out of the land of Egypt. . . . I will place my law within them, and write it upon their hearts; I will be their God, and they shall be my people. They will no longer teach their friends and relatives, "Know the Lord!" Everyone, from least to greatest, shall know me—says the Lord—for I will forgive their iniquity and no longer remember their sin. (Jer. 31:31–34)

Echoes of Jeremiah's prophecy of the implantation of a new heart occur in the prophet Ezekiel: "I will give them another heart and a new spirit I will put within them. From their bodies I will remove the hearts of stone, and give them hearts of flesh, so that they walk according to my statutes, taking care to keep my ordinances" (Ezek. 11:19–20).

These prophecies raise a fundamental question that was later to be probed extensively by Saint Paul, namely the inability of the Law—the Torah—to fulfill the role that came to be assigned to it. The Law had been inscribed in stone and preserved in the Ark of the Covenant so that the covenantal obligations would not be lost or distorted and the promises of YHWH not be forgotten. And yet, the act of preserving the verbatim code in stone tended to mitigate against a deeper, inner assent to the essential covenantal relationship the Law existed to foster. One thinks of Plato's concern in the Phaedrus about the deleterious effect writing might have on the retention of memories, the inculcation of inwardness, and the growth of wisdom—on whose misgivings the present writer can be forgiven for not dwelling except to say that on roughly similar grounds, both Jeremiah and Ezekiel had come to realize that the transmission of religious truth could not be altogether entrusted to the written word, however much the exiled Jews had been forced to rely on it when deprived of more felicitous means. Happily it did not prevent the prophecies of Jeremiah and Ezekiel from being written down. Of course, Paul's concern goes much deeper, but it is cognate with that of Jeremiah and Ezekiel.

"Do not think that I have come to abolish the law or the prophets. I have come not to abolish but to fulfill" (Mt. 5:17). With Jesus, the Jewish Law, the Torah, is being fulfilled by being enfleshed in human form. For this Law—the Logos—cannot be fulfilled prescriptively or proscriptively, but only in life. The *metanoia* that we fallen creatures need amounts to having this Torah written on our hearts. What does it take to write the Torah on our hearts? The answer is an encounter with the Torah in the Flesh. We are endowed with an insatiable mimetic desire, which is an unimaginably fickle but nonetheless indispensable precondition for recognizing—through the unavoidable fog of our lust and lassitude—the Christ, the human Incarnation of the God in whose image and likeness we are made. It is in lovingly "following" Christ and exposing ourselves to the mimetic influence of the Logos Incarnate that the Torah enfleshed is written on our hearts.

## What Do You Want?

The place to begin in trying to refresh our relationship to the mystery that Christianity exists to reveal, the mystery that is inseparable from the man Jesus, is the scene, in John's Gospel, where the two disciples of John the Baptist follow the Baptist's redirection of their mimetic fascination from himself to Jesus. The Baptist had responded to the inquiries of the Pharisees as to his status by saying that he was neither the Messiah, Elijah, nor the Prophet. He was, he declared, the herald of the messiah, "whose sandal strap I am not worthy to untie" (Jn. 1:27). The day following this announcement, John, seeing Jesus coming toward him, declared: "Behold, the Lamb of God, who takes away the sin of the world" (Jn. 1:29). On the day following that, John repeated this startling epithet, directing the attention of two of his disciples to his cousin: "Behold the Lamb of God." John was not known for readily deferring to others, but now, uncharacteristically but unmistakably, he performed his appointed mission with respect to these two disciples. They were quick to respond. Without further ado, they turned from John to Jesus.

We trust we will not violate the serious theological and Christological nuances of this scene by pointing out a humorous feature. To tease out the deeper meaning of this episode, we can imagine John's disciples being drawn almost hypnotically toward Jesus by the sudden transference of their reverent attention from John to Jesus. They move toward Jesus so promptly and unselfconsciously that it hardly occurs to them what they will do once in the presence of this obviously important figure. At some point in their approach to Jesus, it would likely have dawned on them that they could not just stand and stare; they would have to say something to Jesus. But what could they possibly say? We know that one of these men was Andrew, a fisherman and the brother of Simon Peter. Both had been drawn to the fiery preaching of the Baptist, but we needn't assume that either had any great expertise in matters religious. In any case, they were hardly prepared for a colloquy with the Lamb of God, the one poised to take away the sin of the world. Not wanting to make complete fools of themselves, perhaps they tried to quickly formulate questions that might at least appear to be worthy of so exalted a figure, serious questions about the Law, for instance, the weightier and more imponderable the better. In our mind's eye we can imagine them hastily rehearsing the enigmatic puzzles they think commensurate with this man's stature in John's eyes. But suddenly something quite shocking happens: Jesus turns to them, and before they can get a word out, he says: "What do you want?" (Jn. 1:38).

There are many ways this question might be verbally inflected, each decisive for assessing its implications for the two men who stood for a moment speechless before Jesus. "What do *you* want?" "What *do* you *want*?" "What *do* you *want*?" However inflected and whatever its nuances, in the hands of the most theological evangelist, the question resounds with universal meaning, and we ourselves should ponder it further. *What do we want?*

It can hardly be dismissed as merely fortuitous that the first words spoken by Jesus in the most theological and in many respects the most historically reliable of the gospels are: "What do you want?" It would not be too much to say that Jesus came into the world to help humanity come to grips with that question. We spend much or all of our lives wanting, punctuated only momentarily by fleeting moments of satisfaction, rarely pondering the implications of this gigantic fact of our existence or realizing that it is what defines our species. Other creatures don't want as humans do; they don't *desire*. They try to satisfy instinctual appetites: hunger, sexual release, exhaustion, survival. *Wanting* is not what defines them as it does us. Even the mimeticism of our pre-human primate ancestors is constrained by appetite and/or limited to the immediately obtainable. We want. But what do we want? A magazine cartoon comes to mind, one depicting a small child surrounded by toys and clearly pampered by parents who are anxious to satisfy every wish of the child, who nevertheless is obviously bored by the resulting largess. Noticing the child's sullen dissatisfaction, the exasperated mother asks: "Well, what *do* you want?" To which the child, somewhat confused by the question, replies: "I want... I want... I want *to want!*" As Dante among others testifies, we *are* desire. We are creatures who have inexhaustible and insatiable wants. In truth, man's discrete wants or desires are but kaleidoscopic refractions of the single desire to which his teeming desiderata of longings must be properly ordered if he is to flourish and find fulfillment. Writes the Stanford neurobiologist, William Hurlbut: "Desire is essential to having a mental life at all. In California we used to say 'you are what you eat.' It is, perhaps, more true to say 'you are what you want.' Desires, more than pleasures, define and sum up personal identity. 'For where your treasure is, there will your heart be also'" (Mt. 6:21).[6]

Widespread and unconvincing assertions to the contrary notwithstanding, desire today is weak and altogether tenuous, the more tenuous the more fickle, the more fickle the less any object is desired and the more necessarily dramatized is the desire for it.

6 William Hurlbut, "The Deepest Principle of Life: Neurobiology and the Psychology of Desire," *How We Became Human*, 105.

Though testimonials to desire are everywhere to be found, they betoken its attenuation, not its vibrancy. The word, like so many others, has been debased as fast as have the moral constraints that once protected it from debasement. Much that passes for desire today is so ephemeral and evanescent that it must be acted upon posthaste before it dissipates or is replaced by yet another mimetic enticement. Such feeble desires are quickly recycled, each giving rise, phoenix-like, to yet another effervescent faux-desire. Girard has shown that as mimetic desire moves from model to model, with each new mediator the subject surrenders some of its psychological coherence and ontological weight. In advanced stages of this mimetic promiscuity, such as we find in Western post-modernity, the halfhearted impulses that pass for desire are likely to grow more fickle, more impatient, and more in need of external stimulants and pharmacological enhancements. All the more must such evanescent desires be flamboyantly exhibited and promptly—if perfunctorily—acted upon.

Jesus told the Samaritan woman at the well: "Whoever drinks the water I shall give will never thirst; the water I shall give will become in him a spring of water welling up to eternal life" (Jn. 4:14). The Samaritan woman had had five husbands and was living with another man not her husband. We may fairly take this as evidence of a *thirst* that was not being quenched. What she brought to the well was a sufficiently passionate desire for which she had found no satisfaction, but which her encounter with Jesus fully awakened and mysteriously satisfied. Doubtless, prior to encountering Christ, this desire had from time to time welled up, but without Christ it did not well up to eternal life. The merest taste of this life-giving water sent the Samaritan woman running to share what she had found with the people of her village. "Come see a man who told me everything I have done. Could he possibly be the Messiah?" (Jn. 4:29). The welling up of thirst appears to be requisite to the overflowing joy of which Balthasar writes: "In its recipients it transforms itself into the gift that is to be given to others; only by being handed on can it be a true gift

worthy of God."[7] The metaphor of thirst returns in the Book of
Revelation:

> The one who sat on the throne said, "Behold, I make all things
> new." Then he said, "Write these words down, for they are trust-
> worthy and true." He said to me, "They are accomplished. I
> [am] the Alpha and the Omega, the beginning and the end. To
> the thirsty I will give a gift from the spring of life-giving water.
> The victor will inherit these gifts, and I shall be his God, and he
> will be my son. But as for cowards, the unfaithful, the depraved,
> murderers, the unchaste, sorcerers, idol-worshipers, and deceiv-
> ers of every sort, their lot is in the burning pool of fire and sulfur,
> which is the second death. (Rev. 21:5–8)

It is almost certainly true that repentant "cowards, unfaithful,
depraved, murderers, unchaste, sorcerers, idol-worshipers, and
deceivers of every sort" are well represented in heaven. These
vices are not ontological conditions; they are moral vices, which
are very often so gravely compounded by long habit that they
almost—but not quite—take on an ontological status. All these
sins and habits are rooted in distorted desires, desires which
Dante catalogued as insightfully for his age as René Girard has for
ours. The vices enumerated in the passage above can all be traced
back to disordered desires, which is to say desires originating in
the desire of another and in the attempt to preempt it or thwart it.
The cure for such misshapen desires is not the curtailing of desire,
but its redirection toward its true object. Only the thirsty will be
given a gift from the spring of life-giving water. Those juxtaposed
to the assorted enumerated reprobates are not paragons of the
various virtues that stand in opposition to these vices. They are
the thirsty who have come to realize the depths of the desire and
the correlative heights toward which it is properly ordered.

That noted, we return to our reconstruction of the first
encounter of John's disciples with Jesus. We have imagined that
the disciples—scrambling to think of questions worthy of the figure whose importance John has so wholeheartedly endorsed—

---

7 Hans Urs von Balthasar, *Explorations in Theology, Vol. IV: Spirit and Institu-
tion*, trans. Edward T. Oakes, S.J. (San Francisco: Ignatius Press, 1995), 441.

are all but struck dumb when Jesus turns abruptly to them asking: "What do you want?" The quickly rehearsed question about some weighty religious matter of scriptural exegesis vanishes into thin air. Stuttering, one of them blurts out: "Where do you live?" (Jn. 1:38), ("Where are you staying" in the Revised Standard Version). We may perhaps be forgiven for seeing the humor in this reply as well, the importance of this encounter notwithstanding. Not only is the questioner asking where Jesus lives embarrassingly innocuous, it is obviously a complete *non sequitur*, further evidence of how flummoxed the two disciples are at their first encounter with the Incarnate Logos. What else might we expect? We may not want to give in completely to the apparent farcical possibilities of this scene, but we can imagine the man who spoke these words instantly wanting to take them back, realizing how utterly banal they are, just as we can imagine his companion looking at him in consternation, embarrassed to be associated with someone asking so vacuous a question. But, of course, this encounter, whatever its historical kernel, is being narrated by the author of John's Gospel, a theological evangelist in masterful control of his material. Under such inspired literary and theological guidance, even blurted inanities can be counted on to be pregnant with theological depth, and that is certainly true here. The Greek word *menein* means both to dwell and to remain. It is the same word used with such theological intentionality later in John's Gospel in Jesus's vine and branches discourse: "Remain (or abide) in me as I remain (or abide) in you" (Jn. 15:4). Quite obviously, the two (former) disciples of John have stumbled upon precisely the right question. Without knowing it themselves, they have asked not only about Jesus's ontological origin, but about the core of his existence.

To say, as the inspired Genesis author does, that we are made in the image and likeness of God (whose true Trinitarian essence is revealed by Christ) and to acknowledge that our willful godenvy and rivalry have corrupted that likeness without erasing the indelible image—all that is to say that mimetic desire has lost its moorings in the divine Logos. The Trinitarian watermark on the human heart has been effaced by pride and willfulness, but its Christological essence survives. The longing that secretly surges through our mimetic desires is inherently religious. It is a longing for the mimetic wherewithal for efficaciously redirecting desire toward its true object, thereby making it possible for the human subject to fulfill his vocation with all the uniqueness and incomparability proper to it.

The reason human religions emerged from the effort to channel mimetic passions, and that they were able to do so only with great effort and only very precariously, is that mimetic desire itself has a religious provenance and that, as Augustine so famously noted, it is restless until it finds its true object. Human religions, however, remain powerless to alter the underlying dynamism on which they are based. Their only recourse is to repeat the gesture of mimetic misdirection that brought them into existence, and to do so in the least violent way possible. It is worth mentioning in passing that the prospect of channeling these mimetically aroused passions by relying only on secular procedures, legal institutions, or Kantian or Rawlsian moral recipes is completely chimerical.

At the origin of these passions is a mimetic displacement, an original sin—*hamartia* in Greek—the origin of which the Genesis author was perspicacious enough to recognize as a *malevolent mimetic misdirection*. It is malevolent inasmuch as it leads to rivalry, scandal, hatred and violence of the sort that culminates in events structurally identical to the execution of Jesus outside the walls of Jerusalem. What must not be forgotten, however, in the moral revulsion felt by those looking on such things from a safe distance, is that the mimetic longing—the misdirection of which led to such malevolence and madness—is not only of incomparable importance, but is essentially the lost key to the mystery of human meaning. Misdirected though it surely is, its remediation can be effected, usually though not always, over the course of a lifetime, depending on the degree to which one has a reasonably unobstructed encounter with the Incarnate Logos—the predestined, sacramental object of humanity's mimetic aspiration as such. This is why it took the Incarnation to save us, re-forming the human heart by exposing it to the *Logos* made flesh.

## Come and See

"Where do you live?" For what may have seemed to the two erstwhile disciples of John an eternity, the seemingly frivolous question hung in the air, until Jesus finally came to their aid. "Come and see." "So they went and saw where he was staying, and they stayed with him that day. It was about four in the afternoon" (Jn. 1:39). This matter-of-fact conclusion seems at odds with the high Christological resonance of this encounter, but it serves as evidence of the historical authenticity of the scene, the theological implications of which the evangelist has taken care to draw out.

What do we want? We do not know, but the revealed answer to that question is that we want to be in communion with God in Christ. So buried beneath the ruins of our mimetic promiscuity is this deeper desire, that it takes a good deal more than we might expect to bring it to our attention. And there is only one way to enter into that communion with God for which we were made, and that is by way of a communion with Christ. "No one comes to the Father except through me" (Jn. 14:6). When he said to them: "Come and see," this is what he meant. Christianity is not ultimately about ideas or doctrines, much less rules and rubrics. It is about a Person, and the only way to receive the gift of which that Person consists is to be present to Him, with Him, and to abide in Him and give one's life to His inscrutable purpose: to belong to Him.

The Incarnation is not just the manifestation of the divine in human flesh, it is the rendering of the Torah in its totality into the life of one man. The story itself can be retold, but its drama must be re-enacted, Eucharistically by the believing community and improvisationally by each of the faithful. "Come and see." "Come, follow me." Yes, Jesus taught and preached, and he gave his closest disciples special instruction, but always in order that they might come to better know *Him*. He was neither a Greek philosopher nor a moral sage. He asked his disciples to do the truth.

The universal human ability to recognize the One in whose image and likeness we are made is not only impaired, but because of the docility, contrition, and selflessness that an encounter with him demands, it tends to provoke a hostility that is itself a form of recognition. Like a magnet that transfers a certain mysterious polarity to the metal attracted to it, those drawn to Christ can expect to experience, to some degree, the world's reflexive animosity, for Christ came to wrench us out of our anesthetized banality and to set upon our shoulders a yoke that is easy and a burden that is light. What makes the yoke easy and its burden light is not its convenience or comfort, but its correspondence to the deepest desires of the human heart.

Many Christians and a very great many non-Christians find it hard to imagine how so sweeping a Christian truth-claim could possibly be justified. One can hardly blame them. The claim itself was forced on the earliest Christians by experiences they refused to dismiss. Holy and brilliant Christian theologians have been trying to come to grips with that truth-claim for two millennia, even as it was being verified in the sanctified lives of men and women both gifted and humble. The stamina of the theologians striving to understand Christianity's seemingly incomprehensible truth-claims and the perseverance of the saints facing hardship and hostility cannot be easily accounted for, nor would these truth-claims be well served by proof. If these truth-claims could be proven true, the free response of faith would be unnecessary; grace would be superfluous and Christian truth could be preserved on stone tablets. But Christian truth first takes the heart captive, and only then can it set about taking "every thought captive" (2 Cor. 10:5).

Balthasar has given us a marvelously apt metaphor for the gentle but relentless way in which Christ draws alienated man back into the Trinitarian communion for which he was created. It is a metaphor that softens and deepens the meaning of the often neuralgic word, *atonement*, understood here as the musical *tone* in almost unconscious response to which we are being gradually, and perhaps even unwittingly, drawn into the mystery of true freedom ordered by love.

> The world is like a vast orchestra tuning up: each player plays to himself, while the audience take their seats and the conductor has not yet arrived. All the same, someone has struck an A on the piano, and a certain unity of atmosphere is established around it: they are tuning up for some common endeavor. Nor is

the particular selection of instruments fortuitous. . . . The choice of instruments comes from the unity that, for the moment, lies silent in the open score on the conductor's podium—but soon, when the conductor taps with his baton, this unity will draw everything to itself and transport it, and then we shall see why each instrument is there.

In his revelation, God performs a symphony, and it is impossible to say which is richer: the seamless genius of his composition or the polyphonous orchestra of Creation that he has prepared to play it. Before the Word of God became man, the world orchestra was "fiddling" about without any plan: world views, religions, different concepts of the state, each one playing to itself. Somehow there is a feeling that this cacophonous jumble is only a "tuning up": the A can be heard through everything, like a kind of promise.[8]

We have tried to give a dramatic rather than merely logical answer to the question about why it took the Incarnation to save us. Is there a similarly dramatic answer to the question about why man's salvation required the Crucifixion? Perhaps, but it will necessarily be one that recognizes the reciprocal intensification of good and evil, of forgiveness and sinful spite. "There is no doubt about it," Balthasar insists, "the coming of Jesus has aroused the world's slumbering No."[9]

8 Balthasar, *Truth is Symphonic*, 7–8.
9 Balthasar, *Theo-Drama, Vol. IV*, 342.

# Why Did It Take
# the Crucifixion to Save Us?

*San Zeno Altarpiece*, Andrea Mantegna, c. 1457–1460

FROM the Roman point of view, Jesus's execution was so insignificant that it was scheduled to take place in conjunction with that of two other condemned men. Whereas Matthew merely records this fact, Luke relates the now famous story of the two criminals' attitude toward Jesus.

> One of the criminals who were hanged railed at him, saying, "Are you not the Christ? Save yourself and us!" But the other rebuked him, saying, "Do you not fear God, since you are under the same sentence of condemnation? And we indeed justly; for we are receiving the due reward of our deeds; but this man has done nothing wrong." And he said, "Jesus, remember me when you come into your kingdom." And he said to him, "Truly, I say to you, today you will be with me in Paradise." (Lk. 23.39–43)

Luke's inspired account is immensely important. As we earlier argued, it provides the tableau of the co-crucifixion—indeed, co-suffering—of Christ alongside two others reviled by society, a living embodiment of Jesus's words that what was done unto those rejected by the world was also done unto him (Mt. 25). Here, however, we have what seems a clear reference to the fact that the eternal fate of these two criminals on the threshold of their own death depends on their attitude toward "the Pierced One" who has shared in their sufferings. We only mention it in passing here, but we will return below to the eschatological implications of one's postmortem attitude toward this "Pierced One"—the "Lamb Slain." Our focus at this point is on what happens next in the Lucan account:

> It was now about the sixth hour, and there was darkness over the whole land until the ninth hour, while the sun's light failed; and the curtain of the temple was torn in two. Then Jesus, crying with a loud voice, said, "Father, into thy hands I commit my spirit!" And having said this he breathed his last. The centurion who witnessed what had happened glorified God and said, "This man was innocent beyond doubt." (Lk. 23:44–47)

The centurion's instant conversion can be seen as another Lucan innuendo suggesting that the Gentile world has been caught up in the world-transforming event of the Passion. Of all those present at the scene of the crucifixion, surely the centurion was the one who was least likely to recognize Jesus's innocence. After all, he was a hardened Roman soldier assigned to the task of executing the enemies of Rome. Crucifixions were hardly rare in those days, and he is very likely to have assisted at many such executions and just as likely to have grown calloused in the process. Luke has a special eye for gentiles, to be sure, and earlier in his Gospel Jesus cures a centurion's slave, praising the Roman soldier with the words: "I tell you, not even in Israel have I found such faith" (Lk. 7:9). But there is something more remarkable still about the recognition of Jesus's innocence on the part of the centurion on Golgotha.

By Jewish standards, this Gentile was blissfully ignorant of the scriptural traditions that surely made Jews more open to the truth revealed by the dying Christ. Of the story of Abraham and Isaac, of the sufferings of Jeremiah or the Suffering Servant in Deutero-Isaiah, of the trials of Job—the centurion was ignorant of all those things that prepared Jews for the revelation of the Cross. And yet it is precisely this hardened and hopelessly unprepared Roman functionary who blurts out the one thing that the old system of socially unifying violence existed to obliterate: the innocence of the mob's victim. How did he come to this rather astonishing conclusion? One would not expect a man whose professional responsibilities required him to regularly assist in grizzly public executions to feel great empathy for those he tortured. Nor could the cruelty of crucifixion with which he was so familiar have likely so shocked him that he had a moral epiphany. Nor is it likely that he had any familiarity whatsoever with the nature of the charges against Jesus of which he nevertheless unequivocally declared Jesus innocent. Yet, he did just that. He pronounced Jesus innocent with the same breath with which he glorified God. This is the key. He not only recognized Jesus's innocence, but the centurion realized that his capacity to do so had nothing to do with any personal moral perspicacity on his part. His insight into Jesus's innocence was a divine gift. He was the recipient of a divine revelation, and he seems clearly to have known this to have been the case. He "glorified God."

It may seem passing strange for a man with Jesus's blood on his hands—perhaps literally—to glorify God in thanksgiving for the revelation of his victim's innocence. In Jean-Luc Marion's study of Augustine's *Confessions* he argues that man "thinks first by confessing";[1] confession consisting of a *confessio laudis* and a *confessio peccati*—a confession of praise and a confession of sins. This is another indication that the moral conscience has an intrinsically religious ordination, as Newman's designation of conscience as the Aboriginal Vicar of Christ clearly suggests. If the confession of praise is not accompanied by the confession of sins it is an empty and pompous gesture. If the confession of sins is not accompanied by a confession of praise, it is equally vacuous and barren, the stuff of trashy magazines and tabloid newspapers, a self-preening parody of repentance.

It nevertheless remains an odd fact that the first recipient of the revelation of Christ's innocence is both a pagan and a hard-

---

1 Jean-Luc Marion, *In the Self's Place: The Approach to Saint Augustine*, trans. Jeffery L. Kosky (Stanford: Stanford University Press, 2012), 20.

ened functionary for whom the gruesome business of public execution is routine. Implicit in the centurion's recognition of Jesus's innocence, coupled as it was with his spontaneous prayer of thanksgiving to God for having vouchsafed him this awakening, is the fact that what is at work here is not mere human or juridical innocence. For such innocence could all too easily be lost on either an accusing mob or an indifferent and hardened executioner. Jesus's innocence consisted neither of his merely moral impeccability nor his merely juridical innocence of the charges leveled against him. He was *ontologically* innocent. He was like us in all things but sin. This essentially is why it took the crucifixion of Christ to save us. Only the kind of innocence of which we fallen creatures are incapable could have broken the spellbinding power of the system of ritual accusation and immolation by which sinful man has turned mimetic aggravations into social camaraderie and a communal sense of moral rectitude "since the foundation of the world." That the person who recognized Jesus's innocence was the least likely person present to do so, and that he gave praise to God in the same breath, can be read as evidence of the fact that if we humans were to be freed from the grip of the ancient system of ritual scapegoating, we would have to have help from outside. The centurion was a beneficiary of just such divine intervention, the accused having been ontologically innocent, and centurion's *confessio laudis* is evidence of this.

Two thousand years later, the consequences of this event may seem negligible, but when we look more closely, we can see that the revelation of the Cross is slowly changing the human situation. The Christian Gospel is the driving force in human history in the sense that what has been revealed on Golgotha confronts those exposed with a choice between truth and mimetically conjured delusion. A solicitude for victims and those who might remotely be seen as scapegoats is one of the most distinctive features of those societies that have fallen under Christian influence. Nor has this attention to victims or those claiming victim status failed to fundamentally reshape these societies. This is emphatically not to say that this represents an unambiguous moral triumph. Moral improvement operates at the individual level, where each moral agent faces particular dilemmas. But the prevailing ethos in which these dilemmas are faced will either predispose or indispose those facing them to see what the centurion saw. One need not overestimate the moral improvement possible in a world that remains fallen in order to recognize the ethical, social, and cultural benefits that accrue to those societies that have come under Christian influence to one degree or another, especially when that influence has been sustained over centuries. Ironically, the greater personal latitude these cultures made possible also made possible more egregious betrayals of the source of the cultural vitality they enjoyed. Those who failed to interiorly instantiate these moral acuities have tended to squander the freedoms that their cultural instantiation made possible. But none of this should blind us to the fact that the Christianization of cultures has been immensely advantageous to those societies fortunate enough to have undergone it. All the more reason for those aware of these advantages to fret about the consequences of the de-Christianization that has been occurring in many once Christianized societies for many decades, but which is today taking place with great and disturbing rapidity.

The verse immediately following the one that records the centurion's recognition of Jesus's innocence is this: "When all the people who had gathered for this spectacle saw what had happened, they returned home beating their breasts" (Lk. 23:48). The two verses throw light on one another. As extraordinary as it was for a professional executioner to recognize the innocence of one of the many people he had routinely tortured and killed, it is no less amazing to learn how Jesus's death affected the crowd that had gathered to watch "this spectacle."

Seen through a wider anthropological lens, we can see that this "spectacle" for which the crowds had gathered on Golgotha was essentially indistinguishable from the spectacles at which humans have been gathering since the birth of fallen human culture. It is just such spectacles that have always provided humanity with the spellbinding gathering rituals—whether spontaneous or under sacerdotal direction. Cultures are generated or regenerated at such spectacles, but these spectacles are always precarious. A trace of moral ambiguity is indispensable to the spectacles' cathartic dénouement, but anything more than a trace of moral discomfort will destroy the catharsis. Inasmuch as the catharsis is the key to the draining away of mimetic animosities and sundry social aggravations, when the "spectacle" fails to achieve cathar-sis, the community is likely to slide into fractious strife exasper-ated by the ritual failure.

The Greek verb, here translated as "returned," is a cognate of the word, *hupostrepho*, meaning to turn around or to go in another direction, to re-turn. It clearly suggests something more than the decision to go home. It is more than that, but less than what the accompanying phrase—"beating their breasts"—might seem to indicate. In the context of the times, this phrase suggests, not contrition as such, but confusion, bewilderment at what was just seen—what is meant when we speak of people "shaking their heads." In other words, it is a response to this particular example of publicly sanctioned violence which betokens the spectacle's rit-ual failure. In Aristotelian terms, the spectacle, having failed to produce pity and terror in the precise pharmacological ratio, has left the onlookers in confusion and disarray. This happens, it is important to note, at the moment of Jesus's death. It is the crowd's vague and implicit confirmation of what the centurion had explicitly declared. To assess the anthropological implications of this we should remember what Jesus had said, "Whoever does not gather with me scatters" (Mt. 12:30; Lk. 11:23).

As with many of the other facets of the Christian revelation we are exploring, this haunting statement can and should be under-stood at two levels: roughly speaking, at the cultural and anthro-pological level, and at the theological and eschatological level. For the gathering that Christ effects reaches far beyond what might seem its obvious range. It includes far more than just those to whom he spoke in his earthly life and those who have heard his voice through the ecclesial body he commissioned as messen-ger to those living in post-Ascension history. "'And when I am lifted up from the earth, I will draw everyone to myself.' He said this indicating the kind of death he would die" (Jn. 12:32–33).

Again, we have no warrant to limit this reference to "everyone"—variously translated as "all things" or "all men"—to those who were affected by Christ's crucifixion either directly or indirectly. As argued throughout this exploration, we can do full justice to the depth and scope of the Christian revelation only by insisting on the universal impact of Christ's life, death, and Resurrection on everyone who ever has or ever will live and on creation itself—ordained as it is to being brought by human wonder and affection into the everlasting liturgy of Trinitarian communion.

What we are saying is that there is far more at stake in the "Christ Event" than just humanity's moral sinfulness, summed up, perpetuated, and exemplified though that sinfulness is in the ubiquitous rituals whereby humans "take away the sins of the world" by sinful devices of their own making. The long-term consequences of the Passion of Christ on history, culture, and moral lucidity—though for the most part gradually occurring in the course of a long back-and-forth struggle against the conventional procedures of cultural life—are ultimately overshadowed by its less obvious but more all-encompassing effect on every human who ever lived or ever will live.

As we have tried to show, no merely human death or public execution could possibly have had the consequences that Christ's death has had. Its historically, culturally, and anthropologically detectable ramifications can be properly reckoned only with reference to his unique ontological status, at once divine and human. If the Christian claim that Jesus was both God and man cannot be ignored when trying to account for the historical and cultural impact he has made, it looms even larger when we approach Christianity's more sweeping claims which we will explore below.

# Why Did It Take
# the Resurrection to Save Us?

THE ARGUMENT that death did not exist in the created order until the Fall, for all its implausibility at one level, is subtly and beautifully preserved in one of the most easily dismissed Christian traditions: the dormition and bodily assumption of the mother of the Lord. Even those—Christians or otherwise—who might dismiss the Catholic doctrine of the Assumption will need to concede that it is consistent both with the doctrine of the Immaculate Conception and with the underlying anthropology of the Fall story in Genesis. It is hardly coincidental that she who is revered for, among other things, being born sinless, passes from life in a way that the tradition has steadfastly refused to call death. The tradition of her unique exemption from original sin is an ancient one, predating its elevation to dogma by many centuries. Of course we do not know the actual historical circumstances of Mary's departure from this life, but there were no theological reasons at the time to fabricate such a story. It could be counted as evidence for a strikingly unique death that the ancient belief in the "bodily assumption" survived the similarly ancient celebration of her burial site. (A church ostensibly built on her burial site in the Kidron Valley was erected in the fifth century, and another tradition claims that she was buried at Ephesus.) These are contradictions only at a superficial level, overlooking what we have said about the power of sin to terrify death, at the approach of which a sinless person would remain serene, precisely in the way that, first legend and then magisterial doctrine, remembered the death of the immaculately conceived mother of the Lord. The philosopher Josef Pieper has written eloquently on this. Quoting in passing Karl Rahner, Pieper writes:

> [T]he overwhelming necessity of dying which comes to us from outside, the violent rending asunder of body and soul which we

173

must simply undergo and suffer—this was *not* the way it was "in the beginning. . . ." Rather, from the beginning the *posse mori*, the ability to die, belonged to the natural constitution of man, including paradisiacal man. The account of Genesis, therefore, should not be taken to mean that but for the primal sin man's physical existence upon the earth would have been unending. . . . The end of earthly man would have been a "'death' without death," a "pure, manifest, active completion . . . from within." But such a "deadless death," although a free gift, would at the same time have been far more in keeping with the true nature of man as body-and-soul; it would have been "natural" in a far higher degree than what now awaits historical man at the end of his life.[1]

"Had man not fallen," writes Adrian J. Walker in a similar vein, "he would still have had to undergo an earthly end, though he would have known it as a purely joyous transition into the eschatological state, without any stain of constraint, privation, or corruption."[2] Such a view is entirely compatible with the underlying anthropology of the Fall story in Genesis.

Adam lived to the ripe old age of 930. We earlier noted that, notwithstanding the fact that the punishment followed so tardily on the commission of the crime, its essential repercussions were immediately apparent. The man and woman began immediately to shift the blame for the transgression to one another, the purpose of which could only have been to evade the consequence of the transgression—namely death—precisely by transferring it to another. As we pointed out earlier, this attempt to evade death by foisting it onto another is the quintessential function of primitive sacrifice. Whether any individual or any community succeeds in temporarily offloading death on to another, the strategies by which we attempt to do so require that we bow down before the power of death. The author of the Letter to Hebrews writes that Christ underwent death "that through death he might destroy

1 Josef Pieper, *Death and Immortality,* trans. Richard and Clara Winston (South Bend, IN: St. Augustine Press, 2000), 60–61.

2 Adrian J. Walker, "Singulariter in spe constituisti me: On the Christian Attitude towards Death," *Communio: International Catholic Review,* 39 (Fall 2012): 362.

the one who has the power of death, that is the devil, and free those who through fear of death had been subject to slavery all their life" (Heb. 2:14–15). According to this reading, death is the tool of the Evil One. Sin brings about an ontological diminution, which is life lived under the power of death and as a slave of death, that is the fallen condition.

The immediate aftermath of the first sin is not death; rather it is the cowering, the dissembling, the mutual incrimination of the man and woman. What do these things represent if not the *power* of death, the *fear* of death, and the *slavery* that life haunted by that fear entails? We humans instinctively flee from danger and death as do subhuman creatures, but it is in the specifically human realm that we find a strategy for evading death that consists of redirecting death toward another. In its starkest and most grue-some form, the fallen human condition is life lived in the death camp, where the impulse to push death away—even if off on to another—and postpone it as long as possible secretly infects even our noblest principles.

In the spirit of Christian unity, we turn to the former dean of Saint Vladimir's Orthodox Seminary, John Meyendorff, who offered a reading of the bedrock Pauline passage on original sin in the fifth chapter of the Letter to the Romans:

> The scriptural text which played a decisive role in the polemics between Augustine and the Pelagians is found in Romans 5:12, where Paul, speaking of Adam, writes: "As sin came into the world through one man, and through sin, death, so death spread to all men *because all men have sinned [eph ho pantes hemarton]*." In this passage there is a major issue of translation. The last four Greek words were translated in Latin as *in quo omnes peccaverunt* ("in whom [i.e., Adam] all men have sinned"), and this transla-tion was used in the West to justify the doctrine of guilt inher-ited from Adam and spread to his descendants.

Meyendorff proceeds to make the point, however, that the Eastern Fathers—using the original Greek—interpreted this cru-cial text differently.

> *Eph ho*, if it means "because," is a neuter pronoun; but it can also be masculine, referring to the immediately preceding substantive

*thanatos* ("death"). The sentence then may have a meaning which seems improbable to a reader trained in Augustine, but which is indeed the meaning which most Greek Fathers accepted: "As sin came into the world through one man and death through sin, so death spread to all men; and *because of death, all men have sinned.*"[3]

"It is this death," writes Meyendorff, "which makes sin inevitable, and in this sense 'corrupts' nature." We are setting this view in juxtaposition to the familiar Augustinian and Thomist one, not to argue for the replacement of either by the other, but rather for the same reason we are trying to bring theology and anthropology together. These interpretations are not incompatible. The connection between sin and death can be fruitfully explored from each of these interpretations of Romans 5.

The biological death of the individual organism, as we have said, preceded the dawn of humanity. To interpret death as the punishment or consequence of sin, therefore, is necessarily to understand death as something other than biological cessation. On the other hand, to see death as the cause of sin we need only understand it in its wider context as the whole range of anxieties about one's apparent ontological precariousness. As we will see below, these anxieties infect and problematize the heightened mimetic predispositions out of which sin grows.

Since death is the one thing that cannot be fully secularized, those lost in a secular wasteland eventually turn to death, as fallen humanity always has, siding with death against death, turning death into a cure for death, eluding death by exploiting its mystique and becoming its unwitting accomplices, wailing mourners, voyeuristic onlookers, or pious votaries of death in the nihilistic culture of death. In a post-religious world, both those who are desperate for meaning and those who have despaired of it will find in death an unspoken organizing principle. Whether fleeing from it or flirting with it, whether bound to it by fear or fascination, death eventually becomes the default preoccupation, the chief obsession of those who come to regard

3 John Meyendorff, *Byzantine Theology: Historical Trends and Doctrinal Themes* (New York: Fordham University Press, 1974), 144; his italic emphasis and my italic emphasis.

it as the final, incontrovertible fact. Death as the ultimate and final horizon, Sebastian Moore once said, lets sin make as much sense as sin can make.

Both ancient and contemporary societies surround death with rituals that have the effect of forging bonds between the mourners. These rituals are, in their own way, innocuous or even healthy, but they represent an alliance with death. Jesus told a prospective disciple, "Let the dead bury the dead" (Lk. 9:60). To our ears this sounds almost heartless, but this is because we remain largely oblivious to the way the ancient world exploited natural death for its cathartic potential, thus unwittingly colluding with the mystifying power of death. At Bethany, for instance, after the death of Lazarus, Jesus's reaction to the approach of Mary and the ritual mourners is telling. "When Jesus saw her weeping, and the Jews who came with her also weeping, he was deeply moved in spirit and troubled; and he said, 'Where have you laid him?' They said to him, 'Lord, come and see'" (Jn. 11:33–34).

Given the tradition of ritual wailing in Jewish and other cultures of the time, there are reasons to believe that "the Jews" who attended Mary of Bethany, the sister of the deceased, were not simply weeping; they were performing an important ritual; they were wailing. This was a ritual performed by women, and those performing it needn't have been especially familiar with the deceased or particularly distraught over his death. If the weeping of the Jewish women accompanying Mary of Bethany were to be mistaken for a straightforward expression of sadness at the loss of a friend or relative, Jesus's distress would likely be interpreted similarly. But neither the weeping nor the perturbation expressed by Jesus—being "deeply moved in spirit and troubled"—suggests that. Mary was accompanied by ritual mourners, a very common feature of ancient societies and still found in many places today. Anthropologically understood, the role these mourners performed was to amplify the emotions of the grieving relatives and to draw the wider community into it. The effect of this is to foster a quasi-ritual form of a catharsis that would otherwise require the immolation of socially reprobated victims or its carefully choreographed ritual reenactment. If it is easy to miss the ritual nature of the mourners weeping, it is no less easy to misunderstand Jesus's reaction to it. The Greek word—often translated as if it meant sadness—is a good deal more shocking. It carries an undeniable hint of anger which some exegetes try to soften by suggesting that Jesus is distraught by the evil of death itself. There is obvious truth to that, but it must be remembered that it is only when the wailing women approach that Jesus shows signs of indignation. For all their pious intentions and regardless of how socially fruitful and emotionally purgative their ritual wailing might be, it amounts to complicity with death, and Jesus shudders with revulsion.

In the ancient world, death is fungible. In such a world, and, indeed, more often than we realize in our own world, natural death carries with it a sacrificial residue. Though it functions for the most part beneath the level of conscious reflection, the news that another has died or is facing death, however mingled it is with genuine sadness and mourning, can be accompanied by a faint sense of relief—that one has been "passed over" by the angel of death, spared, temporarily to be sure, the same fate. Most people are too decent to allow this sacrificial trace to rise to consciousness. Though it takes quite different forms in the primitive world than in ours, this sacrificial residue is explicitly affirmed in many primitive societies and detectable to the psychologically discerning even in modern ones. In many archaic societies, there is no such thing as natural death. All death is attributable to the malice of evil forces. In cultures where this is true, each death requires that the evil source that brought it about be repaid in kind. In such societies, the elaborate rituals and wars that carry out these reprisals constitute the *raison d'être* of cultural life. And so death becomes the operating principle of cultural survival and intercultural relations. In more self-designated, advanced societies, where the *raison d'être* is avoiding death and postponing it for as long as possible, vestiges of the exchangeability of death nonetheless survive. Like many such subtle outcroppings of our primitive sacrificial history, this one is usually couched in irony and dark humor. Some jokingly refer to the obituary page as the Irish Sporting Green where one reads of those whom one has suc-

ceeded in outliving. Clever or crude, these hints point to something that is both true and profound. Balthasar has argued that to
be a Catholic is to know that somewhere someone is dying on
my behalf. To which the Swiss theologian would surely add that
this interchangeability of suffering and death would likely be conceivable only to those for whom Someone's death and suffering
had *already* removed the sting of the former and the stigma of the
latter. In other words, Christianity rescues what many primitive
societies superstitiously assumed about the fungibility of death,
vestiges of which still operate in our psychological background
today. The death agony of Christ on the Cross, writes Balthasar,
transforms—at a level that is only rarely made fully conscious—
the death of those who have sufficiently assimilated their lives to
his. So that their death agony "is no longer that of man abandoned to his own helplessness but that of participation in the
darkness of the Cross—a participation that is most real, albeit
unconscious, for the one undergoing death in the night of impo-
tency. In the end, each person dies another's death because Christ
has died the death of each of us for us."[4]

At the Resurrection, "the power of death" was broken, but not
the fact of death. Death, the dark curse of human existence since
the relinquishing of our full ontological dignity in return for the
excitations of the mimetic melodrama, has now been turned into
the universal opportunity to enter into the Paschal Mystery, taking up one's own cross, and dying with Christ. Nor does this
reversal shove aside the mimetic predilections in favor of which
we betray our higher calling. Rather, mimesis is given its proper
Object, God, in the only form that is both worthy of human imitation and capable of mimetic attraction: namely divinity incarnate as a man.

Only by acknowledging the fact of death and accepting it as
our opportunity to enter into the paschal drama with Christ can
we keep from slipping back into the old religious swamp out of
which we were dredged at Easter. Post-Christian culture, bereft
of religious vigor, is becoming such a swamp, a culture of death.

4 Hans Urs von Balthasar, *Bernanos: An Ecclesial Existence* (San Francisco:
Ignatius Press, 1996), 467.

Threatened from without by a resurgence of pre-modern forms of sacred violence, it is inwardly imperiled by postmodern forms of nihilistic resignation for which Martin Heidegger was the chief and chilling prophet. The Heideggerian apotheosis of death as one's "ownmost potentiality-for-being, non-relational, and not to be out-stripped"[5] amounts to the dark and brilliant philosopher's unintentional warning about where the post-Christian path leads: to a death-romanticism masquerading as philosophical profundity. This twisted mystification pales in the presence of the Pauline longing to imitate Christ crucified.

> We are afflicted in every way, but not constrained; perplexed, but not driven to despair; persecuted, but not abandoned; struck down, but not destroyed; always carrying about in the body the dying of Jesus, so that the life of Jesus may also be manifested in our body. For we who live are constantly being given up to death for the sake of Jesus, so that the life of Jesus may be manifested in our mortal flesh. (2 Cor. 7: 8–11)

Paul's use in this passage of the first person plural can be read as the repudiation of Heidegger's above quoted solipsistic dicta. Here again the universal meaning of Christian truth emerges. For perhaps the only thing that can absolutely be said of each and every human being is that he will one day suffer death. Christ came to rob death of its sting, not primarily by providing us with consolations or promises of future happiness, but rather by drawing our suffering and death into his and thus assimilating our suffering and death into the redemptive economy in ways that we simply cannot fully fathom. Paul writes: "You were buried with him in baptism, in which you were also raised with him through faith in the power of God, who raised him from the dead" (Col. 2:12).

"The Resurrection delivers men from the fear of death," writes John Meyendorff, "and, therefore, also from the necessity of struggling for existence."[6] Such a struggle for existence is spiritually deadening precisely inasmuch as it inevitably becomes a

---

5 Martin Heidegger, *Being and Time*, trans. John Macquarrie and Edward Robinson (New York: Harper & Row, 1962), 255.

6 John Meyendorff, *Byzantine Theology*, 146.

struggle *against others* for preeminence, material advantage, power, or survival. To the extent that it has been sacramentally instantiated in the life of the believer, the Resurrection of Christ provides the wherewithal required to live responsibly and nobly. Thus it is that the Resurrection has opened up history in a way never before known. As Raymund Schwager observed:

> Through the resurrection of Christ . . . it became possible . . . to see conflicts, persecutions, and defeats in a different way. No longer did immediate this-worldly success have to be decisive. History as the history of victors was, at least in principle, overcome. . . . Truth and immediate this-worldly success were separated.[7]

Though the responsibility for proclaiming the truth and struggling for its triumph in this world is in no way diminished, the Resurrection relieves those on whom the Easter Sun has shone of the desperate project of trying to achieve in history what can be fulfilled only eschatologically—a fool's errand that has turned the late-modern period into a crematoria like no other in history.

The power of death was broken at Easter, but death itself remains. Death has, however, been altered in ways that Christians are in a position to recognize. Postlapsarian death, writes the Catholic theologian Adrian Walker, "is primarily a punishment for sin, but the justice of this chastisement already conceals a medicinal mercy, an opportunity to come to our senses, to wake up from the perverse illusion of godlike autonomy without God."[8] Given the Catholic understanding of original sin as a sin only in an analogous sense, there may be a less forensic way of expressing the mystery of redemption as it relates to death. Nevertheless, Walker has stressed the essential point: the medicinal mercy hidden in the chastisement.

Christ turned the consequences of the Fall—long regarded as the "punishment" for the Fall and, as we have argued, rightly understood as the consequence of sin—into the most propitious occasions for entering into the drama of redemption. Suffering,

---

7 Schwager, *Jesus in the Drama of Salvation*, 153.

8 Walker, "Singulariter in spe constituisti me: On the Christian Attitude towards Death," 355.

utterly unavoidable in this vale of tears, has become a unique opportunity to enter into the Paschal drama as a companion of Christ. And death, the supreme suffering, offers this same opportunity. In each case, the initiate is drawn into the mystery of self-renouncing self-donation, the very mystery of the Trinity, which we pray for the grace to live out "on earth as it is in heaven," knowing all the while that the heavenly expression of that mystery is performed in pure joy while our efforts to replicate it will necessarily be accompanied by pain, suffering, and instinctive resistance.

"One cannot die *for* the true God, who has nothing to do with our sacrifice," writes Rémi Brague, one can only "die *with* him, if he has arranged it to share our condition."[9] Christ has already died our death. We join him in our "hour," making up for what is lacking in the suffering of Christ. Balthasar makes an important observation:

> There are many ways in which even that death which is appointed for the body, although it is a physical event, can be assimilated in advance to that spiritual event that it is meant to be (and shall be, whether or not one wishes it to be), namely the handing over of corporality to the Giver who fashioned the dust of the earth into a human instrument (Gen. 2:7). The Christian's attitude to the body will be governed by this final sacrifice, which he is to perform as a conscious act; even in health and active life he will make the coming final surrender of corporality the inner meaning of all his action.[10]

"Man's final disposition," writes Josef Pieper, "with which he simultaneously concludes and completes his earthly existence, is a religious act of loving devotion in which the individual, explicitly accepting death as his destiny, offers up himself, and the life now slipping from him, to God."[11]

---

9 Brague, *On the God of the Christians (and on one or two others)*, 137; italic emphasis added.
10 Balthasar, *Theo-Drama*, Vol. V, 476.
11 Pieper, *Death and Immortality*, 92.

# Keeping Faith
## and Breaking Ground

CHRISTIANS have been told by Christ that a Spirit would come to lead those trying to be faithful to Christ into ever greater understanding of the truth unforgettably revealed in the drama of his life, death, and Resurrection. Thus instructed by Jesus himself and obliged by the exigencies of history and theological controversy over the course of two millennia, the Church has prayed for the guidance of the Spirit, trusting that the wider horizon of truth to which the Spirit would lead would enrich and not undermine the message of Christ, which, after all, was Himself.

However determined we may be to remain faithful to Christ and his Church, and to submit to magisterial authority, our faithfulness will require the exercise of both our freedom and our intelligence. To realize, as we ought, that we ourselves are "early Christians" is to recognize that, though the revelation of Christ is full and complete, we are far from having surveyed its vast scope and meaning. With the help of the Holy Spirit, those of our descendants who remain faithful to the Church that is "ever ancient, ever new" will discover facets of our faith that mystics and saints may have known in ages past, but which have yet to coalesce into doctrine. They will do so in the fullness of time if and when it becomes indispensable to the full flowering of Christian discipleship. Ours is the responsibility for appreciating whatever feature of this stupendous revelation the Spirit has determined to be apposite to our age and commensurate with its religious and moral needs.

Nor must we underestimate the seductive power of inadequately scrutinized but widely assumed presuppositions. Precisely because our responsibilities relate to the special needs of our time, we must never forget the danger of being bewitched by the spirit of the age, arguably Christianity's chief perennial temptation. It is not enough, however, to resist capitulation to the spirit of the age. Christians must understand that spirit well enough to separate its healthy potential from its poisoned fruit, and they must be able to give an account of their hope that both engages the zeitgeist and attracts those whose hearts are open. It is apposite to remember that the great Catholic historian, Christopher Dawson praised Blessed John Henry Newman as the central figure of his age by saying that he was "at once the embodiment and the contradiction of the spirit of his age."[1] We live in a world whose strategies for expelling the Christian truth draw on underlying forms of Christian thought for their legitimacy. Nonetheless, the political or ideological simulacra of Christianity retain (for a time) the requisite allure to seduce. The extrication of truth from such tangles will necessarily, therefore, have to wrestle with the particular machinations of the age in question.

It is part of the mystery of the Christian revelation that it functions like a time-release medication. The cultural adjustments it demands become imperative only when those called upon to meet these demands have been vouchsafed the moral and religious wherewithal for doing so. Notwithstanding the merciful concurrence between the moral resources the revelation provides and the moral demands it makes, the social and psychological reflexes that predispose fallen humanity to resort to sacrificial subterfuges even after they have lost their efficacy remain powerful.

In the first part of our attempt to bring recently elucidated anthropological insights to bear on an Alpha and Omega Christology—which has fallen into neglect in deference to evolutionary science—we have suggested two distinct but mutually compatible moments of hominization: the birth of the human person and the birth of human culture. In exploring each of these thresholds of hominization we have located traces, respectively, of the Trinitarian mystery and the Christological drama which finally and fully reveals it. We have argued that these Trinitarian and Christological traces warrant a renewed attention to one of the most sweeping of Christianity's teachings: that the Logos

1 Christopher Dawson, "Newman and the Modern World," *The Tablet*, August 5, 1972, 733.

Incarnate in Jesus of Nazareth is the living manifestation of the operating (Trinitarian) principles on which all reality depends, that "all things were made through him, and without him was not anything made that was made" (Jn. 1:3). This is admittedly a novel case for the revival of an Alpha Christology inasmuch as it focuses exclusively on human origination with only a passing allusion to the birth of the cosmic order, the overflowing Trinitarian and paschal dimensions of which we affirm, but for which we cannot here proffer adequate argumentation.

It remains for us at this point to account for an Omega Christology. Here, too, we will be focusing on one particular end-time. Though Omega Christology properly speaking refers to the final end of creation and history, we will be looking for traces of an Omega Christology closer to home, so to speak. After all, at the final end of history, history will already have ended long, long ago for each of us—precisely at the moment of our own deaths. We will be suggesting that each and every person born of human parents will encounter Christ in death and that this encounter will be eschatologically decisive. We are in good company here. Writes Joseph Ratzinger: "Christ as judge is *ho eschatos*, the Final One, in relation to whom we undergo judgment *both* after death *and* on the Last Day. In the perspective we are offered here, those two judgments are indistinguishable."[2]

This is in no way offered as an alternative to the more conventional understanding of the Omega Christology that focuses on the final reconciliation when "God may be all in all" or, according to the more felicitous Revised Standard Version, "God may be everything to every one" (1 Cor. 15:28). We will be arguing for an Omega Christology that consists of the decisive encounter at the moment of death between the sinner and the God-man who died to save him from the consequences of his sin. This premise is scripturally sound and within the broad framework of magisterial teaching, especially as elucidated by Saint John Paul II, Benedict XVI, and a number of the most traditional theologians of

2 Joseph Ratzinger, *Eschatology: Death and Eternal Life*, trans. Michael Waldstein and Aidan Nichols, O.P. (Washington, DC: The Catholic University of America Press, 1988), 230.

recent memory. We will simply be gathering together a number of the theological reflections that lend credence to this idea and presenting them as cogently as we can.

There is one feature of Balthasar's work for which he is increasingly well known and which he was forced to defend against much criticism, namely his Holy Saturday theology. We are in good company in expressing great admiration for this particular facet of Balthasar's work, but we do so fully aware that many find this feature of the Swiss theologian's work entirely too original. "Holy Saturday," Balthasar writes in rebuttal, "stands as the mysterious middle between cross and resurrection, and consequently properly in the center of all revelation and theology."[3]

Comparatively speaking this event has received little of the attention that Christians have rightly lavished on the Incarnation, Jesus's earthly ministry, his Crucifixion, and his Resurrection. We want to suggest, however, that it is the event of Holy Saturday that brings each of these more conspicuous events to completion. The relatively scant attention given to this feature of the Paschal Drama is understandable for both scriptural reasons—the New Testament allusions to the events of Holy Saturday being minimal—and eschatological ones—events occurring in a realm beyond the familiar temporal order can be only speculatively approximated, and a healthy distrust of speculation is not misplaced. Nonetheless, for reasons both historical and theological and thanks in large measure to the collaborative work of Hans Urs von Balthasar and the Swiss mystic Adrienne von Speyr, increased attention is being given today to the feature of Christ's Passion, which Christians have largely, and perhaps prudently, been happy to leave undiscussed.

Inasmuch as many of the great doctrines of the Church were fashioned in response to spiritual crises and doctrinal confusions, however, we must neither overlook the scope of the crisis in the midst of which we are living nor fail to recognize forms of

---

3 *The von Balthasar Reader*, ed. Medard Kehland and Werner Löser, trans. Robert J. Daly, S.J. and Fred Lawrence (New York: Crossroad Publishing Co., 1997), 404.

theological maturation that may be required as we strive to respond to it. Joseph Ratzinger writes:

> Whenever people adopt an absolutely fresh starting point for their investigation of historical sources, this is always a telltale sign of some change in consciousness by which they are looking at reality with new eyes, and so getting new answers from it. In our case, it is surely obvious that the sudden intensification of our capacity to pick up the eschatological undertones and overtones of the New Testament must have something to do with the emerging crisis of European civilization.[4]

The "eschatological undertones and overtones" of the New Testament that our challenging circumstances inspire us to ponder more deeply may not be the obvious ones. For it is not likely that we are approaching the end of the world, though that will surely come one day and we have no idea when that will be. What we are likely witnessing is the death or, when circumstances seem less dire, the near-death of the civilization without which the world will very likely descend into chaos. But it will not be the end of the world. It will be yet another phase of what Balthasar termed history's "grinding, pulverizing witches' millhouse of blood and tears." If we can rely on Saint Paul's reassurance that the Christians faced with these challenges can count on a grace commensurate with the hardship they will suffer, that grace, we feel, will consist in part of a rather more fully developed appreciation for the eschatological meaning, not of the end of history, but of each individual's death. And we feel that the extensive work of Hans Urs von Balthasar has laid the theological groundwork for just such an eschatological renewal. Whether this renewal will so revive the faith and ardor of Christians that they will be able to rescue the civilization that rests on a foundation of that faith remains an open question, but it is not unreasonable to hope that those Christians fortified by a renewed eschatology will be able to conduct themselves as Christians in the midst of the cultural upheavals to come.

These trials will be accompanied by the temptation to accede

---

4 Ratzinger, *Eschatology*, 2–3.

to the worldly dismissal of Christianity as sectarian; that is to say as something of interest only to Christians themselves. To adopt that premise is to surrender the precious gift of faith and to betray the responsibility incumbent on Christians: to profess the universal significance of Christ and to account for that claim in ways that are both faithful and intelligible to others. Such efforts will have as their proximate Magisterial expression the aforementioned paragraph 22 of *Gaudium et spes*:

> The truth is that only in the mystery of the incarnate Word does the mystery of man take on light. For Adam, the first man, was a figure of Him Who was to come, namely Christ the Lord. Christ, the final Adam, by the revelation of the mystery of the Father and His love, fully reveals man to man himself and makes his supreme calling clear. (§ 22)

The future Benedict XVI acknowledged the salience of this text with words that help us understand why we are invoking it at this point in our inquiry:

> We are probably justified in saying that here for the first time in an official document of the magisterium, a new type of completely Christocentric theology appears. On the basis of Christ this dares to present theology as anthropology and only becomes radically theological by including man in discourse about God by way of Christ, thus manifesting the deepest unity of theology.[5]

If Christians are being led to a deeper appreciation for a facet of our faith that eluded our predecessors, it is surely not due to either their shortcomings or our greater theological astuteness. The Spirit who leads us to the whole truth not only does so gradually but as historical and spiritual circumstances make the deepening and maturing of faith imperative. Another way of saying this is to say that faith grows and matures in response to circumstances that compel its maturation. We have earlier noted with appreciation how timely have been the contributions of René Girard and Hans Urs von Balthasar to the renewal of faith in our time. We have no reason to regard the appearance of these contributions to Christian self-understanding as merely fortuitous.

5 *Commentary on the Documents of Vatican II*, Vol. 5, 159.

The Spirit who will gradually lead us to the whole truth (Jn. 16:13) will do so as our historical circumstances require the maturation of our faith. As dangerous as it might be to receive a Spirit-revealed truth when lacking the maturity required to live in fidelity to it, there is danger as well in refusing to explore a feature of the Christian revelation which may now be coming into focus—and on which the vitality of the Church and her mission to the world might very well depend—on the grounds that its unambiguous magisterial formulation is still lacking.

History as Christianity understands it is made dynamic by the leavening effect of two interrelated phenomenon: Christ's life, death, and Resurrection and the gradual theological, cultural, and moral discoveries to which this revelation leads and for which it makes the heart restless. The spiritual barb that was driving ancient Israel to a decision is continually at work in post-Easter history to the same end. "Who do you say that I am?" This continues to be the central question, and those with eyes to see can perceive the subtle presence of this question buried deep within the most seminal events of post-Easter history—no less in our day than in earlier ages. The task of demonstrating this inner dynamic of history is obviously a formidable one, and René Girard is among those who have brought to the task the combination of scholarship and creativity that it requires. However breathtaking Christianity's claim to *historical centrality,* Christians make an even more audacious one, namely that Christ's Passion has altered the *ontological circumstances* and *eschatological destiny* of every human who has ever lived or ever will live. "Fundamentally," Balthasar reminds us, "the understanding that comes by faith embraces more truth than it can understand."[6] And we are here entering an area of great mystery that will ever be immune to our attempts to transpose it into discursive thought. But neither are we dispensed from bringing its ultimate reality more into relationship with the lives that lead finally to it. If only those drawing on the perspicacious resources of faith are likely to find the seemingly preposterous claim of universal efficacy convincing, it was Girard's task to provide anthropological and historical

6 Balthasar, *The Office of Peter and the Structure of the Church,* 250.

corroboration for a corollary that might serve to awaken an attitude congenial to its better appreciation, namely that the Christian revelation is the driving force in post-Easter history. Hans Urs von Balthasar has complemented Girard's work by performing the theological reconnoitering of the event of Holy Saturday, offering fresh new insights into the economy of salvation.

# Why Did It Take
# Christ's Descent into Hell?

It is often the case that a time has to become ripe for a new perspective on the Bible, for a new grace of the Holy Spirit who
casts his light upon a till-now little or not at all attended field of
revelation.[1]—Hans Urs von Balthasar

To hold as authentic and pure only the very earliest expression
of the faith with no other standard than this primitiveness itself,
would be the mark of a very shortsighted positivism.[2]—Henri
de Lubac

WE HAVE thus far tried to show that even as its greatest beneficiaries busy themselves in an attempt to marginalize Christianity,
the dreary consequence of their fool's errand is yet another indication that the Paschal Drama—in its once and for all manifestation of two millennia ago, in its unbroken ecclesial and
sacramental contemporaneity, and in its historically inexorable
role as complacent humanity's ineradicable stumbling stone—is
the central animating agent in human history. This may seem a
breathtakingly audacious—indeed outrageous—claim, but it is
meekness itself compared to the theological and eschatological
claims Christians make about the universal effect of the Paschal
Event. Commenting on the passage in 1 Peter 4:6 about Christ's
preaching to the dead, the *Catechism of the Catholic Church* says
this:

> "The gospel was preached even to the dead." The descent into
> hell brings the Gospel message of salvation to complete fulfill-
> ment. This is the last phase of Jesus's messianic mission, a phase

1 *The von Balthasar Reader*, 404.
2 Henri de Lubac, *The Christian Faith: An Essay on the Structure of the Apostles' Creed* (San Francisco: Ignatius Press, 1986), 64.

which is condensed in time but vast in its real significance: the spread of Christ's redemptive work to *all men of all times and all places*, for all who are saved have been made sharers in the redemption. Christ went down into the depths of death so that "the dead will hear the voice of the Son of God, and those who hear will live."[3]

Michelle Schumacher has written that "there is, in fact, very little that the theologian can actually affirm with regard to Christ's actual descent into hell."[4] Perhaps one not formally trained in the queen of the sciences can nonetheless proffer a conjecture or two as to why this rather surprising and curious feature of the overall Paschal drama might have been necessary, all the while recognizing the tentative and speculative nature of these conjectures. If the Cross is the center of the salvific event of the Incarnation, Christ's descent into the realm of the dead on Holy Saturday is the event upon which the universal efficacy of the Passion depends, its extension "to all men of all times and all places." If the universal salvific efficacy of Christianity is to be defended, then the events—on the actual occurrence of which Christianity stands or falls—had to have been as consequential for those who lived prior to them as they were for those living in their historical aftermath. Similarly, they have to have been as consequential for those whose life circumstances deprived them of contact with Christ—whether in the flesh or in his equally efficacious presence in his ecclesial and sacramental Church—as they were for those who had access to these blessings. The Greek Church Fathers found it necessary to speak of the *supra-temporality* of the events on which faith is based. Expanding on a metaphor Balthasar used to explain this facet of the Christian mystery—namely the ripples radiating out in all directions from a stone dropped into the sea—Edward Oakes, S. J. writes:

> With each human life, except for that of Jesus, effects always work forward in time (Charlemagne might still influence us, however distantly, but he had no influence at all on Cicero). Moreover, the influence ineluctably fades (Napoleon's impact on

3 *CCC* §§634-5, italic emphasis added.
4 Schumacher, *A Trinitarian Anthropology*, 348.

contemporary history feels greater than does that of, say, Julius Caesar). But for Jesus to be the effective savior of the world, his stone must drop into history in such a way that *his* ripples go backward and forward. Furthermore, his ripples must reach us with such immediate directness that he remains ever-contemporary to us (this is the work of the Holy Spirit in the sacraments), without the fading away that characterizes all other events of world-historical time. This requirement is, for Balthasar, the reasoning behind that enigmatic line from the First Letter of Peter—which has often puzzled theologians down through the ages—that, after his death, Jesus descended into the underworld "to rescue those spirits in prison who disobeyed God *long ago*" (1 Pet. 3:19–20).[5]

If Jesus descended into the underworld to rescue those spirits in prison who disobeyed God long ago, what about those who disobeyed God not so long ago? From a strictly eschatological point of view, what does the phrase "long ago" really mean? How would those who disobeyed God long ago differ from those who disobeyed God the day before yesterday? Inasmuch as we can hardly unambiguously impute the temporal order of creation to the reality beyond this life, what eschatological connotations might we ascribe to the phrase "long ago?" If the phrase refers to those who lived prior to the full revelation of God in Christ, how would they differ from those living after the revelation but who were nevertheless not exposed to it? And how could those in either of these categories be differentiated from those whose exposure to Christ and his Church were occluded by any number of factors? Even among professed Christians, how many have had a sufficiently unimpaired encounter with Christ for their Yes or No to his summons to be regarded as eschatologically dispositive? The universal impact of Christ's Passion and death is not

---

5 Edward T. Oakes, S.J., *Infinity Dwindles to Infancy*, 366. To Oakes's beautiful image we can only add a corollary alluded to when the Johannine Christ said that when he was raised up (on the Cross and at the Resurrection) he would draw all men to himself. The life, death, and Resurrection of Christ is the one and only point of concavity on the plane of space and time. It draws all things toward itself, both those lives and events that preceded it and those that followed it in chronological time.

limited to those who lived during and after it happened. Every person who ever lived or whoever will live is affected. The question is: how?

Fr. Oakes, one of the finest readers and interpreters of Balthasar's theology, called attention to one of the Swiss theologian's most important insights, namely that Christ's descent into the netherworld is the key to the supra-temporality and therefore to the universality of the Paschal Drama. "The power of Christ," Joseph Ratzinger writes, "reaches out, not just to those who come *after* him (and how strange that would be!), but to everyone, and of course it puts everyone in the position of being free to make his own response."[6]

The relative neglect theology has given to Holy Saturday and to what the Apostles' Creed refers to as Christ's descent into hell left this admittedly enigmatic feature of the overall Paschal Drama languishing in the background where it tended to be treated perfunctorily as Jesus's triumphant rescue of a few righteous pagans and Old Testament patriarchs. This view helped resolve misgivings that would otherwise have arisen with regard to God's justice and mercy in the case of a few of those who lived before Christ. Beyond this, however, Christ's postmortem journey to the netherworld seemed to have little consequence for those living after Christ.

There is no reason not to regard this theological neglect as providential. Not only is there scant scriptural reference to Jesus's descent into the realm of the dead, but it is distinguished by the fact that it is the only feature of the Paschal drama that occurs entirely off stage, and this feature deserves separate attention. If this descent into the netherworld is as important as both the Catholic *Catechism* and one of the Church's most perceptive theologians insist, why are its putative beneficiaries deprived of details that might aid them in their effort to appreciate its meaning? If Jesus's descent into "hell" was solely for the purpose of rescuing the virtuous pagans and Old Testament patriarchs, the event would be of little concern to those living in post-Easter history.

---

6 Ratzinger, *What It Means to Be a Christian*, 50.

But, as we have pointed out, this is not how the descent is under-stood by the Church. So, why are we left with so little scriptural information? It is our surmise that this is the case because this is one of those things—arguably the most significant one—that Jesus had in mind when he told his disciples: "I have yet many things to say to you, but you cannot bear them now. When the Spirit of truth comes, he will guide you into all the truth" (Jn. 16:12–13). The Church will forever be discovering new and deeper mysteries embedded in the Paschal drama and the life of Christ. What part of that mystery we may be as yet unprepared to assim-ilate we cannot know until in the fullness of time it rises into view and we must grapple with its theological integration and meet the moral responsibilities commensurate with it. Fidelity to tradition and the willingness to be led into a deeper understand-ing of that tradition have always been in tension, and this is as it should be. Writes Balthasar:

> In every epoch, the Church comes to look on the Old and New Testaments in a fresh light, gaining understanding for the value of a particular text in the light of its historical setting, its context in religious history and in the history of revelation. The insights thus gained may lead her to propose criticism (often far-reach-ing) of the traditional exegesis; but as a result of some slight transpositions, they may also bring to light new and valid aspects of traditional thought.[7]

One of Balthasar's most prescient readers, Cyril O'Regan, expresses this same insight in an especially lapidary way: "The tradition is an open-ended process of continual excavation, per-petual quarrying of what has not been said, what has not been said adequately about the exigent reality of love and forgiveness which governs all Christian response and makes it possible."[8]

We may regard the mystery of Holy Saturday as one of those things that, for reasons we cannot fathom, the Church had to await in roughly the way that she only very gradually formulated

---

7 Balthasar, *Explorations in Theology, Vol. I*, 271.
8 O'Regan, *The Anatomy of Misremembering*, 135.

the teaching about purgatory as well as the more recent Marian doctrines. In our view, however, Balthasar, in collaboration with Adrienne von Speyr, has both recognized the need and provided the preliminary theological resources for coming to a richer and more fruitful understanding of Holy Saturday, precisely one that will be indispensable for kindling Christian hope anew and in grounding anew Christianity's assertion of universal efficacy.

We have asked if Jesus had to die to save us, why did he have to die at the hands of a raging mob, which the religious and political powers manipulated and to which they themselves were beholden? In asking that question our emphasis was then on the nature of the death Jesus died. We now want to ask why Jesus had to die at all. Of course, the very idea of the Incarnation necessarily implies experiencing what we humans experience, and though death is not *per se* an experience, dying is, and its elimination would seriously compromise the realism of the Incarnation. And yet that merely raises the question about the Incarnation all over again. Was Jesus's death—regardless of how he died—only an incidental reality required in order that the Incarnation be authentic?

We want to try to show that only by dying and undergoing what every human being in the history of the world has or will undergo could Christ enter into the realm of the dead on the same terms as the sinners languishing there, for this is the only realm from which no one is excluded and from which no one is exempt. There and there only can an encounter occur between the One who died for each human who ever lived and each and every one of those for whom he died. The question we want to ask, in other words, is how might it be possible for everyone who ever lived to experience something of what the centurion experienced at the moment of Jesus's death?

Balthasar's proposal, as we are here re-proposing it, provides a scripturally cogent and theologically inspired account of venerable Christian doctrines whose received intellectual underpinnings the contemporary world has largely found wanting. It removes the historical barrier between those privileged to have encountered Christ or to have lived in anticipation of his revelation and those who have had no exposure to him from cradle to grave. Our exploration of this feature of the Christian mystery begins with a crucial passage from the *Summa contra Gentiles* by St. Thomas Aquinas: "To be sure, the power of the divine Incarnation is equal to the salvation of all men, but the fact that some are not saved thereby comes from their indisposition: they are unwilling to take unto themselves the fruit of the Incarnation; they do not cleave to the incarnate God by faith and love."[9]

This would be more satisfying were it not for the obvious fact that the very access to the invitation to "cleave to the incarnate God by faith and love" is hardly uniformly distributed. Any theological defense of Christian universality that rests on a foundation that has not taken into account this immense variation in exposure to Christianity cries out for more refinement. Just as in the redemptive work of the Cross, God, according to Balthasar, "cannot function as a mere Spectator, allegedly immutable and not susceptible to influence," neither can "man, guilty as he is in God's sight, lie passive and anesthetized on the operating table while the cancer of his sin is cut out."[10]

Atonement theories arose out of the need to account for the universal effect of Christ's death and Resurrection. For, as Cardinal Christoph Schönborn, the editor of the *Catechism of the Catholic Church*, has written: "If Christ's death and Resurrection are to be more than just an example for us, if they are *the* divine act of atonement, embracing all times and ages, then this one act must reach out to *all* men."[11] Balthasar has argued that eschatology "is the storm center of the theology of our times,"[12] and the attempt he made to open new ways of understanding the mystery of Holy Saturday placed him at the center of the storm. That storm, however, is no tempest in a teapot; it goes to the very heart of

---

9 *Summa contra Gentiles*, IV, c. 55, 10.

10 Balthasar, *Theo-Drama*, Vol. IV, 318.

11 Christoph Schönborn, *Loving the Church*, trans. John Saward (San Francisco: Ignatius Press, 1998), 64.

12 Balthasar, *Explorations in Theology, Vol. I*, 255.

Christian faith. Of the four last things, many today regard only one of them, death, with the attention it deserves, and many others don't even do that. But Christianity cannot be this careless, for if Christ is who Christians say he is and if the effect of his life, death, and Resurrection are what Christianity declares them to be, then all four of the last things—death, judgment, heaven, and hell—will be fundamentally determined by Christ. The question is, how?

# Atonement

The conceptuality of St. Anselm has now become for us incomprehensible. It is our job to try again to understand the truth that lies behind this mode of expression. There is no doubt that on this point we are faced with a profound evolution of dogma. . . . Somehow today, the answer to these questions can be formulated in a new way.[1]—Emeritus Pope Benedict XVI

AT THE HEART of Christian faith are events that are so unique and so unparalleled in human history that even those who were present at these events groped awkwardly for appropriate analogies and terminology with which to account for their own experiences. This is no doubt in large part because the epicenter of these events was below and beyond what was accessible to human apperception. Those of Jesus's friends and disciples who were present at his death were not privy to its universal repercussions, not to mention its inner-Trinitarian ramifications. Nor, we hasten to add, are we. Neither are we exempt from the task of giving credible witness to these mysteries as best we can, all the while aware that the task of making the mystery of our redemption intelligible will, at best, succeed only in enhancing our appreciation for its unfathomability.

"In Christ," writes Saint Paul, "God was reconciling the world to himself, not counting their trespasses against them, and entrusting to us the message of reconciliation" (2 Cor. 5:19). Ineffable mysteries are recalcitrant to attempts to render them perfectly intelligible to unaided reason. Nonetheless, the Church, her bishops, and her theologians are obliged to give an account of how Christ had managed to reconcile God and man, and these attempts take various paths and employ various images, often

---

1 Reprinted by the *Catholic News Agency*, November 17, 2016.

images taken from worldly forms of economic exchange and the adjudication of justice. Especially since the high Middle Ages, the term that has dominated this swirling theological discussion is atonement, and that was as it should be since the word is virtually a synonym for reconciliation and Christians had long believed that the Passion of Christ had reconciled God and man. In his survey of patristic and medieval theories of atonement, Junius Johnson writes that the term "expresses the idea that the way has been cleared for humans to enter into the desired fellowship with God."[2] The question is how can this be most properly understood?

The Greek Fathers of the Church tended to credit the Incarnation itself as the key to the reconciliation of God and man, inasmuch as Jesus Christ was both God and man. Clear scriptural testimony that the Passion of Christ was decisive for the redemption of fallen man inevitably turned the focus to Jesus's suffering and death. Appeals were made to the metaphor of ransom whereby a prisoner or slave is ransomed from captivity, a theme found prominently in the Old Testament. No sooner had such theories arisen than the metaphors on which they relied led to quite convoluted constructions, which had dubious theological implications, the inadequacies of which it was necessary to rectify. This is less a defect than it is a sign of the undeniableness of a truth which Christians had experienced, but for which they lacked adequate conceptual tools.

Accounting for universal reconciliation was the challenge, and attempts to do so varied in theological cogency and popular appeal. None of them achieved canonical status. Prominent among the attempts to account for this reconciliation were theories of atonement that admittedly relied on forensic principles drawn too uncritically from human systems of justice. The ideal on which the latter depends is epitomized by the blindfolded goddess of justice holding perfectly balanced scales and a sword. The key to such justice is the strict neutrality of the judge, represented by the blindfold. The simple transposition of this principle

2 Junius Johnson, *Patristic and Medieval Atonement Theory* (Lanham, UK: Rowman & Littlefield, 2016), 7.

200

to the question of divine justice overlooks a fact to which both the Old and New Testaments repeatedly testify: that God is not neutral with respect to the creatures he brought into existence precisely for the purpose of bringing them into the Trinitarian embrace. As Margaret Turek has observed:

> On the basis of the paschal mystery a concomitant asymmetry can be discerned with respect to God's self-disposing *vis-à-vis* sinners: rather than manifesting a disposition equally ready to reject as to forgive, the inter-trinitarian work of judgment that occurs in the Christ event shows itself to be a function of absolute benevolent love, love which as trinitarian aims to enable every human being to re-turn together with the Son toward the Father.[3]

The asymmetry of which Turek speaks is all the more germane inasmuch as it is the very Christ who suffered and died in order to save sinners who is to judge the living and the dead (2 Tim. 4:1). Christ is the righteous judge, not because he is blindfolded and neutral, but because he is Love and Mercy itself: "For God sent the Son into the world, not to condemn the world, but that the world might be saved through him" (Jn. 3:17).

The degree to which the principles of worldly justice apply in the altogether different case of the Paschal mystery is questionable, but to downplay the requirement of justice is surely too facile a response. Human justice is and will always be a crude approximation of true eschatological justice. There will ever be complicating and mitigating factors, which man's judicial systems are incapable of factoring into a judgment and largely incapable of knowing with any degree of certainty. The eschatological judgment by which we will be judged at death or in the Final Judgment cannot be hampered by such limitations. That one's life will one day be judged is a fact that should be conducive to moral seriousness, personal honesty with regard to one's behavior, and most of all to a deep and sincere contrition for one's moral failures. In other words, the certainty of a future judgment has as its

---

3  Margaret M. Turek, "Dare We Hope 'That All Men Be Saved,'" *Logos: A Journal of Catholic Thought and Culture*, Vol. 1, no. 3 (Fall 1997): 96.

goal an increased likelihood that the judgment rendered will be a happy one.

Notwithstanding the unsettled state of atonement theology, versions of it—not always the most felicitous versions—hover persistently in the background of Christian accounts of redemption. Nonetheless, Edward Oakes, S.J. writes:

> [T]he church has never solemnly defined one theory of the atonement as better than another, let alone that a particular version advanced by a theologian is heretical. Why that would be so is itself an interesting question, but perhaps it is due to the fact that the New Testament itself seems willing to draw any number of images for the atonement, which, when put into systematic order, do not seem to privilege one image or theory over another.[4]

Especially in light of its adoption by Thomas Aquinas, Fr. Oakes is surely right when he observes: "Anselm's Christology will never lose its relevance, precisely because his thought is so deeply grounded in the tradition, indeed in the Bible's own images and doctrine."[5] For our part, we bring to these weighty matters little more than a Catholic aversion for acts of theological amputation. Whatever might come of the effort to better clarify the Anselmian doctrine of atonement, we would like to suggest that Balthasar's own original Holy Saturday theology promises to provide a more compelling account of the universal salvific efficacy of Christ's Passion than what atonement theology has heretofore been able to provide.

We needn't rehearse all the theological controversies surrounding atonement theology to suggest that after all is said and done, the integral issue is not how to assuage God's wrath or meet the criteria of divine justice, but rather how the flinty human heart, hardened by the habitual rebellion of sin, might be softened and made sufficiently contrite to avail itself of the mercy of a loving God. That this mercy is available is due to the universal efficacy of Christ's Passion, but a theological puzzle remains:

4 Oakes, S. J., *Infinity Dwindles to Infancy*, 179, n.18.
5 Ibid., 184.

how to account for the extension of this mercy to each individual without abrogating God's greatest gift to our species—human freedom. The bond uniting Christ to the creature would seem obviously to apply only to those who have encountered Christ in one form or another in life. But it is precisely this constriction of the scope of Christ's salvific accomplishment that undermines the universality which, in part at least, the atonement theory was formulated to affirm.

With the help of a theological anthropology to which both René Girard and Hans Urs von Balthasar have made enormous contributions, we may come to a better appreciation for the bond between Christ and every person who ever has or ever will live. Christ is at one and the same time the revelation of the Trinity—in whose image and likeness we are made—and the Enfleshed Logos, the blueprint for both creation as such and for the creature made to bring the created order into the Trinitarian *communio*. These facts, for which a well-founded theological anthropology strives to account, are essential to the task of formulating a theory of universal redemption capable of better performing the explanatory role that the various theories of atonement have attempted in ages past and in our own.

# The Inner-Trinitarian Passion

> Where the Son feels himself weakest, he is strongest: the Church Fathers, mystics and theologians have turned their attention to this paradox thousands of times. Outwardly it may seem that men cause Christ's Passion: they put him in chains, scourge and crucify him; they pierce his heart. But inwardly it is a trinitarian action, in which God has the chief role and men are merely supernumeraries.[1]—Hans Urs von Balthasar

JESUS had warm relationships with his friends and disciples, but in a very real sense, and speaking socially, he was the loneliest man who ever lived. While his life was the Enfleshed Logos, the very revelation of the nature and meaning of the human vocation to which every person is divinely called, he was at the same time in a category of one. His one intimate lifeline is with the Father. The place therefore to begin an exploration of the mystery of Holy Saturday, which may hold an important key to the retrieval of an Alpha and Omega Christology—and which, in turn, may deepen the faith and embolden the witness of contemporary Christians—is the Agony in the Garden: "The Garden of Olives, where the cosmic struggle between the nature of God and the nature of the world took place within a single soul, is not only the center of Christ's work but also the core of the syntheses that were intended to achieve the redemption of all creation by drawing it step by step toward God."[2]

Thus does Balthasar in his study of the seventh century Byzantine theologian, Maximus the Confessor, underscore the importance of Christ's Agony in the Garden. The Incarnation of the second divine Person of the Trinity, Balthasar writes, "does not

---

1 Balthasar, *Truth is Symphonic*, 43.
2 Balthasar, *Cosmic Liturgy*, 271.

leave the inter-relationship of those Persons unaffected."[3] And the first clear hint of the otherwise veiled intra-Trinitarian drama takes place in the Garden of Olives. The curtain goes up on the central event in the drama of salvation. The scene is a garden, reminiscent of the garden in the Genesis story in which humanity's aboriginal rebellion occurred.

In all three Synoptic Gospels, the confession of Peter—his recognition of Jesus as the Messiah, the Son of the Living God (Mt. 16:16)—was followed closely by the Transfiguration at which three disciples were present: Peter, James, and John. It was with these three disciples that Jesus was most intimate. It was to them that his utter uniqueness was unmistakably revealed on Mount Tabor where Jesus's divine Sonship and the Trinitarian reality consonant with it broke through: "This is my beloved Son, with whom I am well pleased; listen to him" (Mk. 9:7). It was likewise only Peter and these sons of Zebedee who were present when Jesus raised the daughter of Jairus from death. As though He was preparing them for a subsequent event—the Agony in the Garden—which might otherwise have been injurious or fatal to their faith in Jesus without this preparatory glimpse of his divine provenance, these, his closest disciples, saw Jesus with Moses and Elijah. Once their eyes had adjusted to the astounding scene of Jesus conversing on equal terms with the proverbial representatives of the Law and the Prophets, his venerable interlocutors disappeared, and "a cloud overshadowed them, and a voice came out of the cloud, 'This is my beloved Son; listen to him.' And suddenly, looking around, they no longer saw anyone with them but Jesus only" (Mk 9:7–8). Gently but authoritatively the disciples had been led to the realization of Jesus's utter incomparability. He is the "beloved Son." The Transfiguration served as the necessary preparation for Jesus's Agony in the Garden of Gethsemane which only these same three disciples witnessed. Arguably even more than the horrors of the crucifixion itself, the Agony in the Garden that preceded it was so disconcerting that only those who had already experienced the revelation of Jesus's divine Son-

---

3 Hans Urs von Balthasar, *Mysterium Paschale: The Mystery of Easter*, trans. Aidan Nichols, O.P. (San Francisco: Ignatius Press, 2000), 30.

ship on Mount Tabor could have safely been exposed to the dark hour of Jesus's anguish at Gethsemane.

The Jews who comprised Jesus's inner circle of friends were neither Hellenized stoics nor death-defying zealots, but they lived in a cultural milieu in which facing death with the resigned serenity of a Socrates or the unflinching defiance of Jewish martyrs was regarded as a reliable measure of one's spiritual stature. Even after experiencing the Transfiguration, the disciples closed their eyes to Jesus's agony. That the evangelists attribute this to weariness and drowsiness hardly distracts from the essential point. Though Jesus's closest disciples physically accompanied him in his hour of agony, and despite the fact that they had been prepared for it on Tabor, they took shelter from the full impact of the event in a lethargy that was more likely to have been a reflexive act of inattention than sleep as such. For, however shocking it must have been to those in earshot of it, the content of Jesus's prayer made its way into the gospel accounts. Moreover, apparently alluding to each of these unforgettable experiences—the Transfiguration and the Agony in the Garden—Peter drew on the strength of what he had witnessed firsthand to exhort the presbyters, reminding them that he was a "witness to the sufferings of Christ and one who has a share in the glory to be revealed" (1 Pet. 5:1). What Jesus's closest friends glimpsed in each of these situations without full comprehension, as Balthasar has argued, were the external signs of an event taking place in the heart of the Triune God.

Not only Jesus's weary disciples, but we too have allowed our fatigue to overtake us when it comes to that part of Jesus's Passion inaugurated in the garden. To see his agony as a recoiling in the face of a terrible death is to fend off a more troubling implication. Jesus is "sorrowful even to death." Before any of the physical tortures begin, he is dying of extreme sadness (peri-lupos), a sorrow unimaginable to us sinners. If we keep that sorrow in mind we will better appreciate the nature of Jesus's suffering, for sorrow remains the Passion's inner core throughout.

It is to be remembered here that the inner condition of the sinner is rarely the inner experience of the sinner. Sin is suffering in its larval stage. Suffering is sin in its symptomatic stage, and godforsakenness is its final terminus. Count it as more evidence of original sin that however profoundly contrite we sinners may be, sin has so invaded our physiology, psychology, and affectivity that we are incapable of experiencing the "sorrow unto death" that a sinless person would experience if he were to consent to be "made sin" on behalf of sinners. Writes Balthasar: "It can even be said that no one can suffer being forsaken by God more profoundly than the Son, whose whole life was unity with the Father, whose meat and drink it was to do his will."[4]

To remove the sin externally, so to speak, to undergo the suffering that sin sets in motion without undergoing the godforsakenness that constitutes its ultimate essence, would be to pluck sin's leaves and leave its rhizome to send up fresh new shoots elsewhere in the garden. This is why it is inadequate—not false—but inadequate to say that Christ came to forgive sins. He came to take away *the* sin of the world—man's ruse for aggregating sins and transforming them into cheap righteousness at the expense of the victims on whom the violence born of sin is vented. If sins are to be forgiven, they must first be recognized for what they are, and for this to happen, the demonic mechanism for evading that recognition had to be crippled. This took place on Golgotha, but if Christ was to rescue all those in bondage to sin—past, present, and future—he would have to reach into its godforsaken core in his own suffering and Passion, there to conquer sin at its monstrous and paralytic worst.

The gospel accounts of the Agony in the Garden foreground Jesus's experience of the loss of companionship at the moment of his great trial, but this receding of human solidarity is the analogue at the human level of a far greater isolation into which Jesus was slipping now that his "hour" had come. On the mountain, the voice of the Father was heard declaring Jesus to be his beloved Son. In the garden, Jesus cries out to his heavenly Father, pleading not simply to be spared the unthinkable tortures to which those executed by crucifixion were subjected, but, at a deeper and vastly more consequential level, not to be cut off

4 Hans Urs von Balthasar, *Does Jesus Know Us?—Do We Know Him?*, trans. Graham Harrison (San Francisco: Ignatius Press, 1983), 36.

from the relationship on which his very existence depended. No heavenly response was forthcoming. Taken together, the Father's silence and the disciples' incapacity to accompany him indicate that *the hour* had finally come. For this is the essence of that hour to which Jesus has consented: abandonment. Henri de Lubac once remarked that he who suffers well hasn't suffered yet, and Simone Weil once noted that countless Christian martyrs have gone to their deaths singing, thanks to the One who went to his death unconsoled. Those who suffer well are able to do so because of some consolation, moral or eschatological. Christians derive the greatest eschatological consolation of all from the agony of the God-man who knew no such consolation, and many non-believers are consoled by an aura of hope with which a society under Christian influence is suffused.

We will have occasion to point out that the sacramental sensibilities which it has been the historical privilege of Catholic Christianity to awaken are essential for recognizing in the concrete details of history the scriptural intimations of "things unseen." Here in the Garden of Gethsemane we are allowed to catch the first glimpse of the intra-Trinitarian drama, the consequences of which are incomparably greater than even those vastly underestimated historical and cultural consequences of Christ's Passion which are available to the senses and to historical and cultural analysis.

## The Cry of the Godforsaken

From René Girard's perspective, the Cross—understood as the revelation of "things hidden since the foundation of the world"—is the "place" to which fallen humanity, driven to ever greater violence by a mimeticism whose religious ordination it has failed to recognize, returns again and again in order to "take away the *sins* of the world" by committing there the *Sin* of the world, the ritual immolation or expulsion upon which human culture has always depended. Just as it is anthropologically correct, therefore, to say that sins eventually accumulate at the foot of the Cross, it is eschatologically correct to say that sins reach their absolute nadir in godforsakenness, and that, unless repented, sins eventually accumulate at the "place" of godforsakenness. Christ, who went to the Cross to ram a stick in the spokes of the ritual for transforming sin into the delusion of righteousness, also went to the realm of lifeless lovelessness, there to break the power of sin at its most hideous godforsakenness simply by sharing—and therefore shattering—the alienated condition of the sinners languishing there. By undergoing the unsurpassable godforsakenness which only God himself could experience, Christ has suffered the supreme weight of sin. He drank to the dregs the sin of the world. He has gone to the depths. The crucified Christ, writes Balthasar, "does not simply suffer the hell deserved by sinners; he suffers something below and beyond this, namely being forsaken by God in the pure obedience of love. Only he as Son is capable of this, and it is qualitatively deeper than any possible hell."[5]

The clearest indication of this ultimate intra-Trinitarian play-within-the-play is the cry of dereliction which brings the anguish that must have shaken Jesus's three disciples in the garden of Gethsemane to its truly shocking conclusion: "From noon onward, darkness came over the whole land until three in the afternoon. And about three o'clock Jesus cried out in a loud voice, *Eli, Eli, lema sabachthani?* which means, My God, my God, why have you forsaken me?" (Mt. 27:45–46).

Theologians as distinguished as Thomas Aquinas and the Church's Magisterium have been reluctant to take these startling words at face value, often suggesting that Jesus retained throughout his Passion and death an unproblematic relationship with his heavenly Father. Most who hold such a view are quick to propose caveats lest it evacuate the Passion of its most obvious features. Attempts to reassure the faithful of an uninterrupted and tranquil rapport between the Father and Son during the Passion, writes Jacques Servais, S. J., "scarcely make the central mystery of the Credo more accessible to believers."[6] Balthasar faults both Anselm and Karl Rahner for focusing exclusively on Christ's

---

5 Balthasar, *Theo-Drama*, Vol. V, 277.

6 Jacques Servais, S.J. "The 'Pro Nobis' in the Consciousness of Jesus," *To the Heart of the Mystery of Redemption*, trans. Anne Englund Nash (San Francisco: Ignatius Press, 2010), 103.

death, and he laments the fact that Thomas Aquinas treats the Passion as a purely bodily event, "with no emphasis whatsoever on Christ's abandonment by God as the center of the Passion."[7] It is surely possible for a theologian to call attention to the relative neglect shown by the stark suggestion of Christ's godforsakenness without going as far as Balthasar goes here in declaring it to be the center of the Passion itself, but it is that claim that deserves our attention. For it is the key to restoring Holy Saturday to its rightful place in Christian thought, and it makes a new understanding of the universal efficacy of Christ's Passion possible.

The fact that both Matthew and Mark refuse to translate this cry of godforsakenness make its historical authenticity all but impossible to deny. The words are from Psalm 22, verse 2, and attempts have been made to soften their shocking implications by reference to the fact that the psalm ends on a more reassuring note. But how likely is it that Jesus, at the nadir of his anguish, was employing a clever literary allusion? It is far more likely that the words that so seared the imaginations of those who heard Jesus utter them meant exactly what they literally mean, and that all the stunned witnesses could do was to render them as faithfully as possible—retaining even in the gospels written in Greek the Aramaic used by Jesus and other Judean Jews at the time. We can be grateful for their reluctance to patch over the scandal that these words must surely have been when they were uttered. We are reminded what an indelible mark these words would have left on those present at the crucifixion when the author of the Letter to the Hebrews declares that Jesus "offered prayers and supplications with loud cries and tears to the one who was able to save him from death" (Heb. 5:7). Writes Fleming Rutledge:

> If Christ entered into Godforsakenness, and if hell is the absence of God, then something happened to him that was unprecedented. God was separated from God—while still remaining God.[8]

7 Balthasar, *Theo-Drama*, Vol. IV, 264.

8 Fleming Rutledge, *The Crucifixion: Understanding the Death of Jesus Christ* (Grand Rapids, MI: Eerdmans, 2015), 407.

We will take up the question of God's wrath below, but suffice it here to say that its essence is godforsakenness. No one who has experienced the least hint of real existential alienation will think it less representative of hell than the kind of physical tortures Christians have too often associated with divine wrath. And so it is here in the cry of dereliction that we see hints of the hidden drama: the beginning of an inner-Trinitarian estrangement, which is the necessary corollary to Jesus's taking on himself the sins of the world. He cannot drag the Father into the Passion which it is his mission to undergo. He can rely only on the Spirit, who has mediated his mission to him moment by moment, to sustain a rapport with the Father of which he will necessarily no longer be a conscious participant. Balthasar describes this hiatus within the Trinity as "a requirement utterly unknown and unimagined, a demand that 'convulses' [Jesus's] whole being to its core, like an earthquake." On the Cross, Jesus—the God-Man—undergoes godforsakenness, thereby shaking, as Balthasar has written, "the foundation upon which the eternal relationship between Father and Son rests."[9] That relationship is the very source of the created order. So it is by bearing in mind, as Jacques Servais reminds us, that the salvific event "concerns creation as a whole" that theological reflection, tempted under such circumstances to take refuge in mythology, must bring into focus the intrinsic Christological link between creation and redemption. For the Logos through whom all things came to be (Jn. 1:3) is the same Logos incarnate in Jesus of Nazareth. Christ as Logos incarnate, in a rather technical formulation by Balthasar, is "a form-phenomenon which comprises within itself both God and world."[10] He is both with God and God himself, the Trinitarian perichoresis constituting precisely the heart of all reality—*perichoresis* being the Greek term used by John Damascene, the eighth century patriarch of Jerusalem, to

9 Hans Urs von Balthasar, *You Have Words of Eternal Life*, trans. Dennis Martin (San Francisco: Ignatius Press, 2004), 147.

10 Balthasar, *The Glory of the Lord, Vol. I*, 154.

refer to the identity-in-otherness of the intra-Trinitarian *communio*.[11]

And now, nothing less dramatic is taking place on Golgotha than a caesura in that perichoresis. Like a cardiologist stopping a patient's heart for a moment in order to restore the proper rhythm, the Trinitarian Heart of the World, the ontological underpinnings of the created order itself, is for one terrible moment in time interrupted in order to restore to creation its original self-sacrificial rhythm. The metaphor is aptly subtle. The interruption is not a rupture but a "momentary" cessation, the interim nature of which Jesus is necessarily unaware. Nonetheless, the break between the Father and the Son, in the words of Martin Bieler, represents "not the end of their love, but on the contrary its resilience under changed conditions."[12] We find a faint scriptural foreshadowing of this in Isaiah, where divine wrath not only serves a redemptive purpose but requires a temporal interruption in the Lord's covenantal solicitude:

> For a brief moment I abandoned you,
> but with great tenderness I will take you back.
> In an outburst of wrath, for a moment
> I hid my face from you;
> But with enduring love I take pity on you,
> says the Lord, your redeemer. (Isaiah 54:7–8)

Here wrath, indeed great wrath suggested by the phrase "an outburst of wrath," appears not only as abandonment, but also as an episode in an ongoing but momentarily eclipsed covenantal relationship, which can be restored to health only by a reparative interruption. The remedial efficacy of the wrath constituted by

---

11 Even though Girard is too reticent to speak in such terms (my own importuning having been to no avail), and perhaps because he is too prudent to appeal to such theologically esoteric terminology, it has been Girard's life work, I believe, to sketch the outlines of just the sort of perichoretic anthropology required to understand creatures made in the image and likeness of the trinitarian God.

12 Martin Bieler, "God and the Cross: The Doctrine of God in the Work of Hans Urs von Balthasar," *Communio: International Catholic Review* Vol. XLII (Spring 2015): 70.

the veiling of the divine countenance is the absence of any confidence in its transitory nature:

> There is a cry that penetrates all the cool pharisaism of our alleged religiosity: "My God, my God, why have you forsaken me?" In the darkest night of the soul, while every fiber of his body is in pain, and he experiences extreme thirst for God, for lost love, he *atones* for our comfortable indifference.[13]

Both our comfort and the indifference it helps to foster can be traced in part to the fact that we live downstream from the atoning Event and in cultures profoundly shaped by it. In other words, unaware though we may be of this fact, we live buoyed by consolations that first washed over the world at the Resurrection, consolations that were the fruit of unconsoled suffering.

Reflecting on the Agony in the Garden, Balthasar writes that "the Father measures out for [the Son] the part of his divine consciousness that he needs . . . according to the demands of his mission."[14] Solomon only prayed for the wisdom required by his royal mission (1 Kings 8:22–61), and Virgil's Anchises tells his son Aeneas to concern himself only with the matters pertinent to founding of Rome and the furtherance of the governing role assigned to it (Aeneid VI: 1235–37). This same epistemic concentration on the matters pertaining to his salvific mission was operative in the case of Jesus. He wished to know only what he needed to know for the fulfillment of his mission. (St. Paul's insistence that he preached nothing more and nothing less than Christ crucified is an apt analogue of this.) Jesus predicted both his Passion and his Resurrection, but these predictions—which the Evangelists have in all likelihood retrospectively reworked—were forthcoming prior to his plunge into the depths of his suffering, in the midst of which any consoling knowledge of his Easter triumph would have constituted a source of moral and spiritual reassurance incompatible with his mission of becoming sin and entering into the experience of godforsakenness. Writes Balthasar:

---

13 Balthasar, *You Crown the Year with Your Goodness*, trans. Graham Harrison (San Francisco: Ignatius Press, 1989), Kindle edition §1085, italic emphasis added.

14 Balthasar, *To the Heart of the Mystery of Redemption*, 81.

# The Inner-Trinitarian Passion

[T]here are some things that must be clear to Jesus as the divine revealer of the Father himself, which he must conceal because only so can he show the essential hiddenness of God; there are other things known to him that he conceals, because, although he is "Lord and Master," he must display the form of a slave; and finally there are some which he must do without knowing, because otherwise the form of a slave and "being like man" (Phil. 2.7) would not be genuine.[15]

Christ, writes Jacques Servais, S.J., "makes no plan, he sets no personal norm or ideal for himself. The only 'rule' he wishes to obey is the one dictated at every instant and in ever unexpected ways by the Holy Spirit, who represents for him the will of the Father."[16] It is here that a feature of Trinitarian theology throws a light on an anthropological issue of very considerable significance, namely the question of volition and the complex reality of human freedom. Jesus was free beyond anything we can imagine, and yet his freedom was inseparable from his obedience to the will of his Father. Up to the moment when he was "handed over" and became a mere object in the hands of his persecutors, the will of his heavenly Father was mediated to him by the Spirit. Christ was the Script (*Logos*) but he was neither its Author (the Father) nor its sanctifying Choreographer (the Spirit). His was a life lived entirely free precisely because he was entirely docile to the will of the Father as it was mediated by the Spirit. In fact, the act of will, in contrast to the state of being willing, hardly even manifests itself in the life of Jesus, except to say that he wills what the Father wills for him. The role of the Spirit here comes to the fore. Jesus's mission is to live out for all to see the manifestation in human existence of the "inner-Trinitarian ecstasy." He remains remarkably untroubled by the many instances in which his message was lost on those to whom he came to deliver it, but his equanimity in the face of rejection is a feature of his confidence that his was the task of surrendering himself, and that the task of showering the commensurate blessings and assigning the corresponding historical responsibilities would fall to the third Hypostasis of the Trin-

---

15 Balthasar, *The Glory of the Lord, Vol. VII*, 325.
16 Balthasar, *To the Heart of the Mystery of Redemption*, 115.

ity, the Holy Spirit. His mission was to leave an indelible and unforgettable imprint on the human imagination of the basic contours of the human vocation.

On the Cross atonement becomes inseparable and largely indistinguishable from abandonment or, more specifically, godforsakenness. To become sin is to take on oneself the final consequences of sin. The God-Man, Jesus underwent this abandonment at two levels. Handed over as only a lifeless object can be handed over, he was the repository of the "wrath" of his righteous contemporaries who took from him his life. As the One who had become sin, he suffered the "wrath" of God, which is the abandonment by the Father. He submitted to a caesura in the Father's sustaining, life-giving love. Thus he took upon himself the "wrath" of sinful humanity as well as the "wrath" of God, the latter being the godforsakenness to which those who reject and revile God condemn themselves. A proper understanding of the atonement is impossible in our view without recognizing divine "wrath" as the godforsakenness suffered by those who have themselves forsaken God. The scant scriptural references to Jesus's descent into the realm of the dead both allude to and veil the full eschatological ramifications of the mystery Balthasar has asked us to reexamine.

Christians and others have long associated perdition with images of gruesome physical torture drawn from Scripture, explicated and elaborated by theologians, and richly embroidered by the popular imagination. Those who have learned to associate the sufferings of hell with Dantesque torments and the ghastly images of the Last Judgment found on the tympanums and doors of many cathedrals might be tempted to think of mere godforsakenness as a welcome alternative. It is easier for us to associate hell with these garish depictions of eternal torment than it is to think of godforsakenness as constituting the very essence of hell. There are several reasons for this. Those who take seriously the prospect of damnation tend to be the beneficiaries of the religious tradition that has encouraged that concern, and as long as they remain within the orbit of a believing community, however remote from its center or religiously disaffected they might be, they enjoy a degree of immunity from the experience of godforsakenness, the unmitigated versions of which they are then likely to vastly underestimate. Those, on the other hand, who have had a brush with real godforsakenness may not recognize it as such precisely because a correct diagnosis of godforsakenness presupposes a degree of spiritual lucidity that is incompatible with godforsakenness.

The richer one's experience of God, the greater the devastation of godforsakenness. Even the experiences of godforsakenness of which we humans are capable, however, are but pale approximations of the unparalleled godforsakenness of which Christ as the Second Person of the Divine Trinity was capable. Even though we who are made in the image and likeness of the Triune God can experience godforsakenness by betraying that image and besmirching that likeness, the relationship we thereby compromise is a covenantal and not a hypostatic one. For the Second Person of the Trinity to undergo godforsakenness is a seeming impossibility, so much so that we prefer to join with the three disciples in the garden and avert our eyes, to treat the godforsakenness of Christ as something other than godforsakenness, to bracket it in some way. In fact, it is the key to understanding the deeper meaning of the Passion.

All efforts to mitigate the meaning of this cry of godforsakenness undercut the mystery they seek to preserve. "The man who cries out knows only that he is forsaken," writes Balthasar; "in this darkness he no longer knows why. He is not permitted to know why, for the idea that the darkness he is undergoing might be on behalf of others would constitute a certain comfort; it would give him a ray of light."[17] At this stage the mortal anguish, which his closest disciples were reluctant to witness at Gethsemane, erupts into something that is not only far more shocking but far more public as well. It was witnessed by all those present at the execution: his persecutors, those taunting him, and those few followers courageous enough to have been within earshot.

The rending of the Father and the Son on the Cross, writes Bal-

---

17 Balthasar, *You Crown the Year with Your Goodness*, Kindle edition §1138 ff.

thasar, "is in truth the ultimate revelation of the tri-personality of God."[18] What prevents this interruption from becoming a world-annihilating breach is that it occurs within the bond of love between the Father and Son—preserved intact by the love of the Holy Spirit. Thus preserved in the very act that both veils and exemplifies it, the Son and the Father are most intimate at the very moment of the Son's godforsakenness. "In this wrathful alienation," writes Balthasar, "Father and Son are closer together than ever."[19] Even as the relationship between the Father and the Son enters into this godforsakenness, observes Martin Bieler, "the bliss of unbroken love" between them survives.[20] At every level the mystery of our redemption is unavoidably paradoxical. "Even when Fatherforsaken," writes John Saward, Jesus is "Father-centered." In fact, simultaneous experience of being Fatherforsaken and Father-centered is the essence of Jesus's Godforsakenness.

The question of divine impassibility so central to patristic thought has been widely challenged in our day. It was not a doctrine that was arrived at casually, and to dismiss it would have broad and serious theological ramifications. For Balthasar, the unreserved and unguarded self-gift that constitutes the life of the Trinity becomes suffering when exposed to the calculating strategies of self-preservation rooted in sin. This stops short of saying that there is suffering in God; rather it reframes the whole problem of divine impassibility. It recognizes "recklessness" and "self-lessness" as the unguarded essence of Trinitarian love, which leaves the Incarnate God defenseless in his encounter with sin. This defenselessness survives as well in the Eucharistic self-offering that deposits the seeds of the Trinitarian self-giving aspiration in both human history and the human heart.

Setting the thorny question of divine impassibility to one side, we would ask a related and rather inelegantly formulated question: Was the outcome of Christ's incarnation and death a foregone

18  Balthasar, *To the Heart of the Mystery of Redemption*, 38.

19  Balthasar, *Theo-Drama, Vol. IV*, 349.

20  Bieler, "God and the Cross," 84.

conclusion, or did something hang in the balance? However the outcome might have been foreknown by divine omniscience (a premise that is itself analogical), was something at stake? Was the Passion of Christ truly dramatic? Did Jesus's Passion pose any risk for the Triune God and for the created order stamped with a Trinitarian ordination? Having chosen to bring the created order into the Trinitarian communion through the one creature endowed with true and truly consequential freedom, was the outcome of the plan of redemption—foreseen by omniscience though it was—nonetheless truly dramatic? Was there a divine gamble on the outcome of which both Jesus's Resurrection and the continued existence of the created order itself depended? "Is there not, right from the start," writes Balthasar, "something we might call 'hope' on the part of Father and Spirit, namely, the hope that the Son's mission will succeed?"[21]

Whatever unimaginable degree of divine condescension the Incarnation itself must have entailed, might we not draw closer to the heart of what Balthasar calls the theo-drama by framing Christ's culminating plunge into the realm of sin and death as quite literally the greatest gamble of all time: the "momentary" interruption within the Trinity of the world-sustaining exchange between the Divine Persons. As preposterous as this may sound, no one has captured this possibility better than did Joseph Ratzinger. Commenting on Jesus's death on the Cross, he writes:

> When the human instrument comes to fall away, the spiritual action which is founded on it also disappears, temporarily. Thus something more is shattered here than in any ordinary death. *There is an interruption of that dialogue which in reality is the axis of the whole world.* The cry of agony in Psalm 21, "My God, my God, why hast thou forsaken me," makes us perceive something of the depths of this process.[22]

The Passion of Christ consists of a series of *the* most important events in history and beyond, but these events are also—and even more importantly—traces of and evidence for an inner-Trinitar-

21 Balthasar, *Theo-Drama, Vol. V,* 181.

22 Joseph Ratzinger, *Journey Towards Easter,* trans. Dame Mary Groves, OSB (New York: Crossroad Publishing, 1987), 109; my italic emphasis.

ian event of literally earthshaking scope and consequence. For what is at stake is the survival of the created order, imperiled by man's misused gift of freedom and threatening the irreversible disfiguration of creatures divinely destined for participation in the communion of Trinitarian Love. Giorgio Buccellati saw the cosmic peril implicit in Christ's godforsakenness prefigured in Jesus's temptation in the wilderness:

> In the tempter's view, the possibility that Jesus might succumb to temptation would have caused a seismic rupture such as to rent asunder (again, in his view) the very core of trinitarian life, hence the order of being in its integrity. If so, it was by avoiding sin that Jesus saved the whole of reality from ontological collapse.[23]

The possibility that a sundering within the Trinity would mean the ontological collapse of "the whole of reality" provides a glimpse into the deeper drama underlying those aspects of the Passion that are accessible to the senses. For Scripture links the devil's wilderness attempt to produce the "seismic rupture" by seducing Jesus into sin with a subsequent assault, which we have every reason to presume had the same goal. "When the devil had finished every temptation, he departed from him *for a time*" (Lk. 4:13). Exegetes agree that this is a reference to the devil's return at the time of Jesus's Passion, and the stakes in this latter confrontation are certainly no less breathtaking than those Buccellati recognizes in the background of the wilderness temptations. On Golgotha Jesus enters into a far darker and more desolate wilderness than the one in which he wandered at the onset of his public mission. Buccellati boldly suggests what these confrontations entailed at their deepest level, namely an attempt to fracture "the very core of trinitarian life." Satan, as Goethe's *Faust* has it, is the dark (non)being who would "ever do evil but ever does good." In that sense, it can be said that Satan's wilderness assault is re-launched at a most propitious moment, the moment when the plan of redemption required an arrhythmic caesura in the Trinitarian perichoresis on which all created reality—cosmic, his-

23 Giorgio Buccellati, "Trinity Spermatiké: The Veiled Perception of a Pagan World (Part 2)," *Communio: International Catholic Review* Vol. XL, No. 1 (Spring 2013): 116.

torical, and eschatological—depends. The attractive and assimilating love at the center of creation itself, the uncreated center which orders created reality, is put at risk for the sake of the lost sheep beloved of God, called by God, and made for communion with God, the only species sufficiently endowed with freedom to be capable of love but that ever and again betrays its high calling, frustrating the plan of creation and threatening to do so irreparably. "Human thought and human language," writes Balthasar, "break down in the presence of this mystery."[24]

With a great deal of help from the theologian who issued that warning, we will proceed with caution, but the mystery we are here circumambulating is such that we can hardly do justice to it by restricting ourselves to boilerplate theological formulations and conventional figures of speech. What was at stake in the wilderness temptations was the bonding power by which the Divine Trinity retains its oneness, the secret ontological source of creation itself. This is even more the case later in Jesus's Passion as he descended into the darkness that he saw approaching in the garden at Gethsemane. For our sake, Saint Paul tells us, "Jesus was made to be sin who knew no sin" (2 Cor. 5:21). He who would remain sinless in the face of the wilderness temptations was ever sinless, but in order to reach into the infected and cancerous heart of sin, he became sin, entering into godforsakenness with consequences for the otherwise inviolable hypostatic communion of Father and Son and for the order of creation dependent upon it. As precarious as was Christ's taking on himself the sin of the world, this was the reason why the Son condescended to pitch his tent among us.

Not only is Christ's abandonment—his godforsakenness—at the heart of his atoning triumph, but it is also—and paradoxically—the essential feature of his revelation of the truth about God. As Benedict XVI put it in his encyclical *Spe Salvi*: "God now reveals his true face in the figure of the sufferer who shares man's God-forsaken condition by taking it upon himself."[25] Writes Balthasar:

---

24 Balthasar, *Mysterium Paschale*, 30.
25 *Spe Salvi*, §43.

If Jesus has suffered on the cross the sin of the world to the very last truth of this sin, namely godforsakenness, then he must experience, in solidarity with the sinners who have gone to the underworld, their—ultimately hopeless—separation from God; otherwise he would not have known all the phases and conditions of what it means for man to be unredeemed yet awaiting redemption.[26]

Just as the Eucharistic Last Supper is the sacramental prefiguration of the inner meaning of the Passion, so the events of the Passion themselves, their facticity and historicity notwithstanding, provide a glimpse into an intra-Trinitarian drama, which it was Balthasar's special mission to foreground. To come to the Christian mystery with a sacramental sensibility, as one must, is to realize that the greater the historical verisimilitude of any given scriptural passage, the greater is its potential for serving as "evidence of things not seen" (Heb. 11:1). Writes Balthasar: "Without the Cross and the Blood of the Cross, and without the permanent wounds of the risen Lord, we would never have guessed the depth of the mystery of the Trinity."[27]

"The anthropocentric tendency," writes Balthasar, "will never be able to keep within view the Trinitarian background of the Cross."[28] The cultural and historical *consequences* of the death of Jesus on Golgotha are so sweeping, so ubiquitous, and so interwoven with post-Paschal world history—especially in those societies that have fallen under Christian influence—that we hardly recognize their Christian source any more. But the *mystery* of the Cross, its world-transcending importance, is far more elusive, for it represents nothing less than an irruption into human history of the timeless Trinitarian reality of God's loving self-gift. "The cross of the New Testament," writes Norbert Hoffmann, "sinks its roots deep into the very being of God."[29]

Lest the idea of a caesura within the Trinity seem utterly heret-

---

26 Balthasar, *Explorations in Theology, Vol. IV*, 408.

27 Balthasar, *Theo-Drama, Vol. V*, 478.

28 Balthasar, *Mysterium Paschale*, 140.

29 Norbert Hoffmann, "Atonement and Ontological Coherence," *Toward a Civilization of Love* (San Francisco: Ignatius Press, 1985), 232.

ical, another of Adrienne von Speyr's insights is to be remembered: "The Father is never more present," writes von Speyr, "than in this absence on the Cross."[30] This is confirmed in the lives of saints and mystics who have testified to the apparent indistinguishability between the presence and the absence of God.

## The Expiration

An incarnational theology requires a sacramental sensibility alert to the theological and eschatological resonances of both the scriptural data and historical events. Far from distrusting the empirical realism of scriptural texts, a sacramental sensibility examines the evidentiary data with greater attentiveness than would otherwise be the case. For instance, experts in forensic medicine have suggested that due to the nature of execution by crucifixion, Jesus was likely to have died from suffocation, preceded by the autonomic gasping for oxygen. Such witnesses as may have been present at his death would have had no trouble recognizing the moment of death: the dreadful moment when Jesus's heavy heaving fell silent. Those of us who have been present at the death of a loved one, however serene and natural such a death might have been in comparison to Jesus's torture, know something of how emotionally intense and religiously profound is the moment of the dying person's last breath. We might regard the religious profundity of such a moment as a faint analogue of the intense experience Jesus's death was for those who witnessed it. They experienced Jesus's last breath as a stirring within themselves of a Spirit somehow cognate with the *expiring* Jesus, though all this would remain inchoate until Pentecost, at which the ex-piration of the crucified Jesus returned as the in-spiration that would henceforth oxygenate and animate his body the Church.

Jesus's body had been "handed over" to his executioners and those calling for his death, but what he retained was the capacity to hand over his Spirit. His breath was choked out of him, but his Spirit, perfectly symbolized by his breath, was his to dispose of in fidelity to his mission. Each of the Evangelists has referred to

30 Quoted: Balthasar, *Theo-Logic, Vol. II*, 352.

Jesus's final breath, and we can be sure that eyewitnesses are in the background of their accounts of this solemn moment.

> "Jesus gave a loud cry and breathed his last" (Mk. 15:37).
> "Jesus cried out again in a loud voice, and gave up his spirit" (Mt. 27:50).
> "Jesus cried out in a loud voice, 'Father, into your hands I commend my spirit'; and when he had said this he breathed his last" (Lk. 23:46).
> "When Jesus had taken the wine, he said, 'It is finished.' And bowing his head, he handed over the spirit" (Jn. 19:30).

With Jesus's last breath, we come to the threshold of the great silence of Holy Saturday and Jesus's descent into the netherworld of the dead. We will not be violating the manifold implications of this emphasis on Jesus's last breath and its relationship to the Spirit (the Paraclete) by noticing what an apt image it is of the Paschal drama's transition from the events of Golgotha to Jesus's descent into the realm of the dead. Inspired by the Fourth Evangelist's sacramental recognition of the meaning of the blood and water from Christ's side and by the liberties the greatest of the Church Fathers took in their effort to discover the hidden depths of the Scripture, we summon something of the same audacity by seeing Christ's last breath in relationship to what immediately follows. In order to rescue the most lost of the lost, Christ had to sink to the uttermost bottom of sinful lifelessness and morbidity. This he could not do other than by exhaling every molecule of the world-animating Spirit that had sustained him throughout his earthly mission. By expiring—breathing out his last breath—Christ allowed himself to be stripped completely of all buoyancy. As a swimmer must empty his lungs to dive to greater depths, Christ had to surrender every trace of that world-creating Spirit that had *animated* his mission. He breathed his last and died.

We can only grope for metaphors, but one presents itself: While the intimacy between the Son and the Father are preserved intact by the Spirit, the direct contact between the Son and the Father ceases at Jesus's death so that the Dead One, the Pierced One, the Lamb Slain can descend to the very depths of death, sin, and godforsakenness as one who is himself godforsaken. The Trinitarian interruption this involves is very real, as is the risk to creation it entails. Jesus expires (*ex-spirate*) and creation itself holds its breath.

Again at the Risen Christ's appearance, attention is called to breath as the sacramental sign of the Spirit, which he bequeaths to his disciples: "He said to them again, 'Peace be with you. As the Father has sent me, so I send you.' And when he had said this, he breathed on them and said to them, 'Receive the holy Spirit. Whose sins you forgive are forgiven them, and whose sins you retain are retained'" (Jn. 20:21–23). Details such as these may awaken skepticism in some as to both their historical veracity and dominical origin, but the One who was himself his message conveyed that message primarily by way of performative gestures—acts not words—which proved capable of releasing over time a wider range of implications and a richer imaginative participation by the faithful than would have been aroused by any mere verbal instruction.

At the Easter gathering in Jerusalem and on the shore of the Sea of Tiberias we learn that the Risen Christ is present bodily: he eats with his disciples. When Christ appears to his disciples in the passage above, we see another sign of his bodily Resurrection. He breathes on them. In the most concrete way the Risen Christ shows that the break, which began with his last breath, is now over. The world need no longer hold its breath. It can breathe a sigh of relief. The perilous descent into death and the rescue of the lost has been accomplished. The same Greek word for "breathed" used here appears in the Greek Septuagint translation of the creation story in Genesis: "then the Lord God formed the man out of the dust of the ground and blew into his nostrils the breath of life, and the man became a living being" (Gen. 2:7). A new creation has been inaugurated.

## Cosmic Signs

History, writes Angelo Scola, "takes a turn in the sepulchre of Christ."[31] Like every historical or mythopoetic detail in the four

---

31 Angelo Scola, *Hans Urs von Balthasar: A Theological Style* (Grand Rapids: Eerdmans, 1995), 109.

gospels, the rending of the temple veil has an eschatological dimension. In addition to the anthropological implication that the work of René Girard brings out (the unveiling at the Crucifixion of the sacrificial violence hidden behind myth and mystifications of both pagan and, to a far lesser extent, Jewish cultic practice), the rending of the temple veil aptly echoes what Balthasar calls the "supreme *diastasis* (rupture)" between the Father and the Son on the Cross. Paradoxically, Balthasar argues that this break within the unbreakable Trinitarian perichoresis "is in truth the ultimate revelation of the tri-personality of God":[32] "And behold, the veil of the sanctuary was torn in two from top to bottom. The earth quaked, rocks were split, tombs were opened, and the bodies of many saints who had fallen asleep were raised. And coming forth from their tombs after his resurrection, they entered the holy city and appeared to many" (Mt. 27:51–53).

Balthasar brackets the Matthean qualification—that the bodies came from the tombs "after his resurrection"—as a later insertion meant to underscore the designation by the early Church of Christ as the firstborn of the dead. In a formulation that captures the richness of Balthasar's own sacramental sensibilities, this transposition of post-Easter symbolism to the moment of Jesus's death is "chronological precision, in the midst of eschatology, in the service of theological exactitude."[33]

Inasmuch as the sanctuary curtain protected Judaism's accommodation with ritual blood sacrifice from Judaism's own misgivings about such things, its rending at the moment of Christ's death stands in a relationship of mutual illumination with the seals in the Book of Revelation, which keep the apocalyptic drama of history from being revealed until the Lamb Slain provides the wherewithal for facing its exigencies. At a still deeper level, inasmuch as, according to Philo and Josephus, the temple curtain was arrayed with cosmic imagery, the rending of the veil can be read as suggestive of the cosmic peril involved in the interruption in the perichoretic exchange within the Trinity itself, something no less unfathomable and shocking than the torture

---

32 Balthasar, *To the Heart of the Mystery of Redemption*, 38.
33 Balthasar, *Mysterium Paschale*, 128.

and death of the Second Person of the Trinity at the hands of creatures made in his image and likeness. Saturated as it is with supra-temporality, the allusion to cosmic disruptions stands as evidence of the instantaneous efficacy of Christ's death, which occurred prior to and independent of the conscious appropriation by its beneficiaries.

## Descent into Hades

> According to the understanding of the New Testament, this is an event that no myth can match or outdo: this is not a living man descending into the underworld to come back up again unchanged and intact; nor has an inhabitant of the underworld been snatched away from death for a limited period of time; nor is it simply a matter of the eternal fluctuation between life and death, of a merely periodic victory of the first over the second. No, it is a definitive, eschatological turn that decides the fate of all in the fate of the one (1 Cor. 15:21ff).[34]—Hans Urs von Balthasar

In what follows, relying heavily on the theology of Hans Urs von Balthasar and, in turn, on his confidence in the general trustworthiness of the Swiss mystic Adrienne von Speyr's religious experiences, we will entertain a few theological speculations not unlike those the mystery of Holy Saturday awakened in our predecessors in the faith. The purpose of these speculations is to arrive at a better understanding of the statement from the Catholic *Catechism* earlier quoted that the preaching of the gospel to the dead mentioned in the First Epistle of Peter was "the last phase of Jesus's messianic mission, a phase which is condensed in time but vast in its real significance: the spread of Christ's redemptive work to all men of all times and all places."[35] In light of so intriguing a catechetical formulation, are we not fairly invited to explore its implications with whatever theological, anthropological, and doctrinal tools might be found to be appropriate? To foreswear such an exploration is hardly synonymous with doctrinal rigor,

---

34  Balthasar, *Explorations in Theology, Vol. IV,* 402.
35  *CCC* §634.

but neither are our meager attempts to imagine what cannot be known to be mistaken for doctrinal claims, much less for dissent from the Church's Magisterium, which, notes Balthasar, has "the duty of living in the tension between having to teach and not being able to arrive at ultimate definitions."[36]

Just as the images of the "harrowing of hell" have enjoyed a status in the religious imagination out of proportion to its scant scriptural allusions, and just as the concept of purgatory only slowly achieved formal recognition many centuries after it had become theologically familiar and popularly accepted as the optimal way for reconciling mercy and justice, so we need not neglect the religious imagination in the ongoing effort to bring the mystery of Holy Saturday into clearer focus and to accord it the status within the overall Passion that it obviously deserves. Caution in these matters must consist of never confusing the speculations we employ in our effort at better and deeper understanding with the underlying mystery for which these speculations will ever be, at best, but gestures toward a reality as yet neither rationally nor imaginatively accessible to us. The task of exhausting the meaning of these references and reconciling the complex theological and doctrinal attempts to account for them is beyond our competence. We can, however, agree with Balthasar's observation: "The fact of [Christ's] being with the unredeemed dead, in the Sheol of the Old Testament, signifies a solidarity in whose absence the condition of standing for sinful man before God would not be complete."[37]

For Balthasar, the exploration of the meaning of Holy Saturday should begin with the adoption of the Old Testament conception of postmortem existence, which is to say Sheol as understood prior to Israel's assimilation of Persian ideas of reward and punishment and Hellenistic ideas of the immortality of the soul. Even though considerable echoes of these Gentile influences are found in both the New and the Old Testament, Balthasar chooses to begin his reassessment of life after death by returning to Sheol as

---

36 Balthasar, *The Office of Peter and the Structure of the Church*, 255.
37 Balthasar, *Mysterium Paschale*, 161.

originally understood. The condition of the upright in Sheol was only marginally better, if that, than the condition of the wicked. Rather Sheol is a place of dreary semi-existence where there is neither happiness nor hope. Throughout most of the Old Testament, the realm of the dead, Sheol, is described in ways that are largely indistinguishable from contemporaneous pagan depictions. It is a place of ontological diminution where the ghost-like shades wander about seemingly incapable of relationship. "The casual reader of many parts of the Old Testament," writes N. T. Wright, "could be forgiven for thinking that ancient Israelite belief about life after death was not very different from that of Homer."[38]

In pagan thought as well as in most early Old Testament thought, death involves the cessation or, at the very least, the radical attenuation of personal relationships, not only the relationships between the living and the dead and (in the Old Testament) the relationship between the deceased and God, but also the relationships, such as they are imagined, among the dead themselves. Stories abound in literature and mythology of attempts to reestablish contact with the dead. These stories typically attest to a persistent disappointment that haunts these efforts. Even in cultural and religious settings where life after death is presupposed, it is often the case that the postmortem existence is imagined to be deficient in important ways.

Might it not be the case that such specters of the afterlife, which arose in both the Jewish and the Gentile imagination, are the projection into the next life of an extant ontological insubstantiality that is camouflaged in the here and now by an ensemble of social and cultural reassurances reinforced by vanity, the imminent collapse of which at death is arguably what makes death so frightening. The image familiar to antiquity of ghostlike shades aimlessly wandering an eerie netherworld can therefore be seen as an intimation of the ontological tenuousness of man's fallen existence. If one can neither fully know himself nor fully reveal himself to another, does that which is recalcitrant to his

38 N. T. Wright, *The Resurrection of the Son of God* (Minneapolis: Fortress Press, 2003), 87.

introspection and his self-disclosure simply vanish at death? Writes Joseph Ratzinger: "In death, a human being emerges into the light of full reality and truth. He takes up that place which is truly his by right. The masquerade of living with its constant retreat behind posturings and fictions, is now over. Man is what he is in truth."[39]

For Balthasar, the key to understanding Jesus's postmortem existence among the dead is his extension of solidarity with those deprived of it, not only those deprived of solidarity with the living by the fact of death, but even more radically those deprived of solidarity by their escalating assertion of autonomy and the godforsakenness that is the final step in that escalation. In either case, however, solidarity is interpersonal; it requires mutual consent. There is nothing automatic about it. Christ shared in the godforsakenness of the languishing dead. His presence among them and more specifically his encounter with *each* of them awakens the very volitional capacity that makes it possible for them to say Yes or No to Christ's offer of solidarity. Any conquering triumph of "hell" of the sort that gradually formed in the Christian imagination is incompatible with this personal dimension of Christ's solidarity with *each* of the dead. He who died, not for the human race generically understood, but for each person in all his uniqueness, did not "conquer hell" by force of an impersonal victory. Personal encounter is indispensable to a Christian understanding. As Benedict XVI writes in his encyclical, *Spe Salvi*: "Christ descended into 'Hell' and is therefore close to those cast into it, transforming their darkness into light."[40] Later in the same encyclical Benedict makes this point in a particularly illuminating way: "The Latin word *con-solatio*, 'consolation', expresses this beautifully. It suggests *being with* the other in his solitude, so that it ceases to be solitude."[41]

As cautious as one should be in trying to exegete what are essentially mythic or at best mythopoetic images, we are invited

---

39 Ratzinger, *Eschatology*, 206.
40 *Spe Salvi*, §37, quotation marks in the original.
41 *Spe Salvi*, §38.

to do just that by Balthasar's contention that the late creedal description of Jesus as descending into the realm of the dead, while understandable, implied activity that, Balthasar argues, cannot be ascribed to a dead man. Admittedly, the Christ who descends to the realm of the dead is surely not the corpse of Christ; that remained in the tomb. Yet it is right to be wary of ascribing to Christ martial activity envisioned in the standard "harrowing of hell" depictions. In the first instance one might ask: If the netherworld prior to the arrival of the dead Jesus was that of Sheol, as biblical and non-biblical thought had more or less consistently imagined, would not the dead Jesus have been at least as animate as were the postmortem shades described in both Scripture and pagan mythology? If, however, as we have argued, our lives—both on this side of death and beyond—are ontologically compromised to one degree or another, it might be supposed that our *animation*—from the word for soul or breath—in the postmortem realm would be a measure of our ontological vibrancy. As hopelessly theoretical as such speculation might be, were we to follow it out we would find ourselves returning to Christ's godforsakenness. To take on all the sins of the world, to become sin itself, is to surrender one's *being* entirely, to ontologically empty oneself. One who underwent so thorough a kenotic emptying would be less, not more, *animate* in the realm of the dead than those whose merely circumstantial godforsakenness was the consequence of congenital and personal sin, but who are far from being sin itself, as was Christ in his Passion. In this sense at least, Balthasar's opposition to the idea of an active Christ in the realm of the dead makes sense. In any case, it helps us realize that the locus of the "triumph" in Hades is not the power of Christ soon to be risen but rather the simple wordless presence of the Pierced One, precisely as motionless as he is on crucifixes throughout the Christian world and down through the ages.

In his wordless condition while in his mother's womb and while lying in the makeshift crib at his birth, Christ elicited a response: from the child in Elizabeth's womb, from the shepherds and magi in the infancy narratives of Matthew and Luke, and from Herod and his royal retinue. At the end of his life the Incarnate Word is returned to this wordless state. Here at the culmination of his salvific descent, he wordlessly and passively *acts* on those lingering incommunicado in the realm of the dead by obliging them to cry out like the inert stones of which Jesus spoke (Lk. 19:14), from which stones he declared God capable of raising up children of Abraham (Lk. 3:8).

The dead Christ *accompanies* the dead in their dreary Sheol/ Hades condition of ghost-likeness. Dead though he is, he does not cease to be the second Person of the Trinity. As such his very nature is self-giving life and interpersonal communion. As the other dead linger and languish in a side-by-side isolation, from which their feeble attempts to extricate themselves are impotent, the dead Christ brings an interrelationship rooted in his unconquerable Trinitarian life. In his presence, those who remain estranged from their fellow ghost-like inhabitants in the realm of the dead feel themselves accompanied. This stirring of communion lifts them sufficiently from their impotent passivity, making possible and unavoidable an all but imperceptible act: assent or rejection.

Christ doesn't need to *do* anything. What needs to happen will happen if and when the souls lingering in Sheol "look on him whom they have pierced" (Jn. 19:37), recognizing at last the One in whose image and likeness they are made, still bearing the marks of the sufferings he underwent for their sins and those of the whole world. Those for whom Christ descends into the realm of the dead encounter precisely the *crucified* Christ, not the Risen Christ. Whether, under the circumstances, human freedom confronted with the Risen Christ could retain enough independent volition to utter a bona fide Yes is a legitimate question. But another is whether or not such a Yes would be morally serious enough without the experience of contrition consonant with an encounter with "him whom they have pierced." The judgment that takes place at death has to do less with how gravely the dead have sinned than with whether or not the sinners have the Roman centurion's capacity to encounter in the crucified Christ the awful truth about moral flaws, spiritual self-deceptions, and habitual self-referentiality they might otherwise have regarded as mediocre shortcomings.

If the centurion's conversion is prototypical, then it is worth noting that his conversion occurred at the moment when the body of Christ became a corpse and hung on the Cross the way it still does in churches and homes all over the world. The exigencies of life rarely provide us mediocre sinners with anything quite comparable. If we are to have the benefit of the shock that brought the centurion first to his senses and then to his knees and if we are *all* to have that benefit, it will have to take place at death. And the outcome of the encounter will very likely determine our postmortem destiny—or at least it would be prudent to regard it so.

The emblematic nature of the centurion's *metanoia* invites a further speculation. Was the sudden moral and religious awakening the centurion experienced at the moment of Christ's death attended by a reevaluation of his prior complicity in comparable acts of cruelty? Speaking metaphorically, might he have seen in the face of the Pierced One the reflection of all the faces of those at whose torture and execution he had presided? Nor is this idle speculation. For even if Christ suffers the sin, heartlessness, and selfishness of each sinner, he does so by being the co-recipient of these things, sharing in the suffering of those who were the direct recipients of the sinful behavior. Thus, in what follows, when we speak of the encounter with the Pierced One at death, we presuppose that the remorse it arouses will have specificity and that the face of the Pierced One will reflect the "faces" of all those whose sufferings Christ has co-suffered.

It may seem entirely fanciful even to try to imagine something beyond senses that are bound by unidirectional chronology and three-dimensional space. These habits of mind may be of little use when creatures cognitively, morally, and imaginatively crippled by sin try to ascertain something as transcendent to these limitations as the inbreaking of eternal reality into a finite world. There is, however, as far as we know, nothing theologically objectionable about the suggestion that the impact of Christ's entry into the realm of the dead need not  indeed, cannot—be limited to those who had already died by the mid-first century AD. Writes Adrienne von Speyr: "He is for every dead person, in every age, the One who is already dead; each of them possesses the reality of his death in him. For the Son has not merely carried each sinner's sins, in order to redeem him; he also died each one's death, so that all the dead might share in his being."[42]

There may be reasons to think that postmortem existence may involve some form of temporality. While we neither dismiss that possibility nor read too much into it, it seems important to point out that there is no reason to suppose that temporal experience operative after death is, as temporality is in this life, either unidirectional or incompatible with simultaneity. Our quantum physicists are fully capable of bewildering us with the mysteries of time. We have no warrant for thinking the mystery beyond the space-time reality our physicists find so marvelously paradoxical will be any less so. Josef Pieper provides a useful reflection:

> [The dead] . . . enter a realm of existence in which a new non-temporal mode of duration reigns and in which our clocks and measurements of time no longer mean anything. The "interval," extending from the moment of death to the Resurrection awaited by faith at the end of days, cannot possibly be of the same type of duration as the time between birth and death. Time, eon, eternity have become, from one moment to the next, and in an entirely new fashion, "simultaneous."[43]

There is just as little reason to be overly chronological in assessing the "moment" of death as there is for imagining the "interval" between the death of the individual and the final Resurrection in crudely temporal terms. However it must elude capture within the temporality familiar to us, the "event" of death surely has *an inside*. It has content that cannot be squeezed into the punctuality of the moment of death. Countless cases have been reported of "near-death" experiences. In some cases, the researchers insist on speaking of *actual death experiences*—situations in which a person is declared dead and remains so until a medical intervention or an unexpected reversal occurs and the person "returns" to life. In this, science is in accord with many religious traditions. Beyond that, a high percentage of those who have survived a near-death or actual death experience report hav-

---

42 Adrienne von Speyr, *The Letter to the Colossians*, trans. Michael J. Miller (San Francisco: Ignatius Press, 1998), 35.

43 Pieper, *Death and Immortality*, 117.

ing their lives flash before them in an instant. One would think that it would take more than an instant for a very long and active life to flash before someone, especially if the ostensible purpose of the review is the deceased's confrontation with the moral failures and spiritual betrayals of his life. It would be a category mistake to rely on such cases in a theological exploration, and we are not intending that. Nonetheless, it is not irrelevant to note that medical and neurological science as well as social science today sees death as a process. Our point is quite straightforward, however. We simply want to argue that while death is punctual inasmuch as a moment comes when the person has exercised his freedom for the very last time, the experience of the dead person after death, however chronologically punctual it might seem from within our space-time continuum, has dimensionality.

When, for instance, the *Catechism of the Catholic Church* declares that: "Immediately after death the souls of those who died in a state of mortal sin descend into hell, where they suffer the punishments of hell, 'eternal fire,'" it hastens to add that: "The chief punishment of hell is eternal separation from God, in whom alone man can possess the life and happiness for which he was created and for which he longs."[44] In the quotation marks around the phrase *eternal fire* one can delineate something of the history of the Church's eschatological understanding, and the word *immediately* is not without a certain ambiguity in this regard as well. There is no less ambiguity in the phrase *postmortem encounter* and the variations on it to which we resort, but it would be as injurious to censure the use of the latter term as it would the former. "To die in mortal sin without repenting and accepting God's merciful love means remaining separated from him forever by our own free choice. This state of definitive self-exclusion from communion with God and the blessed is called 'hell'."[45]

So says the *Catechism of the Catholic Church*. The designation of perdition as "self-exclusion from communion with God" and the quotation marks around the word *hell*, and later in this section of the *Catechism* around *Gehenna* and the phrases *eternal fire*—all

44 *CCC* §1035.
45 Ibid., §1033.

these things represent an entirely appropriate deference by the theological sensibility of a later age toward the venerable theological formulations of an earlier one, but they serve as well to remind the later age of the continuing need to bring Christian theological reflection into ever clearer and more faithful expression.

There are dangers associated with thinking of man's eschatological destiny in ways that are insufficiently Christological. At the heart of Christology, of course, is the mystery of the Trinity. Writes Balthasar:

> If hell is supposed to be a dogmatic truth, then it can have a meaningful and, in faith, intelligible place only within the framework of the doctrine of the Trinity, of christology, and of soteriology. . . . Christ's experience of hell on Holy Saturday is a trinitarian as well as a soteriological experience that forms the necessary conclusion to the cross as well as the necessary presupposition of the resurrection.[46]

Until Christ's descent into the realm of the dead, there is neither heaven nor hell as we (however poorly) understand them. For the chasm between self-sacrificial Trinitarian love and the sin-crippled creature incapable of living in accord with that love remained unbridged. Only when confronted with the invitation to Trinitarian existence offered by Christ does heaven—constituted by the acceptance of the invitation—and hell—constituted by its final rejection—become possible. "God is the 'last thing' of the creature," writes Balthasar. "Gained, he is heaven; lost, he is hell; examining, he is judgment; purifying, he is purgatory." All of these "last things" take place in the encounter with God in the form he has chosen as most conducive to the happy outcome of these encounters, namely as a meeting with the Slain Lamb, the Crucified Christ.[47] In fact, Christianity does indeed involve a radical redefinition of immortality, for it posits Christ as the judge who determines the content of postmortem existence, albeit a

---

46 *The von Balthasar Reader*, 404.
47 Balthasar, *Explorations in Theology, Vol. I*, 260.

judgment that is constituted by whether the deceased—made explicitly aware of the wreckage caused by his sins—experiences a sincere contrition, not motivated by fear for his own suffering, but by remorse over what his sins have done to others and to God in Christ crucified.

"On Holy Saturday," writes the French theologian Louis Lochet, "we observe the fulfillment of the mystery of salvation: from now on, hell belongs to Christ."[48] Although it is a place of desolation, Balthasar insists, hell is "always still a Christological place."[49] It consists precisely of the infernal alienation and loneliness of those who have rejected the offer of communion, either out of sinful self-absorbed rage or by remaining impenitent. In either case, Hell is under new management, and its denizens—if any reside there—are there only as a result of a decision on their part.

## God of the Godforsaken

[T]he time that has passed is sufficient for doing what the Gentiles like to do: living in debauchery, evil desires, drunkenness, orgies, carousing, and wanton idolatry. They are surprised that you do not plunge into the same swamp of profligacy, and they vilify you; but they will give an account to him who stands ready to judge the living and the dead. For this is why the gospel was preached even to the dead that, though condemned in the flesh in human estimation, they might live in the spirit in the estimation of God. (1 Pet. 4:1–6)

Saint Augustine insisted that this passage in First Peter should not be read as indicating that those who did not believe in Christ in life would be offered the possibility of believing in him after death.

But if we accept this opinion, according to which we are warranted in supposing that men who did not believe while they were in life can in hell believe in Christ, who can bear the contra-

48 Quoted: Hans Urs von Balthasar, *Dare We Hope that All Men Be Saved?: A Short Discourse on Hell*, trans. Dr. David Kipp and Rev. Lothar Krauth (San Francisco: Ignatius Press, 1988), 112.

49 *The von Balthasar Reader*, 422.

dictions both of reason and faith which must follow? In the first place, if this were true, we should seem to have no reason for mourning over those who have departed from the body without that grace, and there would be no ground for being solicitous and using urgent exhortation that men would accept the grace of God before they die, lest they should be punished with eternal death.[50]

Balthasar has a quibble of his own. It should not be assumed, he argues, that the "preaching" to the dead was "a subjective kind of preaching, meant to move others to conversion," rather, he writes, "it is the objective announcement (like a herald's signal) of a fact."[51] On this reading, the "harrowing of hell" consisted of an encounter between, on one hand, those whose lives had been intrinsically animated—as all human life is—by an inchoate desire for the embrace of divine love and, on the other hand, the ultimate condescension of that Love: the disarmed and disarming God, the God who "did not destine us for wrath, but to gain salvation through our Lord Jesus Christ, who died for us, so that whether we are awake or asleep we may live together with him" (1 Thess. 5:9–10). The passage above from First Peter suggests that though the demarcation of death is definitive with regard to the moral and spiritual content of the life that preceded it, even those condemned in the flesh in human estimation for having plunged into the swamp of profligacy are to have the gospel preached to them so that "they might live in the spirit in the estimation of God" (1 Pet. 4:6). The Living Logos, the Word made flesh, is the message he came to deliver. This is emphatically the case when the Logos takes on the sin of the world and falls to the farthest realm of lifeless lovelessness. His "preaching" to the dead is what his preaching prior to his Passion was, namely *Himself*. His preaching in the netherworld is as the Pierced One on whom those whose sins pierced him must look and who must at that "moment" face or flee the Truth.

We have yet to free ourselves from the vague forms of universalism so prevalent in Enlightenment and post-Enlightenment

50 Augustine, *Letter* 164 (AD 404), 4.13.
51 Balthasar, *Mysterium Paschale*, 159.

thought. The importance of the Apostles' Creed reference to Christ's descent into hell begins to come into focus against the background of an authentic universalism, one that shakes off the vague and generic connotations conjured up by references to Christ's impact on *humanity*. If death is where we meet Christ crucified, then Christ has upended death and made the supreme punishment for sin (in Western theology) and the supreme cause of sin (according to the Orthodox reading of Romans 5) into the instrument of redemption, thereby making access to that redemption as universal as death itself. "For this is why Christ died and came to life, that he might be Lord of both the dead and the living" (Rom. 14:9). Death, too, is under new management. Christ's Resurrection converts the death that is the punishment for sin—or, according to Meyendorff's Orthodox reading, the cause of sin—into the event conducive to our redemption. In Christ's surrender to death, writes Balthasar, "he brings the deaths of all sinners with him; he envelops them in his uniquely definitive death and gives them a changed value, thereby changing the value of all life destined for a similar death."[52]

Sheol becomes hell for any who refuse the invitation of Christ, but just as the Lamb Slain continues to suffer with the creatures whose vocation he reveals, so too Christ is continually emptying hell by encountering those who would otherwise rage against God for all eternity were it not for the encounter with the Lamb Slain, the Pierced One. Writes Adrienne von Speyr: "God has given two responses to sin: the netherworld and the Son. The netherworld as the necessary consequence of sin, the Son as the free willingness to atone for sin. Now, the two encounter each other."[53]

"When Christ died," wrote Romano Guardini, "something happened to death."[54] Death has been commandeered by Christ for redemptive purpose. Like the proverbial hangman's noose, it focuses the mind. Now, under the right circumstances—precisely

---

52 Balthasar, *Theo-Drama, Vol. V,* 327.

53 Adrienne von Speyr, *The Birth of the Church*, trans. David Kipp (San Francisco: Ignatius Press, 2012); quoted: Balthasar, *Theo-Drama, Vol. V,* 268.

54 Romano Guardini, *The Last Things,* 23.

those fostered by Christianity—the very specter of an approaching finality introduces a moral seriousness and conduces to the awakening or intensification of a religious attitude, which serves to prepare one for the encounter with Christ at death. With Christ's Passion, the Möbius strip of sin and death takes an entirely new twist. The Crucified Christ has turned death itself into the encounter between the sinner and the God who condescended to bring him back into the Trinitarian embrace. The "sacrament of dying," writes Adrienne von Speyr, has been "instituted by the Lord for his inadequate, imperfect Church—a Church into which he accepts everyone who acknowledges him in any way, sinners great and small, and all those in between."[55]

"Jesus's Resurrection," Balthasar writes, "took place in all truth at the end of the world, since he has atoned for those who will come after him in time just as much as for those who were before him and contemporaneous with him."[56] If the Resurrection, as Balthasar avers, is an event at the end of the world, the descent into the realm of the dead on Holy Saturday can be no less so. The preaching of the Good News to the dead, Balthasar writes, "is an event in the world beyond, producing there the effective fruits of Christ's suffering in the flesh—whatever idea of conversion after death may be involved."[57] Father Aidan Nichols has faithfully translated the German original of this text—"*Bekehrung nach dem Tode.*" It is the idea of conversion after death that the Swiss theologian is asking his readers to consider, even if Balthasar himself and most of his interpreters steer clear of this idea for fear of its seeming incompatibility with doctrine and no less because of the danger it poses for the perfectly valid understanding of death as the moment when nothing in the life ended can be changed.

Balthasar elsewhere dismisses the idea that "a further 'conversion' is still possible at the Judgment, after death," insisting that "it is only a question of the Judge's objective evaluation of a life's

---

55 Adrienne von Speyr, *The Cross: Word and Sacrament*, trans. Graham Harrison (San Francisco: Ignatius Press, 1983), 25.

56 Balthasar, *Theo-Drama*, Vol. V, 353.

57 Balthasar, *Mysterium Paschale*, 157–8.

totality."[58] This is the unimpeachable teaching of the Church, but the fact that one of the greatest theologians of recent memory, the theologian who arguably devoted more attention to the catholicity of God's salvific will than any other theologian of his time, chose to put the word *conversion* in the above quoted sentence in quotation marks, should not be overlooked. There are neither theological nor expositional reasons for doing this. If the word conversion implies a determination to live one's life otherwise than the way one has heretofore lived, any such option will obviously have been foreclosed at death. How likely is it, however, that the posthumous encounter with the Living Logos in whose image and likeness the deceased is made would have no repercussions other than the ratification of a *fait accompli*? If Catholic doctrine has long taught that death is the decisive moment after which the person can have no further influence on his own eschatological destiny, it may well be that this understanding is based on an idea of the mystery of death that adopts too much of the temporal constraints that apply only to life prior to death.

It takes no great powers of observation to recognize how happenstantial are our moral and spiritual challenges in this life and how unequally distributed are the religious, familial, and cultural resources conducive to a life of rectitude and religious devotion. How better under the circumstances might Divine Justice be done than by simultaneously confronting each person—*postmortem*—with, on one hand, the Archetype of Trinitarian Love (in whose image and likeness he was made) and, on the other hand, the relative mess he has made of the vocation to approximate that Archetype? Writes Balthasar: "His features come to life, are lit up and deepened, when man beholds not his mirror but his original."[59] We must never underestimate either the love or the transforming power of Christ. As the author of the First Letter of John reminds us: "Beloved, we are God's children now; it does not yet appear what we shall be, but we know that when he appears we shall be like him, for we shall see him as he is" (1 Jn. 3:2–3).

---

58 Balthasar, *Theo-Drama, Vol. V,* 297.

59 Hans Urs von Balthasar, *The God Question and Modern Man,* trans. Hidla Graef (New York: Seabury Press: 1967), 90.

One can approach Balthasar's insistence that Christ's "preaching" was more a manifestation of a fact than the act of persuasion usually associated with the verb preaching by turning to the psalmist:

Do not hide your face from me,
lest I become like those descending to the pit. (Ps. 143:7)

What saves the soul from the pit is the unadulterated vision of the Real—the Real precisely as the *Face* of God—in light of which the entire arsenal of resistance, rebellion, and resentment, accumulated over the course of a lifetime effort to manipulate the mimetic reality to one's own advantage, will either collapse or swell into open rebellion. Balthasar's resistance to the suggestion of an active preaching by Christ in the realm of the dead is in keeping with the psalmist's suggestion that it is the *face* of God that rescues one from the pit of destruction. Writes Balthasar: "Only in absolute weakness does God want to give to each freedom created by him the gift of love that breaks out of every dungeon and dissolves every constriction: in solidarity, from within, with those who refuse all solidarity."[60]

"It is finished" (Jn. 19:30), Jesus had said at the end. Nothing is left to *do*. What remains is only to "reveal" the truth, not defend it. The verbal expression of truth—always inadequate, even when indispensable—gives way to Truth in Person, namely the Logos in whose image and likeness each member of the human race is fashioned, of whose likeness we have all fallen short in ways that may only occasionally weigh on us now but which will be the source of an unspeakable remorse when in the presence of the One whose image and likeness we have so failed to approximate.

Just as the veil of the temple is torn from top to bottom, the doors of hell and the arms of God are thrown open simultaneously. There is no "harrowing of hell," but rather a decision on the part of those who have only two animating sources: the accumulated habits of an earthly life no longer available for remediation and the presence of One who had said—referring to his Crucifixion no less than his Resurrection—"when I am lifted up

60 Balthasar, *Explorations in Theology, Vol. IV*, 422.

from the earth, I will draw everyone to myself" (Jn. 12:32). With his descent into hell, the dead Christ unites himself with those who—on the basis of whatever scraps of evidence they happened upon in their mortal lives and with whatever mediocre volition they managed to summon—have rejected Trinitarian self-giving in favor of either a willful autonomy or a shameless absorption into a mindless and mendacious mob. The only remaining question is how irrevocably the subjects in question have rejected the Trinitarian conditions for the fulfillment of their deepest desires. It is to embrace those most thoroughly lost, those most godforsaken, that the Good Shepherd has left the ninety-nine and come to the netherworld. With those still capable of contrition Christ enters into solidarity. He intrudes into the lifeless loneliness of the lost. "The sinner who wants to be 'damned' by God"—that is, who wants to be left alone in his frozen gesture of defiance—"now rediscovers God in his loneliness," writes Balthasar:

> But this is precisely how he disturbs the absolute loneliness that the sinner strives for: the sinner who wants to be "damned" by God now rediscovers God in the absolute impotence of love. For now God has placed himself in solidarity with those who have damned themselves, entering into non-time in a way we could never anticipate. The verse of the psalm: "If I make my bed in Sheol, thou art there!" (Ps. 39:8) thus receives a whole new meaning. And even the battle cry "God is dead"—that self-asserting *diktat* of the sinner who is finished with God—gains a whole new meaning that God himself has established.[61]

No longer consigned to one rather obscure event that took place on one particular day two millennia ago, thanks to the mystical experiences of Adrienne von Speyr and the theological genius and persistence of Hans Urs von Balthasar, Holy Saturday stands as the icon of an almost incomprehensible hope: that those most determined to wall themselves within a hellish fortress of alienation will find that fortress breached by one who is even more godforsaken than they, whose very presence as the Pierced One, who died for the godforsaken, offers them access to

---

61 Balthasar, *Explorations in Theology, IV,* 421–2.

the Trinitarian communion for which they were made and toward which, unbeknownst to them, their lives were ordered.

"Fear not, I am the first and the last [*eschatos*], and the living one; I died, and behold I am alive for evermore, and I have the keys of Death and Hades" (Rev. 1:17–18). Quoting Joseph Ratzinger, Juan M. Sara writes as follows:

"Christ, the Judge, is the eschatos." He, not the destiny of sinful man, not Hades, is the last thing. He is the eschatological reality in person. An implication of this is that, at the moment of death, every man encounters Christ as his only and final judge. And because Christ's own death has "transmuted" death and separated sin at its root from the sinner, this judgment is, at one and the same time, the severest possible condemnation of sin and the offer of an infinite mercy to the sinner.[62]

62 Juan M. Sara, *"Descensus ad Infernos,* Dawn of Hope," *Communio: International Catholic Review,* Vol. XXXII (No. 3): 554.

# Look on Him
# Whom They Have Pierced

*Last Judgment* by Fra Angelico

IN THE SON who offers himself to our gaze, the Father "draws" those who believe in him—who perceive the love in him—to the Son (Jn. 6:44). In the Son who is "raised on high" defenseless, the Son himself draws all persons to himself (12:32), and all eyes will be fixed in fascination on the one who had been pierced, whether they wish this or not (19–37), so that sooner or later—early enough or too late—all will "recognize that I am he" (8:28). But in the empowering of sight, since it is a question of the power of love, and love can be given only in a free decision, the freedom to say yes or no, the freedom for belief and for unbelief, is operative.[1]—Hans Urs von Balthasar

The provocation of the Lamb lies in the rendering of an unthinkable love, of an unimaginable innocence, and an ungraspable truth. No particular response is compelled; the response can be hate as well as love, deliberate wickedness as well as innocence, articulating the lie as well as expositing the truth [2]
—Cyril O'Regan

1 Balthasar, *The Glory of the Lord, Vol. VII,* 291, spelling adjusted to US English usage.
2 O'Regan, *The Anatomy of Misremembering,* 254.

AM I ANSWERABLE for my life? When will I answer? To whom will I answer? My answer will be: Yes or No. "Let what you say be simply 'Yes' or 'No'; anything more than this comes from evil" (Mt. 5:37). That these are the only two responses does not mean that the initial response will be a fully formed Yes or No. It is far more likely that one person's initial Yes will be as eschatologically indecisive as another person's initial No. The Church's doctrine of purgatory has made it possible for us to imagine the otherwise unimaginable ripening of a feeble Yes into a complete surrender to the attractive power of Christ's love and mercy. We have no similar conceptual aid for imagining that an uncertain No might harden into an adamantine refusal, but to entertain that sobering possibility might encourage the faithful to attend more carefully to their state of readiness for this encounter. It seems completely plausible and in keeping with what we know of sin that a hesitant No might gradually harden into hatred, for a hesitant No will not by itself put an end to the love of God as the Hound of Heaven, refusing to accept as decisive, for as long as some flicker of hope remains, man's determination to remain godless. It seems to us that an ever more emphatic No to the offer of mercy and forgiveness might be set in motion by the sinner's desperate attempt to wall himself off from Love and its blessed responsibilities. However incipient might be the Yes or the No, and however bewildered one might be, *indifference* will no longer be possible. A Yes will be, as Marion's reading of Augustine's *Confessions* suggests, twofold: a confession of praise and a confession of sin, a Yes to God's merciful and glorious love and a Yes to the now irremediable facts of one's sinfulness.

Understood in light of its definitive revelation on Golgotha, divine power is the disarming power of powerless love. The saving capacity of this love to break through the most hardened fortress of the heart should not be underestimated, but no one can be saved against his will. Writes Balthasar:

> [F]rom now on, salvation is offered to all men, in such a way that the dead will decide on their response to that offer, in conformity to what [E. Güder] calls "the human possibility of deciding for or against God's revelation in Christ," under the influence of

the "fundamental orientation of the soul's desire" as shaped during this life.[3]

Since the fourteenth century the Church has equated the blessed state of those in heaven as the beatific vision, the emphasis being on both the glory of God and on the face-to-face experience of God by those made worthy of it. Arguably, the term used to emphasize the deeply interpersonal nature of the blessed state has been less and less successful in doing so in more recent time. We would like to suggest that this characterization of heaven is both too static and ultimately too impersonal. It is too static for it represents only the end point of the entry into the blessed state while conveying nothing of what might have occasioned that entry. It is too impersonal because it is too disembodied. And finally it is insufficiently Trinitarian because it is insufficiently Christological.

In his masterful study of theological aesthetics, Balthasar conducted an analysis of the aesthetic impact that the Christian revelation has had on the very experience of beauty.

> What we are used to calling "aesthetic" is as tinged with the vanity and unreality of original sin as is (enlightened) reason. Only Christ and God's Word in him in the form of suffering (the hiddenness *sub contrario*), the historical word of Scripture, reveals anew God's glory. Both Judaism and paganism are oriented toward this Word, and it brings them both to fulfillment by revealing, through the mystery of its own lowliness, the primal splendor of the love of a God who humiliates himself. This is the true *coincidentia oppositorum* that enkindles not only faith, but also the enthusiasm proper to it: "One and the same proof both of the most glorious majesty and the most radical self-emptying!"[4]

What brought about this aesthetic revolution, Balthasar argues, is the crucified Christ: his wretched, scourged, mutilated, and lifeless body radiated such an overwhelming icon of moral beauty that it shattered the existing aesthetic, the epitome of which in the

3 Balthasar, *Mysterium Paschale*, 178.
4 Balthasar, *The Glory of the Lord, Vol. I*, 81–2.

Greco-Roman world was the Apollonian male body. In Christ, physical beauty is set aside and superseded by moral beauty, the latter emanating from an act of self-sacrifice in which privilege and prerogative is surrendered out of love for those unworthy of such sacrifice. As Joseph Ratzinger has written:

> Yet precisely in this Face that is so disfigured, there appears the genuine, the ultimate beauty: the beauty of love that goes "to the very end" and thus proves to be mightier than falsehood and violence. Whoever has perceived this beauty knows that truth after all, and not falsehood, is the ultimate authority of the world.[5]

If we follow the logic underlying the insights of Balthasar and Ratzinger, we are invited to find the beatific vision in the image of the Pierced One to whom Zechariah and the Johannine author allude. Among the many voices out of which Balthasar fashions a theologically substantial chorus is that of the French philosopher Maurice Blondel who "rejects Dante's inscription on the door of hell": [Abandon hope all who enter here]. Quoting Blondel, Balthasar writes:

> To claim that this dungeon with its punishments is "the work of primal and highest love is to attribute to God a responsibility that only the unrepentant have to bear;" he rejects in disgust the condemning gesture of Michelangelo's Christ and refers us instead to Fra Angelico, who depicts Christ, at judgment, as only displaying his wounds: "And at the sight of this, the unrepentant sinners turn away, beat their breasts to indicate that [as understood in the artist's day] they hold themselves to blame."[6]

In the eschatological image favored by Blondel, the judgment of Christ consists in "displaying his wounds," at the sight of which the unrepentant flee. It was this act of self-damnation that the great fifteenth century painter captured. Elsewhere in the Johannine corpus we have the image of judgment in which the damned cry out to the mountains and the rocks: "Fall on us and

5 Joseph Ratzinger, On the Way to Jesus Christ, trans. Michael J. Miller (San Francisco: Ignatius Press, 2005), 39.
6 Balthasar, Dare We Hope that All Men Be Saved?, 115.

hide us from the face of the one who sits on the throne and from the wrath of the Lamb" (Rev. 6:16).

We pause here to point out that insufficient attention has been paid to the glaringly oxymoronic nature of the "wrath of the Lamb" trope. Although it is accompanied in other passages in the Book of Revelation by similar representations of divine ferocity, rather than being yet another image confirming the righteous fury of divine judgment, this phrase—"the wrath of the Lamb"— might be taken as the inversion from within of all the other more or less explicitly Old Testament references to divine judgment that John of Patmos has assembled, rearranged, and subtly reinterpreted. How strange it would be to think that reference to the Lamb in the phrase "wrath of the Lamb" has no other purpose than to designate the source of the wrath. The main point to consider here, however, is that those under judgment in the "wrath of the Lamb" trope recoil from the *face* of the one on the throne and from the wrath of the Lamb. "God's wrath and the Son's Cross are two sides of a simple reality," writes Balthasar. The judgment then is determined by how the sinner responds to the *Face* of God made visible in the Lamb Slain, that is, the face of the Crucified One whose wounds represent the essential focus of the judgment. This is the key to one's eternal destiny. Those who cling to their godforsaken sinfulness can do so only by shielding themselves from the Lamb by fleeing his presence into the outer darkness or by calling upon the mountains and rocks to fall on them. Judgment consists of the fact that their desire for complete annihilation will be denied them. The tomb of their refusal is the dreary, isolated dungeon they have chosen as sanctuary from the love of God in Christ and the demand of Trinitarian self-surrender, which is its precondition. Short of annihilation, the damned try to mitigate their misery by imagining its source to be God and not themselves. But even this will be denied them.

"God," writes Balthasar, "respects the freedom which God has bestowed upon his creature and with which it is capable of resisting his love." It seems likely that the underlying reason why not even Jesus's closest disciples were vouchsafed a *completely unambiguous* revelation of the Risen Christ and also why he so dramatically drew their attention to his bodily wounds is that the fully glorified

Risen Christ would so compromise one's volitional capacity as to deprive one's assent of its full eschatological consequences. As Balthasar states:

> It remains however to consider whether God is not free to encounter the sinner turned away from him in the form of weakness of the crucified brother abandoned by God, and indeed in such a way that it becomes clear to the one turned away: this (like me) God-forsaken one is so for my sake. In this situation one can no longer speak of any overpowering if, to one who has chosen (maybe one should say: thinks he has chosen) the complete loneliness of being-only-for-oneself, God himself enters into his very loneliness as someone who is even more lonely.[7]

Though man's autonomy is relative and not—as late-modernity has tended to believe—absolute, it is essential to human freedom, which achieves its supreme purpose by assenting to participation, via Christ, in the Trinitarian coexistence for which humans are made and to which they are ontologically ordered. Christ as the refulgence of the Father's glory (Heb. 1:3) appeared in human form in order to mediate the mystery of Trinitarian Love to the one creature ontologically ordered toward it. This he does, not as divine omnipotence but as crucified love. "At the judgment," writes the future pope, Benedict XVI, "in response to our questions, the Lord will show us his wounds, and we will understand."[8]

Perhaps. But there is a danger here, which we overlook, and it is one that may be more perilous to conventional believers and strict adherents to divine and ecclesial law than to others. Recall Peter's reaction when Jesus proposed to wash his feet. Why did he recoil so vociferously? Jesus's act threatened to invert the master-servant hierarchy, but behind this hierarchy stands the grand distinction between the sacred and the profane, the locus of archaic religion's aboriginal taboo. At Caesarea Philippi, Peter was similarly scandalized by the prospect of the God-Man going

---

7 *The von Balthasar Reader*, 422.

8 Joseph Cardinal Ratzinger, *God Is Near Us: The Eucharist, the Heart of Life*, trans. Henry Taylor (San Francisco: Ignatius Press, 2003), 147.

to Jerusalem to be tortured and crucified. The mockery of the crowd at the Crucifixion: "If you are the Son of God, come down from the cross" (Mt. 27:40) may have been more than just a malicious taunt. The fear of tampering with the distinction between the sacred and the profane is deeply rooted in the religious mind, and both the Incarnation and, more especially, the crucifixion and death of Jesus represent an egregious violation of that taboo. Those mocking Jesus may well have been pleased if he had come down from the Cross. That at least would have left the wall separating the sacred and the profane intact. The worldly hope par excellence—the Resurrection without the cross—would have been fulfilled. Conceivably this mockery was the flip side of an earlier enthusiasm for Jesus and his message.

We previously called attention to how easily the attitudinal valence of those who yield to the mimetic attraction of a crowd can shift from adulation to antipathy. In many archaic myths, that moment comes when the "observed of all observers"—the king or "big-man" or high priest—shows some sign of weakness, indicating that he is as mortal and vulnerable as are his adulators, who then turn on him with a ferocity matching their earlier devotion. What this suggests is that the appeal of the Lamb Slain or the Pierced One may well arouse aversion in proportion to the degree that those to whom the appeal is made remained inured within the old order—the anthropological structures limned by the Caiaphas reprising of Thucydides' moral agnosticism regarding violence from which "it was quite clear that the rest of the city, as things were, benefited greatly." Inasmuch as Christianity exists to bring humanity out of this captivity to structural sin and thereby to make it possible for each of its erstwhile captives to recognize the degree of his own culpability in these matters, Christian faith improves man's eschatological fortunes in proportion to how fully he allows himself to be transformed by the renewal of his mind (Rom. 12:2), allowing the mind of Christ to awaken within him (Phil. 2:5). Absent this inculcation of the new order of reality, an encounter at death between someone insufficiently disabused of the old order and the Pierced One might elicit a response similar to Peter's response to Jesus at Caesarea Philippi and at the washing of the feet at the Last Supper.

What began at the Agony in the Garden and reached its earthly apogee with the cry of dereliction on the Cross culminates in a postmortem crescendo of complete godforsakenness indistinguishable, except for the Son's temporarily bracketed hypostasis, from the godforsaken lost sheep. In his Resurrection appearances, Christ's wounds are shockingly conspicuous, and they serve ever after to make it clear that the Cross was not a phase to be left happily behind in the euphoria of Easter. In the realm of the dead, these wounds take the place of any action, for Jesus enters the realm of the dead, as we have suggested earlier, even more kenotically empty, even more ontologically eviscerated, than any sinner could possibly be. Only in such a lifeless and godforsaken state could he sink to the very bottom of sin and despair in search of the lost sheep.

After Jesus's Resurrection, when his closest followers seemed strangely unable to recognize him, his wounds served not only to identify him but to make it clear that the Risen One was and would ever be the Crucified One, pierced by fallen humanity as such and on whom all were now destined to look—in this life and at the threshold of the next—the centurion's sudden transformation being the New Testament augury thereof. This feature of the Passion story—to which our only access is a scant and inconclusive scriptural reference and a few equally tentative attempts at theological reconnoitering—provides us nonetheless with our most compelling account of Christian universality, a universality that must include every person who ever lived or ever will live.

While we cannot imagine what form the encounter between the crucified Christ and the mortals in Sheol might have taken, an analogous situation provides a general suggestion. The enduring centrality and attractive power of the corpse of Christ is as strange as it is a conspicuous fact of Christian faith and Christian iconography. It is both perfectly obvious and passing strange that Christianity's central and defining icon is the crucifix on which Jesus's corpse hangs lifelessly. That this supreme image of defeat should become Christianity's most recognizable representation of Christ's triumph is beautifully baffling precisely because it is the revelation of moral beauty that was as bafflingly transformative of aesthetic sensibilities as it was of the religious imagination. Christians themselves have at times found this image troubling. Acknowledging that the Cross was a scandal to the Jews and foolishness to the Gentiles, Saint Paul tried to fortify the wayward Corinthian Christians by insisting the he (Paul) preached only "Jesus Christ and him crucified" (1 Cor. 2:20). Clinging as steadfastly as Saint Paul did to the crucified Christ, the Catholic faithful have for centuries found the lifeless body of Christ on the crucifix to have something of that magnetic power that Jesus himself confidently predicted his crucified body would have. "The whole of Christianity is contained in the sign of the cross," writes Yves Congar, O.P.; "no theory of Redemption expresses half as much as a simple crucifix hung on the wall, erected as a wayside shrine or put on a tomb or altar."[9]

When the Paraclete comes, Jesus says in John's Gospel, "he will convict the world in regard to sin and righteousness and condemnation" (Jn. 16:8). It is the world's judgment with regard to sin, righteousness, and condemnation that the Spirit will call into question, precisely to the extent, we would argue, that this worldly way of reckoning with sin, righteousness, and condemnation has been overturned on the Cross and in the bowels of the netherworld. Thus it will be, too, at the end of time:

> Behold, he is coming amid the clouds,
> and every eye will see him,
> even those who pierced him.
> All the peoples of the earth will lament him.
> Yes. Amen. (Rev. 1:7)

Every eye will see him, even those who pierced him. Christ, Balthasar writes, "appears before all the peoples as the pierced one, which means as the living, palpable proof of what the sin of

9 Yves Congar, O.P. *The Meaning of Tradition*, trans. A.N. Woodrow (San Francisco: Ignatius Press, 2004), 74.

the world has in reality done to God."[10] The whole elaborate charade of our temporizing, self-exonerating, and rationalizing is destined to collapse—at the moment of our deaths. What Balthasar's Holy Saturday theology brings into focus is the possibility that at the encounter with the Crucified Christ, who has been savaged and slain since the foundation of the world by humans made nonetheless in his image and likeness, each of us will have to say Yes or No to the Truth—the gruesome truth of sin and its consequences and the glorious truth of Christ. The Crucified Christ—the Pierced One—is the beatific vision, and it is in his presence after death that each of us will choose communion with him or rebellion against him. Those who are overly serene about this Omega encounter with the Crucified Christ are almost surely underestimating the gravitational power of a lifetime of habitual self-justification or the surge of rebellion that can be triggered by the sudden demand for the selfless self-gift requisite to Trinitarian existence.

If we should not underestimate how jeopardized our eschatological destiny is by a lifelong habit of self-referentiality, however, we have even more reason not to underestimate the redemptive power of God's love in Christ. Those of us whose sins have been atoned for by Christ's Cross exist under changed existential circumstances whether we know it or not. But the fruit of the redemption that Christ accomplished will not be forced on us, for that would deprive us of the greatest God-given gift our species has: freedom and the capacity for moral reasoning and metaphysical wonder, which give freedom its purpose and true dignity. If we are to be the beneficiaries of Christ's redemptive suffering, we must consent to it and accept its terms and consequences. We must say Yes to our redemption, and this Yes requires an appreciation for the nature of our sinful rebellion and its extensive ramifications, an appreciation of which no earthly examination of conscience is capable.

An assessment of our lives that remains within an exclusively moral framework will have law—revealed law, natural law, and positive law—as the criteria. The whole Pauline corpus testifies to

10 *The von Balthasar Reader*, 416.

the shortcomings of this framework. Indispensable though such an examination of conscience is to the right conduct of one's life, the assessment of how faithfully one is living out the human vocation—and doing so with all the absolute uniqueness demanded by one's own special calling and circumstance—depends on a deeper understanding of the Christlikeness to which we are called than can be constructed from an exclusively moral reckoning. The predominance of mimetic over strictly moral admonition in the New Testament, both explicit and implicit, is instructive. Following Christ is the new Decalogue, one that fulfills the Law of Moses and raises it to new heights. Jesus, and specifically the crucified Christ, the Pierced One, is indispensable to a right reckoning of anyone's life. For He is the Logos, the Template, or (as Kierkegaard would say) the Pattern, which the First Adam forfeited in the very attempt to appropriate it by a prideful act of will, renouncing the promise of his Godlike endowment by trying to procure it as a possession.

Moreover, there is the paradox of sin and forgiveness. Of the sinful woman who anointed Jesus at the house of Simon the leper (identified by the Fourth Evangelist as Mary of Bethany), Jesus said, "the one to whom little is forgiven, loves little" (Lk. 7:47). And Saint Paul famously blurted out: "Shall we persist in sin that grace may abound?" (Rom. 6:1). That Paul promptly answered No to his own question takes nothing away from its suggestive power. Contrition—whether of the sort that we sinners can muster in moments of moral lucidity or the kind that only Christ crucified can elicit—is accompanied by grace commensurate with how thoroughly the sinner has been disarmed in the process. "Every man's final destiny," writes Balthasar, "will be determined by his attitude to Jesus."[11]

## Postmortem "Conversion"

God gives human beings the capacity to perform what seems for human beings to be a definitive (negative) choice against God, but which does not need to be judged/evaluated/assessed by

---

11 Balthasar, *Theo-Drama, Vol. III*, 27.

God as definitive. And not of course in such a way that the human person's choice is called into question from outside—which would amount to a disregard of the freedom bestowed on it—but rather in such a way that God, with his own divine choice, accompanies the human person into the most extreme situation of his (negative) choice. This is what happens in the passion of Jesus.[12]—Hans Urs von Balthasar

We live in a world today that has terribly and tragically come to think of freedom—man's great and mysterious gift—as nothing more than arbitrary self-will, which has no ordination other than that which each person chooses to assign it. The unspoken but implicit assumption that we humans have been endowed with the gift of freedom for no loftier reason than to enable us to chase after whatever desires or compulsions might excite us for the moment is intrinsically nihilistic. We live amid the spiritual wreckage and societal ruin that this implicit understanding of freedom has brought about. In fact, freedom exists to make it possible for the creature possessing it to assent to truth, goodness, and beauty, and by doing so, recognize a harmony underlying the cacophony of the world, celebrate the divine origin of that harmony, and leave further evidence of it by living loving lives. By comparison, an ostensibly free decision in favor of the tawdry, the vile, and the meretricious is a particularly sinister form of slavery.

In contrast to this vacuous and frivolous understanding of freedom, freedom as understood by Christianity is consequential to a frightening degree. The aggregate decisions of one's life not only constitute an infallible spiritual self-portrait, but they massively determine what one's final decision for or against God will be, the very decision on which one's ultimate destiny depends. The question we are exploring here is when does the sinner make this decision? According to Balthasar: "The absolute decision must be made in one's earthly life; in the hereafter, it will be too late."[13] Margaret Turek asks: "Since von Balthasar does not want to allow for a conversion after death [notwithstanding an innuendo to that effect heretofore mentioned], are we to understand the

---

12 *The von Balthasar Reader*, 152–3.
13 Balthasar, *Dare We Hope that All Men Be Saved?*, 182.

sinner's decisive encounter to occur 'in dying'?"[14] The phrase "in dying"—between quotation marks—suggests something that is punctual but sufficiently spacious to allow for a final exercise of freedom. "I am convinced that the fundamental thesis of there being a final decision which must be made and which is in fact made *in dying* expresses an indefeasible truth," writes Josef Pieper.[15] Complete and irreversible though the life now ended is, its eschatological consequence is not yet a foregone conclusion. That will require a final act of freedom, massively determined though it doubtless is by the habits of a lifetime. The question is when exactly might such a decision take place? Josef Pieper answers that it "takes place in a *breathing spell* not yet claimed by the impending catastrophe."[16]

> Christendom, moreover, has never failed to consider a dying person a *subjectum capax* for the sacraments even when he no longer presents any signs of conscious life, or may seem already deceased. That is, he is treated as someone who can and is willing to receive the salvation the sacramental symbols are meant to bestow. Of course the proponents of positivistic enlightenment have always considered this practice as obscurantist magic and dismissed it as prescientific naïveté, a piece of atavistic primitivism. But it is surprising to have that old conviction confirmed by certain findings brought to light in the past few decades by empirical investigation of man in general and death in particular.[17]

Pieper acknowledges the objection that a great many people die in circumstances that hardly seem to allow for a postmortem or intramortem decision—"in an accidental explosion, in an air raid, in a plane crash, in a cerebral hemorrhage." "Do not loss of consciousness, helplessness, inability to communicate, anesthesia, and so on, exclude the act we have been discussing?"[18] But

---

14 Tirolt, "Dare We Hope 'That All Men Be Saved'," 112.
15 Pieper, *Death and Immortality*, 78, italic emphasis added.
16 Ibid., 82, italic emphasis added.
17 Ibid., 89.
18 Ibid., 87–89.

then Pieper asks: "How many units of measurable time do we need for a decision?"[19]

> What is manifest in dreams is that our psyche, our soul, can set aside temporal successiveness to a great extent, and that, as the old writers expressed it, the power of the mind is itself something above and beyond time, *supra tempus.* We know also, on the basis of immediate experience, that for the performance of an act of loving concern (for example) no more than an instant is needed, an infinitesimally small span of time which no one will ever be able to measure with a chronometer. Again and again we hear it reported that people who have been rescued from the imminent threat of death have at the moment before losing consciousness seen their entire life, with all the details thought to be long since forgotten, or actually forgotten, unrolling with perfect clarity before their mind's eye.[20]

Death, concludes Pieper, "turns out to be a process of infinite stages taking place gradually over an unexpectedly long period of time."[21] The Catholic *Catechism* declares: "Death puts an end to human life as the time open to either accepting or rejecting the divine grace manifested in Christ."[22] "Each man receives his eternal retribution in his immortal soul at the very moment of his death, in a particular judgment that refers his life to Christ: either entrance into the blessedness of heaven—through a purification or immediately—or immediate and everlasting damnation."[23]

The rigor of this teaching has long served to sober sinners, to encourage moral rectitude, and to prompt sinners to make recompense for sins before it is too late. Is the postmortem encounter with Christ, then, nothing more than the official certification of the moral *status quo ante*, more or less mechanically consigning the soul to the eschatological destiny corresponding to its moral condition at death? This would seem to rob the *encounter* with

---

19 Ibid., 87–8.
20 Ibid., 88.
21 Ibid., 90.
22 *CCC* §1021.
23 Ibid., §1022.

Christ of the transformative power that must surely be its hall-mark, nor is it easily reconcilable with Christ's "preaching" to the dead so that "though condemned in the flesh in human estimation, they might live in the spirit in the estimation of God" (1 Pet. 4:6). To regard the postmortem encounter with Christ as a *fait accompli* would evacuate the word encounter of its meaning by eliminating its genuine relationality. At the beginning of the conclave that would elevate him to the papacy, Cardinal Joseph Ratzinger said: "Jesus Christ is divine mercy in person: to encounter Christ is to encounter the mercy of God."

> Betwixt the stirrup and the ground
> Mercy I asked, mercy I found.

Thus writes the Elizabethan biographer, historian, and topographer, William Camden. If pleading for mercy can be taken as an indication of a spirit of contrition commensurate with the waywardness of one's life, we have reason to be confident in divine mercy, however necessarily accompanied it is by an ontological and moral reordering to which the word purgatory has long alluded. The question is whether the plea for mercy elicited by fear of punishment rises to the same level as might a plea awakened by an encounter with the God-man who suffered the full consequences of one's sins.

We submit to Magisterial teaching, but, our theological deference notwithstanding, we find no reason to give more weight to the punctual than to the personal, to the chronological than to the Christological, to ascribe more weight to the *moment* of death than to the *encounter* with Christ that coincides with it. At the point of this encounter, of course, nothing in the life of the deceased can be altered. The moral and spiritual facts are now irrevocable, and both the glaring reality of these facts and their irrevocability can now, for the first time, have their greatest chastening effect. If each person's particular judgment consists of an encounter with the crucified Lord, surely the outcome of that judgment will depend at least as much on the sinner's response to

Christ as on his conduct in life. To give more weight to the sins than the encounter with Christ would be, in effect, to succumb to the moral pharisaism against which Jesus persistently inveighed. Since sin destroys the consciousness of sin, how complete can even the most scrupulous examination of conscience be in this life? As we have said, it would be a grave mistake to ignore how much the sinner's encounter with Christ will be determined by the moral habits and spiritual orientation of a lifetime. It is virtually certain that the full revelation of the moral failures of life—finally faced in the presence of the crucified Christ on whose flesh the sinner's sins have left their mark—will be an inducement to repentance greater than any known in life. It seems contrary to the spirit of Christ as transmitted by Scripture and tradition to insist that the Truth—in the person of the crucified Christ, who made that contrition possible—will nonetheless regard it as eschatologically inefficacious simply because it occurs after the electroencephalogram has gone flat. We, in any case, want to propose a more dramatic and consequential postmortem encounter, one in which the deceased sinner finally faces the Truth—the truth of his life no longer held at bay by illusions and self-justifications, on one hand, and, on the other hand, the truth of the love of God in Christ. Here, it seems—and here alone—is the sinner brought out of the fog formed by his own sinfulness into the light of Truth where he can for the first time make a fully informed act of contrition, one which, however influenced by the moral contours of his life, will be even more consequential than his accumulated sins. Douglas Farrow comes to a similar conclusion:

> The sudden and strange power of God is a power applied to soul and body alike in the definitive encounter with the risen Christ that takes place for each person *after death*, for Christ himself is the one through whom and with whom we make our transition to glory—the one who determines both continuity and discontinuity for us.[24]

24 Douglas Farrow, *Ascension Theology* (New York: T&T International, 2011), 135, italic emphasis added.

Still we cannot look away from the sternness of Jesus's warnings.

> Amen, amen, I say to you, the hour is coming and is now here when the dead will hear the voice of the Son of God, and those who hear will live. . . . Do not be amazed at this, because the hour is coming in which all who are in the tombs will hear his voice and will come out, those who have done good deeds to the resurrection of life, but those who have done wicked deeds to the resurrection of judgment. (Jn. 5:25, 28–29)

A cursory reading of this passage easily leads to a sheep and goats division between the doers of good and evil, which hardly corresponds to our lived experience. To support the idea of a simple and easily decided division between those who have done good deeds and those who have done wicked ones, one has to lay aside the glaring fact that everyone has done both. The Greek word here for judgment is *kriseos*, a cognate of our word crisis, a moment when a decision is unavoidable, entailing the gravest of consequences. The outstanding question is who makes that decision and on what basis? According to these verses in John's Gospel, at the otherwise *critical* hour, a doer of exclusively good deeds would face no such crisis. That possibility is only slightly less unlikely than that someone might arrive at that "hour" having done exclusively wicked deeds. So the passage that seems to settle matters simply peals back the outer layer of the mystery.

Drawing on Scripture, there can be no doubt that a reckoning occurs and that it will consist of the encounter between the dead and Christ crucified, but that this encounter can be even roughly approximated or anticipated in terms of a simple moral calculus is highly unlikely. While Jesus occasionally appealed to such a moral yardstick, far more striking, more original to Jesus, and less convergent with the conventional views of his time are his disparagements of this view of the judgment to come:

> From the parables and warnings of the Lord we know that not the number of "talents" received is decisive, but their use (Lk. 19:16 ff), especially not the storing up of religious values against the day of judgment: "Tax collectors and harlots will come into the kingdom of God before you" (Mt. 21:31). "On that day many

will say to me, 'Lord, Lord, did we not prophesy in your name, and cast out demons in your name, and do many mighty works in your name?' And then I will declare to them, 'I never knew you'" (Mt. 7:22ff).[25]

If, as Balthasar writes, "the attitude a man takes toward [Christ] decides the eternal fate of that man,"[26] then when else will this attitude be formally and finally expressed if not at the "moment" of death. For the last moment of life—just before the last breath or the last beat of the heart—rarely affords the moral or mental lucidity necessary for such a decision. Writes the Dominican scholar J. A. DiNoia:

> It by no means follows from the particular and unique role ascribed to Jesus Christ in central Christian doctrines that those who do not *now* acknowledge him will be permanently excluded from sharing in the salvation he both signifies and effects. Rather than attributing an implausible implicit faith in Christ to the members of other religious communities [as, for example, Karl Rahner did with his idea of "anonymous Christians"], theology of religions in a prospective vein contends that non-Christians will have the opportunity to acknowledge Christ in the future. This opportunity may come to them in the course of their lives here on earth or *in the course of their entrance into the life to come.*[27]

How this might happen is of course a mystery known only to God, but following the path Balthasar has charted we feel that the New Testament locus for reconnoitering this mystery is Christ's "descent into hell." As with other discrete and chronologically delimited events occurring between the Annunciation and the Ascension, the events of the Passion most specifically, the temporal punctuality of the crucified Christ's "descent into hell" neither exhausts its eventfulness, consigns it to the past, nor hinders its ever-present contemporaneity. As such, he who took on the sins of the world stands before the deceased sinner as the ulti-

---

25  *The von Balthasar Reader*, 421.

26  Balthasar, *To the Heart of the Mystery of Redemption*, 20.

27  J. A. DiNoia, O. P., *The Diversity of Religions: A Christian Perspective* (Washington, DC: Catholic University of America Press, 1992), 105; quoted: Oakes, S. J., *Infinity Dwindles to Infancy*, 370, n. 45, emphasis added.

mate recipient of the wreckage born of the sinner's forfeited Trinitarian ontology and its moral and social ramifications. The Pierced One is as well the living portal to Trinitarian joy for those who accept its terms and submit to its demands. The distinguished Orthodox theologian, Sergius Bulgakov, has probed this mystery with remarkable deftness.

> The afterlife is not only "reward" and "punishment," and not only a "purgatory," but also a spiritual school, a new experience of life, which does not remain without consequence but enriches and changes each individual's spiritual image. We know nothing about the degree or manner of this process. But it is important to establish that, even in the afterlife, human souls experience and acquire something new, each in its own way, in its freedom. . . . And if one asserts that late repentance is not accompanied by forgiveness, to whom is it given to measure the depth of the mercy of God, who "hath concluded them all in unbelief, that he might have mercy upon all" (Rom. 11:32)? Repentance has an internal dynamism, a self-moving, self-acting power. Can one in general allow that repentance is ineffective?[28]

To read the scriptural and theological data as evidence for what Balthasar calls "post-mortem conversion" is not, therefore, to automatically suggest that the offer of forgiveness and mercy afforded each person at death will be accepted. It is possible for a sinner to remain so annealed against the penitential demands required for his ontological rehabilitation that he clings either to his vaunted autonomy or to his membership in a parochial association defined over-against its non-members. Conceding that the rejection of Christ's offer is possible, however, that possibility should not lead us to underestimate just how disarming a post-mortem encounter with Christ might be even to the most hardened heart. Nonetheless, the responsibility for the decision for or against Christ and the Trinitarian communion, to which Christ came to restore humanity, lies with each person. But it is essential to remember Joseph Ratzinger's insistence that "Christ inflicts pure perdition on no one."

---

28 Sergius Bulgakov, *The Bride of the Lamb*, trans. Boris Jakim (Grand Rapids: Eerdmans, 2002), 363–64.

In himself he is sheer salvation. Anyone who is with him has entered the space of deliverance and salvation. Perdition is not imposed by him, but comes to be wherever a person distances himself from Christ. It comes about whenever someone remains enclosed within himself. . . . Judgment consists in this removal of the mask in death. The judgment is simply the manifestation of the truth. . . . Herein lies that redemptive transformation of the idea of judgment which Christian faith brought about. The truth which judges man has itself set out to save him.[29]

A person is not *sent* to hell at death. Rather the masquerades, the posturings, and the fictions by which he hollowed out his life in an effort to secure it on his own terms suddenly fall away. He faces the cold facts, the truth about whatever degree of lovelessness, selfishness, and indifference have determined his life. Moreover, he does so in the full and painful realization of the now vanished possibility of altering the past in any way. The only question is whether or not he will respond to this encounter with Reality with the contrition commensurate with it or with self-justifying defiance. The latter response turns the veiled hell of sinful earthly existence into the eschatological finality of hell. While it seems highly likely that one's eschatological prospects would be greatly improved were one to face the choice between contrition and defiance in the presence of Christ and the offer of mercy that is constituted by his presence, we would be wrong to take too much solace from this. We know from Scripture and from our own lives how predisposed we are to self-justification and how loath we are to drop our guard and acknowledge our sinfulness. We know—again from Scripture and, if we are honest, from our own lives—that habitual sin both hardens the heart of the sinner and conduces to a reflexive act of self-deluding self-justification. However promising the sinner's encounter with Love in person may be, it would be an act of unwarranted presumption to think it suffices to ensure the humble spirit and contrite heart by which the sinner opens himself to the purgatorial preparation for incorporation into the Trinitarian *communio*.

29 Ratzinger, *Eschatology,* 205–6.

How easy might it be for a person to distance himself from the One who is and has been throughout one's life the secret aspiration of all his desires? How much energy it might take to remain in one's self-justifying self-enclosure, when presented with the easiest of yokes and the lightest of burdens, would depend on how hardened one's heart has become and how habituated one is to self-justifications. Nor is there warrant for minimizing the penitential and purgative consequences of the sinner's Yes to Christ's offer. In the final analysis, writes Joseph Ratzinger, "man becomes his own judgment."[30] Concurring, Josef Pieper argues that if we think of hell as a prison, "we should visualize it as not barred from outside, but from within."[31]

The responsibility for man's sinful rebellion against God and the rejection of his own self-sacrificial Trinitarian provenance lies with each of us. In Christ, however, we have been given—in this life and the next—the grace to say Yes and in doing so to rescue our freedom from its Babylonian captivity to self-will. In a passage in his encyclical *Spe Savli*, which strongly suggests his concurrence with Balthasar's Holy Saturday theology, Benedict XVI writes:

> Some recent theologians are of the opinion that the fire which both burns and saves is Christ himself, the Judge and Savior. The encounter with him is the decisive act of judgment. Before his gaze all falsehood melts away. This encounter with him, as it burns us, transforms and frees us, allowing us to become truly ourselves. All that we build during our lives can prove to be mere straw, pure bluster, and it collapses. Yet in the pain of this encounter, when the impurity and sickness of our lives become evident to us, there lies salvation. His gaze, the touch of his heart heals us through an undeniably painful transformation "as through fire." But it is a blessed pain, in which the holy power of his love sears through us like a flame, enabling us to become totally ourselves and thus totally of God. In this way the inter-relation between justice and grace also becomes clear: the way we live our lives is not immaterial, but our defilement does not

---

30  Ratzinger, *Eschatology*, 207.
31  Pieper, *Death and Immortality*, 59.

stain us forever if we have at least continued to reach out towards Christ, towards truth and towards love. Indeed, it has already been burned away through Christ's Passion. At the moment of judgment we experience and we absorb the overwhelming power of his love over all the evil in the world and in ourselves. The pain of love becomes our salvation and our joy. It is clear that we cannot calculate the "duration" of this transforming burning in terms of the chronological measurements of this world. The transforming "moment" of this encounter eludes earthly time-reckoning—it is the heart's time, it is the time of "passage" to communion with God in the Body of Christ.[32]

In our view, the descent into the realm of the dead, scant though the scriptural references are, is the key to accounting for the universal efficacy of the Christian revelation. Doctrines like the atonement theories and others can be tweaked and contorted in all manner of ways as demanded by objections that arise over time, but, in the end, their account of universality is not entirely convincing. But if the descent into hell and the preaching to the dead is the key to the meaning and universal efficacy of the Passion, why were the scriptural references to these things so scant and why are we just now, thanks to Balthasar and others, coming to grips with their implications? As we have suggested above, it is our opinion that the paucity of biblical references and the seeming tardiness of the Church in bringing them into sharper focus is due to the "time-released" quality of the Christian revelation.

> "I have yet many things to say to you, but you cannot bear them now. When the Spirit of truth comes, he will guide you into all the truth; for he will not speak on his own authority, but whatever he hears he will speak, and he will declare to you the things that are to come. He will glorify me, for he will take what is mine and declare it to you. All that the Father has is mine; therefore I said that he will take what is mine and declare it to you." (Jn. 16:13–15)

The deposit of faith does not change, but its depth, meaning, and ever-widening scope are revealed to the faithful gradually in concert with their capacity to both assimilate the broader impli-

32 *Spe Salvi*, §47.

cations and to live up to the responsibilities they entail. God as the Spirit who blows where he will does not summon his people to a task for which they lack the requisite fortitude, nor does he foster the development of theological doctrine that is beyond their powers of assimilation—that is, their capacity to recognize how apposite the new theologoumenon is to the elucidation of apostolic faith and how germane it is to the exigencies and needs of the era in which the Spirit of Truth has chosen to bring it into consideration. It is our opinion that Balthasar's theology of Holy Saturday represents just such a development—theologically profound and of immense value in rekindling faith in believers and inspiring anew the evangelical and apologetic activities that have lately languished. Inasmuch as it would be inappropriate to confine the descent into hell to the worldly chronology in terms of which the events of the Passion occurred, it opens the possibility that all the dead, regardless of when they die, are confronted by the One who has taken on himself the suffering born of sin. This encounter is the Omega event in the lives of every person who has ever lived or will ever live.

Fleming Rutledge contends that a theology that takes seriously Christ's descent into hell places us "on the front lines of God's apocalyptic war."[33] If this is so, then the decisive battle of that war takes place in circumstances far more reminiscent of the confessional than of the field of valor, and at the moment of death when we ourselves "descend" to the depths of our gravest sins only to find ourselves accompanied there by the One who suffered the full weight of those sins. On this view, what is at stake in the apocalyptic war is precisely God's gamble: whether the divine intention of bringing each and every creature made in the image and likeness of Trinitarian Love into full communion with the Trinity will succeed or be thwarted by human willfulness. *The decisive battle in this apocalyptic war occurs at the death of each and every person endowed with the capacity for the Trinitarian communion. Each death is the decisive battle* precisely because, if

---

33 Fleming Rutledge, *The Crucifixion: Understanding the Death of Jesus Christ* (Grand Rapids, MI: Eerdmans, 2015), 465.

anyone is lost, the divine plan for universal salvation will have been thwarted to that extent.

To believe, as we do, that Tertullian was right to say that the soul is naturally Christian, is simply to believe that Christ is who he said he was and who his Church has ceaselessly declared him to be. Whether in due course or in the fullness of time—in this life or the next—eventually every person will discover that his destiny is inextricably intertwined with that of Christ, and he will have to embrace that fact—with all the humility, gratitude, and moral remorse it entails—or rebel fiercely but impotently against it. Those of us fortunate enough to have received the gift of faith, on the basis of which we have been given advance notice of this extraordinary fact, have a moral obligation to alert those who remain unaware of it. For the outcome of one's eventual encounter with Christ will very likely be significantly improved by having lived a life in relationship with him through the mediation of the Church.

With virtually the entire Christian tradition, Romano Guardini declared that "With death the time for willing and acting is over."[34] But is the postmortem response to Christ—who accompanies us in our deaths as he accompanied the dead on Holy Saturday—necessarily an act of will? Is it, as Pieper suggested, a decision? Arguably the Yes to Christ is more like the relinquishing of willfulness than an "act" of will. In the same way that in his descent into the realm of the dead Christ did nothing, inasmuch as the sublime "act" was simply to accompany the godforsaken, so the dead can do nothing. However unavoidable it is that we transpose the conditions pertaining only in this life to our musings about existence on the far side of death, we have no reason to rule out forms of volition which—though they may not constitute action—may nonetheless represent the assent of the heart.

Imagine a young couple having a candle-lit dinner when a look, a gesture, a confidence shared, a momentarily shared glance into one another's eyes causes one or both to fall in love. Has an act been performed? Something like this may better approximate the

---

34 Romano Guardini, *The Last Things*, 33.

postmortem encounter with Christ than would the more familiar image of Christ the judge. Writes Søren Kierkegaard:

> And what does all this mean? It means that everyone for himself, in quiet inwardness before God, shall humble himself before what it means in the strictest sense to be a Christian, admit candidly before God how it stands with him, so that he might yet accept the grace which is offered to everyone who is imperfect, that is, to everyone.[35]

The encounter with the crucified and risen Christ at death constitutes an unavoidable decision; fundamentally it is the decision between, on one hand, a hard and humble and almost certainly humiliating truth, represented by the Truth in Person, and, on the other hand, a tissue of vainglorious and flimsy lies, each an act of obeisance to the Father of Lies. Arguably, the Yes to Christ's invitation to share in his existence, the accompanying remorse for having squandered the opportunity to live accordingly in earthly life, and the gratitude for having been brought into the Trinitarian communion, arises spontaneously. The dead encountered by Christ in the realm of the dead can do nothing because what is required of them is an assent to what has been the secret desire of their heart, an assent that elicits an act of gratitude without requiring an act of will.

Christ has died our death. Balthasar cites a passage in the diary of the French novelist Georges Bernanos written shortly before his death, declaring this passage to be "the capstone of all his thought."

> We imagine that we fear our death and want to flee from it, whereas we really desire this death as He desired His. Just as he sacrifices himself on each altar where Mass is offered, so he begins to die again in each man at the moment of his agony. We will all that he wills, but we do not know that we will it. Sin makes us live on the surface of our lives; we only enter in ourselves to die, and there it is he awaits us.[36]

35 Søren Kierkegaard, *Training in Christianity*, trans. Walter Lowrie, preface, Richard J. Neuhaus (New York: Vintage, 2004), 61.
36 *Agenda*, January 24, 1948; quoted: Balthasar, *Bernanos*, 468.

Most non-Christians would be offended to be told—and it would surely be a mistake to break the news to them too abruptly—that they are likely to be contrite and newly shriven Christians before rigor mortis sets in at death. But to view everyone we meet in this life with this understanding is surely conducive to the spirit of forgiveness, kindness, generosity, and the spiritual *noblesse oblige* that should characterize the Christian attitude toward those who have not been given the gift of faith or whose full acceptance of that gift awaits exposure to someone who has. And what shines through such a Christian witness without his realizing it and what makes his example compelling—and potentially maddening—to unbelieving onlookers is how the *Imitatio Christi*, as his transcendent model, stabilizes his life and makes him less susceptible to the myriad mimetic allurements that would otherwise lead to his ontological fragmentation.

## Blaspheming Against the Holy Spirit

> Amen, I say to you, all sins and all blasphemies that people utter will be forgiven them. But whoever blasphemes against the Holy Spirit will never have forgiveness, but is guilty of an everlasting sin. (Mk. 3:28–29)

This puzzling statement has received considerable attention, but due to the fact that most of the attention has focused on the question as to what the blasphemy against the (Holy) Spirit might be, many overlook the general claim for which this represents the sole exception. All sins and all blasphemies in Mark's version and all who speak a word against the Son of Man in Luke's will be forgiven. There may be many reasons why this sweeping statement has attracted less attention than the single exception to it, but arguably one of the reasons for this is the emphasis that Christian thought has long placed on avoiding eternal punishment, often enough even at the expense of its opposite: attaining eternal happiness.

"Whoever does not gather with me scatters," Jesus said in Luke's Gospel (Lk. 11:23). The Spirit both dwells in our hearts and gathers the community of those whose form of existence is in the process of being changed. It is not just another community, but a new form of community with a new center of gravity and a radically different gathering principle. The new form of existence represented by faith in Christ cannot reach maturity except with and in the ecclesial communion. This is the anthropological fact that underlies the otherwise contentious proposition, *extra ecclesiam nulla salus*—outside the Church there is no salvation.

Heaven, which is to say the kingdom or reign of the Triune God, consists from all eternity of the Persons of the Divine Trinity. Entry into this supremely loving community begins with an encounter with the Second Person of the Trinity, Christ the Logos or Blueprint for creation itself, into whose incarnational embrace we can be incorporated according to our willingness to find our ultimate freedom in the will of Another. Catholic Christians aspire to that gift of will, and they refer to those who continue that aspiration in the next life as members of the Church Triumphant. Those of us still struggling to overcome the sin-laden circumstances of this life and the wickedness and snares of the Devil are members of the Church Militant. Inasmuch as Christ is the head of the Church, those who through him are brought into the Trinitarian communion are, by that fact, members of his Church. Heaven is the Church Triumphant. In that sense, the principle *extra ecclesiam nulla salus* is a tautology, precisely because *salus*—salvation itself—is participation in the Trinitarian Communion, the Church Triumphant.

The nature of doctrinal development made current by John Henry Newman stands as a reminder that the Church exercises magisterial authority in seeking to refine and deepen doctrines which require such refinement precisely in the interest of remaining true to the Scriptures, the deposit of faith, and the Spirit's guidance in elucidating them. The Church once held that the principle of *extra ecclesiam nulla salus* meant that pagans, heretics, Jews, and infants who die before baptism were condemned to eternal damnation. The Second Vatican Council—especially in *Lumen Gentium*—refined the Church's position on this seminal issue.

The process of maturation almost inevitably involves a process of assimilation during which both the "progressive" and the "reactionary" responses will miss the point and take their toll.

The new openness to the world represented by *Lumen Gentium*, lacking the pastoral and theological care necessary to assure its most fruitful assimilation, has had serious, unhealthy, and unwarranted consequences, and Balthasar has unfortunately become something of a lightning rod for those fearing a drift toward theological relativism, even though he himself spent no small amount of his considerable energy resisting this trend.

When we consider Jesus's warnings about the unforgiveable sin against the Holy Spirit in this context, we are led to surmise that one of the major impediments standing in the way of a sinner's Yes to Christ at the moment of death might well be his refusal to enter into communion with those he regarded in life as irredeemably cursed—an eschatological manifestation of the Pharisees who refused to be associated with Jesus because he refused *not to be associated* with sinners, harlots, and tax-collectors. Both the moral realities of life and the operations of mimetic antagonism foster a binary principle of social organization. One knows his own people in some measure by knowing the alien forces that stand in contrast to his people. If there is any habit that cannot be carried into the Trinitarian communion it is this one. The partisan spirit can be deeply ingrained, and in this life it can at times have considerable justifications, but any attempt to sustain it in the next life disqualifies one from participation in the "all in all" nature of heavenly communion. Writes Fleming Rutledge:

> There is nothing more characteristic of humanity than the universal tendency of one portion of that humanity to justify itself as deserving and some other portion as undeserving. Nothing is more foundational in Christian faith than the recognition that we can never be justified in that way. To speak of "deserving" is to divide up the world in a fashion that is utterly alien to the gospel. Christ came to die expressly for sinners, for the *undeserving*, for the *ungodly* (Rom. 5:6).[37]

37 Fleming Rutledge, *The Crucifixion: Understanding the Death of Jesus Christ* (Grand Rapids, MI: Eerdmans, 2015), 451.

For further elucidation, we turn briefly to a term used by the author of the Letter to the Hebrews: "If we sin deliberately after receiving knowledge of the truth, there no longer remains sacrifice for sins but a fearful prospect of judgment and a flaming fire that is going to consume the adversaries" (Heb. 10:26–7).

Quite obviously this passage alludes to the collapse of the efficacy of ritual sacrifice of the sort that was central to Temple Judaism. For Girard, texts such as this have precisely the apocalyptic implications for which he gave so lucid an anthropological account. At this point, however, we are primarily concerned with the reference to the flaming fire that is to consume rebels. The flames of hell have for centuries dominated Christianity's attempt to imagine the condition of the lost, and this passage has contributed to that stereotypical image. But there is a good deal more here than just another image of torture. The word here translated as "adversaries" is the Greek word, *hupenantios*. It combines the prefix *hupen*—from which we have in English the word *hyper*—and *enantios*—meaning antagonist. It is the partisan spirit that is habitually hyper antagonistic. In some translations, the term *rebel* is used as the English equivalent of the Greek word. In light of our exploration of René Girard's work, we can paraphrase this passage by saying that once the old sacrificial system for "taking away sins" by transferring them to a scapegoat has been crippled by exposure to the truth of the Cross, then those who persist in their hyper-antagonism will face the "fearful prospect of judgment and the flaming fire that is going to consume the adversaries." Who are the *hupenantios*? Who are the raging rebels? They are those whose moral and ontological resources have been so depleted by sin that their "thirst" for truth, goodness, and beauty has degenerated into a hyper-mimetic antagonism of one sort or another. For them the prospect of reconciliation and forgiveness is unthinkable

Inasmuch as the ecclesial *communio* constitutes the preparation for participation in the ultimate *communio* that awaits us, it has early and long warned against the sectarian spirit. Understanding how strong the mimetic impulse is and how readily it fosters a

273

sectarian spirit, René Girard credited Paul's immunity to such things to the depth of his conversion:

> Paul was more radical than Peter. He lectured Peter, and often strongly disapproved of him. But in the end Paul always gave into him because he knew that Christ had wanted Peter to speak for him. Paul went right to the heart of the matter in everything, and here he recognized the authority of tradition—a tradition that had only been in existence for a quarter-century! And it is because he was perfectly aware of what was at stake that he acted as he did. If he hadn't, Christianity would never have survived; it would have fallen apart at once. To understand Christianity and orthodoxy one must think of Paul. Paul was indeed stronger than Peter, better educated, more cosmopolitan, but he always yielded to Peter's primacy.[38]

Paul's deference with regard to Peter was not motivated by a solicitude for tradition, *qua* tradition. Rather, he knew that at the heart of any hope for the survival of a healthy Catholic tradition is *catholicity* itself, that is, a need to avoid schism and the sectarian spirit that is its harbinger. It was this same Paul, of course, who so forcefully chastised the Corinthian Christians for the incipient forms of division and rivalry that had been called to his attention:

> For it has been reported to me about you, my brothers, by Chloe's people, that there are rivalries among you. I mean that each of you is saying, "I belong to Paul," or "I belong to Apollos," or "I belong to Cephas," or "I belong to Christ." Is Christ divided? Was Paul crucified for you? Or were you baptized in the name of Paul? (1 Cor. 1:11–13)

Saint Paul was hardly chastising the Corinthians for expressing their gratitude to those from whom they had come to know Christ. Rather, he was alerting them to the dangers of the partisan spirit which has its source in the *diabolos*, the demonic sower of discord. Inasmuch as the Church exists to reconcile the world to God and its inhabitants to both God and one another, it must

---

38 René Girard, *The One by Whom Scandal Comes*, trans. M.B. DeBevoise (East Lansing, MI: Michigan State University Press, 2014), 78.

forever resist captivity to a partisan spirit, as Paul did. There may be many ways of sinning against or blaspheming against the Holy Spirit, but surely one of them is the harboring of a sectarian, pharisaical, or Gnostic spirit of division. It is a mistake to think, as do many whose de-Christianization has taken its intellectual toll, either that unity trumps difference or that difference can be maintained only by compromises constantly adjudicated and re-adjudicated. Nevertheless there is a distinctly Catholic way in which seeming antinomies of this sort can be reconciled. As Michele M. Schumacher observes with reference to the writings of Adrienne von Speyr, "all that is recognized in the world as polar, is shown by Adrienne to be first and finally—that is to say, *archetypally*—Trinitarian."[39] Thus is the well-known Catholic principle of *both/and*—and all the paradoxical perplexities flowing therefrom—grounded in the mystery of the Trinity.

Meanwhile, those stuck in a partisan or hyper-partisan stance find the apparently paradoxical and ultimately Trinitarian anthropology—on which Catholic ecclesiology is based—offensive. Hell is for the hyper-antagonistic, which is to say it is the inner experience of someone who, consumed by the scandals born of misdirected mimetic desire, refuses to be gathered into a community consisting of their erstwhile antagonists. Hell consists of those who are so addicted to the energy of animosity that they resist being gathered by the Good Shepherd into the communion where all energy is the energy of love.

Blessedness consists of entering into full participation in the unique ecclesial form of existence of which Christians are privileged to partake by faith (1 Cor. 13:12). As John R. Sachs, S.J. has written: "'We and They,' the saved and the damned, are not and cannot be categories into which faith and hope, if they are truly Christian, divide humanity."[40] Saint Paul was quick to recognize the seeds of the division that would ultimately lead to destruction. "While there is jealousy and strife among you, are you not of the flesh, and behaving like ordinary men? For when one says,

39 Schumacher, *A Trinitarian Anthropology*, 27.
40 Sachs, "Current Eschatology," 243.

'I belong to Paul' and another, 'I belong to Apollo' are you not merely men" (1 Cor. 3:3–4)?

The Holy Spirit who guides the Church not only breaks down the barriers that separate partisans, but he leads us to the whole truth. To blaspheme against this mysterious reality is to refuse the divine invitation. Again in *Spe Salvi*, Benedict XVI expresses this horror aptly:

> There can be people who have totally destroyed their desire for truth and readiness to love, people for whom everything has become a lie, people who have lived for hatred and have suppressed all love within themselves. This is a terrifying thought, but alarming profiles of this type can be seen in certain figures of our own history. In such people all would be beyond remedy and the destruction of good would be irrevocable: this is what we mean by the word *Hell*.[41]

We have heretofore mentioned research on what some call "near-death" experiences and others insist on referring to as events experienced *while dead*, and before resuscitation restored them to life. Medical advances have greatly increased the number of people who have survived clinical death, and a very great many of them describe experiences in terms of light and love and a welcoming presence. Those reporting such things were not necessarily moral paragons or particularly religious. As we have said before, such experiences hardly constitute theological evidence, but neither should they be dismissed as eschatologically uninteresting. Mention is here made of them in support of our two suggestions: First, that, the revelation of the Lamb Slain, the Pierced One, set in motion an alteration in man's religious, aesthetic, and moral sensibilities and, secondly, that the asymmetry between man's final Yes and the No to Christ is rooted in the fact that Christ's yoke is so easy and his burden so light that, unless choked back with the force of a titanic will, it is as forthcoming as

41 *Spe Salvi*, §45.

an expression of gratitude for an unearned gift. This at least would correlate with the rapidly accumulating research into after-or near-death experiences.

We earlier made reference to Balthasar's important study of theological aesthetics and his insistence that the Cross inaugurated a deepening of man's understanding of beauty. Henceforth, the moral beauty of complete self-sacrifice for another or others is found to be more aesthetically compelling than merely physical beauty.[42] In light of the aesthetic revolution radiating out from the Cross, there is no reason to dismiss the likelihood that, for all but a very few, the encounter with the Pierced One can be conflated with the loving light to which many survivors of the so-called "near-death" experience testify.

It is only the No to the invitation that the Pierced One wordlessly issues that requires an act of will, and it is the very attempt to sustain such an absurd act of negation—*non serviam*—that constitutes the soul's suffering. Fully acknowledging the impenetrability of this mystery, we may nevertheless surmise that the absurdity of this refusal of love, mercy, and forgiveness is not lost on one attempting it. The distinction between what we call purgatory and hell may turn on the question as to whether the refusal—and therefore the suffering that accompanies it—subsides or becomes all-consuming. For the knowledge of how preposterous this refusal is will by no means lead to its abandonment. The more ontological deficit one suffers, the more exhilarating and intoxicating a fit of rage can be. One can cling to rage and intensify it in a desperate attempt to fill the void. So it is that the impotence of self-will in the next life can lead, not to the abandonment of so futile an act, but to its hypertrophic swelling into the madness of hellish rebellion as such. Nothing short of this maddened rage at God could hold out against the love of

---

42 The crisis into which so-called modern art has descended may be due to an intuition, untutored by faith, of the aesthetic superiority of something other than worldly loveliness. If so, it is yet another sign of the danger involved in being exposed to Christian revelation while remaining hostile to the Christian faith.

Christ, and we have no evidence that a fellow human has ever been able to sustain such hellish fury. Even a Yes that is, so to speak, all but inaudible sets one on a path of ontological rehabilitation in preparation for the divine communion for which one was created in the first place.

# The Raging Rebels

The pit into which the sinner falls by his No, the Son reaches by his Yes.[1]—John Saward

I could swear indeed that until I was put under a master, I did not so much as know what it was to want my own way.[2] —Jean-Jacque Rousseau

EDWARD OAKES asks, "If the gospel means good news, what is the bad news it means to rescue us from?"[3] A one-word answer to Oakes' question might be *hell*, but it might more precisely be *unforgivenness*, a state that consists of the effort to extricate one-self from the resentments born of mimetic aggravations by repeatedly reasserting one's autonomy. Remember Dostoevsky's underground man:

> I am a sick man. . . . I am a spiteful man. I am a most unpleasant man. I think my liver is diseased. . . . I know perfectly well that I can't possibly "get even" with doctors by refusing their treatment; I know better than anyone that all this is going to hurt me alone, and no one else. Even so, if I refuse to be treated, it's out of spite.[4]

The weight of the theological sources we find most compelling is that perdition is not something imposed on the sinner, but rather it is the result of the sinner's rejection of the forgiveness

1 John Saward, *The Mysteries of March: Hans Urs von Balthasar on the Incarnation and Easter* (Washington, DC: The Catholic University of America Press, 1990), 47.

2 Jean-Jacques Rousseau, The Confessions, trans. J.M. Cohen (London: Penguin, 1953), 22.

3 Edward T. Oakes, S.J., "Saved from What? On Preaching Hell in the New Evangelization," *Pro Ecclesia*, Vol. XXII, No. 4: 380.

4 Fyodor Dostoyevsky, *Notes From Underground*, trans. by Michael R. Katz (New York: W.W. Norton & Company, 1989).

offered by Christ, the divine Logos in whose image and likeness we are made and the human face of the loving Trinitarian communion to which we humans are intrinsically ordered. Reprising a mystery that Saint Paul circumambulates in more complex ways, Rémi Brague insists that "sin is what is forgiven. One can even say: it has no other meaning than to be forgiven." Sin can be rightly understood only by one who has experienced its forgiveness. "Sin is like a precipice toward which one returns after having risked falling in. If he had fallen in, he would not have seen its depth, not having survived the fall."[5] Brague reminds us that the very idea of sin has its true meaning only for those who have experienced sin forgiven. Mercy and sin are realities that elude those who have never experienced the mystery of their inner connection.

We have ample scriptural warrant—especially from Johannine sources—for saying that Christ provokes a decision. Moreover, any attempt to remain neutral or indifferent will fail. Christ will have to be loved or hated, served unreservedly or opposed with all one's strength. He is heaven if loved and served and hell if rejected and hated. To think that there is a middle option is to vastly underestimate the breathtaking drama that will occur at the moment of the postmortem encounter with Christ. In the presence of the truth as the Pierced One, a decision is required: A Yes, accompanied by contrition for one's acts of rebellion, great or small, or this encounter will elicit an unavoidably hate-filled No. Just as we imagine a period of purgation during which the sinful habits of a lifetime are slowly overcome—conceding the dubious importation of temporality into these imaginings—we might as well imagine an analogous process going in the other direction, beginning with an attempted indifference and forced by the "insistent feet" of the Hound of Heaven to grow ever more intensely antagonistic, and ending in a state of full rebellion. "[A]ll true freedom rests upon the overcoming of the power to say no," writes Balthasar in his treatise on the writings of Vladimir Solovyov, rather ominously adding that "the depth of denial that is possible increases in proportion to the increase of

---

5 Brague, *On the God of the Christians (and on one or two others)*, 150.

consciousness and spirituality."[6] This rebellion, in other words, becomes truly titanic in those whose prodigious spiritual and intellectual gifts have been squandered on their own Promethean stratagems.

We noted above Balthasar's insistence that a characteristic of hell is the hatred of God. In this sense we might propose two forms of the cry of dereliction, Jesus's "My God, my God, why have you forsaken me?" and the truly hellish one of the sinner, as astonished as the psalmist of Psalm 139—but clinging to his own godforsakenness—who cries, "My God, my God, why have you not left me alone? Why can I not—even in my bitter hatred—rid myself of you? Why do you hover so persistently, haunting my willful attempt to think of you no longer?"

To insist on fleeing farther and farther into the netherworld to escape from the encounter is to grow ever more antagonistic to God in Christ, the Hound of Heaven. If such antagonism persists the result is the "hyper antagonism" about which the author of Hebrews speaks. Just as there is no hell until there is a total and complete rejection of love, mercy, and forgiveness, so such rejection can have as the object of its antagonism only love, mercy, and forgiveness in person. "Strictly speaking," writes Jean-Luc Marion, "hatred can *truly* be directed against the truth only if it is directed against a witness who dares to say: 'I am the way, the truth, and the life' (Jn. 14:6)."[7] To fortify oneself against the Truth—in Person—to the point of hating him is hell itself.

Willing one's own damnation may not be as easy as some suppose, for the decision for damnation is the decision to refuse an unimaginable offer of forgiveness and mercy, accompanied though it necessarily must be by the sinner's willingness to undergo whatever anguish might be involved in recognizing the damage his sins have done to others and to himself and how shamefully he has squandered the precious opportunity to live a nobler and more selfless life. There remains, however, the all-important *mysterium iniquitatis*, declared by Balthasar to be "the central mystery of the theo-drama" and summarized thusly:

6 Balthasar, *The Glory of the Lord, Vol III*, 340.
7 Marion, *In the Self's Place*, 102.

"God's heightened love provokes a heightened hatred that is as bottomless as love itself (John 15:25)."[8] As Balthasar elsewhere writes, "love reveals the depths of hatred, and indeed in a certain sense generates hatred."[9]

## Milton's Satan

The attempt to rid oneself of the God revealed by Christ, may well begin with mere indifference, but, if it persists, this refusal will necessarily be driven to ever more emphatic forms of rejection leading finally to a hatred of God that is fueled by a self-hatred that secretly wells up in hate-filled hearts. In his *Paradise Lost*, John Milton has given us a vivid picture of the rejection of God by Satan, a rejection that both constitutes hell itself and, in Milton's telling, captures its quintessence. Milton's depiction begins with lines about God's response to the existence of a rebellious will and the evil born of that rebellion, lines that raise the perennial theodicy question: How could a good God allow the suffering born of sinful humanity? In general, this question raises the issue of freedom and the role of moral reason associated with it. To prevent evil from occurring, God would have to extinguish freedom and thus undermine the moral seriousness of life, essentially abandoning the prospect of bringing the created order into a free and loving communion with the uncreated Trinitarian life of God. Since the misuse of freedom could not have been unforeseen by God, there must have been from the beginning a plan for reconciling with the mortal miscreants who were amenable to reconciliation and for quarantining those who were not. Of the latter, Milton presents the quintessence of Satan, the aboriginal rebel against God. Anticipating by three centuries Joseph Ratzinger's assertion that God "leaves to the damned the right to will their own damnation,"[10] Milton acknowledges that evil would have to be tolerated, but that it would also have to be ultimately impotent:

8  Balthasar, *Theo-Drama: Theological Dramatic Theology, Vol. V,* 285.
9  Balthasar, *The Glory of the Lord, Vol. VII,* 382.
10  Ratzinger, *Eschatology,* 216.

# The Raging Rebels

> ...the will
> And high permission of all-ruling Heaven
> Left him at large to his own dark designs,
> That with reiterated crimes he might
> Heap on himself damnation, while he sought
> Evil to others, and enrag'd might see
> How all his malice serv'd but to bring forth
> Infinite goodness, grace and mercy shewn
> On Man by him seduc't, but on himself
> Treble confusion, wrath and vengeance pour'd. [211–220]

We are citing Milton's great poem primarily because the poet has provided lines that help us come to a better understanding of what postmortem perdition consists. The raging soliloquy that Milton puts into the mouth of Satan distills the essence of sin: the self-annihilating mutation of freedom into the defiant and rebellious triumph of the will. Milton's Satan chooses hell and in explaining his reason, defines the essence of hell itself:

> The mind is its own place, and in it self
> Can make a Heav'n of Hell, a Hell of Heav'n.
> What matter where, if I be still the same,
> And what I should be, all but less then he
> Whom Thunder hath made greater? Here at least
> We shall be free; th' Almighty hath not built
> Here for his envy, will not drive us hence:
> Here we may reign secure, and in my choyce
> To reign is worth ambition though in Hell:
> Better to reign in Hell, then serve in Heav'n. [254–263]

Even the self-damned house themselves in hell in the cause of freedom. How conspicuous are the many manifestations of this paradox in our world today, where impotent compulsions and gesticulations designed to demonstrate one's freedom from constraint serve only to confirm—to the perceptive—the tragedy of the degeneration of freedom, first into self-will and then into fleeting spasms of impotent but compulsive desire. The blame for the fact that Milton's Satan was to be transfigured into a dark hero cannot be laid entirely at Milton's door, though the verve with which the blind and splenetic poet depicts the great Rebel shows how readily those who rebelled against the given order of the world gradually reject all normativity and eventually adopt the strutting and sputtering *non serviam* form of pride. Balthasar quotes Blondel:

> The Christian concept of punishment can, therefore, arouse absolutely no suspicion of divine vengeance. For the old law of fear, it might be appropriate to speak of the wrath of a vengeful God infuriated by rabble-rousers and idolaters; the truth of the New Covenant knows only one punishment, which allows the irretrievably hardened to dismember and incinerate themselves. The prosecutor and executioner is none other than the rebel who can place the blame only on himself. Damnation is brought by the guilty upon themselves, once they have become conscious of their perversity. Thus hell has not been created by God; it is the logical and moral consequence of the sin of the guilty.[11]

Milton draws on the legends of a Luciferian rebellion, derived in part from the reference in the Book of Revelation to a war in heaven. Milton's Satan exists prior to the human Fall which he—as Serpent in the Garden—brings about as the mimetic source of the original act of rebellion. Read in the opposite order, however, the Genesis author's account of the Fall—the story of an attempted usurpation of divine prerogatives prompted by the serpent—represents the incipient form of the ferocious raging of Milton's Satan. Seemingly mild by comparison, the author of the second creation account in Genesis describes the beginning of the process that, if left to run its course, leads to the blind and envious animosity of Milton's Satan. The serpent in the garden delivers the essential message: he who created you in his own image and who wants to lead you gradually into the whole truth (Jn. 16:13) is not to be trusted; rebelling against him is the essence of freedom and the key to becoming godlike yourself. You, not the Lord, are the arbiter of what is good and what is evil. No one can make that decision for you. You create good and evil precisely by defining them as you see fit.

This condition can be variously described. Let us look at one feature of it: the secret dependence of the will on the affective

---

11  Balthasar, *Dare We Hope that All Men Be Saved?*, 115–6.

stimulation of a counter-will. This is patently clear in both the Genesis story and in Milton's great poem. Balthasar quotes Karl Rahner to the effect that the possibility of refusing God "must not be considered an option of free choice on the same level as the possibility of accepting God; for such a No can be defined only in reference to the corresponding Yes."[12] Anselm of Canterbury says something comparable: "The will that cannot turn aside from the rectitude of not sinning is more free than the will that can."[13] To fully explicate this terse comment, we would need to bring René Girard's insights into our mimetic predicament to bear on the asymmetry of the Yes and No. To say Yes to the model of desire is, in itself, both an unproblematic and an entirely free decision, free and unproblematic, that is, until the imitator begins to envy the model and to desire not just what the model desires but all the prerogatives the model enjoys by virtue of what the imitator imagines—wrongly—to be the model's spontaneous and *sui generis* desire. At that point the competition for preeminence begins and the No begins to incubate. This No is unfree inasmuch and to the extent that it is animated by resentment of the model-turned-rival. This No is an act of will, but one that is affectively dependent on the counter-will of a mimetic antagonist.

Comparing the Yes and No, one could say that the Yes is *dramatic*, inasmuch and to the extent that it involves a genuine and uncoerced Yes that accepts its unforeseen ramifications. The No, on the other hand, is *melodramatic*, inasmuch as it involves a contest, a struggle against the model for preeminence and control. Even though the melodrama that results from the No arouses passions, it extinguishes *the passion*, the essence of which is self-renunciation performed for the sake of another. If allowed to fester and spread its infection, the nay-saying rival pronounces the defiant non serviam (I will not serve), so marvelously depicted by Milton. If such a maniacal reviling of God seems something to which we are unlikely to succumb, we should not be so sure,

[A] sinner might so identify himself with his No to God that trinitarian love would be unable to loosen the resultant snarl, with

12 Ibid., 248.
13 *De libertate arbitrii*, quoted: Balthasar, *Theo-Drama, Vol. V,* 402.

the result that the fiery torrent of eternal love that flows around and through him would remain a torrent of eternal wrath. Hence the words, "it is a terrible thing to fall into the hands of the living God." (Heb. 10:31)[14]

If, as we must assume, the full encounter with Christ involves a demand for selflessness far beyond anything we have ever experienced and if, as also seems likely, that demand awakens a counter-will in creatures who have forfeited their divinely endowed god-likeness, it is by no means out of the question that a love as demanding as that offered by the crucified Christ would be met, not with a childlike and disarming gratitude for the opportunity to repent, but with a ferocious clinging to one's pride and autonomy. We cannot avert our eyes from the *mysterium iniquitatis*, the essence of which is the inveterate *hupenantios* (hyper-animosity) of which the author of the Letter to the Hebrews speaks.

For Balthasar the "basic christological law regarding the (horizontal) history of the Church and the world" is "that there is an ever-intensifying No to the Yes uttered by God in Christ." This Balthasar calls "the law of the reciprocal intensification of Yes and No."[15] The world will forever be a battlefield between these two responses to the gift Christ has held out to us. Along similar lines, Douglas Farrow has persuasively argued that the very preaching of Christ produces the Antichrist and that the very law of freedom about which Saint Paul preached so passionately awakens in sinful hyper-antagonists the mystery of lawlessness.[16] The Trinitarian kingdom into which we are called, and for which Jesus is the ultimate Evangel, can be entered only at the expense of the reflexive self-preservation and self-regard that has become deeply embedded in postlapsarian humanity and that instinctively reacts to the revelation of its insubstantiality with antipathy. In considering our eschatological prospects, we are well advised to reckon with "the reciprocal escalation of love and sin" and Balthasar's insistence that "ever greater mercy arouses ever-greater anger."[17]

---

14 Balthasar, *Theo-Drama*, Vol. IV, 350.
15 Balthasar, *Theo-Drama*, Vol. V, 22–3.
16 Farrow, *Ascension Theology*, 95.
17 Balthasar, *Theo-Drama*, Vol. IV, 342.

## Nietzsche's Antichrist

We pause at this point to explore this *non serviam* phenomenon more closely, turning to the case of Friedrich Nietzsche for further insight. For all his passionate rhetoric about the will and the will-to-power, Nietzsche seems to have instinctively grasped the asymmetry between the Yes and No to Christ to which Fr. Rahner alluded. For all its centrality in Nietzsche's thought, the German philologist knew that his paean to the will-to-power was founded on an unexamined premise. In *The Gay Science*, he writes:

> The thoughtless man thinks that the Will is the only thing that operates, that willing is something simple, manifestly given, underived, and comprehensible in itself. He is convinced that when he does anything, for example, when he delivers a blow, it is *he* who strikes, and he has struck because he *willed* to strike. . . . Of the mechanism of the occurrence, and of the manifold subtle operations that must be performed in order that the blow may result, and likewise the incapacity of the Will in itself to effect even the smallest part of those operations—he knows nothing. . . . [V]olition is in fact such a cleverly practiced mechanical process that it almost escapes the observing eye.[18]

The metaphor Nietzsche uses to illustrate his point perhaps illustrates it all too well, thanks to which what almost escapes the observing eye may not altogether escape it. It is the *will to strike a blow* and the *mechanism* that gives rise to that will with which Nietzsche seems fascinated. Make no mistake, the mechanism Nietzsche has in mind is not the autonomic nervous system. The "manifold subtle operations" of which he speaks are *social* operations, that is to say, mimetic ones, followed in short order though they usually are by visceral, psychophysiological phenomenon, in the Pauline lexicon: the flesh. "Will," writes Nietzsche elsewhere, "can of course operate only on 'will' and not on 'matter'."[19] The will that strikes a blow depends quite obviously on

18 Friedrich Nietzsche, *Joyful Wisdom*, edited and introduction by Kurt F. Reinhardt (New York: Frederick Ungar, 1964), 169 ff.

19 Friedrich Nietzsche, *A Nietzsche Reader*, selected and translated by R.J. Hollingdale (London: Penguin, 1977), 229.

the counter-will of the rival to whom the blow is delivered. Such a will is but a crippled form of volition inasmuch as it is thoroughly predicated on the existence of an adversarial counter-will. *"The Antichrist* is a description of Nietzsche's hell," writes Giuseppe Fornari, "a crazy and brilliant formulation of the infernal underground of the modern world."[20]

> Nietzsche, and much of the Western world with him, rebels against God because he hates and *envies* him. Nietzsche's envy of God is not a simple psychological attitude on his part, it is, in biblical terms, the expression of mankind's constitutive wrong, the ancestral, ontological propensity to evil, no longer covered up in any way. Nietzsche's rebellion cannot be understood unless we understand the anthropologically objective, founding nature of Satan. *The Antichrist*, in its enormous pretensions (though not necessarily in its final significance), is a satanic work, it is a satanic interpretation of Christianity, with its history and message considered from Satan's viewpoint. Because Satan is the antichrist.[21]

Before moving on, we call attention to the point Fornari makes explicitly, a point to which René Girard has often alluded, namely that the appearance of Nietzsche at the end of the nineteenth century is hardly coincidental. At the moment when the Christian influence on Western civilization was waning, Nietzsche had the combination of brilliance, resentment, and pride to give voice to sentiments that would only gradually begin to surface, aided no doubt by the infectiousness of Nietzsche's provocative rhetoric. Nietzsche is famous for predicting that the forces he was letting loose at the end of the nineteenth century were premature but that these ferocious sentiments were destined to overtake a once Christian civilization. The carnage of the twentieth century and the moral and anthropological breakdowns of the twenty-first hardly amount to evidence to the contrary.

---

20 Giuseppe Fornari, *A God Torn to Pieces*, trans. Keith Buck (East Lansing: Michigan State University Press, 2013), 82.
21 Ibid., 87.

# The Unperson

> [S]in is depersonalization . . . the one called "the devil" is the personification of the impersonal as such.[22]—Rémi Brague

We are *persons* from the moment of conception, the moment at which the embryo achieves the biological status of a member of the human family and the spiritual dignity commensurate with that status. Nonetheless, the full flowering of this endowment takes many years in the course of which we may be so corrupted either by our penchant for self-regarding autonomy or by our assimilation into a mindless mob or impersonal social aggregation that our personhood remains inchoate or is subject to the diminution of ontological density of which Henri de Lubac has written.

The word *person* (*hypostasis* in Greek) is a Christian word, given philosophical and theological weight in the patristic age as the Church was giving birth to the doctrine of the three *Persons* of the one God. The word today has lost all of the richness once associated with it, but serious theologians, philosophers, and even social anthropologists have come to realize that the person, properly understood, always presupposes a relationship with another. To be a person in any serious sense of the term is to be in communion with others. Writes Balthasar:

> Precisely this, however, would no longer be predicable of a being that had, in its entirety, made a radical decision against God, or absolute love; thus, we would have to join J. Ratzinger in speaking of an "un-person," of the "decomposition, the disintegration of being a person," for which reason it is characteristic of the devil "that he appears without a face, that unrecognizableness is his real strength." E. Brunner says quite appropriately: "He works in an impersonal, indeed, in a virtually person-dissolving way."[23]

Along with the moral and ontological dignity of the human person comes the freedom to betray that dignity so thoroughly and renounce the human vocation so irrevocably that one

---

22 Brague, *On the God of the Christians (and on one or two others)*, 149.
23 Balthasar, *Dare We Hope that All Men Be Saved?*, 145–6.

becomes soulless—to speak in more traditional terms. Soulless-ness, like Ratzinger's characterization of the "un-person," has an affinity with the passage in the twentieth chapter of the Book of Revelation which Balthasar cites as the place where "for the first time the New Testament concept of Hell makes its appearance."[24]

> Next I saw a large white throne and the one who was sitting on it. The earth and the sky fled from his presence and there was no place for them. I saw the dead, the great and the lowly, standing before the throne, and scrolls were opened. Then another scroll was opened, the book of life. The dead were judged according to their deeds, by what was written in the scrolls. The sea gave up its dead; then Death and Hades gave up their dead. All the dead were judged according to their deeds. Then Death and Hades were thrown into the pool of fire. (This pool of fire is the second death.) Anyone whose name was not found written in the book of life was thrown into the pool of fire. (Rev. 20:11–15)

Those whose names are not found in the Book of Life are the un-persons, those who so completely crippled their capacity for genuine relationship in the interest of self that they instinctively refuse even—and especially—the demanding invitation to par-take of the joys of Trinitarian communion. Their refusal of the demands of true relationship in favor of either radical autonomy or the mindless absorption in antagonistic mobs has render them soulless. Even though the path to this soullessness is begun in this life, it cannot be declared irreversible until it pronounces a defini-tive No to the Second *Person* of the Trinity—the Pierced One who took flesh so that the world could see what the vocation of the human person actually is. We may—indeed, we must—pray that in the end there will be no such soulless un-persons, and we must live in the certain knowledge that it is a fate from which we are not ourselves immune. Balthasar adds another feature of the soulless un-person by quoting the Austrian theologian Alois Winklhofer: "The sufferings of Hell . . . contain absolutely no longing for God. The damned person wills himself as he is, and hell as it is."[25]

---

24 Balthasar, *Mysterium Paschale*, 168.
25 Balthasar, *Dare We Hope that All Men Be Saved?*, 129.

The foregoing is offered as a counterweight to the hope for universal salvation for which the Church encourages us to pray and the possibility of which cannot therefore be ruled out. What we have tried to bring out with our brief discussion of Milton's Satan and Nietzsche's Antichrist is that the mimetic entanglements of which life consists are capable of drawing us into frenzies of resentment and making us into the *hupenantios* of which the author of Hebrews writes. Working out our salvation in fear and trembling—as the author of Philippians exhorts—remains ever valid. Hope remains at the bottom of Pandora's Box, however, as Anthony Kelly notes:

> Human freedom is obviously capable of ultimate perversion. It can set itself up in opposition to the will and claims of the infinite Other. It can project its own violence and pride onto God. Thus, this "other," this "god," appears only as the most threatening and absolute rival. However, in Christ's descent into the realm of the lost, this hitherto menacing "other" is revealed as searching out those who have damned themselves with the offer of infinite mercy.[26]

Dramatists and artists have long appreciated how much more dramatic depictions of evil are compared with which portrayals of goodness seem tepid. Both Milton's Satan and Nietzsche's Antichrist bear witness to the fascination that is easily aroused by a will in rebellion. We must not allow ourselves to become complicit with this dramatic asymmetry. If these are examples of hellishness, are we able to locate rarer, but no less compelling, images of the will operating in a graceful rather than rebellious modality?

Milton has left us with a vivid image of the will among the damned. We now turn from the seventeenth century British Puritan to the fourteenth century Italian Catholic, the greatest poet of his age. In his *Paradiso,* Dante meets Piccarda Donati, whom he questions about the unequal degrees of blessedness in paradise, an ostensibly eternal inequality of the kind that the

---

26 Anthony Kelly, C.SS.R., *Eschatology and Hope*, 91.

pilgrim Dante obviously suspects might give rise to resentment. He asks his heavenly interlocutor whether or not those in lower stations envy the higher states others enjoy. She answers:

> What we desire, we have,
> There is in us no other thirst than this...
> the essence of this blessed state of being
> is to hold all our will within His will
> whereby our wills are one and all-agreeing...
> In His will is our peace. (III:79 ff)[27]

In order to better grasp what the poet has offered here, we conflate it with a correlative comment by Balthasar: "In the harmony of all freedoms, the freedom of each individual retains its own timbre. The divine freedom is so all-encompassing that it makes room, within its single Truth, for countless aspects; thus it does not override or infringe the area of mystery of each individual's creaturely spontaneity."[28]

Just so, Satan's rebellious will is his self-damnation. In heaven wills are not made to conform by obedience to extrinsic rules as even rightly-ordered wills very often are in this life. The blessed enter into the Trinitarian communion in which the loving self-gift of being is pure joy. As noted earlier, in the Lord's Prayer, we pray that we may conform to the Father's will on earth as do the souls of the blessed in heaven. In the blessed state we call heaven the will operates entirely free from mimetic enticements. It functions according to the intersubjective mystery by means of which the will of the creature and the will of the Creator are conformed *gracefully* rather than impersonally by mechanical acts of obedience. Grace effects a richer conjugation of the divine and human wills than any that could be brought about solely by prescription or proscription. Only when the Law is written on hearts by an encounter with Christ might we understand what otherwise might seem—to an age in which the will has undergone an apotheosis—to be the incomprehensible words of Piccarda Donati: "In His will is our peace."

27 Alighieri Dante, *The Paradiso*, trans. John Ciardi (New York: New American Library, 1970).

28 Balthasar, *Theo-Drama, Vol. V,* 485.

The value of being a Christian is that it is better to live in the truth than in illusion, but it is also because faith forms the dispositions most congenial to Trinitarian existence, which one day each person must embrace or repudiate. If we take Piccarda Donati and Milton's Satan as the two ends of a spectrum, faith in Christ and full participation in the sacramental life of the Church is what fosters the attitude captured by the Florentine poet and dissolves the pride and resentment made so graphic by the English one.

## The Just Judge

Sin destroys the consciousness of sin, and sin corrupts and destroys relationships. The same can be said of intoxicants and drugs, and there is probably an apt analogue between the two when considering the postmortem consequences of a life of sinful self-absorption. Hard drugs create a physiological dependency which is very often impervious to the drug addict's sincerest determination to abandon the habit. A lifetime of sin—even of the run-of-the-mill selfishness and hypocrisy—may result in spiritual habits that are as recalcitrant to remediation as heroin or morphine.

Karl Rahner emphasized the decisiveness of the "fundamental option" for or against God consisting of the decisions and actions of a lifetime. At death this fundamental option has already been determined. It is, in one sense, irreversible. But, as stated previously, this does not mean that the encounter with Christ will amount to no more than a ratification of this fundamental option, for it would otherwise fail to be a genuine encounter. In this vale of tears we humans know ourselves imperfectly, and we are buoyed up or dragged down by circumstances not of our own making. Only God knows us and only God knows how our lives have been influenced for good or ill by people and events over which we have little, if any, control and for which we bear correspondingly little responsibility. Joseph Ratzinger is helpful here:

> The truth of a man that judgment renders definitive is that truth which has emerged as the fundamental orientation of his existence in all the pathways of his life. In terms of the sum total of

decision from out of which an entire life is constructed, this final direction may be, in the end, a fumbling after readiness for God, valid no matter what wrong turnings have been taken by and by. Or again, it may be a decision to reject God, reaching down into the deepest roots of the self. But this is something that only God can determine. He knows the shadows of our freedom better than we do ourselves.[29]

## Omnisubjectivity

> O Lord, thou hast searched me and known me!
> Thou knowest when I sit down and when I rise up;
> thou discernest my thoughts from afar.
> Thou searchest out my path and my lying down,
> and art acquainted with all my ways. (Ps. 139:1–3)

Cardinal Ratzinger's suggestion that God knows the shadows of our freedom better than we do can be found as well in Balthasar's theology of the Passion. Jacques Servais, S.J. noted that for Balthasar, Christ understood that his mission was not only to suffer and die for sinners, but "to freely assume the inner condition of the sinner."[30] These insights bring us to Linda Zagzebski's argument that divine omniscience presupposes omnisubjectivity, a concept which has great bearing on the eschatological mystery of justice and mercy. If God is omniscient, as longstanding doctrine and tradition have affirmed, then Dr. Zagzebski argues that he would have access to the very personal and private knowledge of his creatures. That seems unproblematic, but she further insists that this would mean not only that God would know our deepest thoughts, fears, and desires but that he would know—by experience so to speak—what it is like to have these thoughts, fears, and desires. He would know what it is like to be each of us. Augustine long ago declared that God knows us better than we know ourselves. Zagzebski brings this Augustinian insight into sharper focus. God knows our moment by moment experience

---

29 Ratzinger, *Eschatology*, 209.

30 Jacques Servais, "Postscript: The Thomist Doctrine of Redemption," Balthasar, *To the Heart of the Mystery of Redemption*, 100–1.

just as we do. God enters into our subjectivity, for a feature of divine omniscience is omnisubjectivity. "An omnisubjective being would know what it is like to be you," Zagzebski writes. "If God is omnisubjective, God knows you as well as you know yourself. God could not only write your biography, God could write your autobiography."[31] Balthasar provides Christological evidence corroborating Zagzebski:

> The motif is constant: Jesus knows the hidden thoughts of the hearts of the disciples (Lk. 9:47), of those who put him to the test (Lk. 11:17), of the Pharisees (Mt. 12:25), of the man who invites him to a meal (Lk. 7:39ff.); he "at once" sees through the thoughts of the scribes (Mk. 2:8), he "sees through their hypocrisy" (Mk. 12:15); but he also sees at once the faith of those who stand before him (Mt. 9:2; Mk. 2:5; Lk. 5:20), or their lack of faith (Lk. 8:25), and he knows his betrayer (Mt. 26:20ff.; Jn. 13:21ff.). In John, he measures with his glance Simon who appears before him, and tells him who he really is (1:40ff.); not only does he see through Nathanael when he is presented to him, but he has already seen the one who looks at him now ("Come and see," 1:46) when he was hidden (1:48); he knows all about the Samaritan woman's past and present, and discloses this to her, judging her, but bringing her salvation (4:16ff.).[32]

Whereas we empathize with another by imagining their subjective state—their heartache, their joy, their distress—God empathizes by actually entering into the very same heartache, joy, or distress and experiencing it as they experience it. This is surely the divine incarnational thrust operating in its most penetrating, empathetic, and intimate modality. Dr. Zagzebski argues that though God would know that a falsehood sincerely held by someone is false, he would nonetheless also know exactly what it is like to believe, as that person does, that the falsehood is true. It has long been assumed that God would know if a person who fancied that he was feeling love was actually being driven by lust,

---

31 Linda Zagzebski, "Omnisubjectivity," *Oxford Studies in Philosophy of Religion* (Vol. 1), edited by Jonathan Kvanvig, 2008.
32 Balthasar, *The Glory of the Lord, Vol. VII*, 119–20.

but according to Zagzebski's notion of omnisubjectivity God would also know what it is like to think that the lust was actually love. God would know when someone mistakes his rage or vengefulness for righteous indignation, but he would also know what it is like to believe that his rage is righteous indignation. Perhaps it should also be said that an omnisubjective God would know what it is like for someone to know in his heart that his lust or rage was lust or rage even as he was deluding himself into believing that it is love or righteous indignation. What Zagzebski is proposing is that "God lives through the conscious experience of each being who possesses consciousness."[33] Balthasar anticipated Zagzebski when he writes that God "becomes involved, right along with men, in accomplishing their spatial and temporal movements within the sphere of their lives, and this is not only as an observer who steers things from above, but as one who journeys and experiences with creatures on their level."[34]

Obviously divine omnisubjectivity would be operative—and necessary to the perfect convergence of mercy and justice—only in the case of creatures endowed with subjectivity and interiority. Zagzebski captures this nicely when she writes that divine omnisubjectivity "would not apply to non-human conscious animals, animals who cannot pray."[35] Of course, non-human creatures are not judged, inasmuch as they are animated by instinct and have neither free will nor the full mimetic endowment by which man is summoned to fulfill his greater and more perilous destiny.

The Church has declared Christ to be "the righteous judge" (2 Tim. 4:8). The concept of omnisubjectivity, congruent with the doctrine of divine omniscience and a further refinement of it, bears on the intimacy of the encounter which we have suggested awaits us at death. "For the word of God is living and active, sharper than any two-edged sword, piercing to the division of soul and spirit, of joints and marrow, and discerning the thoughts and intentions of the heart. And before him no creature is hid-

---

33  Zagzebski, *Omnisubjectivity: A Defense of a Divine Attribute* (Milwaukee: Marquette University Press, 2013), 33.

34  Balthasar, *The Glory of the Lord, Vol. VI*, 47.

35  Zagzebski, *Omnisubjectivity,* 34, italic emphasis added.

den, but all are open and laid bare to the eyes of him with whom we have to do" (Heb. 4:12–13).

Acknowledging how difficult it is for human reason to understand what takes place in the Passion, Balthasar notes how incomprehensible is the Son's abandonment by the Father inasmuch as it is the key to the event "affecting God's Trinity itself" in such a way that "this event can embrace all past and future times."[36] On the Cross Christ takes on himself the weight of all sin. In doing so, he lifts this weight off the shoulders and the moral scales of the very sinners whose imperfect lives helped amass this weight of sin. The mystical experiences of Adrienne von Speyr led her to the novel but richly suggestive conclusion that Christ takes on himself all sin, including the crushing weight of *remorse*—a "sorrow even unto death"—(which those who committed these sins largely managed to evade) in order to make a confession of sins with the thoroughness of which he alone is capable.

Thus has Adrienne von Speyr given us a key for unlocking the atonement theory that—however it might need to be refined and reconciled with other such theories—charts a fresh new course for Catholic soteriology. Von Speyr, who had an incalculable impact on the theology of Hans Urs von Balthasar, mystically experienced her solidarity with saints and sinners to an extraordinary degree. She experienced her own sins as well as her inclination to sin as intimately linked to all the sins and sinfulness of humanity throughout history. She came to understand how morally and existentially interrelated we humans are, how fungible is our suffering and death. She writes: "As soon as a person has inwardly said Yes to some trial, to suffering, it is used further afield and has an effect on other people. Even without explicit offering up . . . or special prayer."[37]

Von Speyr's experience of an all-encompassing moral and existential solidarity mystically available to a very rare few—none-

36 Balthasar, *Theo-Logic, Vol. II*, Kindle edition, §5132ff.
37 Adrienne von Speyr, *Erde und Himmel: Ein Tagebuch, Vol. I* (Einsiedeln, 1975), 341; quoted: Saward, *The Mysteries of March*, 98.

theless touches on a feature of human solidarity that goes to the heart of the mystery of Christian redemption. "On the Cross," writes von Speyr, "Christ confesses to the Father the sin of the whole of humanity: the monstrous reality of the world's sin, already committed and still to be committed."[38] Novel though von Speyr's thought is in this regard, it rests on a Thomist foundation. In the *Summa Theologica* Thomas writes:

> Christ grieved not only over the loss of His own bodily life, but also over the sins of all others. And this grief in Christ surpassed all grief of every contrite heart, both because it flowed from a greater wisdom and charity, by which *the pang of contrition* is intensified, and because He grieved at the one time for all sins, according to Is. 53:4: "Surely He hath carried our sorrows."[39]

Christ not only suffers the sins of all humanity but he identifies with those sins. *He owns them.* Though he remains morally sinless, he adopts as his own the sins of the world, not only in order to undergo the suffering to which these sins inevitably lead, but in order to *confess* these sins with all the penitential remorse of a contrite sinner. *Owning these sins as his own and confessing them as though they were his own*, he not only undergoes the godforsakenness (wrath) to which unforgiven sin finally leads, but he accepts the Father's forthcoming absolution on behalf of all sinners, thereafter holding this absolution in safekeeping and offering it to each sinner at the moment of his death, conditioned only on a willingness to face the truth with a humble and contrite heart.

An even deeper feature of God's omnisubjectivity than Zabzebski herself surveyed comes to the fore here, and it helps us better understand the descent into the realm of the dead. The Second Person of the Trinity enters so unreservedly into the human predicament that he knows the inner life of each and every human as though it were his own. Whereas the sinner might know the sin at one level, he will know the sugar-coated delectation of sin's allure while remaining largely ignorant of the suffering toward which it inevitably moves. Christ, however, would know sin all the way

38 Adrienne von Speyr, *Kreuz und Hölle, Part I: Die Passionen* (Einsiedeln, 1966), 365; quoted: Saward, *The Mysteries of March*, 165, n. 27.
39 *Summa Theologica*, III, q.46, a.6 obj.4, italic emphasis added.

down, so to speak. He would know it from within its pestilential core, and his appropriation of sin would unavoidably include the anguish at its heart.

A hundred years ago or so, prior to his conversion, G. K. Chesterton said that if a person lived to be a thousand years old he would end in utter pessimistic skepticism or as a member of the Catholic Church. Correlatively, only by living a very, very long life could a person discover the suffering toward which every sin and every self-serving and self-aggrandizing act inevitably moves. Only a sinless person would be capable of the immediate recognition of the suffering lurking beneath sin's glamorous façade, and only a person endowed with omnisubjectivity could undergo that suffering on behalf of those otherwise destined for it. Not even the sinner's most scrupulous and thoroughgoing examination of conscience could sufficiently unravel the twisted skein of sinful self-regard and self-justification to make a clean sweep of his complicity in his own fallen condition. Only One who has both taken on the sins of each and every person and who has known that person's moral life from the inside—with an omnisubjectivity of the kind that Linda Zagzebski has explored—could make a perfect and comprehensive confession of sins with the requisite awareness of their gravity. And yet this confession of sin must arise wordlessly from the Penitent crushed by the full weight of sinful lovelessness in all its hideousness.

Thereafter Christ serves as the custodian of the Father's absolution, held in trust on behalf of each sinner, awaiting only the sinner's Yes to the particulars of the indictment whose thoroughness he could not himself have supplied. To the extent that we can predict the emotional character of this Yes to this indictment, we might assume that it would be an amalgam of the deepest possible regret and the greatest possible gratitude. In other words, a purgatorial joy. With this joyful but contrite spirit each will be able, so to speak, to redeem the redemption Christ has effected on his behalf.

As to whether human freedom is capable of sustaining a sufficiently rebellious spirit to thwart the redemptive will of God in Christ, we must remain agnostic. It would be prudent to assume that we can finally cut ourselves off from God and to take precautions in one's own life against so dreaded an eventuality. Balthasar, however, suggests that we must not overestimate the power of human free will, which is unavoidably benighted by its fallen condition even before actual sins further cripple it.

> However hard it may try, in fact, the creature can never betray and profane its mystery as completely as it might intend by its sin. The mystery, in other words, is never given into the creature's possession in such a way that it ceases to remain, at the same time, in God's safekeeping. This is the seal that the Creator has imprinted upon his creature, thereby branding it as his property.[40]

While the creature remains ever "in God's safekeeping," he is not thereby relieved of the need to appeal to his Divine Benefactor for the absolution of his sins obtained on his behalf by Christ's Passion. Only the Son could gather into himself the aggregated sins of humanity without being turned in the process into something like Milton's Satan. He gathered these sins to himself precisely to be able to repent of them in the crushing sorrow of Good Friday and Holy Saturday and confess them to the Father. In absolving these sins, the Father pronounces a second Yes to the creation of the world. The fallen condition would remain and the world would continue on its careening course, but the absolution for these sins and the hand that would wipe away the tears they caused would be offered to each sinner at his death, requiring only the contrite surrender of his pride and self-absorption.

Thereafter Christ is the non-judging Judge who holds the Father's absolution in trust for each sinner, who only has to say Yes to this offer and to consent to the requirements of Trinitarian existence. That this consent is neither a forgone conclusion nor painless is what justifies the trepidation one ought to feel when contemplating it. We want to argue that this is what Balthasar's Holy Saturday theology brings into focus and that, once subjected to the appropriate theological scrutiny, it will provide an immensely important contribution to the Church's ongoing task of bringing the mystery of Christ's redemption into ever clearer focus.

---

40 Hans Urs von Balthasar, *Theo-logic: Theological Logical Theory, Vol. I: Truth of the World*, trans. Adrian J. Walker (San Francisco: Ignatius Press, 2000), 231.

# Dare We Hope?

O my Jesus, forgive us our sins, save us from the fires of hell, and lead all souls to Heaven, especially those in most need of Thy mercy.—The Fatima Prayer

> I look at the church again, and yet again,
> And think of those who house together in Hell,
> Cooped by ingenious theological men
> Expert to track the sour and musty smell
> Of sins they know too well;
> Until grown proud, they crib in rusty bars
> The Love that moves the sun and the other stars.[1]
> —Edwin Muir

AS JOHN PAUL II writes in his 1990 encyclical *Redemptoris Missio*, "It is necessary to keep these two truths together, namely, the real possibility of salvation in Christ for all mankind and the necessity of the Church for salvation" (§9). In 1964, a predecessor of St. John Paul II, Paul VI, promulgated the Vatican document *Lumen Gentium*, the sixteenth section of which sent shock waves through the Church. Paul VI declared:

> In the first place we must recall the people to whom the testament and the promises were given and from whom Christ was born according to the flesh. On account of their fathers this people remains most dear to God, for God does not repent of the gifts He makes nor of the calls He issues. But the plan of salvation also includes those who acknowledge the Creator. In the first place amongst these there are the Muslims, who, professing to hold the faith of Abraham, along with us adore the one and merciful God, who on the last day will judge mankind. Nor is God far distant from those who in shadows and images seek the

---

1 "The Church," *Edwin Muir: Collected Poems* (London: Faber and Faber, 1979), 263–4.

unknown God, for it is He who gives to all men life and breath and all things, and as Saviour wills that all men be saved. (§16)

This passage has been criticized for expressing a universalism more in keeping with the spirit of the conciliar age than with Christian universality, and especially for glossing over the very substantial differences between Islam and Christianity. No one entirely avoids being influenced by the spirit of the age, and at the time of the Council many in the Church shared in the hope that the bitter divisions and conflicts that had repeatedly burdened our predecessors might be a thing of the past. Be that as it may, the irenic tone of this passage is perfectly apt inasmuch as Christ died, descended into the realm of the dead, and rose thereafter precisely on behalf of *every human* who has ever lived regardless of the age in which he lived or his religious affiliation. The Council's misstep was a theological one only insofar as the Council Fathers rather too cavalierly declared the God worshiped by Jews and Christians to be indistinguishable from the God (Allah) to whom Muslims submit. Arguably, what haunts *Lumen Gentium* is historical naïveté. The idea that Christians and Muslims worship the same God depends for its validity on a studied inattention to certain very glaring differences. Recognizing the traditional doctrine—outside the Church there is no salvation—the Vatican document is more generous in its assessment of non-Christian and non-Catholic religions and almost Pelagian in its confidence in the eschatological efficacy of the well-formed moral conscience. It is true that the good pope hastened to add that the Christian is commanded in all urgency to preach the Gospel to those without it, but the argument that made it necessary to emphasize the urgency of the Church's missionary responsibility had the effect of weakening the Christocentric essence of salvation. The Church is the original and only indispensable mediator of Christ, but others, touched by her mediation—some very remotely so—perform intermediating roles to one degree or another. Inasmuch as the Church is the Body of Christ in history, her mediation justifies the religious devotion of those in formal communion with her, but neither can we fail to honor auxiliary mediators of the Church's moral, intellectual, and cultural patrimony—whatever their formal relationship to the Church. The

Spirit blows where it will and the efficacious operation of such mediation may elude detection.

In his 1990 encyclical *Redemptoris Missio*, John Paul II accounts for Christian universality with more theological and ecclesial sobriety, but in ways that were no less generous. Citing in passing the now famous paragraph 22 of *Gaudium et spes*, Saint John Paul II writes:

> The universality of salvation means that it is granted not only to those who explicitly believe in Christ and have entered the Church. Since salvation is offered to all, it must be made concretely available to all. But it is clear that today, as in the past, many people do not have an opportunity to come to know or accept the gospel revelation or to enter the Church. The social and cultural conditions in which they live do not permit this, and frequently they have been brought up in other religious traditions. For such people salvation in Christ is accessible by virtue of a grace which, while having a mysterious relationship to the Church, does not make them formally part of the Church but enlightens them in a way which is accommodated to their spiritual and material situation. This grace comes from Christ; it is the result of his Sacrifice and is communicated by the Holy Spirit. It enables each person to attain salvation through his or her free cooperation.
>
> For this reason the Council, after affirming the centrality of the Paschal Mystery, went on to declare that "this applies not only to Christians but to all people of good will in whose hearts grace is secretly at work. Since Christ died for everyone, and since the ultimate calling of each of us comes from God and is therefore a universal one, we are obliged to hold that the Holy Spirit offers everyone the possibility of sharing in this Paschal Mystery in a manner known to God."[2]

One needn't gainsay the underlying theological and pastoral perspective of these two important encyclicals to note that despite their efforts to the contrary, they were sometimes interpreted in ways that led to an attenuation of the Christocentric universality and ecclesial indispensability that they sought to clar-

2 *Redemptoris Missio*, §10.

ify. Of course, this brings us back to the question we have been exploring in what has gone before: Can we account for the universal reach of Christ's sacrifice in ways that underscore rather than mitigate Christ's indispensable role as the sole means of salvation? "I am the way, and the truth, and the life; no one comes to the Father, but by me" (Jn. 14:6). John Paul II's successor on the Chair of Peter weighed in on the neuralgic issue that *Lumen Gentium* §16 raised:

> Everything we believe about God, and everything we know about man, prevents us from accepting that beyond the limits of the Church there is no more salvation, that up to the time of Christ all men were subject to the fate of eternal damnation. We are no longer ready and able to think that our neighbor, who is a decent and respectable man and in many ways better than we are, should be eternally damned simply because he is not a Catholic. We are no longer ready, no longer willing, to think that eternal corruption should be inflicted on people in Asia, in Africa, or wherever it may be, merely on account of their not having "Catholic" marked in their passport. . . . The question that really troubles us is not in the least concerned with whether and how God manages to save *others*. The question that torments us is, much rather, that of why it is still actually necessary for us to carry out the whole ministry of the Christian faith—why, if there are so many other ways to heaven and to salvation, should it still be demanded of us that we bear, day by day, the whole gravamen of ecclesiastical dogma and ecclesiastical ethics? . . . What actually is the Christian reality, the real substance of Christianity that goes beyond mere moralism? What is that special thing in Christianity that not only justifies but compels us to be and live as Christians?
>
> We are staring at the trials of everyday Christianity and forgetting on that account that faith is not just a burden that weighs us down; it is at the same time a light that brings us counsel, gives us a path to follow, and gives us meaning. . . . [W]hat a strange attitude that actually is, when we no longer find Christian service worthwhile if the denarius of salvation may be obtained even without it![3]

3 Ratzinger, *What It Means to Be a Christian*, 43–49.

# Dare We Hope?

The theory that in the end the whole of creation will be restored and reconciled is called *apokatastasis*. It was a position supported—ostensibly at least—by a number of early theologians, notably Origen, Gregory of Nyssa, and—more discretely and less consistently—Maximus the Confessor. In his famous work, *Contra Celsum*, Origen drew back from broadcasting too widely the possible scope of divine mercy:

> Whatever may be said about this question is not to be displayed in front of everybody and has no bearing here. It is even dangerous to commit such things to paper; for most people it suffices to know that sinners will be punished. To go beyond that would scarce benefit those who can barely be restrained a while from evil and its resulting sins by fear of everlasting punishments.[4]

Origen never doubted the suffering that awaited after death. The only question was whether it would be purgatorial and temporary or eternal and everlasting. He seems clearly to have favored the former possibility, while aware of the ineffable nature of the question and the need for great discretion in pondering such mysteries, especially within earshot of those who could "barely be restrained a while from evil." According to Maximus, as Balthasar reports: "the whole species will be saved from death, 'the works of sin will disappear into nothingness,' all will share in the resurrection, the whole world, in the Son, will be 'subject' to the Father [1 Cor. 15:28]. . . . The whole world will be brought home by the Logos, for he saves everyone, the whole race, just as his ineffable mystery embraces all ages and every place."[5] Balthasar does not claim that such references to universal salvation completely eclipse other Maximus references that are problematic for so merciful an eschatological vision. He rather cites texts in which Maximus, like Origen, seems reluctant to speak more publicly about universal salvation for fear of scandalizing or seriously misleading those for whom such a view would compromise

---

4 Quoted: Balthasar, *Dare We Hope that All Men Be Saved?*, §1963 ff.
5 Balthasar, *Cosmic Liturgy*, 355–56.

either their moral resolve or their missionary spirit. John R. Sachs, S.J. provides the relevant summary:

> Origen, the first truly great Christian theologian, wrestled with this problem, wondering which was greater, human freedom (and its ability to reject God) or God's love for sinners. . . . Thought by some to have taught the eventual conversion and salvation even of the demons, Origen's school of thought was condemned by the Provincial Council of Constantinople in 543. Nonetheless, several other important patristic authors, such as Clement of Alexandria and Gregory of Nyssa, argued for some form of *apokatastasis* and were not explicitly condemned.[6]

This account of the sixth century Synod of Constantinople is contested, most recently and most robustly by the Orthodox scholar David Bentley Hart, who notes that the fifteen anathemas—in the eleventh of which Origen was condemned—were appended to the Council document long after the Council. Hart assesses this to be no less than "the most shameful episode in the history of Christian doctrine," expressing his vexation with almost Pauline straightforwardness:

> For one thing, to have declared any man a heretic three centuries after dying in the peace of the Church, in respect of doctrinal determinations not reached during his life, was a gross violation of all legitimate canonical order; but in Origen's case it was especially loathsome. After Paul, there is no single Christian figure to whom the whole tradition is more indebted. It was Origen who taught the Church how to read Scripture as a living mirror of Christ, who evolved the principles of later trinitarian theology and Christology, who majestically set the standard for Christian apologetics, who produced the first and richest expositions of contemplative spirituality, and who—simply said—laid the foundation of the whole edifice of developed Christian thought. Moreover, he was not only a man of extraordinary personal holiness, piety, and charity, but a martyr as well: Brutally tortured during the Decian persecution at the age of sixty-six, he never recovered, but slowly withered away over a period of three years. He was, in short, among the greatest of the Church Fathers and

---

6 Sachs, "Current Eschatology," 230.

the most illustrious of the saints, and yet, disgracefully, official church tradition—East and West—commemorates him as neither.[7]

We will leave this historical controversy to those better qualified to adjudicate it, but we might find some Catholic corroboration of at least the general thrust of Hart's judgment in the fact that theologians as distinguished as Henri de Lubac and Hans Urs von Balthasar devoted considerable attention to Origen, esteeming him and his contribution to Christianity no less enthusiastically than did David Bentley Hart.

The most powerful critique of *apokatastasis*—or what has come to be called Origenism—is that it does not take the essential principle of human freedom sufficiently into account and thus it makes a mockery of the moral dignity of each individual. (Of course freedom that is not ordered to truth is not freedom at all; it is arbitrary self-will, and it is quite literally the opposite of real freedom. That said, however, it must be said as well that the responsibility for ordering freedom toward truth is, precisely, the act of freedom par excellence.) Balthasar has been sharply criticized for putatively espousing something very much like the *apokatastasis* that the Church has (according to received opinion) condemned. The Swiss theologian famously argued that we have both scriptural warrant and Christ's admonition for hoping and praying for the salvation of all, but he emphatically insisted that this hardly justifies a doctrinal assertion of the universal salvation long rejected by the Church. If such a happy eventuality could be assured, there would be no reason for either the hope or the prayers that it might be so. We are encouraged to pray and hope but by no means to do anything that would undermine the moral seriousness of our lives or diminish the Christian duty to bring the Gospel of Christ to the whole world. Balthasar was surely right when he insisted that: "Only by hewing to the thought of God's judgment will Christian theology be able to preserve its authenticity against the ever-present danger and temptation of Origenism."[8]

---

7 David Bentley Hart, "Saint Origen," *First Things* (October 2015).

8 Hans Urs von Balthasar, *The Theology of Karl Barth*, trans. Edward T. Oakes, S.J. (San Francisco: Ignatius Press, 1992), 260.

On the other hand, to vindicate the truth of divine justice and in the process becloud the truth of divine love and mercy would be a serious mistake. The question is whether it is possible for a creature made in the image and likeness of God and intrinsically ordered to communion with God to completely extinguish the longing for this communion. God's love for those of his creatures with whom he has entered into a covenant is not likely to accept as eternal and ever-binding a refusal that is accompanied by even the faintest forms of equivocation. Only a hatred of God that is never, and can never be, accompanied by flickering misgivings could be said to be eschatologically irreversible. The merest hint of remorse at so great a loss may well be sufficient to turn an ostensible hell into a pre-purgatory.

Few deny that the eternal destiny of each person is a subject that deserves further reflection and that there is no prospect of a clear resolution of this issue. Such reflection will be fruitful to the extent that it recognizes its limitations and resists the temptation to declare further theological exploration unnecessary. Margaret Turek has stated the matter succinctly: "Nothing," she writes, "forbids the theologian to turn his attention to one of the possible outcomes [all are saved or some are eternally damned] in an attempt to render it consonant with reason, so long as his reflections do not rule out the other possibility."[9]

As we have tried to stress, we live amid cultural forces and attitudes which foster precisely the rebellious and resentful habits that if not rectified might well lead to the kind of hell represented by John Milton's Satan. Moreover, we see today—in faraway lands—many who have grown so filled with hatred and rage and soulless evil that they do not shrink from beheading children, and—in our own land—many who stand by or justify the merciless severing of the spinal cords of the most defenseless children of all. Such soulless indifference to cruelty has consequences, and it

9 Turek, "Dare We Hope 'That All Men Be Saved,'" 98.

would be a mistake to dismiss the possibility that these consequences might replace the human heart with a heart of stone so
hardened that its adamantine condition becomes eschatologically
irreversible. Nor, however, can we be sanguine about the failure
of the divine plan, about which Saint Peter said that the Lord is
"forbearing toward you, not wishing that any should perish, but
that all should reach repentance" (2 Pet. 3:9).

Though Balthasar attracted the ire of those who fear the
revival of Origenism and the perceived theological errors associated with it, in fact, his exhortations were aimed simply at keeping the question open, as any fair appraisal of the scriptural
evidence requires. Nonetheless, just as the Yes and the No to God
in Christ cannot be given the same weight—God's desire for the
salvation of all not being irrelevant—so the prospect that some
suffer eternal damnation and the prospect that all are finally
saved might be assigned an equally asymmetrical place in the
Christian worldview. Balthasar has simply proposed that we who
have been commanded by Christ and his Church to hope and
pray for the salvation of all should at least entertain the possibility that this prayer might be answered affirmatively. Nor was he
making this proposal in a vacuum; he was making it in a world
where Christians have for centuries been made keenly aware of
the flames and torments of hell and encouraged to believe that
this view was unambiguously doctrinal. It is in the face of such a
widely held and long unquestioned eschatological presupposition that the fervor of Balthasar's eschatological theology can be
best explained. But the Swiss theologian had no trouble in citing
doctrinally impeccable voices within the Church in support of
keeping open the possibility that all might be saved. He cites, for
instance, the French priest and philosopher Maurice Nédoncelle:

> I renounce, vehemently and decisively—and this seems to me of
> the greatest importance—the idea that has poisoned us for cen-
> turies, not to say millennia, namely that God hates sinners and
> the damned. I regard this as absolutely intolerable, just like the
> notion that God's love could fail to have an effect on any one of
> his creatures.[10]

10  Quoted: Balthasar, *Theo-Drama*, Vol. V, 278.

Thomas P. Rausch draws attention to one particularly vivid example of the way in which the idea that God hates sinners has "poisoned us for centuries."

> From the seventh century on, confidence in God's mercy for those who had died began to give way to the fear of judgment. . . . One has only to contrast the joyful exclamation of the primitive church, "Come, Lord Jesus," with the *Dies Irae*, the thirteenth-century hymn once used as the sequence at the Roman Catholic Requiem or funeral Mass. Full of the fear of judgment, it looks toward that "day of wrath and day of mourning" when Christ who so suffered on the cross comes in judgment, a day when "even the just are mercy needing." Hardly a message of hope.[11]

Writing some years before his ascension to the papacy, Joseph Ratzinger issued a similar caution:

> We cannot start to set limits on God's behalf; the very heart of faith has been lost to anyone who supposes that it is only worthwhile, if it is, so to say, made worthwhile by the damnation of others. Such a way of thinking, which finds punishment of other people necessary, springs from not having inwardly accepted the faith; from loving only oneself and not God the Creator, to whom his creatures belong. That way of thinking would be like the attitude of those people who could not bear the workers who came last being paid a denarius like the rest; like the attitude of people who feel properly rewarded only if others have received less. This would be the attitude of the son who stayed at home [in the Prodigal Son story], who could not bear the reconciling kindness of his father.[12]

This unflinching assessment does not, however, mitigate the equally resolute warning about the almost shrugging belief in universal salvation that many inside and outside the Church rather casually adopted in the postconciliar years. "God gives man the capacity to make a (negative) choice against God that seems *for man* to be definitive," Balthasar writes, "but which need

11  Thomas P. Rausch, S.J., *Eschatology, Liturgy, and Christology* (Collegeville, MN: Liturgical Press, 2012), 4.
12  Ratzinger, *God Is Near Us*, 35–6.

not be taken *by God* as definitive."[13] Balthasar is hardly incautious
on this matter, but neither does he mince words. "The certainty
that a number of men, especially unbelievers, must end in hell we
can leave to Islam,"[14] he writes. Nor should we be quick to adopt
the "hellfire decrees of the God of Tertullian, Calvin, and Janse-
nius."[15] Balthasar concludes unceremoniously: "this whole con-
struction must be laid to one side, since before Christ (and here
the term 'before' must be understood not in a chronological
sense but in an ontological), there can be neither Hell nor Purgatory—and as for a Hell of infants, of that we know nothing."[16]
Echoing the above quoted position of Thomas P. Rausch, Balthasar elsewhere writes:

> The claim to know the outcome of the judgment (in the sense of
> certain knowledge that the Judge will condemn some) . . . took
> on that dark and menacing aspect which brought untold suffer-
> ing to mankind in the Middle Ages and the Reformation, even to
> the men of the Counter-Reformation. It was a spirit in strong
> contrast with that of early Christianity and the patristic era. We
> are just now beginning, in conformity with scripture, to grope
> our way by degrees to a more objective position.[17]

On the other hand, however, Balthasar warns against the very
universalism of which he is routinely accused: "But the desire to
conclude from this that all human beings, before and after Christ,
are henceforth saved, that Christ by his experience of Hell has
emptied Hell, so that all fear of damnation is now without object,
is a surrender to the opposite extreme."[18]

Matthew declares that "the Son of Man did not come to be
served but to serve and to give his life as a ransom for *many*"
(20:28; Mk. 10:45). Balthasar points out that the reference to *many*
is "a Semitism equivalent to 'for all', whereby the Old Testament
barrier which excluded the pagans from eschatological salvation

13 Balthasar, *Explorations in Theology, Vol. IV,* 411.
14 Balthasar, *Dare We Hope that All Men Be Saved?,* §1719ff.
15 Balthasar, *Man in History,* 72.
16 Balthasar, *Mysterium Paschale,* 177.
17 Balthasar, *Explorations in Theology, Vol. I,* 266–67.
18 Balthasar, *Mysterium Paschale,* 177.

is broken down."[19] *Many* is not juxtaposed to *many others*, or *some others*, but rather to *one* as in one chosen people. Similarly, in the reference to the "many" in the extraordinarily central passage in Paul's Letter to the Romans we find this: "But the gift is not like the transgression. For if by that one person's transgression the *many* died, how much more did the grace of God and the gracious gift of the one person Jesus Christ overflow for the *many*" (Rom. 5:15).

Obviously all humans die, and Paul cannot have used the one/many contrast to suggest otherwise. A few verses later, in fact, Paul conjoins in two verses the reference to "all" and to "many" in a way that makes it abundantly clear that the latter is a synonym for the former. "Just as through one transgression condemnation came upon all, so through one righteous act acquittal and life came to *all*" (Rom. 5:18). The critical point is not whether acquittal will not be offered to all, but that it will come with conditions which it is conceivable may be found unacceptable to those to whom it is offered:

> Those who are to be judged do not stand over against either Jesus or his church as alien. He has become their brother, yes, much more: their advocate before God. He has borne their guilt. . . . By him they have been ontically changed in the most profound way, whether or not they acknowledge it or let it happen—this would be the essential part of their redemption—or whether or not they, *if they are capable of it*, refuse it and so harden themselves in their guilt as their own.[20]

Among the Church Fathers who espoused some version of *apokatastasis*, there was a tendency to distinguish between those Christians who might safely be exposed to such an idea and those for whom the fear of punishment continued to serve as an indispensable aid in their effort to avoid moral and spiritual pitfalls. The Church Fathers who recognized this admittedly real issue

---

19 Ibid., 97. It is true that the original "for many" has been retained in the latest translation of the Catholic liturgy, but this deference to the original scriptural text can hardly be read as a repudiation of the original understanding of what the original text meant to those who originally heard it.

20 *The von Balthasar Reader*, 419, emphasis added.

were prone to speak of the possibility of universal salvation exclusively in their more rarefied theological treatises rather than in popular preaching. This is in keeping with Paul's warning (in 1 Cor. 8) to those who understood how irrelevant were the dietary laws that they should not ignore these laws in ways that would scandalize the faithful who had yet to recognize their religious inconsequence. In either case, a certain deference is simply an act of courtesy, but it can nonetheless have the effect of retarding the natural maturation of faith, an outcome no less harmful to many.

Among the prestigious figures to whom Balthasar attributed an open-ended eschatology like his own were Erich Przywara, Henri de Lubac, Charles Péguy, Paul Claudel, Gabriel Marcel, Joseph Ratzinger, and Leon Bloy. Some disputing Balthasar's Holy Saturday theology have questioned whether all on his list of theological allies can be counted as such.[21] As more or less representative of these distinguished Catholic philosophers, theologians, and literary figures, Balthasar quotes at greater length than shall we, Gustave Martelet, S.J.:

> [W]e must read the New Testament, and read it ever anew, in the light of divine love. Certainly there is talk of fire, worm and the second death that excludes one from the kingdom. Christ does not recognize the evildoers, distances them from him. But hell, as a refusal of divine love, always exists on one side only: on the side of him who persists in creating it for himself. It is, however, impossible that God himself could cooperate in the slightest way in this aberration, above all, not for the purpose of vindicating the magnificence of his denied love through the triumph of his righteousness, as has, unfortunately, often enough been claimed.... If Christ speaks to us in the Gospel of the possibility of man's becoming lost through a refusal of love, then certainly this is not in order that it should happen, but only in order that it should not happen.[22]

---

21 See Ralph Martin, *Will Many Be Saved?* (Eerdmann, 2011) und Thomas Joseph White, OP, *The Incarnate Lord: A Thomistic Study in Christology* (Catholic University of America, 2015).

22 Gustave Martelet, SJ, *L'au-delà retrouvé. Christologie des fins dernières* (Desclée, 1974), 181–91; quoted and abbreviated: Balthasar, *Dare We Hope that All Men Be Saved?*, 53 ff, n.10.

In other words, the specters of hellish torture or interminable languishing in misery have an exhortative or paraenetic function. However much the moral catastrophes within us and around us may lead to the assumption, not just that hell is possible, but that it is well populated, we are positively commanded to pray to the contrary that the *First* Word—the Logos through whom all things came to be and without whom nothing came to be—will prevent sin and death from having the *Last* Word. As Balthasar writes:

> [Christ] will therefore take every available path to bring back the person whose sins he has borne, even if this person rejects him; and, if this proves impossible, he will not positively thrust him from him (the reader will recall the protests of Nédoncelle, Martelet and Ratzinger) but will negatively leave the sinner to his blinded will.[23]

Among the several places where Joseph Ratzinger has signaled his broad agreement with Balthasar's eschatological views is this from his own early book on eschatology: "Christ allots perdition to no one. . . . He does not pronounce the fatal verdict. It happens where a person has held aloof from him. It comes about where man clings to his isolation."[24]

Hope that all will be saved might well have significant social consequences in the here and now. The specter of an eschatological abyss separating the elect and the damned reinforces the human tendency to overlook the fact of a universal "brotherhood" which Christianity has proclaimed for two millennia. Are there those who have nothing to do with me, and with whom I need not have anything to do? Must I shun some for fear of being contaminated? Not if I am destined not only to be with them in the next life, but, where necessary, to forgive them and be forgiven by them. (Jesus readily mingled with lepers, harlots, tax collectors,

---

23 Balthasar, *Theo-Drama*, Vol. V, 299.

24 *Eschatologie* (Regensburg: Pustet, 1970), 169: quoted: Balthasar, *Theo-Drama*, Vol. V, 278.

and other social outcasts.) Simply to know that we are destined to be companions in the next life would mitigate the sinful tendency of regarding some of our brothers and sisters with indifference or worse: as mere social ciphers with whom we have no relationship and for whom we bear no responsibility. To the extent that our hope for salvation or fear of damnation and the moral efforts made in connection with these hopes and fears are premised on the casual and unproblematic assumption that some others will be damned, we remain beholden to the fallen and pharisaical calculus against which Jesus persistently inveighed. For the moral shortcomings of one's earthly life are symptoms of the fallen condition, but not its essence, as the smug and sanctimonious Mrs. Turpin in Flannery O'Connor's short story "Revelation" discovered when, staring into the pigsty, the following vision appeared:

> There was a purple streak in the sky. . . . She saw the streak as a vast swinging bridge extending upward from the earth through a field of living fire. Upon it a vast horde of souls were rumbling toward heaven. There were whole companies of white-trash, clean for the first time in their lives, and bands of black niggers in white robes, and battalions of freaks and lunatics shouting and clapping and leaping like frogs. And bringing up the end of the procession was a tribe of people whom she recognized at once as those who, like herself and Claud, had always had a little of everything and the God-given wit to use it right. She leaned forward to observe them closer. They were marching behind the others with great dignity, accountable as they had always been for good order and common sense and respectable behavior. They alone were on key. Yet she could see by their shocked and altered faces that even their virtues were being burned away.[25]

Not one of the saved, insists Balthasar, "has saved himself on condition of the exclusion of others. Each one has had the love that 'seeks not its own' (1 Cor. 13:5), that does not gather merits for itself, but rather in a Christian and christological sense radiates

---

25 Flannery O'Connor, "Revelation," *The Complete Short Stories of Flannery O'Connor* (New York: Farrar, Straus and Giroux, 1973), 508.

the grace received: to others, for others."[26] This was the lesson that constituted the revelation for Mrs. Turpin in O'Connor's aptly titled short story.

## Maturation

> [O]bedience in the Church is nothing other than love, the form and fruitfulness of bridal love. And thus the juridical-moral concept of merit, in use till now, is irresistibly giving way—in keeping with revelation.[27] —Hans Urs von Balthasar

Like his venerable predecessors who considered the possibility—not the certainty—of universal salvation, Balthasar was keenly aware such a possibility might lead some to the sin of presumption and others to moral recklessness. He hastens to admonish:

> We should not, then, be more curious than Scripture allows us to be. With Paul, we may say that grace is far more powerful than sin, that all die in Adam, but that all will also be raised to life in Christ, who will lay a perfected creation at the Father's feet [Rom. 5:12–21; 1 Cor. 15:21–22, 28]. But we must also stand with Christ himself, and with his gospel, at the edge of eternal destruction and gaze down into it. To want to overcome this final antinomy through a premature "synthesis" is not appropriate for theology in this present age. The serious possibility of being lost must never be watered down, if the seriousness of Christian life is not to be transformed into a mere game.[28]

We must be mindful of the empty churches and the shrugging reluctance on the part of many to proclaim the faith to non-believers—both of which lamentable developments have risen sharply since the Second Vatican Council. Many have cited as the epicenter of these disappointing trends the conciliar document *Lumen Gentium*, especially its paragraph 16 quoted above. Taken alone, this section of the document might reasonably undermine

---

26 *The von Balthasar Reader*, 419.

27 Hans Urs von Balthasar, *Razing the Bastions*, trans. Brian McNeil, C.R.V. (San Francisco: Ignatius Press, 1993), 40–41.

28 Balthasar, *Cosmic Liturgy*, 358.

evangelical ardor, the reverence for Christianity's traditional doctrines, and the moral resolve of Christians. These concerns are perfectly warranted, but we want to suggest that they must not cause us to retreat from responsibilities arising from a deeper and more universal understanding of our faith. We concur with the French historian and philosopher, Rémi Brague: "What might be thought to lead to libertinage in fact places us before a somewhat terrifying responsibility. Each way of behaving contains an internal logic that, in the final analysis, causes it to lead necessarily either to life or to death."[29]

It is possible to save orthodoxy in ways that are destined to hobble it going forward, which amounts to letting heresy determine the terms in which orthodoxy feels obliged to express itself. What Henri de Lubac said of an earlier controversy bears repeating, "that [the] ultraorthodox fell into the trap which the heretic had set up for them."[30] This might well apply to the very real contemporary need to recover the distinctively Catholic understanding of the mystery of faith and to return to fidelity to the tradition. The prospect of effecting this recovery by returning to the fear of hell as a dominant motivation would amount to being formally faithful while neglecting the opportunity presented by the current crisis to discover richer and more theologically foundational motivations for the life of faith.

Heaven is not a reward; it is our home which we have never known but for which we nonetheless feel nostalgic. Hell is a punishment only in the sense that living contrary to the inner law of one's being leads to misery, resentment, and self-loathing, in the final stages of which it is possible to revel in one's own misery, the condition Milton depicted so graphically. The vocabulary of rewards and punishments, scriptural allusions to them notwithstanding, are very clumsy ways of speaking of our eschatological prospects, one all too often saturated with either pride or vindictiveness, both of which infect and corrupt Christian reflection on the meaning of the moral life and its consequences on the far side of death. We have entered into a period in the history and life of

29 Brague, *On the God of the Christians (and on one or two others)*, 122.
30 Quoted: McPartlan, *The Eucharist Makes the Church*, 84–5.

the Church in which, Balthasar felt, "the preaching of the dogma of hell in the way that we have become used to is no longer possible." Neither however, he insisted, can we treat "this important and not to be demythologized facet of biblical revelation with a deathly silence."[31]

We have argued above that the desacralizing effect of the Christian revelation poses the greatest possible challenge, inasmuch as the various ruses by which violence and sacral awe were conflated in history and culture have long seemed indispensable to moral and cultural order. Once the perversities of the old system of sacred violence on which humanity has ever relied were exposed as definitively as they were by the biblical tradition generally and the revelation of the Cross specifically, the slow attenuation of what René Girard calls humanity's "sacrificial resources" began. In concert with this diminution of the old order, the responsibilities from which the old order insulated man began to devolve upon him. Certain props upon which man could rely in earlier ages slowly lost their compelling power, often becoming sources of scandal.

There is an analogue of this touching on the question of hell. Hanna Arendt once argued that we cannot persuade people of the truth, for the truth cannot be the object of persuasion. But we can persuade people of almost anything else, and if we persuade them of the existence of heaven and hell they are more likely to live as though they knew the truth. We share neither Arendt's agnosticism nor her condescension, but her point need not be lost. Both Jesus and Saint Paul warned against scandalizing those whose faith, though sometimes stronger and more resilient than that of the more theologically informed, is often composed of deference to familiar conventions and the admonitions and reassurances concerning the rewards and punishments associated with moral conduct and ecclesial obedience. The sincerity and legitimacy of this concern is not one that either this author or the theologians he finds most convincing care to casually dismiss. Nonetheless, the patronizing tone of Arendt's remark points to the dangers of using solicitude for those of simple faith as a reason for resisting

31 *The von Balthasar Reader*, 403.

the task of maturing in the faith. When intimidation ceases to be a convenient substitute for persuasion, its attempted revival will only compound the crisis and delay the evangelical and catechetical renewal required to make the truth itself credible and the Truth Himself (sacramentally) palpable. It is worth noting that the postconciliar theological school most often accused today of clinging to tradition—the "Communio theologians"—is precisely the school that has discovered within that tradition new horizons for which it is today criticized by not a few of the Church's self-proclaimed "traditionalists."[32]

When this author was a child, church attendance, meatless Fridays, and a number of other healthy tokens of cultural Catholicism and/or faithful Catholic practice were enforced by reference to eternal punishment. Such threats, however well-intentioned and issued with sincere concern for the eternal welfare of the faithful, are no longer effective. Once again, as often in the Church's history, it proves to be the case that shortcuts sincerely made for the best of reasons eventually become detours and dead-ends. Regardless of how useful it once might have been and of any unhappy moral consequences that are coincident with the loss of these moral expedients, fewer people today choose the moral high ground out of fear of eternal punishment. Undoubtedly, one of the reasons for this is the blasé and unwarranted underestimation of the moral seriousness of life. But it is partly due to the fact that people cannot be bullied into living a Christian existence. In the absence of the intimidation once used to encourage moral responsibility, the faithful need to discover the intrinsic value of selflessness, self-gift, moral virtue, regular worship, the supreme importance of the Eucharist, and the value of those simple acts of piety and devotion that help form, enrich, and sustain the culture

---

32 By "Communio theologians" we mean those who collaborated in launching the journal *Communio* and those who have more or less adopted their theology, ecclesiology, and eschatology: Joseph Ratzinger, Henri de Lubac, Hans Urs von Balthasar, Louis Bouyer, Karol Wojtyla, among others.

of faith. In short, as the fear of eternal damnation plays less a role in the lives of the faithful, this negative motivation will need to be replaced by the love of charity and virtue as well as a genuine attraction to the saving sacraments of the Church, most particularly the regular reception of the Eucharist. We fully recognize the dangers of moral laxity and the decline in both sacramental participation and in the sacramental sensibility requisite to it. But we sense that something far more important and more promising for the future of our faith is at work here.

"Conversion to God," writes John Paul II in his encyclical *Dives in Misericordia*, "always consists in discovering His mercy."[33] A moral and religious life that is dominated by the fear of hell and the need to avoid that fate tends to reinforce the life of self-reference that is the essential barrier to the blessed life. On the other hand, when the knowledge of one's unworthiness encounters the mercy and forgiveness of God, the experience opens one to the mystery at the heart of a Trinitarian and eucharistic way of life that is the preparation for the *communio sanctorum* to which we are ultimately called. We think in this regard of that well-known passage from the prophet Jeremiah: "Everyone, from least to greatest, shall know me—says the Lord—for I will forgive their iniquity and no longer remember their sin" (Jer. 31:34). We know God, not first because we have come to our senses and repented, but because God has chosen to forgive sins so as to free us from the moral and mental shackles that blind us to divine truth, which is Love itself. "For God has consigned all men to disobedience, that he may have mercy upon all" (Rom. 11:32).

The knowledge of the true God begins with an encounter with divine mercy; the spirit of contrition that floods from a once hardened heart upon exposure to this mercy is, of course, indispensable to having the covenant written on one's heart, but it is the mercy that triggers the moral remorse and the realization of ontological vacuity that underlies it. The Spirit that guides the Church seems to be urging her toward a greater appreciation of this in our time. If Balthasar assigned great importance to the mystical experiences of the woman whom he helped bring into the Church, the

---

33 *Dives in Misericordia*, §10.

pope who insisted on overriding Balthasar's reluctance to be made a cardinal in the Church relied no less on the mystical experiences of a vowed religious woman whose visions centered around the theme of divine mercy, the recently canonized Saint Faustina Kowalska. The work of probing the overlapping mystical experiences of these two twentieth century women has only just begun, but for our purposes we can simply call attention to how the theme of divine mercy has been taken up by popes who might otherwise be thought to have quite distinct ecclesial aspirations: Saint John Paul II and Pope Francis. The former delivered a homily at the canonization of Faustina in which he said:

> It is not a new message but can be considered a gift of special enlightenment that helps us to relive the Gospel of Easter more intensely, to offer it as a ray of light to the men and women of our time. . . . What will man's future on earth be like? We are not given to know. However, it is certain that in addition to new progress there will unfortunately be no lack of painful experiences. But the light of divine mercy, which the Lord in a way wished to return to the world through Sr. Faustina's charism, will illumine the way for the men and women of the third millennium.[34]

Emeritus Pope Benedict XVI has added his voice to those of both his predecessor and successor on the Chair of Peter: "For me it is a 'sign of the times' the fact that the idea of the mercy of God should become more and more central and dominant— starting from Sister Faustina, whose visions in various ways reflect deeply the image of God held by the men of today and their desire for the divine goodness."[35]

For every person whose moral rectitude depends on the fear of hell, there are many others whose understanding of the God revealed by Christ is distorted in some way by the specter of a

---

34 John Paul II, *Mass of Canonization for Sister Faustina Kowalska*, April 30, 2000.

35 Reprinted by the *Catholic New Agency*, November 17, 2016.

God who would countenance the eternal damnation of the creatures he created out of love. Fear of damnation cannot be laid
aside, but it necessarily reinforces a self-referentiality that
remains fundamentally at odds with the self-forgetfulness and
self-gift appropriate to Trinitarian existence. "Perfect love casts
out fear" (1 Jn. 4:18). One trusts that when a deeper understanding makes it possible and more spiritually efficacious to motivate
the faithful by appeals to loving self-donation rather than the self-
obsessed fear of punishment that the grace to do without these
training wheels will accompany their superannuation.

The historian of Christianity, Jaroslav Pelikan, quoted with
approval the second century apologist, Tatian: "The only man
whom God grants the life eternal is the man who refuses to grasp
for immortality on his own."[36] Eve famously snatched at a godlikeness, seeking to possess what could be received only as a gift
by one humble enough to recognize the unattainability of the gift
by any other means. How reminiscent of this it is for someone to
calculate how best to ensure his eternal happiness—or worse still,
how best to elude his eternal perdition—by taking moral precautions and attending scrupulously to ecclesial demands. Even
when these things encourage a morally upright life and sacramental participation, they may do so at the cost of fostering a preoccupation with self that is antithetical to both ecclesial charity in
this world and its eschatological fulfillment in the next.

It would be in keeping with the Devil's modus operandi to convince us that the sole key to our salvation is our moral rectitude.
For in most cases, the assessment of one's moral state of affairs
will be performed by way of comparison with others, and here is
the mimetic fly in the ointment. Far from alleviating the destructive potential of a mimetic melodrama, the introduction of moral
competition tends to greatly intensify the rivalry. The fact that
this rivalry will often be carried out with far more subtlety means
only that the rivals caught up in it will be even less likely to recognize how the road to hell is being paved with their moral good
intentions. The reason that the harlots and tax-collectors will

36 Jaroslav Pelikan, *The Shape of Death* (Nashville, TN: Abingdon Press,
1961), 27.

enter the Kingdom before the fastidious Pharisees is that the pride of the latter is more resistant to the contrition requisite to the sinner's salvation than is the waywardness of the former.

Every challenge is accompanied by a commensurate grace, and every grace is accompanied by a mission. It is our opinion that the doctrinal angst of our age is accompanied by a grace that will inspire a deeper appreciation for the faith than that which relied too heavily on the fear of everlasting punishment. Few Catholics the age of this writer can honestly say that they would have lived more moral or religious lives without the encouragement provided by the threat of Church censure or unwanted eternal consequences, but neither can we fail to recognize that this is no longer the case for a very great many of the faithful today. To pretend otherwise is to cling to forms of dependency that unnecessarily postpone the maturation process that now awaits us.

Among the many reasons some have resisted Balthasar's eschatology is his insistence on the inseparability of his work from that of the lay mystic for whom he served as spiritual director, Adrienne von Speyr, whom he received into the Church and with whom he founded *The Community of Saint John*. One of the reasons why Balthasar was more open to the lay mystic than other Church theologians might be suggested by what he has to say in lamenting both the theological and the practical repercussions of Augustine's recourse to the theory of predestination:

> High Scholasticism entertains no other eschatology than this, and here the Doctor Seraphicus [St. Bonaventure] is even more uncompromising than Aquinas. This is also the period in which Christian princes hold banquets in the halls of their castles and citadels while their enemies languish in lifelong imprisonment in the dungeons below. Somehow Christian reflection seems to have stopped at a preliminary stage—except in certain women, such as Hildegard of Bingen, the two Mechthilds or the Lady Julian of Norwich.[37]

37  Balthasar, *Theo-Drama, Vol. V*, 317.

Few would dispute the importance of the "Sibyl of the Rhine" (d. 1179), the "Nightingale of Helfta" (1240–1299), mystic Mechthild of Magdeburg (1221–1285), and the incomparable author of the justly famous line, "All shall be well, and all manner of thing shall be well" (Julian of Norwich, ca. 1342–ca. 1416), but Balthasar seems to esteem these remarkable women of faith for having resisted what was at the time the eschatological complacency of their age, a complacency hardly less perilous than the equal but opposite Pollyannaish complacency of our time.

The prospect of hell in Balthasar and von Speyr may seem less ominous than the medieval specter of torture chambers, but that isn't the case. For one's postmortem encounter with Christ is very likely to mirror one's earthly life, and in any case it will be strongly determined by the habits of a lifetime. In assessing one's own prospects it might be useful to ask: How would I react if without warning I were to face a terrifying danger, with no onlookers to influence my choice, and be obliged to choose between mortally dangerous heroism, on one hand, or, on the other, an act of self-preservation reinforced by powerful instincts and a lifetime of prudential regard for my own safety? Those who are perfectly confident that they would make the noble decision under these circumstances may not have actually faced a comparable situation. Those who have will know how powerful are the instincts and the psychological and social reflexes that have to be overcome if one is to act in a truly noble way when one's life is endangered. This, roughly speaking, suggests that whether the decision required at the moment of the encounter with Christ is made in a truly Christ-like way will be greatly determined by how congruent that decision is with the earthly decisions that preceded it and the moral virtues and spiritual reflexes these decisions have fostered.

Balthasar's critics have accused his eschatological propositions of giving rise to the widespread spirit of religious indifference adopted today by so many as well as the dramatic attenuation of the missionary spirit that is the hallmark of a healthy Christian faith. A case could be made, however, that these lamentable developments are due precisely to an older over-insistence on the avoidance of hell as a principle concern, in some cases *the* principle concern, of the faithful. As early as the 1930s, Henri de Lubac was pointing to this overly individualist preoccupation as a serious error in the Catholicism of his day. In reality, de Lubac writes, "Catholicism is essentially social. It is social in the deepest sense of the word: not merely in its applications in the field of natural institutions but first and foremost in itself, in the heart of its mystery, in the essence of its dogma."[38] The social dimension of our lives comes to the fore when one realizes that some and perhaps most of the consequences of one's life, for which one has to take moral responsibility, occur after one's death, which is why the final judgment awaits the unfolding of history in its entirety. Arguably, purgatory may consist first and foremost of the anguish of watching one's often casual hardheartedness ripple out into the lives of others, for whose spiritual and material injuries one is justly accountable.

The problem to which de Lubac alludes is not just an excessive individualism. Rather it is that this reinforcement of self-referentiality is very likely to have a deleterious effect on the spirit of self-gift that is the key to the Trinitarian existence toward which we are ordered. Pope Benedict—speaking magisterially—writes in *Spe Salvi*:

> Our lives are involved with one another, through innumerable interactions they are linked together. No one lives alone. No one sins alone. No one is saved alone. The lives of others continually spill over into mine: in what I think, say, do and achieve. And conversely, my life spills over into that of others: for better and for worse. . . . As Christians we should never limit ourselves to asking: how can I save myself? We should also ask: what can I do in order that others may be saved and that for them too the star of hope may rise? Then I will have done my utmost for my own personal salvation as well.[39]

Balthasar eloquently concurs:

38 De Lubac, *Catholicism*, 15.
39 *Spe Salvi*, §48.

We are at the heart of the unfathomable mystery of the exchangeability of all spiritual goods in the household and circulatory system of the mystical body of Christ: "If one member suffers, all suffer together; if one member is honored, all rejoice together" (1 Cor. 12:26). . . . The penance of one can effect for another the grace of conversion, without that person's ever knowing—prior to the judgment—from where it comes to him. . . . Even non-Christian religions have known about this mystery, although mostly in a limited sense. However, certain of the Christian confessions derivative from the Catholic church have almost entirely forgotten it out of pure concern for personal salvation. Yet in the midst of the *Catholica* lives the knowledge of this marvelous mystery.[40]

We can be confident that in the days and hours immediately ahead we will face perils aplenty and, God willing, the grace to face them as Christ would have us do. We turn at this point, therefore, to the supreme resource bequeathed to us by Christ himself for entering into communion with him and with one another and for radiating to the larger world the Spirit of Christ.

40  *The von Balthasar Reader*, 420.

# "Abide With Us"

*Supper at Emmaus* by Caravaggio, 1601

IN THE second canto of the *Paradiso*, Dante warns the readers who have followed his poetic journey through the *Inferno* and the *Purgatorio* of the demands of the celestial regions to which this last phase of his pilgrimage is to lead. He clearly indicates that most of his readers should go no farther, a remarkable suggestion for an author to make and certainly not one we care to second with regard to these final pages of the journey we have taken together. What fascinates, however, in this Dantean conceit is the sole exception to his warning. The readers the poet declares capable of following him into the bewildering empyrean regions are those who have regularly eaten the *panis angelicus*.

> You other few who have set yourselves to eat
> the bread of angels, by which we live on earth,
> but of which no man ever grew replete;
> you may well trust your keel to the salt track
> and follow in the furrow of my wake
> ahead of the parted waters that close back.[1]

---

1 Dante, *Paradiso*, II: 10–15; italic emphasis added.

This is obviously a reference to the Eucharist. Why might Dante feel that those who feed on the Bread of Angels are better able to appreciate his description of the heavenly regions? Might it not be something like the *sacramental sensibility* to which we have frequently referred? It is something more than the ability to imagine the reality of the Eucharist or to affirm Church teaching on the matter. It is an ability to enter into the reality of the Eucharist, an ability which the Florentine poet seems to feel has epistemological benefits, making those who feed on the Bread of Angels capable of understanding his most demanding poetry. It is, as we have said, a poetic conceit. But it is one we find fascinating enough to mention as we ourselves take up the Eucharistic theme.

And so we come at last to the misplaced center of this book, as it is the center of its author's life and, in fact, the largely lost center of history itself, the midpoint in the *meantime*: the Table of the Lord. With so few pages given to so imponderable a mystery, we can only hope that the pedantry and parsimony of these concluding words will serve at least as fitting analogue for the all too ordinary scraps of bread and sips of wine of which the sacrament in question appears to consist.

Max Weber gave sociological prominence to the term *disenchantment*, by which he designated the triumph of the analytic, rationalistic, bureaucratic secularism of the modern era. Like the vocabulary of sacrifice and the sacred, disenchantment carries both a positive and a negative connotation. It is the cure for the dreamlike and superstitious cast of mind found among primitive peoples and contemporary utopian ideologues, but it is a curse when it represents an incapacity to perceive or acknowledge the subtle realities that elude the merely practical or strictly rationalistic mind. In fact, the form of rationalism that survives in this our irrational age is not truly rational, for it fails to recognize, much less appreciate, the myriad ways in which truth, goodness, and beauty interweave, enchant, and summon us to fulfill our ultimate human vocation. A mind so impervious to mystery and miracle and the ways of the Spirit who both dwells in our heart and leads us to the whole truth is a mind devoid of what we have repeatedly characterized as man's sacramental sensibilities. Today, the dreary disenchantment of the materialist and rationalist lives side by side—and often enough within the breast of one person—with a dreamily enchanted ideological or political credulity which ascribes religious meaning to worldly causes to which one can consecrate oneself wholeheartedly. In such a world, one who has managed to retain a sacramental sensibility will feel himself something of an interloper. But he is also a spiritual aristocrat, enjoying unearned privileges he has no right to squander only on his own behalf and which it is his responsibility to dispense to those who lack these gifts and from whom what little they have might otherwise be lost.

We have used René Girard's work to foreground the role Christianity has played in exposing and delegitimizing the age-old procedures for bringing order out of disorder by means of violence that climaxes in catharsis and emerges from the mystical fogs of the manifold ritual religions of antiquity. Traces of this ritualistic violence—and often more than traces—can be found in the religious traditions of our own time. Modernity can be characterized most succinctly as the age that (implicitly) thought it possible and preferable to eliminate these traces of sacrality and, with equal confidence, (implicitly) believed that the resulting systems of secularized religiosity—some religious in a conventional way and some more or less political or ideological faux-religions—were sturdy and sustainable enough to fulfill the role of religion in man's life. And yet it grows clearer by the day that the secular is utterly incapable of replacing the sacred as a cultural foundation. Thoroughly secularized systems today either dissolve back into structures of sacred violence too poorly mythologized to ward off moral revulsion or squander their meager assimilating power and drift slowly into nihilism and anarchy. Now that we are living in so advanced and perilous a stage in the worldwide cultural diaspora that was set in motion on Golgotha, the question is: How might this scattering be countered by a gathering principle more worthy of the human vocation? What, if anything, does Christianity offer in place of the gravitational

power of the structures of sacred violence—whose moral legitimacy it has compromised—and those clumsily de-sacralized religious alternatives, whose assimilating power and cultural efficacy
are dissolving before our eyes?

Recounting the events just after Jesus's death, the Fourth Evangelist tells us that the Jews, anxious that the three men executed on
Golgotha be buried before the Sabbath, asked Pilate to hasten
their deaths by breaking their legs. The latter practice was recognized in Roman law, and reference to it reinforces the Gospel's
historical reliability. Since Jesus was already dead, the soldier
thrust a lance into his side, "and immediately blood and water
flowed out" (Jn. 19:34). It can be counted one of the miracles of
Gospel origination that, while in each of the synoptic evangelists
Jesus's death is followed immediately by the rending of the temple
curtain, in the Fourth Gospel it is followed by the piercing of
Jesus's side by the soldier's lance. At this rending of the side of the
Pierced One, blood and water flowed out, which both the Johannine author and his early Christian contemporaries were quick
to understand as the sign of the sacramental foundation of an
altogether new *form* of community, one ultimately grounded in
the Trinitarian communion and the sacramental participation
therein. Thus it is that taken together, the synoptic and the Johannine Gospels spell out symbolically not only the theological significance of Jesus's death, but no less strikingly its anthropological
ramifications: the world has shifted on its true axis, the Cross of
Christ, and henceforth history will consist of the long, slow, and
often tragic reorientation from a (primitive) sacred to a sacramental form of religious meaning and social solidarity.

These juxtaposing references to the desacralizing effect of the
Gospel—the exposé of the system of sacred violence exemplified
by the rending of the temple veil and the sacramental alternative
to the old sacred system symbolized by the blood and water
flowing from the side of the Crucified Christ—acquit Christianity
of the charge that it is responsible, not for making secularity possible, which it did, but for making hypertrophic irreligious secu-

larism inevitable, which it most certainly did not. These charges fail to recognize the sacramental alternative to the primitive sacred, which is at the center of the lived experience of apostolic Christianity. It has been the historical privilege and responsibility of Catholic Christianity to fashion, within the Church herself and for the sake of the world outside her immediate embrace, a sacramentally grounded *communio*, one far worthier of man's supreme calling than was the old "sacred" anthropology, at the occluded heart of which was violence. A Catholic with his sacramental sensibilities intact will find himself liturgically participating in a cosmic drama when beholding the elevation of the consecrated host at a Catholic Mass. Someone else—suffering from what William Blake calls "single vision and Newton's sleep"—would see nothing more than a piece of bread and a silly ritual. But that little piece of bread and that little cup of wine represent the entire created order that Christ is entering, transforming, and eventually bringing into the Trinitarian embrace. The Eucharist, writes Emery de Gaál, "is woven into the ultimate destiny of humankind and the cosmos."[2]

Judaism, Islam, and Protestantism are "religions of the book," often quite overtly declared by their adherents to be so. For all its dependence on Scripture and (written) tradition—including its punctiliousness about Magisterial teaching—Catholicism is not a religion of the book. Romano Guardini reminds us of this when he writes: "Jesus knew that he and his message were absolutely decisive, so he wished this to be carried on 'to all nations and even to the end of the world' (Matt. 28:19–20). But in his comments about this continuation of his message, the concept of a book does not occur."[3]

To say that the Christian Bible was written at the Table of the Lord, the Eucharistic celebration, is to speak metaphorically, but it is also to speak a truth that could hardly be better spoken. Karl Adam concurs with his contemporary: "The Catholic does not come to Christ by literary channels, as by the Scriptural records,

---

2 De Gaál, *The Theology of Pope Benedict XVI*, 240.

3 Romano Guardini, *The Church of the Lord* (Chicago: Henry Regnery Company, 1966), 64.

but through his sacramental and personal incorporation in the living Church."[4] In due course, a book would be written and redacted for the purpose of preserving the living testimony of the apostolic generation, and the New Testament is the indispensable textual touchstone of Christian faith, an inexhaustible treasure. But it remains ancillary to the Eucharistic sacrament of Christ's abiding. The beating heart of Catholic Christianity is the Eucharist, which is not fundamentally an act of remembrance or symbolic reenactment. Nor is the socially bonding power of the Eucharist something that happens at the moral, psychological, or social level. Though it is the ecclesial source of the binding up of man's fallen, fractured unity—"By this all men will know that you are my disciples, if you have love for one another" (Jn. 13:35)—the bonds formed in the Eucharistic liturgy are far more than merely social; they are the outworking in this life of the bond that unites the Trinity, the bonds of love that move the sun and the other stars. To the extent that one is actually brought into the orbit of Trinitarian Love, one is brought into a more meaningful unity, first with one's fellow communicants and then with all those everywhere for whom Christ died. "To be in communication with Christ," writes the future pope, Joseph Ratzinger, "is by its very nature to be in communication with one another as well. No more are we alongside one another, each for himself; rather, everyone else who goes to [Eucharistic] communion is for me, so to speak, 'bone of my bone and flesh of my flesh' (cf. Gen. 2:23)."[5]

Jesus often both acted and spoke in ways that proved disconcerting to his audience, precisely because they seemed to violate in one way or another the paramount distinctions between the sacred and the profane, between Jew and Gentile, between the spiritual and the material, or between the Sabbath and the rest of the week. These distinctions gave rise to dissension even among

4 Karl Adam, *The Spirit of Catholicism* (New York: Crossroad Publishing, 1997), 54.

5 Ratzinger, *On the Way to Jesus Christ*, 117.

his disciples over the most essential features of Jesus's mission. Arguably, the words that most disturbed his own followers are those recorded in the famous bread of life discourse in John's Gospel:

> I am the bread of life. Your fathers ate the manna in the wilderness, and they died. This is the bread which comes down from heaven, that a man may eat of it and not die. I am the living bread which came down from heaven; if any one eats of this bread, he will live forever; and the bread which I shall give for the life of the world is my flesh. (Jn. 6:48–51)

Quite understandably, the reaction to the obvious grotesqueness of this image was one of revulsion. "How can this man give us his flesh to eat?" (Jn. 6:52). Had Jesus inadvertently employed a metaphor that proved to be too shocking and too easily misunderstood, one would have expected him to clarify the misunderstanding by toning down the off-putting imagery. He did no such thing. Rather he drove home, in an unequivocal way, the most repellent features of the image he had used.

> So Jesus said to them, "Truly, truly, I say to you, unless you eat the flesh of the Son of man and drink his blood, you have no life in you; he who eats my flesh and drinks my blood has eternal life, and I will raise him up at the last day. For my flesh is food indeed, and my blood is drink indeed. He who eats my flesh and drinks my blood abides in me, and I in him." (Jn. 6:53–56)

Jesus could not have been surprised by the disciples' reaction nor by the fact that his response to it compounded the visceral revulsion of those who heard it, most of whom forthwith abandoned him. The Fourth Evangelist, who wrote his Gospel no earlier than the late first century, had either known Jesus, himself the Johannine Beloved Disciple, or he had relied on the eyewitness testimony of the apostle John. His access to historical details, long overlooked by exegetes, has recently been better appreciated. The fact that the Johannine author doubtless seized on the sacramental implications of this event to which he was personally privy or of which he was well informed by someone who was and which he recounts with theological deftness, takes nothing away from the unavoidable supposition that nothing less than an explicitly cannibalistic image—the hardly unexpected damage to Jesus's reputation notwithstanding—would convey the message Jesus was trying to communicate.

The invitation was, and will ever be, to respond with Abrahamic simplicity and Marian trust. Jesus said, take this and eat it. He did not say: take this and explore its metaphorical possibilities. Romano Guardini brings us back to the irreducible realism that so startled even Jesus's closest disciples and that would prove a stumbling block to so many of their descendants in the faith.

> For almost two thousand years men have prayed and probed and fought over the meaning of these words. They have become the sign of a community that is holier, more intimate than any other, but also occasion for profoundest schism. Hence, when we ask what they mean, let us first be clear as to how they should be taken. There is only one answer: literally. The words mean precisely what they say.[6]

The aforementioned Kierkegaardian distinction between an *admirer* and a *follower* is pertinent here. Almost inevitably one who is to become a follower will in the first instance be an admirer, for as Kierkegaard observes, admiration is "requisite in one sense in order to get people enlisted." But the moment comes when something more demanding is required:

> But when "the truth," true to itself in being the truth, little by little, more and more definitely, unfolds itself as the truth, the moment comes when no admirer can hold out with it, a moment when it shakes admirers from it as the storm shakes the worm-eaten fruit from the tree. And it is Christ's life precisely which has made it evident, terribly evident, what a dreadful falsehood it is to admire the truth instead of following it, a thought which in the prosperous days of Christendom, when peace and security favor this misunderstanding, ought if possible to be brought to remembrance every Sunday. For when no danger is present, when there is a dead calm, when everything is favorable to Christianity, it is only too easy to mistake an admirer for a follower, and this may pass quite unobserved, the

6 Romano Guardini, *The Lord*, trans. Elinor Castendyk Briefs (Chicago: Henry Regnery, 1954), 369.

admirer may die in the illusion that the relationship he assumed was the true one.[7]

So unexpected and so ravaging of conventional Jewish sensibilities was this particular storm that it not only shook the worm-eaten fruit of mere admiration from the tree but it left even those who had begun the transition from admirers to followers completely perplexed:

> After this many of his disciples drew back and no longer went about with him. Jesus said to the twelve, "Do you also wish to go away?" Simon Peter answered him, "Lord, to whom shall we go? You have the words of eternal life; and we have believed, and have come to know, that you are the Holy One of God." (Jn. 6:66–69)

It was the impulsive and outspoken Peter who had the temerity to speak out when he felt the ground beneath him giving way. Remember his rebuke to Jesus's Caesarea Philippi announcement of his impending Passion and death (Mk. 8:32) and his post-Easter shock at the idea of violating Jewish dietary laws (Acts 10). Characteristically, Peter vehemently objected to having Jesus wash his feet at the Johannine Last Supper (Jn. 13:8). Why? Balthasar answers:

> Because this means the collapse of the total religious order of values of the natural man. God is above, man is below. The saint is above, the sinner is below. It is not enough to accuse Peter here of obstinacy and blindness; it is the *homo religiosus* who speaks or shouts out of him. The answer is: "If I do not wash you, you have no fellowship with me." On the one side stands the world's order of things, on the other side, fellowship with Jesus.[8]

In the famous bread of life discourse in John's Gospel there is reason to assume that Jesus's question to Peter—"Do you also wish to go away?"—was elicited by some indication that Peter too had found such graphically shocking imagery profoundly disturbing. By asking Peter whether he wished to abandon him, Jesus was putting into words precisely the terrible thought that Peter

7 Kierkegaard, *Training in Christianity*, 223.
8 Balthasar, *Explorations in Theology, Vol. III*, 220.

himself would surely have been reluctant to bring into consciousness, namely that circumstances might lead to a break with Jesus
and a return to the life he had lived prior to his discipleship.

What does it cost a person to utter Peter's words: "Lord, to
whom shall we go? You have the words of eternal life; and we have
believed, and have come to know, that you are the Holy One of
God" (Jn. 6:68–69)? According to Glenn W. Olsen, participation in
the sacramental and ecclesial communion bequeathed to us by
Christ requires the "resacralization of intelligence."[9] With neither
Olsen's pithiness nor the Johannine author's economy of expression, but nonetheless quite magnificently, Romano Guardini has
captured the essence of the conversion experience—the *metanoia*—which brings an incipient form of Christian faith to its
maturity.

> Unconverted man lives in the visible world judging all that is or
> may be by tradition's experience and by the rules of logic. But
> when he encounters Christ, he must either accept him and his
> revolutionary approach to truth or lose him. If he attempts to
> judge also the Lord by the standards of common experience, he
> will soon notice that he is dealing with something outside expe-
> rience. He will have to discard the norms of the past, and take
> Christ as his new point of departure. When he no longer
> attempts to subject Christ to immediate reason and experience,
> he will recognize him as the supreme measure of all possible real-
> ity. The intellect jealous for its own sovereignty rejects such rec-
> ognition, which would put an end to its world-anchored self-
> glorification, and surrender it into the hands of the God of Reve-
> lation. This is the "risk" any would-be Christian must take. If he
> takes it, a profound revolution begins. It may take a disquieting,
> even frightening form; may demand passage through stifling
> darkness and perplexity. All that until now has seemed certain
> suddenly becomes questionable. The whole conception of real-
> ity, the whole idea of existence is turned upside-down. Only the
> haunting question persists: Is Christ really so great that he can be
> the norm of all that is? Does the world really lose itself in him, or
> is the whole idea only another (magnificent) example of the

9 Olsen, *Beginning at Jerusalem*, 174.

human tendency to make that which it reveres the measure of all things; another proof of the blindness inherent in all love? Yet the longer the intellect continues to grope, the clearer it becomes that the love of Christ is essentially different from every other love. And to the degree that the searching individual experiences such spiritual revolution, he gains an amplitude, a superiority, a synthesizing power of reason that no natural insight can match.[10]

Where in life is one confronted with the decision of which Guardini speaks? There may be many situations in which one is forced to decide between the norms of the past and the standards of common experience, on one hand, and, on the other hand, Christ as the new point of departure; but entering fully into the mystery of the Eucharist is clearly one of these situations, and it may be the supreme one.

There is a link—subtle but significant—between the explicitly Eucharistic account in John's Gospel and Luke's equally significant Eucharistic story of the two disciples on the road to Emmaus. In Luke's road to Emmaus story, the Risen Christ accompanies the disciples as they are leaving Jerusalem because, as we learn in the course of the story, Jesus's execution had crushed their hope. In leaving Jerusalem they were leaving behind their discipleship and their faith in Jesus as the messiah. The risen Christ joined them on their journey. As was typically the case with Jesus's Resurrection appearances, he was not immediately recognizable, "their eyes were kept from recognizing him" (Lk. 24:16).

Let us pause for a moment on this prominent but puzzling aspect of the encounters between the risen Christ and his disciples. It has perhaps not received the attention it deserves, namely his unrecognizability. As we will see below, even after having seen the risen Christ on two prior occasions, the disciples on the shore of the Sea of Tiberias fail to recognize the risen Christ. "This was now the third time that Jesus was revealed to the disciples after he was raised from the dead" (Jn. 21:14). After the work of Christ

10  Guardini, *The Lord*, 460.

is finished (Jn. 19:30), the criteria for recognizing him changes. The visual recognition had always been the weakest and most unreliable form of recognition. Once they had seen him, even his enemies and those who managed to remain indifferent toward him—how hard that must have been!—were able to pick him out in a crowd. They were able to recognize him. But were they really? Of course not. After the Resurrection, this weak and spiritually ineffectual form of recognition was eliminated, not for the purpose of playing cat and mouse with his disciples, but in order to bring them—and us—to a true recognition of Christ.

Thus it was with the two disciples on the road to Emmaus. Their conversation with the Stranger began with them pouring out their disappointment, telling Jesus of the rumor that women among the disciples had gone to the tomb in which the body of Jesus was laid and found it empty.

> And he said to them, "O foolish men, and slow of heart to believe all that the prophets have spoken! Was it not necessary that the Christ should suffer these things and enter into his glory?" And beginning with Moses and all the prophets, he interpreted to them in all the scriptures the things concerning himself. (Lk. 24:25–27)

In these three verses we have a synopsis of what took place among the disciples of Jesus in the first few decades following the Passion, Resurrection, Ascension, and Pentecost. These seminal Christian events were utterly unique and unexpected even to those who were closest to Jesus prior to his Passion. Far from causing the dominical generation and its immediate successors to renounce its Jewish heritage—that would become a temptation later—the shock of these events inspired the early Church instead to pour over the Jewish Scriptures where they found recognizable foreshadowings of Christ, his life, death, and Resurrection. In doing so, they had something of the same experience that the reader of a detective novel has when the mystery is finally revealed. (G. K. Chesterton opined that the story Christians had to tell was more like a detective novel than a romance novel.) Suddenly all the otherwise puzzling and disconnected clues fall into place and make sense. The history of first century Christianity is therefore encapsulated in these three verses in Luke.

On the road to Emmaus, Jesus explained how the Jewish Scriptures led to him and provided the antecedent narratives for understanding why this was so. Alas, we do not have the transcription of that discourse, but Christians for two thousand years have been discovering its essential content, as they lavish attention and affection on the Hebrew Scriptures and derive from them a richer understanding of the basic principles of their faith. It bears noting at this point that it was René Girard's intellectual achievement to have recognized the stunning structural similarities between the Passion story in the Gospel and the myths and rituals of pagan antiquity. In effect, Girard has appended a footnote to the Emmaus road discourse of the Risen Christ, citing the many ways in which the pagan religions can also be read as harbingers of the Christian revelation.

Turning again to Luke's account: When the two disciples and the mysterious man who accompanied them approached the village of Emmaus, Luke tells his readers that the unrecognized Jesus "appeared to be going further" (Lk. 24:28). This brief but puzzling comment, at first so seemingly gratuitous but on reflection so fascinating, might be read as the supremely succinct Lucan summary of the farewell discourse in John's Gospel (Jn. 16ff). But to what purpose is that reference in this story? We can surmise. Jesus's bread of life discourse and the reaction it caused in both the gathered crowd and his own disciples represented a critical moment in the discipleship of Simon Peter. He suddenly came face to face with the possibility of living without what he had found in Jesus. The alacrity with which Simon Peter rejected the suggestion that he and his fellow disciples might cease to follow Christ is echoed in the Lucan account at precisely the moment when it appeared that Jesus intended to part company with the two disciples at Emmaus.

Arguably it is the shocking possibility of watching Christ leave the erstwhile Christian behind that brings faith in Christ to maturity. It bears mentioning in this context that many Christians today, in starkly different social and cultural contexts—from the murderous persecutions in Muslim lands to the various efforts to marginalize Christianity in the Anglo-European cultures once thought to be its natural and perennial home—have a vague but disconcerting sense of Christ receding from their world. We can pray that the shock that accompanies that apprehension will elicit something comparable to the Emmaus disciples' plea—"stay [abide] with us"—or St. Peter's exclamation: "Lord, to whom shall we go? You have the words of eternal life; and we have believed, and have come to know, that you are the Holy One of God."

In both the Johannine and Lucan accounts there seems to have been a hurdle for his disciples to overcome and only on the far side of that hurdle would their discipleship be mature enough to recognize precisely how it was that he intended to abide with them after his earthly departure. Perhaps blurting out—as reflexively as had the disciple of John in the Fourth Gospel who said "Where do you *abide*?"—the two disciples respond to the dreaded possibility that the man who had opened the Scriptures to them might leave them behind by urging: "Stay with us, for it is toward evening and the day is now far spent" (Lk. 24:29). *Abide* with us. How, then, does Jesus abide with his disciples, both in Luke's unforgettable post-Easter story and in history after Christ's Ascension?

> So he went in to stay [*abide*] with them. When he was at table with them, he took the bread and blessed, and broke it, and gave it to them. And their eyes were opened and they recognized him; and he vanished out of their sight. They said to each other, "Did not our hearts burn within us while he talked to us on the road, while he opened to us the scriptures?" And they rose that same hour and returned to Jerusalem. (Lk. 24:29–33)

In the Greek of Luke's Gospel, the verb for *rising* ("they rose that same hour") is the same word used to speak of the rising of Christ from the tomb. The risen Christ was gone, but departed in such a way as to remain not merely in the memory, but in the hearts and minds of those whose existence he had assimilated to himself precisely in the Eucharistic sharing of himself. "This absence knows itself to be henceforth in-dwelt by a presence," as Louis-Marie Chauvet puts it.[11] He who rose from the tomb has departed, but only after depositing himself within the commu-

---

11 Louis-Marie Chauvet, *The Sacraments: The Word of God at the Mercy of the Body* (Collegeville, MN: The Liturgical Press, 2001) 21.

nity of his disciples and thereby empowering them to rise and return to the work of announcing the Good News of the Gospel.

Just as the flight from Jerusalem, which had become a dangerous place for the followers of Jesus, represented the initial decision by the two disciples to put their lives back together in the aftermath of their disappointment, so the abrupt return to Jerusalem—"that same hour"—represents Christian discipleship fully fledged and emboldened by the encounter with Jesus in the breaking of the bread, his chosen way of abiding with his disciples. This dramatic climax can and should be seen as Jesus's answer to the invitation to "abide with us." The Eucharist and the larger sacramental economy by which the ecclesial anthropology is fleshed out and inculcated is precisely his way of abiding with us.

Upon their return to Jerusalem the Emmaus road disciples found the eleven apostles gathered, to whom they recounted their experience and from whom they learned that the Risen Lord had appeared to Simon Peter. As they were exchanging these accounts:

> Jesus himself stood among them. But they were startled and frightened, and supposed that they saw a spirit. And he said to them, "Why are you troubled, and why do questionings rise in your hearts? See my hands and my feet, that it is I myself; handle me, and see; for a spirit has not flesh and bones as you see that I have." And while they still disbelieved for joy, and wondered, he said to them, "Have you anything here to eat?" They gave him a piece of broiled fish, and he took it and ate before them. (Lk. 24:36–43)

When we say that Christ abides sacramentally with the Church, the verb seems too strong to some and the adverb seems too weak to others to justify what has been the Eucharistic experience of Catholic Christians since the Emmaus meal, the sharing of the broiled fish in the Jerusalem gathering of the eleven, and the breakfast on the shore of the Sea of Tiberias. This central sacrament of the Church cannot be adequately understood solely as a meal, but the role of meals, most especially in the Resurrection appearances, quite obviously was intended—by Christ and the Evangelists—to throw light back on the sacramental gathering and sharing in which Christ abides with his people after the Ascension.

The material evidence for the Eucharistic presence of Christ is a good deal less compelling than were his post-Easter appearances, but it must be borne in mind that the appearance of the Risen Lord left a remarkable degree of doubt even in those whose faith in the Resurrection would eventually grow strong enough to withstand persecution and martyrdom. The historical reliability of the Resurrection appearances is significantly bolstered by the persistent suggestion that the risen body of Christ was insufficiently dispositive. Questions lingered. It is important to note that in the Risen Lord's attempt to convince the disciples that he was in reality standing in their midst—abiding with them—what we might call his last resort was to share a meal with them, the Eucharistic implications of which must not be overlooked. It was with gestures conspicuously reminiscent of the supper he shared with them the night before his Passion that the Risen Christ made himself known to disciples who lacked the sensorium for recognizing him in a more straightforward way. "Jesus said to them, 'Come and have breakfast.' Now none of the disciples dared ask him, 'Who are you?' They knew it was the Lord" (Jn. 21:12).

How did they know? This verse captures both the difficulty the disciples had in recognizing the Risen Christ by his physical appearance alone and how readily this perplexity was remedied by Jesus's invitation to share a meal. This same matrix of confusion and clarity lives on in the Body of Christ in history: the Church. She rarely, if ever, seems worthy of such a lofty title, and those who have come to recognize how apposite that title is, are those who have discovered this truth within the orbit of the Eucharist.

Our world is becoming a spiritual desert, but there is an Oasis hiding in plain sight. Writes Bevil Bramwell, OMI:

> In a society with almost no formal moments that stand apart from the jeans-and-track-shoes culture, liturgy is the last bastion of the authentic meaning of human posture and gesture, speaking and silence. It should be where we recover the core meaning of life again. We can learn how to stand respectfully, to kneel devoutly, to put our heart and soul into our words, to be silent

and open our hearts to what we are hearing and seeing, and how to dress to show that we are genuinely conscious of *who* is with us. . . . Most important, liturgies remind us of our part in the salvation that is always unfolding, inside us and around us. We participate and, for a short while, we know what is truly important. We see with the light of grace where we fit into the great drama.[12]

He who wrote not a word (except in the dust at the scene of the imminent stoning of the adulterous woman) and who made not the slightest effort to codify his instructions to his disciples is not likely to have chosen to reach those future disciples of his down through the ages with a book. When he used words in healing and forgiving those who came to him, he used them as he used other gestures, sacramentally not pedagogically. He was himself the source of healing, forgiveness, and grace. Nor would he rely on words alone—or even on words primarily—to heal, forgive, and bestow grace on the generations to come after him, for whom he was as solicitous as he was for those who stood in his presence. As Denis Farkasfalvy, O. Cist. has written:

The Eucharist is the context in which history does not undergo a *rigor mortis* by becoming both stiff and irrelevant, hopelessly and irredeemably glued to long-past events and states of mind. Instead, in this medium of the church's continued sacramental practice, Jesus's universal mission (Matt. 28:16–20) successfully extends the chain of the gospel episodes so as to reach all times and all places and make his journey transcend the limits of history without rendering it ahistorical.[13]

The Incarnation is the center of history, and the Easter exclamation—He *is* alive!—announces his enduring presence sacramentally within the Eucharistic community and through the Church's sacramental presence to the world beyond her confessional

12 "Liturgy: The Benchmark of Life," The Catholic Thing, accessed March 8 2015, http://www.thecatholicthing.org/2015/03/08/liturgy-the-benchmark-of-life/.

13 Denis Farkasfalvy, "The Eucharistic Provenance of the New Testament Texts," *Rediscovering the Eucharist: Ecumenical Conversations*, ed. Roch A. Kereszty, O. Cist. (New York/Mahwah, NJ: Paulist Press, 2003), 45.

bounds. The celebrant at the Mass and all those in attendance are literally standing and kneeling at the center of history. However momentous are, in relative historical terms, the events happening in the world outside that celebration, all of these events lack any serious claim to historical centrality. The Eucharist, on the contrary, reaches back into the mists of time to the earliest religious rituals of man, which were almost certainly cannibalistic. In this sense the French *Encyclopédie*, that massive effort to catalogue and recalibrate all knowledge in accord with the shrunken forms of reason advanced by the French *philosophes*, touched on a truth when the listing under Eucharist simply said: see cannibalism. But if the Eucharist reaches back to the savage origins of man, it reaches with equal audacity into the eschatological future, for the Mass represents the inbreaking into time of the Messianic Banquet. In Balthasarian terms, the Eucharist is *anamnesis* (memory) under the sign of *maranatha* (the Lord is coming, come Lord).

Those who might otherwise be lost without a story—lost in the cosmos as the novelist Walker Percy put it—can find both that story and the invitation to participate personally in it at the Eucharistic altar. It is precisely the event at which the Christian community enters into the sacrifice of Christ, each communicant assimilating the sacrifices required by his faith and circumstances with Christ's sacrifice on the Cross. As such, the Eucharist, as Joseph Ratzinger notes, "is not an isolated cultic act but a way of existence."[14] His predecessor on the Chair of Peter concurred, for instance, in this passage from John Paul II's 2004 Apostolic Letter, *Mane Nobiscum Domine* ("Stay with us, Lord"):

> The Eucharist is a mode of being, which passes from Jesus into each Christian, through whose testimony it is meant to spread throughout society and culture. For this to happen, each member of the faithful must assimilate, through personal and communal meditation, the values which the Eucharist expresses, the attitudes it inspires, the resolutions to which it gives rise.[15]

---

14 Joseph Cardinal Ratzinger, *Called to Communion: Understanding the Church Today*, trans. Adrian Walker (San Francisco: Ignatius Press, 1996), 43.

15 John Paul II, *Mane Nobiscum Domine*, §25

We earlier spoke of the unique role that Jesus's mother played in the Incarnation, providing the unreserved Yes to God's redemptive will, unencumbered by the preoccupation with self that is rooted in sin. Mary's pure consent comes into the drama of salvation once again—and even more elusively and perhaps decisively—at the Cross. Before turning to a few reflections on the abiding presence of Christ in the Eucharistic communion of the Church, therefore, we will pause to reflect on Mary's consent at the foot of the Cross. We begin with an insight for which Balthasar credits Adrienne von Speyr concerning the roles played in the New Testament by three women: Mary of Nazareth, Mary of Bethany, and Mary of Magdala.

> The mystery of the three Marys would thus consist, according to Adrienne von Speyr, in giving ecclesial consent to the fundamental articulations of the Christ event: Incarnation, Passion, Resurrection. Christ in his Incarnation did not wish at any moment to act alone, without the accompaniment of his Church. An isolated man has never existed; he was unthinkable: "It is not good," said God of this unhappy Adam in the midst of Paradise, "that the man should be alone." (Gen. 2:18)[16]

Jesus interpreted Mary of Bethany's anointing as preparation for this death and burial, which von Speyr in turn interprets as her consent to Jesus's Passion. On Easter morning Mary Magdala, in von Speyr's reading, does not cling to the risen Jesus, consenting to his eventual withdrawal from his earthly presence. In each case, Jesus is accompanied precisely during his necessary withdrawal from worldly companionship. Framed by the gestures of Mary of Bethany and Mary Magdala is the most essential act of accompaniment-and-consent, that of Mary, the mother of the Lord. The Incarnation awaited the pure Yes uttered by Mary of Nazareth at the conception of Jesus, but this same woman would be asked to utter an unfathomable and unspeakable Yes at the foot of the Cross.

In our chapter on hominization and the origin of culture, we

---

16 Balthasar, *To the Heart of the Mystery of Redemption*, 47–48.

dilated at some length on the nature of the catharsis that was key to aboriginal cultural formation and on how dependent a cathartic climax was on an entirely subliminal trace of moral remorse. Thanks to Girard's work, we know that the crucifixion reveals and reverses "things hidden since the foundation of the world." Now we want to suggest that the trace of remorse buried deep inside the otherwise unanimous assent the beneficiaries of primitive culture expressed at having offloaded their violence onto the perceived monster they immolated finds its inverted analogue when the mother of the Lord utters a wordless Yes to the horror to which her son consented in the Garden of Olives. This assent, wrenched from the heart of the Mother of Sorrows at the depth of her anguish, is the history-altering and world-redeeming inversion of the faint trace of moral compunction that, as we have argued above, was the secret key to the inauguration of fallen human culture and to its hidden Christological structure. Whereas the cultural efficacy of the primitive sacrificial violence depended on an inaudible trace of remorse in its participants and onlookers, both the religious and the cosmic efficacy of Christ's Passion depended on an assent made on behalf of all its beneficiaries, an assent that brought the *fiat* at the annunciation to its final fulfillment and which could only have been uttered at the death of Christ by the woman who consented to his conception. Just as only the New Adam, ontologically innocent, could have broken the mesmerizing power of the system of sacred violence, so only the New Eve, immune by her privileged status to what must have been a deafening mimetic vortex of taunts and tears could have kept even these most wretched things in her heart (Lk 2:51) with sufficient repose to allow an even more incomprehensible *fiat* to arise all but unbidden from within her grief. Thus was the Yes of the Lord's mother—first at the Lord's conception and finally at his death—indispensable to the inauguration of a new creation. In this her soul-piercing final *fiat* she merged her own "final surrender of corporality" with that of her son, rendering her subsequent bodily expiration a *fait accompli*, remembered thereafter by the faithful as her dormition.

All this pertains to these our final concerns inasmuch as something analogous to Mary's Yes at the foot of the Cross is asked of

each participant present at Christ's Eucharistically contemporaneous Passion. This consent is what draws the participant into
the heart of the ongoing drama of redemption, and it constitutes
a Yes, not only to the suffering and death of Christ, but a willingness to be assimilated to Christ's sacrifice for the sake of others.
Writes Balthasar:

> Just as every one of the baptized enters into the death of Christ,
> so everyone does likewise who assists at the eucharistic celebra-
> tion by being prepared to offer himself together with Christ in
> the Church's gifts of bread and wine at the offertory. If he is pre-
> pared to surrender (to "sacrifice") his most precious possession
> —his Lord and Savior—for the salvation of the world, how
> much more his own self, which is as nothing in comparison!
> "*Meum ac vestrum sacrificium*," [my sacrifice and yours] says the
> priest. . . .[17]

She who puts up no resistance embodies the promise that we
who resist are nonetheless capable—in this life and the next—of
following her example. The school par excellence where this Yes is
learned and practiced is the Eucharist. For the disposition proper
to the reception of the Eucharist is that of Mary's *fiat*: consenting
to receive Christ with complete equanimity, both from the hands
of the Eucharistic minister and from within the unknowable and
unmanipulated events of one's life. Writes Balthasar:

> We do not know whether Mary ever communicated at a celebra-
> tion of the Eucharist. But she knows better than any saint or sin-
> ner what it means perfectly to receive the Son into oneself. She
> stands, as it were, behind every Holy Communion, as the *Eccle-
> sia Immaculata*, bringing to perfection what we accomplish
> imperfectly.[18]

Again, we turn to Balthasar to help us appreciate how germane
this hidden and vastly underestimated event is to the theme of this
chapter.

---

17 Hans Urs von Balthasar, *New Elucidations*, trans. Sister Mary Theresilde
Skerry (San Francisco: Ignatius Press, 1986), 181.

18 Hans Urs von Balthasar, *Maria für heute* (Freiburg, 1987), 39; Quoted:
Saward, *The Mysteries of March*, 83.

I believe that the expression "sacrifice of the Mass" will remain obscure so long as we have not encountered that veiled woman at the foot of the Cross, who is the Mother of the Crucified and at the same time the icon of the Church. She is present at the self-gift of the Son, not able to intervene; but she is far from passive; a superhuman action is asked of her: consent to the sacrifice of this man who is the Son of God but also her own son. She would prefer a thousand times over to be tortured in his place. But this is not what is demanded of her; she has only to consent to it.[19]

Mary's Yes at the foot of the Cross and our joining in that Yes as we receive the Eucharistic Body of Christ is what warrants, in Balthasar's view, the appellation *Sacrifice of the Mass*. In it we perform the act immortalized by Michelangelo in his *Pietà*. In consenting to her Son's Passion, Mary entered into his death so completely that her own bodily death was incorporated into it—giving us yet another trace of the mystery of her deathless death. So, too, are we invited in the act of consenting to Christ's death—as enacted in the Eucharist—to assimilate our death to his. While we cannot do so as thoroughly as could one who was exempt from sin, we can consent in such a way that we might be capable of saying, with St. Paul, "if we have died with Christ, we believe that we shall also live with him" (Rom. 6:8). This Eucharistic consent to Christ's death on the Cross—which is at the same time our consent to conjoin our own death with his—is the consent to martyrdom, regardless of whether the executioner in our case is a worldly enemy of Christ and his Church or, in most cases, simply the blind force of nature that rends from us our bodily life.

To join in Mary's Yes at the foot of the Cross is to declare oneself ready to undergo the Cross of Christ in whatever form one's faith and circumstances might require. To say Yes to that daunting possibility is not to know for certain that one possesses the capacity to carry through with that pledge. For the capacity to do so requires grace over which we have no control. What we do have is the assurance that where sin—or evil or hardship or persecution—abound, grace superabounds. That is all we need to

19 Ibid., 46.

know in order to commit with our feeble will to endure the Cross of Christ in whatever form it might take in our own lives, and the premier place where the decision to do so is made is at the Eucharistic table of the Lord.

To the extent that they are able to enter more fully into the Paschal mystery, the participants in the "sacrifice of the Mass" will be drawn into the Passion of Mary, experiencing in some small way—not the Aristotelian terror tinged ever so slightly with pity—but the inverted analogue toward which it was ordered and in which it was finally consummated: a heart choking with anguish but from which a mysterious and inexplicable Yes arises—an assent to her son's suffering uttered from within her own vicarious participation in that suffering. To the extent that a worshipper at Mass is drawn into this assent to Christ's Passion, his own suffering and confusion can be lifted out of its mediocrity and brought within the theodrama of world redemption. Adrienne von Speyr, a woman who knew great suffering, has given us a glimpse of this mystery:

> We must not fear this and let ourselves take back, in the night of suffering, the joy underlying this being allowed to suffer with Christ. The joy may have been sent as a deposit; it may have become insensible; it must above all be there, even in the most profound suffering, as grateful joy that we know to be so profoundly anchored in the Lord that it does not disappear even when our whole capacity for feeling is required by the suffering.[20]

If the worshippers at the "sacrifice of the Mass" are only very remotely able to share in this Marian participation in the Passion, they can at least aspire to it and pray for the grace to enter ever more fully into this salvific mystery. Neither sinner nor saint is capable in this life of properly receiving the full measure of grace that accompanies the reception of the Eucharistic Body and Blood of Christ. Had such a Eucharistic communicant been on his deathbed or faced with a comparable threat to his existence, he would almost certainly have been more open to the grace of

---

20 Quoted: Balthasar, *To the Heart of the Mystery of Redemption*, 82.

the Eucharist. According to Adrienne von Speyr, however, the graces that the communicant is incapable of receiving are never lost; they are held in reserve, so to speak, for those moments in life when the person is more open to grace due to the mortal or moral gravity of a situation, or these graces flow toward others in the ecclesial communion as their needs and circumstances require. Like so much else in Catholic Christianity, suggestions such as this find reception only among those whose sacramental sensibilities have survived the toxins and abrasions of our contemporary deracinated age.

We have sought to better appreciate the gathering event offered by Christ and Christianity as an alternative to the old gathering principle rooted in sacred violence, which was exposed and crippled by the Incarnation and Crucifixion of Christ. We have spoken of a new form of community at the center of which is the Eucharist. It remains to say something about the mystery of incorporation that Eucharistic communion fosters. Few have summarized the uniqueness of the Eucharistic liturgy as well as has Romano Guardini, nor have the personal and interpersonal demands of this new form of community been sketched so well or so starkly contrasted with the spirit of our age.

> The individual has to renounce his own ideas and his own way. He is obliged to subscribe to the ideas and to follow the lead of the liturgy. To it he must surrender his independence; pray with others, and not alone; obey, instead of freely disposing of himself; and stand in the ranks instead of moving about at his own will and pleasure. . . . He must shake off the narrow trammels of his own thought, and make his own a far more comprehensive world of ideas; he must go beyond his little personal aims and adopt the educative purpose of the great fellowship of the liturgy.[21]

---

21 Romano Guardini, *The Spirit of the Liturgy*, trans. Ada Lane (New York: Crossroad, 1997), 38.

# "Abide With Us"

The God who chose history's forgotten people as his own and who came into the world in obscurity and ignominy and who thereafter inserts himself into human history by way of a Church as outwardly motley as a Bethlehem cowshed and inwardly magnificent as a Marian *fiat*, today enters "the rag and bone shop of the heart"[22] as a little piece of bread. Could the Good News get any better than this? Is there any form of transmission more egalitarian than this? Could anything resist the speculative takeover or gnostic dissolution of Christian realism more triumphantly than this? To put it more indecorously still, could Christ have offered us a more idiot-proof access to himself than by entering our souls by way of our bodies in what outwardly appears to be but a little piece of bread and a sip of wine? So simple and inauspicious is the gift, in fact, that it is often received more readily by the humble and the unlearned than by the worldly-wise sophisticates. We cannot resist punctuating this last remark with a marvelous passage from a 1955 letter by Flannery O'Connor:

> I was once, five or six years ago, taken by some friends to have dinner with Mary McCarthy and her husband, Mr. Broadwater. (She just wrote that book, *A Charmed Life*.) She departed the Church at the age of 15 and is a Big Intellectual. We went at eight to one, I hadn't opened my mouth once, there being nothing for me in such company to say. The people who took me were Robert Lowell and his now wife, Elizabeth Hardwick. Having me there was like having a dog present who had been trained to say a few words but overcome with inadequacy had forgotten them. Well, toward morning the conversation turned on the Eucharist, which I, being the Catholic, was obviously supposed to defend. Mrs. Broadwater said when she was a child and received the Host, she thought of it as the Holy Ghost, He being the "most portable" person of the Trinity; now she thought of it as a symbol and implied that it was a pretty good one. I then said, in a very shaky voice, "Well, if it's a symbol, to hell with it." That was all the defense I was capable of but I realize now that this is all I will ever be able to say about it, outside of a story, except

---

22 From William Butler Yeats' poem, "The Circus Animals' Desertion."

351

that it is the center of existence for me; all the rest of life is expendable.[23]

In David Samuels' *The New York Times Magazine* article with which we began, Mr. Samuels lamented that "the old rules no longer apply" and that "coherent narratives, the stories that tell us who we are and where we are going, are getting harder and harder to find." In the midst of this cacophony of ad hoc and incoherent stories, Flannery O'Connor—her sacramental sensibilities as acute as anyone of her generation—told her readers parables suffused with intimations of the larger story about who we are and where we are going. Moreover, she tells us—in the wry letter to a friend quoted above—where to look for the source of her remarkable storytelling genius. It was the Eucharist, which itself remained so ineffable a mystery that its deeper meaning could only be coaxed out in narratives, many of which seemed to have nothing whatsoever to do with it. The ever-contemporaneous story relived at each celebration of the Lord's Supper in the upper room and death on Golgotha is the narrative Rosetta Stone for deciphering the meaning of reality itself, the human vocation as such, and the nature and purpose of human history. It is the dramaturgical equivalent of the Wardrobe in C. S. Lewis' Narnia chronicles. It is where all the truly exciting adventures begin.

One of the epigraphs with which this book began was taken from a 1953 book by Jean Daniélou. Nothing is more fitting as an epilogue than another passage from that book, all the more so inasmuch as the title of that book was "The Lord of History." At the time the book was written, of course, the vexing challenge to Christianity and to the civilization underwritten by Christian faith came from Marxism. Daniélou's answer to that challenge, however, was the perennial Christian one: the renewal of faith in

---

23 *The Habit of Being: Letters of Flannery O'Connor* (New York: Macmillan, 1988), 125.

the sacramental life of the Church, the source and summit of which is the Eucharist.

> For Christians, the structure of history is complete, and its decisive event, instead of coming last, occupies the central position. Nothing can ultimately go wrong. . . . But this does not mean that we have no more to do; after the central, decisive event, the task remains of ensuring that all men come into effective possession of the gift once secured in principle for all mankind. Sacred history is thus also the history of our own time. In this later current period of time the outstanding events are those of the sacramental life. This is something vastly more important than the achievements of modern thought, or the discoveries of science, or victorious wars, or successful revolutions, all of which things make up the tissue of recorded history, but leave no trace at the deeper levels where real history is enacted.[24]

---

24  Daniélou, S.J., *The Lord of History*, 82–3.

# INDEX

# Index

# Index

# About the Author

Gil Bailie is the founder and president of *The Cornerstone Forum*, a founding member of *The Colloquium on Violence and Religion*, a member of the *College of Fellows of the Dominican School of Philosophy & Theology* and the *Fellowship of Catholic Scholars*. For many years Mr. Bailie has worked to bring René Girard's extraordinary anthropological contribution to human self-understanding into fruitful dialogue with the theological tradition represented by Benedict XVI, Henri de Lubac, Hans Urs von Balthasar and others. He is the author of *Violence Unveiled: Humanity at the Crossroads* (1995).

.